Self-Defence as a Fundamental Principle

HAGUE COLLOQUIUM ON FUNDAMENTAL PRINCIPLES OF LAW

SELF-DEFENCE AS A FUNDAMENTAL PRINCIPLE

Edited by

Arthur Eyffinger
Alan Stephens
Sam Muller

Hague Academic Press
An Imprint of T·M·C·ASSER PRESS

Published by Hague Academic Press, an imprint of T·M·C·Asser press
P.O.Box 16163, 2500 BD The Hague, The Netherlands

<www.asserpress.nl>

Hague Academic Press' English language books are distributed exclusively by:

Cambridge University Press, The Edinburgh Building, Shaftesbury Road,
Cambridge CB2 2RU, UK,
or
for customers in the USA, Canada and Mexico:
Cambridge University Press, 100 Brook Hill Drive, West Nyack, NY 10994-2133, USA

<www.cambridge.org>

The *Hague Colloquium on Fundamental Principles of Law* Series is based on the results of the bi-annual HCFPL Colloquium, which is an integral part of the Hague Prize for International Law. Held in honour of the Laureate its topic is selected by the Laureate and covers a fundamental principle of law. The Hague Colloquia are designed as high level expert workshops guided by multi-disciplinarity, where practice and academia meet.

ISBN 978-90-6704-287-1
ISSN 1877-279X

INTRODUCTION

The book which you have in your hands has been a long time in the making, for which the Editors make no apology! The topic of self-defence in both national and international law is notoriously difficult to define and to circumscribe. Historians, philosophers, military officers, diplomats, lawyers and theologians, as well as legislators, judges and the executive arm of government, are among the many who have wrestled with the concept from the earliest days of recorded history until today. A subject-matter which includes the right of a householder to repel or discourage intruders, the right of a woman to resist an abusive partner, the right of a State to deal with actual or planned attacks by other States, by armed groups or even by individuals, cannot fail to be a subject-matter worthy of deep study and analysis. Add to this the fact that the contemporary debate on self-defence is interwoven with debates on environmental damage, energy (in)dependence, water-resources, terrorism, self-determination and human rights, and it becomes crystal clear that self-defence is a topic that cries out for discussion and research-based writing.

The Editors decided to respond to this challenge soon after the first Hague Prize for International Law was awarded to Professor Shabtai Rosenne in the year 2004. We had three objectives in view: to honour the Hague Prize Laureate; to inaugurate a new periodic forum for scholarly discussion in The Hague, and to organise a symposium on self-defence. We are delighted to say that all three objectives have been fulfilled.

The Hague Prize Foundation willingly and cooperatively adopted our suggestion that its Laureates should be associated with the new periodic forum, which we have called the Hague Colloquium on Fundamental Principles of Law, and which is already a fixture in the Hague calendar. The structural link which has been established is that the Laureate is a full participant in choosing the topic and speakers for each Colloquium, so that Professor Rosenne was our partner on self-defence, while the second

Hague Laureate, Professor Cherif M. Bassiouni, worked with the T.M.C. Asser Instituut and the Hague Institute for the Internationalisation of Law (HiiL), the current organisers of the Hague Colloquium, to accomplish the 2008 session on 'Jihad and the challenges of international and domestic law.'

Our hope is that this volume will contribute constructively to stimulating scholarship and research in the field of self-defence, that it will provide food for thought, and that it will inspire more colloquia and publications on the topic. The volume does not contain the proceedings of the Colloquium, though all the presentations were indeed recorded and transcribed by HiiL. Rather, we have chosen to publish four* brilliant essays on self-defence written by participants in the Colloquium subsequent to its having taken place. The essays are accompanied by a remarkably full and useful bibliography and by documentary materials, many of which are difficult to obtain elsewhere. We have throughout seen this project as 'work in progress,' and look forward eagerly to further developments.

We would like to thank Doron Kerbel, Galia Haver, H.E.Ambassador Eitan Margalit, Jos Kapteyn, Marjolijn Bastiaans, Frans Nelissen, Peter Kooijmans, Bob Lagerwaard, and the City of The Hague.

Ueberlingen, The Hague, Zichron Yaacov
November 2008 THE EDITORS

---

* *Modesty compels Arthur Eyffinger to disassociate himself from the number 'four.'*

TABLE OF CONTENTS

Part I

SELF-DEFENCE AS A GENERAL PRINCIPLE OF LAW AND ITS RELATION TO WAR

Peter Haggenmacher*

This Chapter aims to provide some introductory observations on the concept of self-defence, 'tracking its evolutionary path and the various meanings attributed to it throughout history, in different legal and belief systems,'[1] and also attempts to give some observations on self-defence as a general principle of law in the sense of Article 38, paragraph 1 (c), of the Statute of the International Court of Justice.[2]

As is well known, this provision – and its progenitors in the Committee of Jurists called upon to devise the Statute in 1920 – initially had in mind a number of basic principles 'recognised by civilised nations' owing to an intrinsic or systemic necessity; that is, a set of substantive or procedural concepts and norms that were thought to be indispensable in any developed legal order. Inasmuch as these principles were not just speculative but positively enacted in municipal law, they were also considered to be valid in international law, and hence applicable by the Permanent Court of International Justice that was being set up in The Hague. This could either be seen as a natural law concept (which was doubtless in the mind of Baron Descamps, the president of the Committee and the originator of this clause, although he might rather have called it 'objective law', in line with the sociological theories that were fashionable in his day) or (in the wake of the dominant positiv-

* Graduate Institute of International Studies, Geneva, Switzerland.

[1] The phrase is freely arranged from the title and subtitle of the Colloquium.

[2] Cour permanente de Justice internationale, Comité consultatif de Juristes, *Procès-verbaux des séances du Comité*, 16 juin-24 juillet 1920, pp. 293-297, 307-321, 331-336.

A.C.G.M. Eyffinger, A. Stephens and A.S. Muller (eds.), Self-Defence as a Fundamental Principle

ist concepts of his opponents in the Committee) as an analogical transposition of municipal law principles to international law.

Be that as it may, what all the members of the Committee were thinking of when speaking of 'general principles of law recognised by civilised nations' were essentially those found in the European legal orders and their various overseas extensions. In practice, this mainly consisted of two legal families: Continental civil law and English common law. In fact, modern international law has been decisively shaped by this twin source of inspiration, and this would seem to hold good, among many other concepts and institutions, for self-defence.[3] The following summary observations, which do not pretend to be more than a very tentative sketch, will therefore stay within this 'Western' horizon.

1. Self-Defence as 'the Primary Law of Nature'

There is a venerable chain of authorities and testimonies regarding self-defence as a basic principle, so intimately linked with human nature itself that it is supposed to precede instituted legal orders. Dryden calls it 'Nature's eldest law';[4] and Blackstone holds that, 'as it is justly called the primary law of nature, so it is not, neither can it be in fact taken away by the law of society'.[5] Isidore of Seville, more than a millennium earlier, considered *violentiae per vim repulsio* as part of natural law which is 'everywhere observed by natural instinct rather than by some legal enactment'.[6] Writing his

---

[3] Self-defence did not figure among the examples of general principles mentioned by the members of the Committee. Hersch Lauterpacht, the author of the first important monograph on general principles drawn from private law, mentions self-help and necessity, but not self-defence; *Private Law Sources and Analogies of International Law*, London 1927, p. 152. Symptomatically, Lauterpacht was writing just before the time when self-defence started to be discussed as a technical concept in international law with the signature of the Pact of Paris in 1928. Bin Cheng's classic study of 1953 on the general principles of law deals with self-defence under 'the principle of self-preservation', together with necessity and self-help; *General Principles of Law as applied by International Courts and Tribunals*, London 1953, pp. 77-97.

[4] John Dryden, *Absalon and Achitophel*, i, 458, following *The Compact Edition of the Oxford Dictionary*, Oxford 1971, v° Self-defence, p. 2717.

[5] William Blackstone, *Commentaries on the Laws of England,* Oxford 1765-1769, bk. III, ch. 1, 1, p. 4.

[6] 'Ius naturale [est] commune omnium nationum, et quod ubique instinctu naturae, non constitutione aliqua habetur; ut...violentiae per vim repulsio. Nam hoc, aut si quid huic simile

influential *Etymologies* in the first third of the VIIth century, Isidore was tributary to the Roman jurisconsults, who saw self-defence very much in the same light. Phrases such as 'vim enim vi defendere omnes leges, omniaque iura permittunt' were common among them, as we shall see.

By the same token one is reminded of the language of Article 51 of the United Nations Charter mentioning 'the inherent right of self-defense'. This is rendered in the French text of the Charter by 'droit naturel de légitime défense', and the two formulas are indeed equivalent, in spite of an apparent discrepancy. Both are in fact used interchangeably in a well-known American note of 1928 relating to Kellogg's draft of the future Pact of Paris. The proposed text, it says, purposely avoids mentioning self-defence, because this right is supposed to be '*inherent* in every sovereign state and is implicit in every treaty'; inasmuch, therefore, 'as no treaty provision can add to the *natural* right of self-defence, it is not in the interest of peace that a treaty should stipulate a juristic conception of self-defence'.[7] In 1945 States thought differently on this matter, when they deemed it appropriate to add an express provision on self-defence to the initial draft of the Charter. Both the English and French formulations of Article 51 find some basis in the American note of 1928. They are substantially equivalent inasmuch as they refer to an original right that precedes the written law of the Charter (and especially its article 2, paragraph 4, which by contrast in 1945 was, at least partly, new law).

Such an original, unwritten right of self-defence was precisely what Isidore of Seville had in mind when he derived it from natural law. In this respect his 'etymological' argument concerning *ius naturale* deserves attention: it is so named, he explains, because it is *commune omnium nationum,* and this in turn is so because it is valid everywhere *instinctu naturae*. For once Isidore's explanation makes sense: the words *natura* and *natio* stem indeed both from the verb *nasci*; natural law is 'inborn', and therefore common to all 'nations', considered not as States but as so many human families. By the same token self-defence appears as a 'natural' right 'born' with us, and hence 'inherent', not derived from any human legislation.

The fountainhead of this whole tradition of self-defence as a natural right is the passage from Cicero's *Pro Milone* that serves as a motto for the present

est, numquam iniustum [est], sed naturale aequumque habetur.' Isidorus Hispalensis Episcopus, *Etymologiarum sive originum libri viginti*, ed. Lindsay, Oxford 1911, bk. V, IV.

[7] Note of the Government of the United States to the Governments of Australia, Belgium, Canada, France, Germany, Great-Britain, etc., of June 23rd, 1928. A. Lysen (ed.), *Le Pacte Kellogg.* Documents concernant le traité multilatéral contre la guerre signé à Paris le 27 août 1928, Leiden 1928, p. 54.

Colloquium. It may be worthwhile to recall the circumstances that gave rise to this speech. Titus Annius Milo was accused of having deliberately caused the death of his enemy Publius Clodius Pulcher during an affray in 52 B.C. at Bovilla on the Via Appia where the two had come across each other with their armed escorts. The incident caused an enormous upheaval in Rome, where Clodius had been very popular with certain circles. This is why Cicero (a deadly enemy of Clodius) had to plead the case in a hostile atmosphere, which strained his rhetorical powers and caused him to lose his client's (and friend's) case.[8] The speech for Milo as it has come down to us was written after the event; had it really been proclaimed as written, it might have won the case. Although it is therefore surrounded by a degree of unreality, it is still, at least on paper, one of Cicero's most accomplished speeches, and certainly a classic text on self-defence. Cicero indeed tries to show that Milo had been the victim of an ambush laid by Clodius and that he therefore had to 'repel force by force'. This is the context of the well-known episode that figures in the introductory part of the speech where the legal problem is set out. If a man has been killed, Cicero explains, the accused usually either denies having done it at all or tries to defend his act as legal: 'aut negari solere omnino esse factum, aut recte ac iure factum esse defendi'. He continues: 'And if there is any occasion (and there are many such) when homicide is justifiable, it is surely not merely justifiable but even inevitable when the offer of violence is repelled by violence. ... against an assassin and a brigand what murderous onslaught can want justification? What is the meaning of the bodyguards that attend us, and the swords that we carry? We should certainly not be permitted to have them, were we never to be permitted to use them. There does exist therefore, gentlemen, a law which is a law not of the statute book, but of nature; a law which we possess not by instruction, tradition, or reading, but which we have caught, imbibed, and sucked in at nature's own breast; a law which comes to us not by education but by constitution, not by training but by intuition – the law, I mean, that, should our life have fallen into any snare, into the violence and the weapons of robbers or foes, every method of winning a way to safety would be morally justifiable. When arms speak, the laws are silent; they bid none await their word, since he who

---

[8] For these facts see e.g. Cicéron, *Discours*, t. XVII, Paris: Société d'édition 'Les Belles Lettres', 1967, pp. 47-60; Cicero, *Pro Milone*, ed. by A.B. Poynton, 2nd ed., Oxford 1902, pp. xi-xxiii; William Forsyth, *Life of Marcus Tullius Cicero*, 2nd ed., London 1867, ch. XVI, pp. 287-307; R. G. M. Nisbet, 'The Speeches', in T. A. Dorey (ed.), *Cicero*, London 1965, pp. 69-72.

chooses to await it must pay an undeserved penalty ere he can exact a deserved one'.[9]

Cicero's conception of self-defence as an elementary primeval right had a lasting influence over the centuries. Let it suffice to mention one author who had a long-standing familiarity with his works, Hugo Grotius, who quotes that very passage from *Pro Milone* to establish the legitimacy of recourse to force according to natural law; following a Stoic tenet reported by Cicero, he relates it with the *prima naturae*, the 'first things according to nature', which impel any animal, as soon as born, to provide for its own conservation and the maintenance of its proper condition, as well as to avoid its destruction and to repel whatever may cause it.[10] Self-defence is therefore paramount among those *prima naturae*, as Grotius confirms at the outset of his discussion of just causes of war. The first of these causes is indeed *defensio sui et rerum*. If an attack is directed against one's body and threatens one's life, he explains, it may be repelled even by killing the aggressor if there is no other escape. He adds: 'Note that this right of defence as such primarily arises from the fact that nature entrusts every one to himself, not from the injustice or sin of the one who is the source of the danger'.[11] This allows him to justify defence even against someone posing a threat without any bad intent. While he refers to medieval jurists and Spanish scholastics, this is in line with the Ciceronian *prima naturae*.

2. Self-Defence as an Institution of Positive Law

There is, however, another way of looking at self-defence, whereby it actually becomes a technical notion. Instead of being a pre-social right of nature, it can be seen as existing only within an instituted legal order, and by virtue of that order. Conduct beyond this social horizon should bear other names such as self-preservation or self-help. Self-defence itself is conceptually linked to a legal order that forbids recourse to force by its members, as an authorised exception to this prohibition. Such a prohibition in turn becomes practically

---

[9] Marcus T. Cicero, *Pro T. Annio Milone*, 8 (III) - 11 (IV), in Cicero, *The Speeches*. With an English translation by N.H. Watts, Cambridge, Mass., and London 1964, pp. 14-17.

[10] Hugo Grotius, *De iure belli ac pacis libri tres* (1625), Aalen 1993, bk. I, ch. II, §§ I (1) and III (1), pp. 48 and 53.

[11] *Op. cit.*, bk. II, ch. I, § III, p. 171.

possible only if legitimate force is effectively monopolised in the hands of central organs endowed with public powers. Rather than being an original right that subsists despite the legal order, self-defence in this perspective is an authorisation handed down by the legal order itself.

This is why it is strictly circumscribed by that order as to its conditions and extent. Its basic condition is an illegal attack raising an instant danger for one's person or property, which cannot be averted except by an immediate reaction. The attack has to be illegal, which excludes coercive acts carried out lawfully, such as by an official within his competences. The attack has to jeopardise an essential value: one's life and physical integrity in the first place, but also moral or material goods, as the case may be. Each legal order is free to determine the range of values it deems essential in this respect, through legislation (in municipal law) or custom (in international law), both being supplemented by case-law. These regulations will usually narrow down to the utmost the modalities of self-defence, which end up by being fairly similar from one legal order to the other.

As a rule, self-defence requires a situation of pressing necessity, which leaves no room for any choice: the danger therefore has to be overwhelming, that is, immediate or at least imminent, which excludes preventive action. On the other hand, self-defence may not be exercised after the fact, for by then it would cease to be defence and would turn into revenge. In addition to these limits in time, there are restrictions as to the action itself, which should be reasonably proportioned to the danger incurred (although some measure of disproportion will usually be dealt with leniently in view of the exceptional circumstances). This condition of proportionality is but another expression, in the exercise of self-defence, of the necessity condition that stands at its beginning. Necessity and proportionality are indeed the cornerstones on which the whole of self-defence is said to rest, be it in municipal or in international law.[12]

Most jurisdictions also allow for the defence of third persons, necessity combining with solidarity. In German terminology this is *Nothilfe*, while ordinary self-defence is *Notwehr*. The word *Not* is akin to the English *need* and stands for necessity. This leads to another related concept, *Notstand,* which in English is rendered by the very term 'necessity', in French by *état*

---

[12] International Court of Justice, *Case concerning Military and Paramilitary Activities in and against Nicaragua* (Nicaragua *v.* United States of America), Merits, 1986, § 176, p. 94, and § 194, p. 103.

de nécessité. These expressions apply to situations where one strives to preserve an essential interest against an impending danger by a measure which is normally unlawful inasmuch as it prejudices an innocent third person. The danger here may stem from any source, except from an attack: this is what differentiates *Notwehr* from the wider notion of *Notstand.* Both are sometimes subsumed under the heading of *self-preservation*, self-defence appearing as a particular case of necessity. They are usually considered separately in modern legislation. The same seems to hold good in international law, as witnessed by the recent draft on State responsibility by the International Law Commission in which self-defence and necessity are listed as distinct circumstances excluding wrongfulness.[13] Obviously the latter gives rise to more doubts than the former as to its legitimacy; but again, each legal order is free to sanction it on its own conditions as a rightful form of action along with self-defence.

These two forms of self-preservation should in turn be distinguished from *self-help.* The natural place of self-help is in so-called 'primitive' or 'weak' legal orders, which have only rudimentary central organs, and whose subjects therefore have 'to take the law into their own hands' to enforce it. While self-preservation has a mainly defensive connotation, self-help is distinctly active since it aims at the pursuit of a right.[14] Self-help is practically banished from modern municipal law, except in well-defined cases where it is explicitly authorised. It was prominent in classical international law when States enforced their claims by so-called measures of coercion short of war, such as intervention or reprisals; war itself was but an extreme means of self-help — 'die äusserste Selbsthilfe' in Heffter's words — inasmuch as it consisted of unilaterally imposing one's view on the adversary in order to 'settle a dispute'. Plainly, self-help is often a mere euphemism for power politics.[15]

[13] Report of the International Law Commission, Fifty-third session (23 April – 1 June and 2 July – 10 August 2001), General Assembly Official Records, Fifty-sixth session, Supplement No. 10 (A/56/10), *Draft Articles on Responsibility of States for Internationally Wrongful Acts*, chapter V, art. 21 and 25.

[14] Yet, as these concepts do not have a proper technical meaning, they are sometimes used interchangeably. See however the helpful clarification by Hans Kelsen, 'Collective Security and Collective Self-Defence under the Charter of the United Nations', *American Journal of International Law*, 42 (1948), pp. 783-796.

[15] It was rejected on these grounds by the International Court of Justice in the *Corfu Channel Case* (Merits) in 1949. See on this generally, René-Jean Wilhelm, 'La réalisation du droit par la force ou la menace des armes. Considérations sur l'arrêt de la Cour Internationale de Justice en l'affaire du Détroit de Corfu', *Annuaire Suisse de Droit International*, 15 (1958), pp. 93-130.

3. The Caroline Case: Self-Defence, Self-Preservation, or Self-Help?

The famous *Caroline* incident of 1837 could probably best be described as a case of self-help, although the parties discussed it essentially in terms of self-defence and self-preservation. It has indeed become a *locus classicus* on self-defence owing to Daniel Webster's well-known letter of April 24th, 1841, to the British Minister at Washington.[16] Here, the Secretary of State set out the conditions that should have been met in order for the Canadian raid on the *Caroline* to qualify as self-defence; in his mind these very stringent conditions – 'necessity of self-defence, instant, overwhelming, leaving no choice of means, and no moment for deliberation', etc. – were clearly not met. There is little doubt indeed that they were not, and this may account for the term self-preservation being used in conjunction with self-defence by the British in their correspondence with the American Secretary of State. Self-preservation was a much vaguer notion than self-defence, and it suggested at least a situation of necessity; but even this may have been somewhat exaggerated, in spite of the very real problems raised for the British authorities by the Canadian insurrection of 1837 and the aid it received from like-minded American citizens. The British raid could however pass muster as a measure of self-help, inasmuch as it purported to quell activities supporting the insurgents which should have been checked by the local American authorities themselves: 'At the time when the event happened, the ordinary laws of the United States were not enforced within the frontier district of the State of New York. The authority of the law was overborne, publicly, by piratical violence.'[17] This is what Fox, the British Minister at Washington wrote five weeks after the incident in response to the American complaint. In his opinion the Canadian authorities had to 'consult their own security, by pursuing and destroying the vessel of their piratical enemy, wheresoever they might find her', even on the American shore of the Niagara. It was the very negligence or inability of the American authorities to enforce their own law that

---

[16] R.Y. Jennings, 'The *Caroline* and McLeod Cases', *American Journal of International Law*, 31 (1938), pp. 82-99, at 89. For a full account of the incident in its context, see Kenneth R. Stevens, *Border Diplomacy*. The *Caroline* and McLeod Affairs in Anglo-American-Canadian relations, 1837-1842, Tuscaloosa and London 1989; an excellent study which, however, strangely does not mention Jennings's brief but (as usual) most perceptive note on the case.

[17] Letter of February 6th, 1838, in R.Y. Jennings, *op. cit.*, p. 85.

had therefore prompted the British to 'take the law into their own hands', even at the price of 'some little overstepping of the boundary of the Union' (as Palmerston put it in a despatch to Fox).[18] This is precisely what self-help is about.

The fact is, however, that the *Caroline* affair was seen by the parties as a case of 'self-defence and self-preservation'.[19] While this designation may seem somewhat incongruous to us, there was nothing strange about it at the time. It is enough to open Wheaton's *Elements of International Law*, which had appeared the year before the incident, to see both notions in narrow association. They are dealt with at the beginning of the second part, which bears on 'absolute international rights of states'. These absolute (or primitive) rights are accorded to every State 'as an independent moral being', simply 'because it is a state', whereas conditional (or hypothetical) rights, 'arise from international relations existing either in peace or in war', and hence only 'under particular circumstances'. Among the absolute international rights of States, the right of self-preservation is 'one of the most essential and important, and that which lies at the foundation of all the rest'. As such, it 'necessarily involves all other incidental rights, which are essential as means to give effect to the principal end'.[20]

Immediately after this sentence the text continues in the same paragraph: 'Among these is the right of self-defence'. The close relationship between self-preservation and self-defence could not be stated more clearly; they would seem to be almost identical, the latter being but a particular expression of the former. Wheaton's brief explanations concerning the right of self-defence wholly confirm this impression. It consists in the general right of a State to provide for its security by all reasonable means, which 'involves the right to require the military service of all its people, to levy troops and maintain a naval force, to build fortifications, and to impose and collect taxes for all these purposes'.[21] Significantly, this short passage on self-defence is immediately followed by a lengthy development on the 'right of intervention',

[18] Letter of December 15th, 1838, *ibid.*, p. 87, note 13.

[19] See e.g. Fox's letter of February 6th, 1838, *loc. cit.*

[20] Henry Wheaton, *Elements of International Law: With a sketch of the history of the science*, London 1836, vol. I, part II, §§ 1-3, pp. 107- 108. See also 8th ed., by R. H. Dana, Boston 1866, part II, ch. I, §§ 60-61, p. 75 (re-ed. in The Classics of International Law, Oxford and London 1936).

[21] *Loc. cit.*, § 3, p. 108 (= § 62, p. 75).

which amounts to the 'right of every independent State to increase its national dominions, wealth, population, and power, by all innocent and lawful means'.[22] Obviously Wheaton's concept of self-defence is a far cry from ours. Yet again, there was nothing unusual about this in his time. It can be traced to Klüber and to Martens, whose manuals were among the most influential during the XIXth century.[23] Some decades earlier, in the same vein, we find Vattel's *droit de sûreté*, which is dealt with in a separate chapter in the second book of his *Droit des Gens*:

'C'est en vain' [says Vattel] 'que la Nature prescrit aux Nations comme aux particuliers le soin de se conserver, celui d'avancer leur propre perfection & celle de leur état, si elle ne leur donne pas le droit de se garentir de tout ce qui peut rendre ce même soin inutile. ...Toute Nation, comme tout homme, a donc le droit de ne point souffrir qu'une autre donne atteinte à sa conservation, à sa perfection & à celle de son état, c'est-à-dire, de se garentir de toute lézion.... C'est ce droit de se garentir de toute lézion que l'on appelle *Droit de sûreté*'.[24]

From this basic right of security flows a threefold right of resistance, of seeking redress, and of punishment.[25] The right of resistance in fact amounts to self-defence, and Vattel's explanations show that his view of it is quite a generous one: it includes not only the right of warding off an actual attack, but also of anticipating 'machinations', provided one does not attack on the basis merely of 'vague and uncertain suspicions', lest one become an aggressor oneself.[26] This is all he has to say about self-defence in this place. He is hardly more explicit in the following chapter bearing on the 'observation of justice among nations', although he speaks here more specifically of 'the right of defence' belonging to any nation, that is, 'le droit d'opposer la force à quiconque l'attaque elle & ses droits'.[27] Nothing more is said about the conditions of self-defence. All we can surmise, again, is that Vattel has a rather broad conception of it. This may be explained by the fact that he examines defence only inasmuch as it is relevant as a just cause of war. Signifi-

---

[22] *Loc.cit.*, § 4, p. 109 (= § 63, p. 76).

[23] Johann L. Klüber, *Droit des gens moderne de l'Europe* (1819), ed. by M.A. Ott, Paris 1861, §§ 36-44, pp. 57-65; Georg F. Martens, *Précis de droit des gens moderne de l'Europe* (1788/1802/1821), ed. by Ch. Vergé, Paris 1864, bk. IV, ch. I, §§ 116-117.

[24] Emer de Vattel, *Le droit des gens*, London 1758, bk. II, ch. IV, § 49, p. 295.

[25] *Loc. cit.*, §§ 50-52, p. 296.

[26] *Loc. cit.*, § 50, p. 296.

[27] *Op. cit.*, bk. II, ch. V, § 67, p. 307.

cantly, the above-quoted passage is immediately followed by this short sentence which ends the paragraph: 'C'est le fondement de la Guerre défensive'.[28] The next paragraph deals symmetrically with the right to obtain redress by armed force, which in turn is seen as 'le fondement de la Guerre offensive'.[29] There is no marked difference between defensive and offensive warfare, since both consist of preserving one's rights: both are direct emanations of the Vattelian *droit de sûreté*.

This is obviously what we find in Wheaton's *Elements of International Law* eight decades later, Vattel's *droit de sûreté* being merely renamed *right of self-preservation*; both occupy the same central position, and the notion of self-defence derived from them is in substance the same: it is more or less what the parties had in mind in the *Caroline* case. Maybe Vattel gives us a clue to this wide notion of self-defence which seems so difficult to reconcile with our current, much narrower conception. As we have just seen, his *juste défense* is immediately linked with war; and inasmuch as recourse to war remained a legitimate means of preserving one's rights, there was little point in restraining self-defence to strictly defined conditions.

4. Self-Defence and Defensive War

Vattel's 'right of just defence', merely as the basis of 'defensive war', should indeed not be confused with the technical concept of self-defence as we know it from municipal law. The latter by definition excludes the very idea of war, which is incompatible with a State governed by a centralised public power. One of the basic features of any civil order is precisely to banish war. Recourse to force in self-defence, admitted as it is by all domestic orders, is therefore categorically distinct from war.

This is why self-defence did not properly become a subject of debate in international law before the time when States resolved to 'outlaw' war. As we know, this was only the case after World War I. Before 1914, peaceful settlement of disputes was of course considered desirable – as witnessed by the first Hague Convention of 1899/1907 – but war, and any measure short of war, still lay within the sovereign powers of States. Even the Covenant of

[28] *Ibid.* For a more restrictive notion of self-defence in Vattel, see *op. cit.* bk. IV, ch. IV, § 43, p. 284.

[29] *Loc. cit.*, § 68, p. 307.

the League of Nations did not radically exclude war. Such a stance was only taken by the Kellogg Pact in 1928, which for the first time aimed at abolishing war as a legal institution. Whereas war had until then been construed as a kind of duel between sovereign nations, it was now split into wrongful aggression on the one hand, and legitimate defence on the other. The negotiations leading up, from Briand's first proposal of April 6th, 1927, to the signature of the Pact on August 27th, 1928, reveal, however, that aggression and defence were still both largely considered in terms of aggressive and defensive *war*.[30]

Only in 1945, after an almost six year worldwide struggle fought on all sides as a classic, albeit total, war, did the language change from war to *force*. War no longer figures in the United Nations Charter in its technical meaning; in all the relevant provisions it has been carefully avoided and is superseded by the term force. Not only is force wider than war so as to include what had formerly been measures of coercion short of war; above all it is axiologically neutral: it can designate an illegal (Article 2, paragraph 4) or legal (Articles 44 and 46) use of force; it may consist of acts of aggression (Article 39) or armed attacks (Article 51), or of lawful measures (Article 39) or action by the competent United Nations organs (Article 42), or of self-defence by member States (Article 51).

Thus self-defence is henceforth to be considered as lawful use of *force*. It is no longer *war*, legally speaking, even if it results in major military operations (these, however, remain, as to their conduct, subject to the ordinary rules applying to armed conflicts). Significantly, the word *force* corresponds to the Latin term *vis*, which was the one used by Roman jurisconsults with respect to self-defence, as appears in the above-mentioned phrase.[31] By the same token we are led back to the idea voiced at the beginning of this Chapter: self-defence would indeed appear to qualify as a general principle of law in the sense of Article 38 of the Statute of the International Court of Justice. Its origins doubtlessly lie in municipal law. Being found in all developed jurisdictions, it was only natural that it should also crop up in international

[30] See e.g. A. Lysen, *op. cit.* (*supra*, fn. 7), pp. 27, 37, 43, 62, 66-7, 74, 75. There are other statements, however, which show that some of the negotiators at least (starting with Briand and Kellogg themselves, of course), had a clear consciousness that what was at stake was the very institution of war as it had been admitted hitherto; see e.g. pp. 17, 19, 20, 23, 28, 32, 41, 64, 83.

[31] See above, p. 4, and below, pp. 19-20.

law, once the latter had done away with war, at least nominally, even if for the time being the international community had not yet reached the degree of integration that characterises municipal law. The mere fact that recourse to force by individual States is prohibited by the United Nations Charter logically calls for the complementary principle of self-defence,[32] all the more so as the central organs remain weak and their action insufficiently detached from the interests of the member States.

In fact things are less clear-cut in their historical development. While the origins of self-defence indeed to a great extent lie in municipal law, especially criminal and tort law, the concept was also decisively shaped by the scholastic theory of war. It is mainly this latter aspect which will be highlighted here, but we shall start by a few considerations on the former.

5. Various Approaches to Self-Defence in Municipal Law

In municipal law, self-defence appears either as a right or as a mere excuse. Moreover it can be either seen as an autonomous principle excluding wrongfulness or as a particular circumstance excluding wrongfulness with respect to specific delinquencies. Most of today's criminal legislation considers it as a right and as an autonomous principle. Such is the approach of the Swiss Code of 1942 (the one least unfamiliar to the author, who had to study it some forty years ago!). At the centre of its article 33 ('légitime défense')[33] stands an illegal attack that may be repelled by proportionate means. Neither the object of the attack or its intended result, nor the outcome of the defensive action, are specified. This had also been the solution of the preceding cantonal codes, some of which, however, enumerated the categories of goods

---

[32] Hans Kelsen, *op. cit.* (*supra*, fn. 14). One has to remember, however, that article 51 of the United Nations Charter did not figure in the original Dumbarton Oaks Proposals; it was added in San Francisco at the request of several Latin-American States; J.L. Kunz, 'Individual and Collective Self-Defence in Article 51 of the Charter of the United Nations', *American Journal of International Law*, 41 (1947), pp. 872-879, at 872-873; see also Stanimir A. Alexandrow, *Self-Defence Against the Use of Force in International Law,* The Hague 1996, pp. 77-93.

[33] 'Celui qui est attaqué sans droit ou menacé sans droit d'une attaque imminente a le droit de repousser l'attaque par des moyens proportionnés aux circonstances; le même droit appartient aux tiers.' The second paragraph of the article concerns defensive acts in excess of what was required by self-defence (*Notwehrexzess*). See also Paul Logoz, *Commentaire du Code pénal suisse*, 2nd ed., Neuchâtel and Paris, 1976, pp. 168-174.

that could be protected, such as one's life, physical integrity, or property.[34] The same approach had been taken by the Prussian Code of 1794.[35]

Some decades earlier this position had similarly been adopted by Blackstone at the beginning of the third book of his *Commentaries,* in which he deals with 'private wrongs', in other words the law of torts. It is in fact the very passage where he calls self-defence 'the primary law of nature'. If someone is forcibly attacked in his person or property, it is lawful for him to repel force by force; and the breach of the peace, which happens, is chargeable upon him only who began the affray. For the law, in this case, respects the passions of the human mind; and (when external violence is offered to a man himself, or those to whom he bears a near connection) makes it lawful in him to do himself that immediate justice, to which he is prompted by nature, and which no prudential motives are strong enough to restrain.[36]

Clearly, this passage is in harmony with the above-mentioned Ciceronian tradition: self-defence appears as an absolute right of the attacked individual, a conception that tends to prevail in modern law, be it of torts or of crimes, even in the prevailing positivist perspective.[37] Historically, things have been quite different, and Blackstone also bears witness to this other tradition in book four of his *Commentaries*, in which he deals with public wrongs, that is, criminal law. Not only is self-defence there considered as a mere excuse, but moreover it appears only in the specific context of homicide. 'Homicide in *self-defence*, or *se defendendo*' is one of two sorts of 'excusable homicides', the other being 'homicide *per infortunium*, or *misadventure*'. Blackstone asserts 'that whereby a man may protect himself from assault, or the like, in the course of a sudden brawl or quarrel, by killing him who assaults him'. ...'and since in quarrels both parties may be, and usually are, in some fault; and it scarce can be tried who was originally in the wrong; the law will not hold the survivor entirely guiltless'.[38] This is why homicide in self-defence is considered 'excusable, rather than justifiable'.[39]

---

[34] Carl Stooss, *Die schweizerischen Strafgesetzbücher zur Vergleichung zusammengestellt*, Basel and Geneva, 1890, pp. 80-87. Ernst Hafter, *Lehrbuch des schweizerischen Strafrechts.* Allgemeiner Teil, Berlin 1926, § 29, pp. 135-143.

[35] *Allgemeines Landrecht für die Preussischen Staaten.* Neue Ausgabe, Berlin 1817, part II, title XX, sect. IX (Von Privatverbrechen), §§ 517-524.

[36] W. Blackstone, *op. cit.* (*supra*, fn. 5), bk. III, ch. 1,1, pp. 3-4.

[37] 'Die Notwehr ist ein subjektives Recht des Angegriffenen. Notwehrhandlung ist Rechtsausübung. Sie ist nicht nur straflos'. E. Hafter, *op. cit.* (*supra*, fn. 34), p. 143.

[38] W. Blackstone, *op. cit.* (*supra,* fn. 5), bk. IV, ch. 14, II, 2, pp. 184 and 187.

[39] *Loc. cit.*, p. 183.

This position is in keeping with an old English (and French) tradition which held the person responsible for this type of killing to be guilty, so that its author had to ask for pardon in order to be acquitted. Blackstone is clearly conscious of this legislative policy when he says that '[t]he law besides may have a farther view, to make the crime of homicide more odious, and to caution men how they venture to kill another upon their own private judgement; by ordaining, that he who slays his neighbour, without an express warrant from the law to do so, shall in no case be absolutely free from guilt'.[40] In any event, the practical consequences of this policy, as reported by Blackstone, forfeiture of one's goods and chattels, were already strongly attenuated in his times: 'the delinquent', he says, 'has now, and has had as early as our records will reach, a pardon and writ of restitution of his goods as a matter of course and right, only paying for suing out the same'.[41] In XVIIth century France, Jean-Baptiste Domat equally considered that 'he who is attacked by robbers or other armed persons, so as to be exposed to the danger of losing his life if he does not defend himself, may kill the robber or the aggressor without fearing that he be punished for homicide'.[42]

Yet, even if it was considered as a right and not as a mere excuse, self-defence still appeared in this tradition only as a particular case in the specific context of homicide or other delinquencies, as was the case in the French and Belgian codes of 1810.[43] Further back in time it had been the solution adopted in the *Constitutio Criminalis Carolina,* the criminal code edicted by Emperor Charles V in 1532, where *recht notweer* is dealt with in connection with *etlich böse tödtung.* The seven articles concerned are part of a development on *entschuldigte entleibungen* which aim at instructing the judges 'who have not been taught in the laws' how to distinguish such cases of 'pardonable manslaughter' from 'wicked killings'.[44]

---

[40] *Loc. cit.*, p. 187.

[41] *Loc. cit.,* p. 188.

[42] Jean-Baptiste Domat, *Les loix civiles dans leur ordre naturel* (1689/1697), Paris 1777, tome II, liv. III (suppl.), tit. VII, § 6 (Cas d'une légitime défense), p. 156.

[43] Art. 328 of the French *Code pénal* of 1810: 'Il n'y a ni crime ni délit, lorsque l'homicide, les blessures et les coups étaient commandés par la nécessité actuelle de la légitime défense de soi-même ou d'autrui.' See also G. Vidal, *Cours de droit criminel et de science criminelle*, 6ème éd., par J. Magnol, Paris 1921, p. 331.

[44] *Hals- oder Peinliche Gerichtsordnung Kaiser Carls V. und des H. Röm. Reichs nach der Originalausgabe vom J. 1533 auf das genaueste abgedruckt...*von Dr. Johann Christoph Koch, 8th ed., Marburg 1824, art. cxxxix-cxlv, pp. 67-71. Similarly, medieval German books

The same approach can be noticed in the highly influential Dominican and Jesuit Thomists of the XVIth and XVIIth centuries;[45] and it was indeed Aquinas himself who had given it a classic expression in an article of his *Quaestio de homicidio* entitled *Utrum alicui liceat occidere aliquem se defendendo*. He famously applies the theory of double effect: homicide in self-defence is but an accidental result of an action that aims at saving one's life. The moral qualification of the action being solely determined by its fundamental intent, self-preservation, the killing appears as a mere side-effect that lies beyond one's intention (we would nowadays speak of 'collateral damage'). No guilt at all attaches to such a *defensio,* which is declared *licita,* provided it remains proportionate in view of the concrete situation; and the killing has to be really unintended, for only public authorities are entitled to inflict death intentionally, and only in view of the public good.[46] In the language of the time this is called 'revenge', *vindicta* or *ultio*, and it remains strictly distinct from *defensio*. While the principle of double effect seems to have been contributed by Aquinas himself, the distinction between retributive vengeance and legitimate defence was common among the theologians and canonists who preceded him. They had mainly developed it with reference to the problem of war. It is to this aspect that we now have to turn.

6. The Roman Law Background of Our Theory of Self-Defence: The Medieval Glossators

Our modern theory of self-defence dates back to the medieval scholars just mentioned. It is essentially a creation of the jurists and theologians of the XIIth and XIIIth centuries. The materials for its construction were gathered

---

of law such as the *Schwabenspiegel* (ca. 1275) predicate self-defence (*reht nôtwer*) on homicide, whether the slain aggressor had struck at one's body or at one's goods (*nôtwer lîbes unde guotes*); *Das Landrecht des Schwabenspiegels*, ed. Wilhelm Wackernagel, Zurich and Frauenfeld 1840, § 194, p. 186; see also §§ 63, 310, 360, pp. 185-6, 298-9, 317-8. For the mature theory of the pandectists, see Chr. F.G. Meister, *Principia iuris criminalis Germaniae communis* (1755), 5th ed., Goettingen 1780, sect. II, part II, ch. IX, pp. 70-74.

[45] See e.g. Leonardus Lessius, *De iustitia et iure caeterisque virtutibus cardinalibus libri quatuor* (1605), Milan 1618, bk. II, ch. 9, dubitationes VIII-XIII, pp. 72-78; Ioannes Azorius, *Institutiones morales* (1602-8), Brixen 1622, part III, bk. II, ch. I, col. 113-119; see also below, pp. 33-35.

[46] Thomas de Aquino, *Summa theologiae,* Alba and Rome 1962, IIa IIae, q. 64, art. 7, pp. 1365-1366.

from Roman law, as they rediscovered it in the legal compilations ordered by Emperor Justinian in the VIth century, which were retrieved from oblivion and put to use in the Catholic stream of Christianity during the so-called XIIth century Renaissance. The Romans themselves had no proper, comprehensive theory of self-defence.[47] They did, however, take into consideration lawful resistance in a number of situations, as witnessed by several legislative texts figuring in Justinian's *Code* and by doctrinal writings collected in the *Digest*. It is from these passages that our theory of self-defence was pieced together by the medieval legists and canonists.

To be sure, at the very beginning of the *Digest* there is an extract of Florentinus that looks like a general theory of self-defence. It asserts anybody's right to repel force and injury: 'Ut vim atque iniuriam propulsemus'. Florentinus sets out that 'it is indeed by virtue of this law (i.e. the law of nations) that what is done to protect one's body is supposed to be rightfully done', and he explains this principle by a natural kinship among humans which makes it wicked for one man to pursue his fellow beings malignantly.[48] The passage was inserted here by Justinian's jurists to illustrate the notion of *ius gentium* as set forth by Ulpian in the text that precedes (and which in fact amounts to natural law applying among human beings, in contrast to his *ius naturale* which extends to all animals).[49] Florentinus's phrase is drawn from the first book of his *Institutes* and must have figured there as a fairly basic principle, echoing some philosophical teaching like the one in Cicero's *Pro Milone* (and echoed in turn by Blackstone's 'primary law of nature').

The principle is mentioned by several other jurisconsults in more specific contexts. One of its best known expressions figures in a passage by Paulus relating to the *Lex Aquilia*: 'Vim enim vi defendere omnes leges, omniaque iura permittunt'.[50] In the same context Gaius holds that one may without guilt kill a slave who is laying an ambush as a brigand: 'Nam adversus periculum naturalis ratio permittit se defendere'.[51] Another formulation of the principle is given by Cassius as quoted by Ulpian, this time in the context of possessorial interdicts. It figures in a lengthy comment on the interdict

[47] This is the case although such a theory is suggested by weighty authorities; see e.g. Theodor Mommsen, *Römisches Strafrecht* (1899), Graz 1955, pp. 620-21.

[48] *Digest*, 1, 1, 3. See also below, at fn. 81.

[49] *Op. Cit.*, 1, 1, 1, §§ 3 and 4.

[50] *Op. Cit*, 9, 2, 45, § 4.

[51] *Op. Cit*, 9, 2, 4, i. pr.

Unde vi: 'Vim (vi) repellere licere, Cassius scribit: idque ius natura comparatur.'[52] Pomponius, again quoted by Ulpian, renders it in yet another manner in a passage on invalidation of legal acts performed under threat. To this purpose a *restitutio in integrum* has to be ordered by a pretorial decree. Such an invalidation is not necessary, however, if the threat answers a threat by the other party, who is then merely suffering what he did himself: 'Nam cum liceat', says Pomponius 'vim vi repellere, quod fecit, passus est'.[53]

The very fact that the maxim *vim vi repellere licet* occurs in various contexts shows that it enjoyed an almost proverbial status. Nor was it merely a doctrinal principle, for we find it also in imperial legislation. To defend one's possessions by proportionate force is allowed, says a constitution of Diocletian and Maximianus Herculius of 290 A.D.: 'inculpatae tutelae moderatione illatam vim propulsare licet.'[54] The same principle is given effect in a series of constitutions relating to the *Lex Cornelia de sicariis et veneficiis*, where it is not one's possessions but one's life which is at stake: 'quia defensor propriae salutis in nullo peccasse videtur'.[55]

While the maxim *vim vi repellere licet* is thus fairly certain, nothing indicates that the Romans had any articulate theory of self-defence. They usually had in mind a given legal institution and its application in various circumstances. (It is the same approach as was noted above with respect to homicide). Their turn of mind was essentially casuistic and pragmatic. They did however display a wealth of legal arguments which could be exploited in another perspective by subsequent jurists – which was indeed done by their medieval successors.

When the Byzantine compilations were rediscovered during the XIIth century, they first had to be re-appropriated. This was the task of several generations of glossators who interpreted and annotated the texts as they were successively exhumed. Their glosses in fact often went beyond mere exegesis; many of them contained the first lineaments of new legal theories that were to be developed by the coming generations of jurists who are called post-glossators or commentators. This is also what happened in the case of the theory of self-defence. It was extracted from the various Roman texts in a manner certainly unforeseen by their authors.

---

52 *Op. Cit,* 43, 16, 1, § 27.
53 *Op. Cit,* 4, 2, 12, § 1.
54 *Code,* 8, 4, 1.
55 *Op. Cit.,* 9, 16, 3.

7. The Elements of the Theory Assembled: The Medieval Canonists

Apart from those legists (as the scholars of Roman 'laws' were collectively named) there was another family of medieval jurists, the canonists, whose field of study consisted of 'canons', the steadily growing corpus of church law. Its two main components during the XIIth and XIIIth centuries were Gratian's *Decretum* (ca. 1140) and the pontifical *Decretals* collected by order of Pope Gregory IX (1230). Although these texts had not come down from Antiquity, and were therefore readily understood, they too were glossed and commented by generations of 'decretists' and 'decretalists', who were also conversant with Roman law. They in their turn made a significant contribution to legal theory, not least in the field of self-defence. It was by them, in particular, that our concept of self-defence was properly defined and was to gain currency as a technical term[56]; and by them the notion of *defensio*, which had remained confined to private law relationships with the legists, was linked to the medieval theory of war.

That theory provided for two fundamental cases of just war: war declared by the emperor or an independent prince to avenge an injury, and self-defence, which was allowed by natural law and was therefore open to any human being. It may seem strange to us – as strange as it would have seemed to the Romans – that self-defence by mere individuals was considered as 'war'. Yet, the medieval notion of *guerra* (which is the same word as war[57]) was much wider than the Roman *bellum* which corresponds to the classical concept of war, restricted to sovereign entities. This is why the medieval jurists could deal with self-defence in terms of war and even see it as a basic expression of just war.

---

[56] To Romans, *defensio* and *defendere* had technical meanings in procedural and military matters; otherwise they had a merely factual connotation, even in situations of self-defence like Milo's *pugna Bovillana* on the via Appia; see Cicero, *Pro Milone*, IV (11) (quodam modo tacite dat ipsa lex potestatem defendendi ... sui defendendi causa); V (14) (non enim est ulla defensio contra vim umquam optanda).

[57] The term *war* derives from old high German *werra* (confusion, discord, strife) and *werran* (bring into confusion): see *The Oxford Dictionary of English Etymology*, ed. by C.T. Onions, with the assistance of G.W.S. Friedrichsen and R.W. Buchfield, Oxford 1966, sub verbum war. The derivation from German *wehren* is inaccurate, although commonly held (even by Leibniz himself!). The basic meaning of *wehren* is to hold in check, to hinder, to counteract, to obstruct.

The driving force behind this conception were the canonists. The identification of self-defence with a form of war was initiated by the decretists commenting on Gratian's celebrated *Causa 23*, which marks the beginning of the scholastic doctrine of just war. The first question raised by Gratian in that case deals with the apparent incompatibility between Christ's commands of love and charity and the profession of bearing arms: the purpose of soldiering is indeed to repel injury or to inflict vengeance, both of which are contrary to the Gospel.[58] After refuting the objection, in his second question Gratian sets out the requirements of just war. The decretists were to attach two important glosses to the very first sentence of the *Causa 23*. Taken together, these glosses lay down a theory of self-defence and link it to the doctrine of just war, which was in turn decisively shaped by Gratian.

The first of these glosses (*Hic quaeritur an militare*) states that the profession of bearing arms and war (*militare seu bellare*) are compatible with the Christian conscience; and it pronounces war to be free of sin in particular if it is declared by a prince, or if it aims at self-defence (*pro defensione sua*), or the defence of the country or of the paternal laws. *Defensio sua* is therefore clearly perceived as a case of just *war*.[59]

The second gloss (*Qui repellere possunt iniuriam*) follows immediately and bears on the word *propulsandam* in Gratian's opening sentence. It is unusually long and consists of a whole disquisition on the conditions of self-defence. Is it permissible for clerics or only for lay persons? The gloss holds that both may repel injury, but it goes on by distinguishing between injuries against the person and against property. In the first case it can be repelled preventively; if it has already occurred, it can be repelled on the spot (*incontinenti*); otherwise defence becomes revenge, and it is presumed to be revenge if the aggressor did not appear to strike a second time; in any event defence has to be blameless and proportionate (*cum moderamine inculpatae tutelae*); however, no blame will be incurred if this limit is exceeded unin-

---

[58] 'Quod militare alienum videatur ab Evangelica disciplina, hinc videtur posse probari, quia omnis militia, vel ob iniuriam propulsandam, vel propter vindictam inferendam est instituta. Iniuria autem vel a propria persona, vel a socio repellitur: quod utrumque Evangelica lege prohibetur.' *Decretum divi Gratiani ... una cum glossis*, Lyon 1554, part II, Causa 23, dictum Gratiani ante can. I, pp. 839-840.

[59] 'Hic quaeritur an militare seu bellare sit peccatum? et dicendum est quod non ... et hoc verum est, si a principe indicatur bellum ... Similiter pro defensione sua vel patriae vel legum paternarum...' Gloss on Causa 23, dictum Gratiani ante can. I (militare), *Ibid.*

tentionally. As to property, an injury can be repelled preventively, but it should preferably be repelled while it is ongoing.[60]

This gloss contains in a nutshell the basic elements of our modern theory of self-defence. It draws on canon and civil law sources which do not seem to have been combined into a coherent whole before. Especially, the two conditions of immediacy and proportionality for the first time appear in conjunction, both being required to keep self-defence from degenerating into revenge, which is reserved for public powers.

8. Self-Defence as a Form of Just War: Raymond of Peñafort and William of Rennes

From the beginning, this theory enjoyed a kind of double status. On the one hand, considering the gloss *Qui repellere possunt iniuriam* in itself, it appeared as self-contained; as such it did not have any specific link to the problem of just war. A link of this sort was, however, suggested, on the other hand, by the case dealt with in *Causa 23*, an armed repression of heretic bishops by order of the pope. This ambivalence explains why the gloss could

[60] 'Qui repellere possunt iniuriam, & qualiter possit repelli, & an tantum personae iniuria, vel etiam personae & rerum possit repelli, videndum est. Et quidem videtur, quod non solum laici sed etiam clerici possunt repellere iniurias & rerum & personae. . . E contra videtur, quod clerici non possunt ... Ad hoc dicunt quidam, quod nulli licet vim repellere repercutiendo, sed tantum impediendo. Alii dicunt quod licet laicis repercutere [,] clericis non. Ego credo quod Et clericis & laicis licet repercutere : distinguitur tamen, quia Aut vis infertur personae, aut rebus. Si personae, tunc est vis repellenda priusquam sit illata. Sed quidam dixerunt quod nullus vim repellere debet nisi illatam: imo insidiantem licitum est occidere ... si tamen aliquis vim factam repellat, potius praesumi debet quod defendendi quam ulciscendi causa fecerit id... & hoc si primus percussor volebat percutere denuo, alioqui si nolebat denuo percutere & alter repercusserit, potius est vindicta quam repulsio iniuriae. & sic intelligo quod dicitur iniuriam incontinenti posse repelli. Requiritur ergo, quod defendendo repercutiat, non ulciscendo... & cum moderamine se defendat... si quis tamen moderamen excedit, & non ex proposito, non tenetur .... Item incontinenti debet vim vi repellere .... Si autem vis infertur rebus, & illatam & inferendam licitum est repellere, sed potius illatam quam inferendam.' Gloss on Causa 23, dictum Gratiani ante can. I (propulsandam), *Ibid.*The references to canon and civil law texts have been omitted. For an English translation of this gloss, see Gregory M. Reichberg et al. (eds.) *The Ethics of War*, Classic and Contemporary Readings, Oxford, etc., 2006, pp. 109-111.On the theory of self-defence of the decretists and early decretalists, see St. Kuttner, *Die kanonistische Schuldlehre von Gratian bis auf die Dekretalen Gregors IX.*, Vatican City 1935, pp. 335-379.

become relevant in various contexts, especially in criminal law. For the time being, however, its influence was mainly felt in the field of war. This was above all due to the use made of it by one of the foremost canonists of the age, Raymond of Peñafort, a Black friar from Catalonia.

Raymond had not only compiled the pontifical decretals by order of Pope Gregory IX, he was also the author of the *Summa casuum poenitentiae*, a new type of canonistic manual for the use of confessors. The work seems to have been written between 1222 and 1228 in its first version, and revised between 1235 and 1245. During that time it was, most importantly, commented on by another Dominican, William of Rennes, whose glosses became an integral part of Raymond's text.[61] The combined work of Raymond and William exerted a considerable influence on the notions of self-defence and of just war.

Self-defence appears in three different places in Raymond's *Summa*: under homicide, duelling, and war. Self-defence is a valid excuse in case of homicide 'by necessity', provided the author had no other means of escape; while no penance is incurred in this case, Raymond holds that he should still feel guilty in conscience on account of the ambiguous situation in which he found himself; like Blackstone centuries later, he seems to consider it 'excusable rather than justifiable'.[62] Raymond is even more severe on duelling in court. The use of duels as a method of proof, though very common, was disparaged by the Church, not least because it often ended in homicide. Yet a party could be compelled to accept fighting lest he lose his case. While Raymond recognised this as a situation of necessity, he still was not ready to concede more than a reduced culpability.[63] This restrictive attitude is probably due to the element of homicide which is common to both passages; it is in keeping with medieval criminal law in France and England, as noted above. Strangely, however, Raymond's argumentation is not couched in terms of self-defence; it is only William of Rennes who adds the language of self-defence in his glosses.

---

[61] On Raymond of Peñafort and his *Summa de casibus*, see St. Kuttner, 'Zur Entstehungsgeschichte der Summa de casibus poenitentiae des hl. Raymund von Penyafort', *Zeitschrift der Savigny-Stiftung für Rechtsgeschichte*, kan. Abt., 70 (1953), pp. 419-434. On William of Rennes, see Ludwik Ehrlich, 'Guillaume de Rennes et les origines de la science du droit de la guerre', *Mélanges G. Gidel*, Paris 1961, pp. 215-227.

[62] Raymundus de Peniafort, *Summa de poenitentia et matrimonio*, Rome 1603, bk. II, tit. 1 (De homicidio), § 3, p. 149; see also above, pp. 16-17.

[63] *Op. cit.*, bk. II, tit. 3 (De duello), pp. 162-164.

The situation is different in the third passage, which deals with war: this time self-defence is already widely present in Raymond's text; here, too, however, William's glosses do add quite a few specifications. This is therefore to be considered the main passage on self-defence in the *Summa Raymundia*. It comprises three paragraphs, which are part of a long chapter dealing with rapine, brigandage and arson, three types of patrimonial delinquencies that were common in medieval warfare.[64] Yet, as far as depredations were committed in the prosecution of a just war, they could be condoned. This is why Raymond first sets out the conditions of a just war. To that purpose he puts to use an important gloss on the *Decretum Gratiani* enumerating five ways in which a war can be unjust (*Bellum dicitur iniustum quinque modis*); he changes these five possible deficiencies into as many positive requirements that have to be cumulatively fulfilled for a war to be just. Last and yet foremost among them is princely authority, which is indeed the pivotal condition for a full-fledged war.[65] He then proceeds by stating in the following paragraph that this authority can be dispensed with in the case of a merely defensive war: 'for the law itself allows every one to repel force by force, instantaneously and with blameless moderation'.[66] There follows a lengthy disquisition on this type of war; in fact Raymond closely follows the decretist gloss *Qui repellere possunt iniuriam*.[67] The theory of self-defence it contains is thereby explicitly connected with war. And William's marginal comments greatly enhance this impression. Both scholars obviously have in mind small scale violence among minor potentates, not the 'princely' war of the preceding paragraph. But these numerous *guerrae* were not essentially different from war waged by sovereign persons. This is precisely why the Church endeavoured to restrain them by grafting a Romanistic theory of self-defence onto them. Yet, given the mentality and conditions of the time, these restrictions could not be all too drastic if they were not to lose all credibility. Some of William's glosses vividly illustrate this dilemma.

---

[64] *Op. cit.*, bk. II, tit. 5 (De raptoribus, praedonibus, & incendiariis), §§ 17-19, pp. 184-188. The paragraphs do not figure on the manuscripts; they were only introduced in the first printed edition of the work, which is being referred to here.

[65] *Loc. cit.*, § 17, pp. 184-185. For the gloss *Bellum dicitur iniustum quinque modis*, see *Decretum divi Gratiani* (*supra*, fn. 58), part II, causa 23, quaestio II, dictum Gratiani ante can. I, p. 844.

[66] *Loc. cit.*, § 18, p. 185.

[67] *Loc. cit.*, § 18, pp. 185-187. For the gloss *Qui repellere possunt iniuriam*, see above, fn. 60.

Two of them refer to Raymond's passage concerning defence of things, which reproduces the short sentence that ends the decretist gloss *Qui repellere possunt iniuriam*: 'If on the other hand force is directed against property, then one is permitted to repel it, whether it has already occurred or is planned, but rather (that is, above all) when it has already occurred.'[68] Self-defence may thus be preventive, but it is preferably exercised against an ongoing attack, and Raymond stresses this point even more than does the gloss. He continues by adding: 'provided this happens immediately, that is, as soon as one knows that the attack has occurred, and before one turns to a contrary action'[69] (that is, a different activity). This time he has in view the period *after* the attack has occurred. As a rule, self-defence is legitimate only on the spot; in the language of the scholastics it must be *in continenti*. There has to be a seamless continuity between attack and defence, otherwise defence becomes revenge (*ultio*).

This being posited in terms of principle, William's glosses are most instructive as to the way in which this immediacy-condition was interpreted in practice. It had to be determined according to the quality of the activity, depending on the more or less time required for preparation. Thus, if some nobleman with a whole army invades the territory of another nobleman and occupies a castle or takes booty there to carry it off to his own territory, if the second nobleman upon hearing this, unable to gather troops and recover the booty or liberate the castle immediately, sends messages or envoys to levy an army, though he cannot do so before one week, or two, or more, he is still deemed to defend himself and to liberate the castle and to recover the booty immediately, even if his adversary has already secured it behind his walls.[70]

Whole weeks can therefore elapse during this preparation, 'or more', and it will still be *in continenti*, depending on the concrete situation. Later manuals of penitence developing that theme would even stretch the time to six months or a year, provided the wronged nobleman does not turn to a 'contrary action'. William explains this notion in another gloss:

It is not considered to be a 'contrary action' if one eats, drinks, or sleeps in the meantime, or prepares to drive the enemy out of an unjustly occupied possession or recover booty brought away by him, even if this preparation demands a period of delay (as has been said); but if one disregards the injury

[68] *Loc. cit.*, p. 186. For the gloss, see *supra*, fn. 60,

[69] *Loc. cit.*, p. 187.

[70] *Loc. cit.*, pp. 186-187.

and gives up the intention to pursue one's goods, turning to other occupations, then this is a 'contrary action'.[71]

Very logically, the 'immediacy' will therefore stretch even beyond the time of the preparatives: it will in fact extend to the whole war that ensues, which will not cease for that matter to be defensive. Again, William's comment is eloquent:

I also believe that, while he is thus pursuing the booty and cannot manage to recover it, perhaps because it has been brought to impregnable places, if he seizes some of the goods of his adversary or his attendants or of those who thwart his pursuit of the goods, he can retain some of their goods and indemnify himself for the losses incurred.[72]

William's notion of *defensio* is obviously quite elastic; it seems to comprise any means to put oneself again into possession of one's property. By the same token, the second major condition of self-defence, proportionality, is in turn stretched very far. This condition is expressed by a formula borrowed from Roman law, *moderamen inculpatae tutelae.*[73] Legitimate defence is supposed not to exceed the 'moderation of blameless protection'. This condition had given rise to a number of discussions and distinctions among the decretists, as reflected in Raymond's text. It was mostly examined in respect to the defence of persons rather than of property, but it obviously also applied to the latter. Overstepping the 'measure of blameless protection' again gave rise to the risk of passing from mere defence into revenge. But to prove such an intention on the part of the person hitting back was not easy. Here is what William had to say on the matter:

This moderation has its place when someone, to protect, that is, to defend himself, resists the adversary with such moderation that the defence or protection is blameless, that is, without fault because it does not exceed the limits of defence nor harms the adversary more – especially on purpose – than is required on account of his violence.[74]

This purely formal definition leaves a wide latitude in its concrete application, and it is easy to imagine how far it could go in a scenario like the one of the two warring noblemen described by William.

---

[71] *Loc. cit.*, p. 187.

[72] *Ibid.* In fact, without being named, this is already a case of medieval 'reprisals', i.e. 'taking back' the equivalent of one's loss.

[73] See *supra*, fn. 54.

[74] *Loc. cit.*, p. 185.

Raymond's and William's teachings were soon reproduced in combined form in another penitential manual, the *Summa perutilis* authored by Monaldus de Capo d'Istria in the second half of the XIIIth century.[75] They recur in a whole series of such manuals written over more than two centuries. It is noteworthy that in all of them self-defence remains included in the entry bearing on 'war'. Such is still the case in the most important of these manuals, which sums them up in a culminating composition, the *Summa summarum* published by Sylvester de Prierio around 1515.[76] But before getting there we have to consider an important medieval treatise by another canonist, John of Legnano.

9. Self-Defence as 'Particular War': John of Legnano and Sylvester de Prierio

John of Legnano's treatise on war, written around 1360, is nothing less than a general theory of war setting out the various categories of conflict which were considered as 'war' in his time.[77] After a shorter disquisition on 'spiritual' wars, it deals with four types of 'corporeal' wars: 'universal corporeal war' as waged by sovereign powers, and three forms of 'particular corporeal wars' which include, apart from reprisals and six different types of duels, 'particular war as waged for one's protection'. This is nothing other than self-defence. It is examined in a substantial section, which forms a diptych with the section on reprisals: while self-defence aims at the protection of the 'true' body of the individual, reprisals protect the 'mystical' body of the city.

It is immediately apparent how closely integrated self-defence is in John's system. There is no doubt that in his view it represented a genuine form of war. This is partly due to a common perception which he shared with his contemporaries; and partly it is the result of his philosophical outlook, which tends to consider any sort of conflict as war. John obviously had a solid philosophical, essentially Aristotelian background, and he liked to show it.

---

75 Monaldus de Capo d'Istria, *Summa perutilis* (ca. 1254-1274), Lyon 1516, fol. xix^{r}-xix^{v} (De bello iusto), and fol. ccxvii^{r}-ccxviii^{r} (De restitutione damnorum in bello iusto facienda).

76 See below, p. 33.

77 The work was first printed in 1477 under the title *De bello, repraesaliis et duello*, and this title was maintained in subsequent prints. The original title, however, seems to have been simply *De bello*, as shown by the manuscript of Bologna (B. 1393) reproduced in T. E. Holland's edition of the work (The Classics of International Law, Washington 1917).

To this trait we owe what is certainly the most coherent and best articulated account of the medieval conception of self-defence.

It is precisely owing to his philosophical leanings that he is the first to give a genuine definition of self-defence, just as he is in fact the first to define war as such – if we set apart what Isidore of Seville had to say of it in his *Etymologies*.[78] War in general is defined as 'a contention arising by reason of something discordant offered to human desire, tending to exclude the discordancy'.[79] From this very comprehensive and abstract formula derive six more specific definitions relating to the various types of war, spiritual or corporeal, universal or particular, as the case may be. Among them, self-defence figures as 'a contention arising on account of something alien, presented to human desire, proceeding from the infliction of particular violence and tending to its exclusion'.[80]

Having defined self-defence, John inquires into its legal basis. His starting point is the gloss to Florentinus's fundamental passage declaring resistance to violence and injury to be licit: 'Nam iure hoc evenit, ut quod quisque ob tutelam corporis sui fecerit, iure fecisse existimetur'.[81] The glossators had deemed it necessary to restrict the word *iure* by adding: 'scilicet iure fori, non caeli', to wit by human law, not by divine law. No further explanation is given, but the restriction probably alludes to the Christian injunction of non-resistance. At any rate John considers this reservation as inaccurate. In his opinion all laws, human or divine, authorise what he calls *defensa* or *defensio*.

Its first basis is natural law: 'war for one's protection stems from natural law, not from positive law, be it civil or canonical'.[82] 'For nature, whatever thing it produces, tends to its conservation, as far as the strength of the natural agent goes, and strives to expel whatever is opposed to it', as shown in Aristotle's *Physics*. At the root of defence lies 'natural instinct', as Isidore of Seville had already observed. Positive law does no more than approve of it and regulate it as to its exercise in society.

After natural law John examines divine law, which seems to harbour some serious objections to self-defence on the grounds already put forth by Gratian:

---

[78] *Op. cit.* (*supra*, fn. 6), bk. XVIII, I.

[79] Iohannes de Lignano, *De bello, repraesaliis et duello* (ca. 1360), ed. T.E. Holland (*supra*, fn. 77), ch. i, pp. 78 (text) / 126 (translation).

[80] *Op. cit.*, chap. lxxviii, pp. 130/277.

[81] See *supra*, at fn. 48.

[82] Iohannes de Lignano, *op. cit.* (*supra*, fn. 77), ch. lxxx, pp. 131-2/278-280.

'Non vos defendentes' is the command handed down by Saint Paul, in the wake of Christ himself. John considers however *defensa sui ipsius* to be quite consonant with charity, since the latter implies not only love of others but also 'dilectionem sui, et sui conservationem', and if so, 'ergo defensam'.[83] Therefore divine law allows one to defend oneself. 'Moreover, divine law does not entirely abolish acts proceeding from natural law, but modifies and refrains them'.[84] John thus holds the gloss to be wrong inasmuch as it affirms self-defence to be contrary to divine law. Like Gratian, he thinks that the teachings of the Gospel are addressed to the inner realm of the heart, not to outward deed.

Thereupon he asks 'what persons may declare this particular war', and at the outset he makes an interesting distinction: 'It is one thing to ask who may *defend* himself, and another to ask who may declare the *war* above defined, the object of which is defence'.[85] Defence as such, he states, 'is allowed to all natural created and corruptible beings'. But as to the 'war above defined', only humans are entitled to wage it. This can indeed be deduced from his definition of that particular type of war which is directed against 'something alien presented to *human* desire'. Although this systemic reason is in itself enough to justify John's position, he may also have had in mind the gloss to Florentinus's text: it specifies that the violence one is allowed to repel must be 'inferred unjustly by some private person', which excludes resisting *justly* inferred private violence as well as resisting coercion by a superior; the gloss ends by stating that beasts too are allowed to repel violence, although they are not capable of committing injury nor of suffering it. Legal relationships can only exist among human beings: such is therefore the case also for self-defence properly speaking, that is, in John's conception, when it is seen as a form of war.

After these introductory observations John examines in detail what persons are entitled to 'declare' this particular war in self-defence. He successively considers the cases of clerics, priests, monks, slaves, and banished individuals, in sometimes awkward situations. Is a cleric, while celebrating, allowed to ward off an attack and, if the aggressor is killed, to continue to celebrate his office?[86] And what about a priest attacked while he is baptizing

[83] *Loc. cit.*, pp. 132/279.
[84] *Loc. cit.*, pp. 132/280.
[85] *Op. cit.*, ch. lxxxi, pp. 133-4/280-1.
[86] *Op. cit.*, ch. lxxxiv, pp. 135-6/283-4.

a child in mortal danger? May he turn to his defence or has he first to carry out the sacrament to its end, lest the child die without being baptised?[87]

John then comes to the other questions raised at the beginning, which are mostly answered in the same casuistic manner: against whom is self-defence allowed? in favour of what persons? for what things? in what manner? and to what end? The legitimate end of self-defence is 'conservatio sui ipsius et bonorum ... et propter hoc est permissum'.[88] As to the legitimate manner in defending oneself, it hinges on the two well-known conditions established by the decretists: *cum moderamine inculpatae tutelae* and *in continenti*, that is, proportionality and immediacy. If one or the other condition is exceeded, defence threatens to turn into revenge and thereby to go beyond the legitimate end of 'conservatio sui ipsius et bonorum'.[89]

We may here set aside the lengthy disquisitions on the three remaining questions, however precious they may be in conveying a more concrete idea of the sort of situations John and his contemporaries had in mind when they talked of *defensio* as a 'particular war'. To a large extent these were clearly cases that would nowadays fall under the description of self-defence, such as the said clerics fending off an attacker while celebrating their office. The same holds good when it is asked whether a son may defend himself against his father, or a servant against his master.[90] Other situations, however, are obviously part of medieval warfare: is a vassal held to assist his lord or a knight his commander?[91] Or again, if a vassal sees that his lord and his father are being attacked at the same time, both being threatened with death, whom has he to assist, given that he cannot assist them both?[92] In fact all these were seen as cases of 'war' in John's times, the notion of war being considerably wider than ours.

It was only normal that this general conception should be reflected in the writings of the jurists. At the same time it should be noted that it was above all the canonists who developed this medieval theory of self-defence as a form of 'war'. The legists, their Romanist colleagues, had little part in it, which may seem strange, given that it was 'their' law, as gathered in the

[87] *Op. cit.*, ch. lxxxvi, pp. 136-8/284-6.
[88] *Op. cit.*, ch. cxxi, pp. 154/306.
[89] *Op. cit.*, ch. cxi-cxiv, pp. 151-2/302-4.
[90] *Op. cit.*, ch. xci and xciii, pp. 141, 142/290, 291.
[91] *Op. cit.*, ch. xcix, pp. 145/295.
[92] *Op. cit.*, ch. cii, pp. 146/296-7.

Digest and *Code*, that furnished the basic materials concerning self-defence. The paradox is easily explained by the fact that their teaching naturally had to closely follow the texts upon which they were commenting. These texts did touch upon self-defence in several places, but did not consider it in any way as war. Bartolus and his colleagues therefore saw no reason to consider it in these terms; they were content with analysing the texts as they stood. For instance in Bartolus's important comment on Florentinus's passage *Ut vim* the term 'war' does not once occur, while it was greatly to inspire his younger contemporary John of Legnano in his treatment of 'particular war' in self-defence.[93] Yet, so deeply was the assimilation of self-defence and war engrained in the mentality of the time, that even the legists, once they enjoyed some leeway with regard to their texts, would easily slip into the register of war. Thus Oldradus da Ponte, an elder contemporary of Bartolus who gave a great number of consultations, states in one of them that moderate defence or blameless protection cannot be specifically defined, but only with reference to the circumstances of the *war*; that is, [taking into account] the person inflicting violence or injury, the person defending himself, the cause of the *war*, the thing that is at issue, the place, the occasion, and all other arguments of that sort... Besides, moderate defence can be generally defined and the legitimate form of *war* understood in three ways. First, one should not rashly take up *arms*, that is, not without great necessity and deliberation. Further, one should see not to exceed the measure required to repel the violence and injury; for why kill someone who can be captured? Thirdly, the *victory* should not be pushed to the point of insolence; for many made better use of *war* than of *victory*.

Oldradus's considerations are reported in Johann Kahl's *Lexicon iuridicum* compiled around 1600 and they would therefore seem to have had some relevance up to that time.[94]

---

[93] Bartolus de Saxoferrato, *Prima super Digesto veteri,* Lyon 1533, ad legem *Ut vim* [= *Digest,* 1, 1, 3; *supra* fn. 48], fol. 6^r – 6^v. See more generally Georg Dahm, *Das Strafrecht Italiens im ausgehenden Mittelalter*, Berlin and Leipzig 1931, pp. 115-151.

[94] Iohannes Calvinus, *Lexicon iuridicum iuris caesarei simul, et canonici, feudalis item, civilis, criminalis*, Geneva 1670, p. 266 b. Italics supplied. It was not possible for the author to obtain a copy of Oldradus's original text in order to ascertain its context; probably some situation of medieval *guerra* as the one described above at pp. 25-28. Kahl also quotes a definition by one Salomonius which is much nearer to our modern conceptions of self-defence: 'Defensio est instantis imminentisve offensionis propulsatio: ubi haec cessat, non est, quod propulsari queat, ab offensione enim omnis defensionis pendet ratio...' *Ibid.*

No wonder that the medieval conception of self-defence should still prevail at the threshold of modern times in Sylvester de Prierio's *Summa summarum*. This canonist deals with war in three separate entries bearing respectively on public war, private war, and 'common war inasmuch as it impinges on clerics or churches'. The second entry is entirely devoted to self-defence.[95] But the subject is already touched upon at the beginning of the first entry, where Sylvester explains the basic distinctions between public and private war (respectively identified with John of Legnano's common and particular wars, although the two pairs do not entirely coincide).[96] It is worth noting that *repraesaliae* and *duellum*, the two major forms of particular war in John's system, appear under separate headings[97] (as had already been the case in earlier penitential manuals, mainly for practical reasons). Only self-defence therefore remains in the orbit of *bellum*: unlike the other two forms of 'particular war', *defensio* had not yet reached an autonomous status. This underlines all the more that it was still normal, at the beginning of the XVIth century, to perceive it as a form of war.

To be sure, Sylvester concedes that *defensio* is not war in the full meaning of the word, it is only *bellum improprie*, as Pope Innocent IV had already stated by the middle of the XIIIth century in his classical commentary on the *Decretals*; only war declared by a prince was *bellum proprie dictum*, invoking the full effects of war as laid down by Roman law.[98] Though Sylvester recalls this restrictive definition of war, which ever since Innocent's days had become a standard conception in decretalist literature (including the *summae confessorum*), he still deals with *defensio* as war, just as Raymond of Peñafort, William of Rennes, and John of Legnano had done. These are in fact Sylvester's main inspirators in his second entry on war, 'when it is private', which to all intents and purposes can be considered as a full summary of the medieval theory of self-defence.

10. Defensive War in Sixteenth Century Thomism: Cajetan

While the theory described above would in itself remain fairly stable during the following centuries, its relation to war was partly changed with the in-

---

[95] Sylvester de Prierio, *Summa Sylvestrina quae summa summarum merito nuncupatur*, Antwerp, 1581, part I, v° Rursus de bello II. Quando est privatum, pp. 80-82.

[96] *Op. cit.*, pp. 75-76.

[97] *Op. cit*, part II, pp. 301-302 and 26-27, respectively.

[98] *Op. cit.*, part I, v° De bello publico, pp. 76-80.

tellectual and political revolutions of the XVIth century. To be sure, it recurs almost in its medieval guise in some of the main treatises on the law of war, not least in Francisco de Vitoria's *Relectio de iure belli* (1539) and even more so in Hugo Grotius's *De iure belli ac pacis libri tres* (1625). In both works self-defence still figures as a basic cause of war, a kind of war that could be legitimately waged by anybody, including private persons. Yet this wide notion of war was getting anachronistic in a political environment increasingly dominated by the emerging sovereign States. In this altered political and legal framework war and self-defence as hitherto understood would necessarily drift apart. War became an exclusively public and interstate relationship soon to be governed by emerging international law. Self-defence for its part would recede into municipal law, mainly as part of criminal jurisdiction, such as it appears in the *Constitutio Criminalis Carolina* of Emperor Charles V.[99] This institutional development had a doctrinal counterpart in Cardinal Cajetanus's commentary on Aquinas's *Summa theologiae*. Written at about the same time as Sylvester's *Summa summarum*, it was to enjoy a quasi official status, very much as had been the case with the ordinary gloss to the great legal collections of the Middle Ages. The effect of the commentary was to enhance the relevance of Aquinas's *Summa*, which became the leading textbook of the Catholic Church during the Counter-Reformation. Through the lectures and treatises elicited by generations of Dominicans and Jesuits it became immensely influential in fashioning conceptions in the field of moral philosophy in general and of legal theory in particular.

This was the case also for Aquinas's doctrine of war and self-defence. As they figured under distinct headings of his *Summa* – war under the theological virtue of charity, self-defence under the cardinal virtue of justice – they were dealt with separately by Cajetan. Self-defence was thus discussed in its own right in the context of homicide, without any link being established with war.[100] As to war, it was curiously Cajetan who introduced the idea of defence, which did not figure in Aquinas's original article.[101] He did it, not to perpetuate medieval conceptions of war, but to clarify Aquinas's first requirement of just war, the *auctoritas principis.* What sort of prince exactly had he meant? For, apart from true princes, there are others who depend on a superior and are princes only in name. The latter, Cajetan explains, have but

[99] *Supra*, fn. 44.
[100] *Supra*, fn. 46.
[101] *Op. cit.* (*supra*, fn. 46), IIa IIae, q. 40, pp. 1266-1269.

a limited capacity to wage war, for strictly defensive purposes. Only the former are invested with full powers of war including offensive war to inflict revenge and punishment on the adversary; and this is the sort of war and type of prince Aquinas was talking about. Otherwise, the prince would not represent a 'perfect republic'; his commonwealth would not be autarchic, having to rely on a superior to assert its rights beyond mere defence. In modern terms, it would not be a fully sovereign State. This is therefore the limited yet crucial part played by self-defence in Cajetan's argumentation: 'Ad euidentiam authoritatis requisite ad bellum sciendum est, quod non est questio de bello defensiuo: quando scilicet aliquis bellum facit defendendo se ab indicto sibi bello. hoc enim a nature iure quilibet populus habet'. 'Any people has indeed the right to defend itself, just as any private person has the right to 'uim ui repellere cum moderamine inculpate tutele'. But it is beyond such moderation of inculpable protection for a private person to take vengeance for himself or for others.[102] Thus, while Cajetan does recall in passing that private persons are entitled naturally to defend themselves against attacks, this serves him only to characterise the powers of war of non- sovereign *princes*. Rather than self-defence in the technical sense, it is defensive *war* he has in mind.

Cajetan's *bellum defensivum* is the ancestor of Vattel's *guerre défensive*. Its counterpart, *bellum offensivum*, was only coined by Cajetan's successors, especially Vitoria, Molina, and de Valentia;[103] others such as Bañes or Suárez would rather speak of *bellum aggressivum* (without any negative connotation).[104] The terminology, which became current in the course of the XVIth century, clearly referred to war by public authorities, be it offensive or defensive. The link between *bellum offensivum* and 'private' self-defence – *propria defensio*, as Suárez calls it[105] – was in fact never entirely forgotten, it was indeed regularly referred to by all the Spanish scholastics; but it was increasingly perceived as a mere analogy.

---

[102] *Secunda secundae Sancti Thomae, cum commentariis Cardinalis Caietani*, Lyon 1548, fol. 69r-69v.

[103] Franciscus de Vitoria, *Relectio de iure belli*, n. 1, in *Relecciones teológicas*, ed. T. Urdánoz, Madrid 1960, pp. 817-818. Ludovicus Molina, *De iustitia et iure* (1593-1600/1615), Geneva 1733, tract. II, disp. 100, n. 1-2. Gregorius de Valentia, *Commentariorum theologicorum tomus tertius* (1595), Lyon 1619, q. 16, punct. 2, col. 711 D-E.

[104] Dominicus Bañez, *De fide, spe, et charitate,* Salamanca 1584, q. XL, art. 1, col. 1351-1353. Franciscus Suárez, *Opus de triplici virtute theologica, fide, spe, et charitate,* Coimbra 1621, disp. XIII, sect. 1, n. 4-6, pp. 798-799.

[105] *Loc. cit.*, n. 4, p. 798.

11. Gentilis and Grotius on Self-Defence, Defensive War, and Prevention

A similar attitude can be observed in a jurist like Alberico Gentili, the author of an important treatise on the law of war published at the end of the XVIth century. While his concept of war is essentially public and international – *publicorum armorum iusta contentio*[106] – subject to a specific *ius gentium bellicum*, Gentili remains deeply attached to the Italian civilists he had studied in his youth at Perugia and would later teach his students as a Regius Professor of Civil Law at Oxford. He does refer to their theory of self-defence in the chapters bearing on defensive war; at the same time, however, he stresses the limited relevance of this private law analogy in conflicts between independent nations. This appears especially in his treatment of what he calls *defensio utilis*, that is, preventive war. Summing up the teachings of civil law in this matter, he holds that 'it is lawful to anticipate a wrong', and therefore also 'to attack a man who is making ready to attack me'. 'One ought to provide not only against an offence which is being committed, but also against one which may possibly be committed. Force must be repelled and kept aloof by force... These things are clear and well established and thoroughly adapted to a treatise on war.'[107] This point being settled, he continues:

What follows is more doubtful, namely, the question when a matter may be said to have reached the point where it is necessary to resort to that expedient defence. A just cause for fear is demanded; suspicion is not enough. Now a just fear is defined as the fear of a greater evil, a fear which might properly be felt even by a man of great courage. Yet in the case of great empires I cannot readily accept that definition, which applies to private affairs. For if a private citizen commit some offence against a fellow citizen, reparation may be secured through the authority of a magistrate. But what a sovereign has done to a sovereign, no one will make good.[108]

As appears in this passage and in some others, Gentili, while remaining fully a jurist in municipal law, had an open ear for the requirements of *ragione di stato* in the realm of the law of nations. He willingly acknowledged his admiration for Machiavelli.[109]

---

106 Albericus Gentilis, *De iure belli libri tres* (1598), Hanau 1612, bk. I, chap. 2, p. 17.

107 *Op. cit.*, bk. I, ch. 14, pp. 98-99 (p. 62 of the translation).

108 *Loc. cit.*, p. 99 (page 62).

109 A. Gentilis, *De legationibus libri tres* (1585), Hanau 1594, bk. III, ch. 8, p. 168 (marginal reference), and more explicitly at ch. 9, pp. 171-175. He has in mind the author of the *Discourses* on Livy, not of the *Prince*.

This was not to the taste of Grotius, who firmly rejected the intrusion of politics in his treatise on the law of war.[110] He pointedly reproved Gentili precisely on this question of preventive war.[111] A closer reading shows that the two authors are less far apart than a first impression might suggest; the main difference, as usual, lies in Grotius's construction. His terse observations on this point figure at the very end of his chapter on *defensio sui vel rerum*, almost as a sort of appendix on self-defence among nations.[112] Taken as a whole, the chapter presents us, by contrast, with a markedly 'privatist' theory of self-defence, as could have figured in a XVIth century treatise by some Thomistic theologian like Domingo de Soto[113] (one of Grotius's first readings when he studied law as a precocious youth). It seems to have no relevance at all to war as commonly understood by his contemporaries. And yet the whole chapter is supposed to be relevant to war, inasmuch as self-defence remains for Grotius a legitimate ground for war, just as it had been for the medieval canonists. It applies above all to private war, he explains, that is, to the sort of conflicts occurring among ordinary people, although it may be made applicable also to public war, if the difference in condition be taken into account. In private war this right is, so to say, momentary; it ceases as soon as circumstances permit to appeal to a judge. But public war, since it does not arise except where there are no courts, or where courts cease to function, extends in time and is continually fostered by renewed losses and injuries. Besides, in private war, self-defence is generally the only consideration; but public powers, in addition to defence, have the right to inflict punishment.[114]

It is indeed owing to their criminal jurisdiction that preemptive war becomes possible for public powers:

Hence they are allowed to forestall violence which is not present, but which is seen to be threatening from afar, not directly (for that, as we have shown, would work injustice) but indirectly, by inflicting punishment for a crime commenced but not yet carried through.[115]

In modern parlance this faculty of 'praevenire vim non praesentem, sed quae de longo imminere videtur' amounts to preemptive, rather than preven-

[110] H. Grotius, *op. cit.* (*supra,* fn. 10), prolegomena, n. 57, p. 27.
[111] *Op. cit.*, bk. II, ch. I, § XVII, p. 183.
[112] *Loc. cit.*, § XVI, pp. 182-183.
[113] Dominicus de Soto, *De iustitia et iure*, Salamanca 1556, bk. V, q. 1, art. 8.
[114] H. Grotius, *op. cit.* (*supra*, fn. 10), bk. II, ch. I, § XVI, pp. 182-183.
[115] *Loc. cit.*, p. 183.

tive war, which is clearly dismissed in the following paragraph with a marginal citation to Gentili's above-mentioned chapter on 'expedient defence'. Grotius completes his explanations under the chapter 'on punishments' which deals with criminal law and penal war: for such a war to be lawful in case of a merely inchoate crime, he requests some real damage having already occurred, or at least a tangible danger, not just speculations on a future political equilibrium and dangers, merely *verisimilia* and *possibilia* as Gentili would to some extent admit.[116]

While the substantive difference between the two authors thus is minimal, the important point here is that Grotius moves the problem of prevention away from defence to punishment and thereby allots it a new systematic place. This allows him to maintain self-defence as such within strict limits, and it explains why he considers it mainly in relation to private persons. Still, he seems to stand fully in the tradition of the medieval lawyers when he considers self-defence by private individuals as a real form of war, against the dominant trend of the XVIth century. His intention was certainly not to revive medieval feuding. Rather, it was to give self-defence its proper place in a general system of lawful recourse to force, or, in other words, in a comprehensive theory of 'just war.' In his system any use of force, *vis,* would indeed automatically give rise to a *bellum*. Accordingly, his definition of war was very wide: *status per vim certantium,* 'the condition of those contending by force.'[117] While Gentili's earlier definition included only what nowadays would be called international war, Grotius's formula meant to encompass any form of violent struggle between any sort of persons. 'War' thus became a somewhat abstract concept with an almost philosophical touch (not unlike the one we met in John of Legano's treatise, which was perfectly familiar to Grotius). War starts where jurisdictions end –'ubi iudicia deficiunt, incipit bellum'[118] – was the axiomatic phrase repeatedly used by Grotius. War stands

[116] *Op. cit.* bk. II, ch. XX, § XXXIX (4), p. 509; see also bk. II, ch. I, § XVII, and compare with A. Gentilis, *op. cit.* (*supra*, fn. 106), bk. I, ch. 14, p. 106 ('a defence is just which anticipates dangers that are already meditated and prepared, and also those which are not meditated, but are probable and possible. This last word, however, is not to be taken literally, for in that case my statement would be that it is just to resort to war of this kind as soon as any one becomes too powerful, which I do not maintain. For what if a prince should have his power increased by successions and elections? Will you assail him in war because his power may possibly be dangerous to you? Some other reason must be added for justice's sake.').

[117] *Op. cit.*, bk. I, ch. I, § II, p. 30.

[118] *Op. cit.*, bk. II, ch. I, § II, p. 170.

in the extension of a legal action. To be lawful, it must be fought for a just cause and in the absence of a competent judge. If these conditions are met, even 'private war' remains legitimate as fought by common individuals defending or prosecuting their rights.

To establish a complete system of these natural rights was one of Grotius's chief endeavours. They were defined as enforceable claims, and hence a just grounds for war. Based on natural law as it derived from the rational and social nature of man, his system of rights was supposed to be exhaustive, therefore allowing one to distinguish infallibly just causes of war from mere pretexts. The system included four general categories of legal claims, each answering a specific type of injury committed by the adversary. First among them came self-defence, as a reaction to 'injury not yet done'.[119] Such are the philosophical premises of Grotius's conception of *defensio sui et rerum*. What looks like private law is in fact part of a general system of natural law.

It was precisely to this fresh natural law spirit and to its renewed systematic context that the Grotian theory of self-defence owes its influence, in spite of its obvious lack of originality. As we have just seen, it found itself integrated into a general system of substantive law which was in turn identified with a system of rightful claims. The function of the latter in the overall framework of the treatise was to allow an exact determination of the rightful causes of war in any given situation, which was the centrepiece of Grotius's just war theory. In this respect self-defence moved back into the orbit of war, from whence Cajetan and his followers had withdrawn it. But the legal system of which it had become an integral element had an autonomous significance, and it could therefore be detached from the particular context of just war. Owing to its intrinsic coherence it was apt to become the main platform for the subsequent development of jurisprudence, going beyond what the Spanish scholastics had achieved in terms of moral theology. It was in this new jurisprudential atmosphere that the theory of self-defence would from then on evolve and become an autonomous principle of law.

---

[119] *Loc. cit.* See generally on this question, P. Haggenmacher, 'Droits subjectifs et système juridique chez Grotius', in L. Foisneau (ed.), *Politique, droit et théologie chez Bodin, Grotius et Hobbes,* Paris 1997, pp. 73-130.

12. SELF-DEFENCE DISTINGUISHED FROM DEFENSIVE WAR: PUFENDORFF

This new type of legal philosophy is none other than the celebrated School of the Law of Nature and Nations. It came into being during the second half of the XVIIth century through the Saxon jurist Samuel Pufendorff, whose major treatise appeared in 1672 and bore precisely the title *De Jure Naturae et Gentium*. Pufendorff considered Grotius as the founder of this new school of jurisprudence, and himself as his continuator. At the same time he was clearly under the spell of Hobbes, whose political theory contained an implicit criticism of Grotius's conceptions of man, of society, and law. Pufendorff acknowledged this twofold debt in the preface to his first work, the *Elements of Universal Jurisprudence* published in 1660.[120] As the title insinuates, it was written in an Euclidean spirit, which was due to the influence of his professor of mathematics at Jena, Erhard Weigel, whom Pufendorff mentions as the direct inspirator of the work.[121] While this taste for 'demonstrative sciences'[122] may explain his fascination for Hobbes, he emphatically opts for the Grotian conception of man as a sociable creature whose normal condition is peace, not war. Two fundamental laws preside over his conduct in the state of nature: first, he should protect his life and limb, and preserve himself and his belongings; second, he should not disturb human society, and therefore avoid anything whereby it might become less tranquil. Pufendorff brings this twofold imperative into one synthetic formula: 'That everybody strive to preserve himself in such manner as not to disturb the society among men.'[123]

This key formula, which in essence was to remain constant in Pufendorff's *scientia iuris et aequi*,[124] appeared to be Grotian, echoing as it did the Stoic distinction between *prima naturae* and *quaedam consequentia*.[125] But in its vagueness it was quite compatible also with Hobbes's conception of the natural

[120] Samuel von Pufendorff, *Elementorum jurisprudentiae universalis libri duo* (1660), 2nd ed., Cambridge 1672, praefatio (no pagination). It proved impossible to compare this 'editio novissima & emendatissima'(reproduced in the *Classics of International Law* series as No. 15, Oxford and London 1931) with the first edition of 1660. In any event, it is interesting to note that it was reedited in the very year that Pufendorff's main treatise was published.

[121] *Ibid.*

[122] *Ibid.*

[123] *Op. cit.*, bk. II, observatio IV, § 4, p. 284.

[124] *Op. cit.*, preface, i. pr.

[125] H. Grotius, *op. cit. (supra,* fn. 10), bk. I, chap. II, § I (1).

condition of man, provided the latter was given a little twist. Instead of seeing it as a lawless condition of war, one could interpret it as a mere condition of instability and precariousness from which law was not excluded. Hobbes himself, after all, had postulated, beside his natural *right,* a *law* of nature inducing man to rational conduct in order to survive in the best possible way, that is, in striving for peaceful coexistence with his fellow beings.[126] While Hobbes's law of nature was in essence prudential rationality, Pufendorff instilled it with legal validity (just as Locke, his exact contemporary, was to do three decades later). Natural law being thus properly law (edicted by a proper lawgiver, God), the state of nature was in turn a lawful and basically peaceful condition.[127] But owing to its intrinsic precariousness it was constantly in danger of collapsing into a state of war. Behind the Grotian smile loomed a Hobbesian grin.

Peace is declared to be man's natural and normal state: it is the one that prevails as long as the second fundamental law is observed, as long as men fulfil their mutual duty not to disturb their social link, in other words, as long as they consent to settle their differences peacefully. As soon however as this (procedural) duty ceases to be observed, as soon as legal claims come to clash, the parties being unwilling to settle the dispute peacefully, the state of nature breaks down and gives way to the state of war, in which the contestants strive for their rights by force. While Pufendorff considers war only as a *status subsidiarius,* because it is not the *natural* way for man to pursue his rights, he still terms it a *necessary* means of last resort, and it becomes very easily so owing to the instability of the state of nature.[128] War is always lurking, and it brings to the fore the first fundamental law which enjoins men to fulfill their duties toward *themselves*. In the end Pufendorff's *lex de*

---

[126] Thomas Hobbes, *Leviathan* (1651), ed. by W. G. Pogson Smith, Oxford 1909, part I, chap. 14, p. 99.

[127] S. v. Pufendorff, *op. cit.* (*supra,* fn. 120), bk. II, observatio IV, §§ 1-5, pp. 280-285. For Locke, see *The Second Treatise of Civil Government* (1690), chap. II (Of the state of nature) and chap. III (Of the state of war), in *Two Treatises of Government,* ed. by T.L. Cook, New York 1947, pp. 122-132. Locke's conception of the *state of nature* is slightly more 'Grotian' than Pufendorff's, owing to his 'strange doctrine' of natural 'jurisdiction' of the individual, everyone having power to 'execute' the law of nature against its transgressors in the name of mankind. But his *state of war* is quite as Hobbesian as Pufendorff's, giving way to a *ius belli infinitum.* See on this question Richard Cox, *Locke on War and Peace,* Oxford 1960.

[128] S. v. Pufendorff, *op. cit.*, bk. I, definitio III, §§ 5-6, pp. 11-14.

conservando se ipso is thus paramount, just as the principle of self-preservation had been in Hobbes's system.[129]

The principle finds various expressions, two of which are particularly relevant in our context: a theory of necessity in the first place, and secondly a theory of self-defence.[130] They are treated in this order, because necessity is supposed to remain within the state of peace, whereas self-defence opens on war. It may well be that the two theories appear side by side for the first time, as they normally do nowadays in criminal codes[131] or in the draft articles of the International Law Commission on State responsibility.[132] In fact, Pufendorff seems to be the first author to draw an autonomous and coherent theory of necessity;[133] in Grotius it had remained an elusive white knight appearing here and there to save a desperate situation, as it had in the scholastics who preceded him. As to self-defence, it constitutes the very point where the natural order of peace breaks down and gives way to the 'subsidiary' order of war. In this reversed perspective, war all of a sudden becomes the vantage point, and self-defence finds itself engulfed in it. The explanations that follow are styled in terms of war. In a truly Hobbesian manner, anybody is allowed to defend himself by any means, including preventive war, and the rights of war stretch as far as needed to exact guarantees and to secure a peaceful future.[134] The classic conditions of self-defence, instantaneousness and proportionality, are only relevant within States; outside, the

---

[129] Th. Hobbes, *loc. cit.* (*supra*, fn. 126). Self-defence proper has only a restricted place in Hobbes's system: it is a residual (and inalienable) nucleus of man's original natural right of preserving himself in the state of nature, once he has submitted to the public power of a commonwealth; *op. cit.*, part I, chap. 14, pp. 101-102, and part II, chap. 21, pp. 167-168.

[130] S. v. Pufendorff, *op. cit.*, (*supra*, fn. 120), bk. II, observatio IV, §§ 6-10, pp. 285-294, and §§ 11-20, pp. 294-304.

[131] The Swiss criminal code deals with both in articles 33 and 34 respectively. Self-defence tends to be considered as a special case of necessity; see E. Hafter, *op. cit.* (*supra*, fn. 34), § 29, pp. 135-136, and § 30, p. 144.

[132] Art. 21 (self-defence) and 25 (necessity) of the draft articles as adopted in 2001 (*supra*, fn. 13); compare art. 33 (necessity) and 34 (self-defence) in Special Rapporteur Roberto Ago's original draft, with his comments, *Annuaire de la Commission du droit international*, 1980, vol. II, 2nd part, pp. 33-59.

[133] See on this Paola A. Pillitu, *Lo stato di necessità nel diritto internazionale*, Perugia 1981, pp. 29-35.

[134] S. v. Pufendorff, *op. cit.* (*supra*, fn. 120), bk. II, observatio IV, §§ 12-13 and 16, pp. 295-297 and 298-299.

sole limitations are those deriving from humaneness and prudential considerations, both being favoured by nature herself as means to restore peace.[135]

In this first sketch of Pufendorff's system, self-defence thus appears completely entwined with war, both being immersed in the philosophical tonality struck by Grotius and Hobbes. While this atmosphere and the basic principles were to be fully maintained in his mature treatise, *The Law of Nature and Nations*, the two concepts would henceforth be clearly dissociated and partly rearticulated. Self-defence and necessity are presented (now in this order) in two separate chapters at the end of book II, which deals with man's natural condition and his duties toward himself,[136] while war figures at the end of the work, in book VIII, which bears on sovereign power and its various 'parts', in the manner of Bodin and Hobbes.[137] To be sure, Pufendorff does not hinge his concept of war exclusively on sovereign power; his chapter *De jure belli* sets out from a general notion of war involving any sort of belligerents, and then only focuses on war between States.[138] In the first half of the chapter we meet with the distinction between defensive and offensive war[139] inherited from the Spanish scholastics: *bellum defensivum* seems to be war proper, even if waged by non-sovereign persons, and it is clearly dissociated from *defensio sui* as dealt with in book II.[140] The theory of self-defence, for its part, constitutes as it were a linear extrapolation of the one sketched in the *Elementa*, but freed from any intermingling with war. It is built on the same dichotomy of self-defence in the state of nature and in civilisation,[141] thereby conciliating the two traditions, naturalist and positivist, that were described at the beginning of our considerations.[142]

---

[135] *Loc. cit.*, § 18, pp. 301-303. These limitations, however, are described in terms that fit only war among nations, without any clear indication being given as to its possible differences with war between individuals.

[136] S. v. Pufendorff, *De jure naturae et gentium libri octo* (1672), Amsterdam 1688, bk. II, ch. V (De defensione sui) and chap. VI (De jure et favore necessitatis), pp. 181-212.

[137] *Op. cit.* bk. VIII, ch. VI (De jure belli), pp. 879-895.

[138] *Loc. cit.*, §§ 1-7 and 8-16, pp. 880-885 and 886-895, respectively.

[139] *Loc. cit.*, § 3, pp. 881-882. Pufendorff's main point in this brief paragraph is to justify preventive warfare.

[140] 'Quanquam autem singulis in civitate quandoque concedatur licentia propriis se viribus defendendi; ea tamen proprie jus bellandi vocari nequit.' *Loc. cit.*, § 8, p. 885. The individual does however recover his primeval 'jus defensionis, quale in libertate naturali est' if he finds himself in places 'quae ad nullam civitatem pertinent', such as the ocean; but while granting this *jus defensionis* Pufendorff avoids calling it a *jus belli gerendi*, especially if the aggressor is a compatriot; *ibid.*

[141] *Op. cit.*, bk. II, ch. V, §§ 1-3 and 4-19, pp. 182-186 and 186-202, respectively.

[142] See above, pp. 4-9.

Pufendorff's mature theory of self-defence is in this respect a landmark. It was to become one of the main references for future codifications, in conjunction with the sister theory of necessity set out in the following chapter.[143] Their combined influence could only be enhanced by their simplified restatement in one single chapter (though again neatly separated) in Pufendorff's third jurisprudential work, *The Duty of Man and Citizen.*[144] Published the year after his main treatise, this compendium was meant 'for beginners', but it became one of the most authoritative manuals up to the French Revolution, especially in Barbeyrac's translation.

13. Self-Defence Identified with Defensive War: Wolff

After the founder of the School of the Law of Nature and Nations we have to come to the philosopher who brought it to full blossoming, Christian von Wolff. He is at the same time Vattel's direct model, so that we again reach the point to which we had stepped back when we were searching for the roots of the argumentation in the *Caroline* incident. While Pufendorff had built a homogeneous natural law system, rejecting in a Hobbesian vein Grotius's conception of a distinct law of nations grounded on the positive consent of States, Wolff considers that such a law of nations does exist apart from natural law; not just as a loose set of rules and institutions as in Grotius (or in Suárez for that matter), complementing natural law, but as a separate and autonomous system of norms specifically applying to States as members of a higher community of nations (*civitas maxima*). This is why he divides his major legal work into a *Jus Naturae methodo scientifica pertractatum* (in eight books, published almost yearly from 1740 to 1748) and a *Jus Gentium* no less 'scientifically treated' (in a single volume, following in 1749). Although they form distinct 'sciences', owing to their respective objects, the law of nations is connected in many ways with the law of nature, as appears tangibly through Wolff's demonstrative method which is rigorously (and tediously) applied throughout the two works, with many references from one to the other.

---

143 Blackstone refers to Pufendorff's chapter on self-defence in his *Commentaries on the Law of England*, bk. IV, ch. 14, II, 2, p. 185.

144 S. v. Pufendorff, *De officio hominis & civis juxta legem naturalem libri duo* (1673), Cambridge 1682, bk. I, ch. V, §§ 1-17 (self-defence) and 18-24 (necessity), pp. 31-41.

Self-defence has a place in both, and in both it is considered as a form of war. In Wolff's *Jus Gentium* it figures as defensive war among States, along with offensive war, just as it was to be in Vattel's *Droit des Gens*, with hardly more explanation.[145] For a proper theory of self-defence we have to turn to the *Jus Naturae*, where Wolff's philosophical underpinnings are better elaborated.

In spite of some ostensible differences from Pufendorff, Wolff's natural law principles are equally Hobbesian in their Grotian (and Leibnitzian) attire. While Pufendorff had dealt with self-defence under man's duties toward himself, Wolff examines it under man's duties toward others.[146] We owe to others what we owe to ourselves, provided they are unable to procure it by themselves, and as far as we can procure it without neglecting our duties to ourselves. Those duties of charity owed to others, also termed duties of humanity, are 'internal' duties weighing on our conscience; they are matched only by 'imperfect' rights which are not enforceable.[147] On the other hand, we have a 'perfect' right to enforce 'external' obligations owed by others to ourselves (and reciprocally). Such rights may be grounded in some specific relationship like a contract; but we also have a general right not to suffer any 'lesion' (*laesio*), that is, 'any action rendering us or our external condition less perfect'.[148]

This general right, which is a corollary of our natural liberty, is called *jus securitatis*.[149] Wolff considers it as the master right which commands, and

[145] Christian von Wolff, *Jus gentium methodo scientifica pertractatum*, Halle 1749, §§ 615-617, pp. 490-491, and § 629, pp. 501-502.

[146] Chr. v. Wolff, *Jus naturae methodo scientifica pertractatum*, part I, Francfort and Leipzig 1740, chap. III, §§ 973-1057, pp. 634-704. Necessity for its part is relegated to the law of property; *op. cit.*, pars sexta, Halle 1746, ch. IV; see also Wolff's *Institutions du droit de la nature et des gens*, ed. by E. Luzac, Leiden 1772, part II, chap. IV.

[147] The distinction between 'perfect' and 'imperfect' rights (and correlative duties) stems from Pufendorff, who had derived it from the Grotian distinction between 'expletive' and 'attributive' justice (redefining the Aristotelian notions of commutative and distributive justice). Wolff moreover correlates perfect and imperfect rights with 'external' and 'internal' obligations respectively, another Grotian pair which, however, originally had a different meaning: it concerned law in the objective sense (*op. cit. supra*, fn. 10, bk. I, ch. I, § IX), whereas the first pair concerned law as a subjective right (*op. cit.*, bk. I, ch. I, §§ IV-VIII). See P. Haggenmacher, *op. cit.* (*supra*, fn. 119), pp. 121-130. The concept of duties of humanity was equally coined by Pufendorff, *op. cit.* (*supra*, fn. 136), bk. III, chap. III (De promiscuis officiis humanitatis).

[148] Chr. v. Wolff, *op. cit.* (*supra*, fn. 146), part I, chap. II, § 669.

[149] *Loc. cit.*, § 917, pp. 602-603.

guarantees as it were, all other rights: 'Jus adeo securitatis tuetur jura cetera omnia'.[150] It applies to individuals as well as to States.[151] The expression seems to have been coined by Wolff himself; Vattel's *droit de sûreté* is its direct offspring.[152] The underlying idea is obviously Hobbes's principle of self-preservation: ever since Hobbes, security has indeed been a central value in Western political thought.

From this universal, cardinal right flow two more specific rights which are still fairly general: the right to defend oneself against an impending *laesio* and the right of punishing its author in order to forestall any future offence and thereby to 'secure' one's 'perfection'.[153] Both these rights are intimately linked to each other in Wolff's conception, punishment being in fact a sort of prospective defence. The resulting theory of self-defence appears in a renewed light, not only through its rearticulation *more geometrico*, but also by its general spirit which brings it nearer to self-preservation than previous authors, including Pufendorff, had ventured.

Laesio is indeed a wider notion than *iniuria* (although sometimes one stands for the other), and it correspondingly extends the sphere of self-defence.[154] It has a technical value, and Wolff himself seems to have intro-

---

[150] *Loc. cit.*, § 920, p. 604.

[151] Chr. v. Wolff, *op. cit.*, pars octava, Halle 1748, ch. I, §§ 12-13, pp. 9-10; *op. cit.* (*supra*, fn. 145), ch. V, § 580, pp. 462-463, and § 636, pp. 509-510.

[152] See above, pp. 12-13.

[153] *Op. cit.* (*supra,* fn. 146) part I, chap. III, §§ 972-1057 (defense), pp. 634-704, and §§ 1058-1100 (punishment), pp. 704-729.

[154] *Op. cit.*, § 669, pp. 440-441. Wolff's explanations in his *Institutes* are helpful: 'Au reste quoique la lésion & l'injure consistent, en un acte; elles diffèrent cependant en ceci, que le mot de lésion a rapport à la personne dont on viole le droit, exprimant un acte que cette personne ne doit point souffrir; au lieu que l'injure est considérée comme une violation du droit lui-même, sans égard à la personne à qui on l'a fait, ou comme un acte illicite en soi, où l'on regarde au droit-même qui est violé.' *Op. cit.* (*supra*, fn. 146,), part I, ch. III, § 88, pp. 36-37. The term *laesio* and its verbal form *laedere* were already amply used by Wolff's forerunners, especially Pufendorff (see e.g. *op. cit. supra*, fn. 136, bk. I, chap. VIII, §§ 15 and 16, p. 89, or bk. III, ch. I, esp. §§ 1-3 and 5-6, pp. 213-215 and 216-219, and *op. cit. supra*, fn. 144, bk. I, ch. VI, esp. §§ 1-4, pp. 42-43); but it was not yet properly a technical concept, still less so in Grotius (see e.g. *op. cit. supra*, fn. 10, bk. II, ch. I § X (3), p. 178; bk. II, ch. XX, § V (1), p. 469; bk. II, ch. XX, § VIII (4), p. 475; bk. II, ch. XX, § XL (4), p. 511; bk. II, ch. XXI, § III (2), p. 534). After Wolff the concept of *laesio* found its way, through Achenwall, into Kant's doctrine of law; see *Metaphysik der Sitten, Rechtslehre* (1797), 2nd part (public law), § 56. The remote ancestor of the notion is of course Ulpian's *alterum non laedere*, *Digest*, 1, 1, 10. (*supra*, fn. 48)

duced it as a negative counterpart to the Leibnitzian idea of self-perfection, which is a fundamental component of his system. Natural law itself orders us to do what renders us and our condition more perfect and to avoid what tends to the contrary. We therefore have a perfect right to act in consequence of this natural obligation of self-perfection.[155]

Self-defence is an immediate outgrowth of it. Not only is it therefore a perfect right, but Wolff terms it an infinite right (like Pufendorff), meaning that its limits cannot be assessed beforehand in the abstract, but depend on the concrete situation created by the aggression.[156] The principle of proportionality still remains valid, and Wolff insists that it be measured with reference to the end, not to the initial attack, being understood that the least damaging means always have to be preferred.[157] If proportionality is exceeded, defence turns into aggression, and the aggressor is on his part entitled to defend himself. A warlike situation thereby ensues, the more so as third persons can be implicated in the fight on either side.[158]

Wolff does in fact consider self-defence among individuals as a form of war, just as inflicting punishment is a form of war. Both indeed aim at pursuing one's right, which in his definition amounts to war: 'Jus itaque belli est jus vi persequendi jus suum adversus eum, qui idem nobis tribuere non vult'.[159] The individual in the state of nature is thus seen as a potential belligerent endowed with a proper *jus belli* (a Grotian conception which was to be angrily rejected by Rousseau a few years later).[160] Self-defence is hereby caught again in the net of war, six centuries after the net had been cast by the decretists in their glosses on Gratian's *Causa 23*.

There is of course a marked difference between medieval *guerra* as a daily reality in the life of most people, and Wolff's concept of *bellum* which had a semblance of life only in an enlightened philosophical key. War as a political reality in his time had long since become a public venture exclusively conducted by States and their sovereigns on the level of the law of nations. It is all the more remarkable that Wolff develops his theory of self-

---

[155] Chr. v. Wolff, *op. cit. (supra,* fn. 146), part I, ch. III, § 920, pp. 603-604.

[156] *Loc. cit.* §§ 975 and 977-978, pp. 635-638.

[157] *Loc. cit.* §§ 983-984, pp. 640-642.

[158] *Loc. cit.* §§ 1001-1009, pp. 654-661.

[159] *Loc. cit.* §§ 1101-1103, pp. 729-730.

[160] *Loc. cit.* §§ 1104-1114, pp. 730-736. Cf., Jean-Jacques Rousseau, *Du contrat social* (1762), bk. I, ch. 4.

defence in both his *Jus Naturae* and *Jus Gentium* on parallel lines with reference to a wide concept of war. This is clearly at variance with our modern notion of self-defence (much better stated by Pufendorff) which, as was shown, excludes by definition the very idea of war, be it in municipal or international law.[161] What we dare say, however, is that self-defence appears in Wolff's theory as an institution perfectly consonant with the idea of a 'general principle of law recognised by civilised nations', even if its full implications were only drawn in the XXth century. 'Quod erat demonstrandum', as the great pedant of Halle would have said.

---

[161] See above, pp. 13-15

SELF-DEFENCE AND THE NON-USE OF FORCE: SOME RANDOM THOUGHTS

Shabtai Rosenne*

When we talk about self-defence, we are really addressing the use of armed force in self-defence. Under the regime of the United Nations Charter, use of armed force in self-defence has to be reconciled with the fundamental precept of Article 2, paragraph 4, of the Charter, the modern reincarnation of the Briand-Kellog Pact of 1928.[1] That provision, which the International Court of Justice has termed 'a cornerstone of the United Nations Charter',[2] requires all members of the United Nations to refrain in their international relations from the threat or use of force against the territorial integrity or political independence of any state or in any other manner inconsistent with the Purposes of the United Nations. The principle of the non-use of force enunciated in this way runs in tandem with the right of self-defence, a right which exists independently of the Charter and which for the purposes of the Charter is formulated in Article 51.[3]

* Honorary member of the Institute of International Law, awarded The Hague Prize for International Law (2004).

[1] General Treaty for the Renunciation of War as an Instrument of National Policy, the Pact of Paris, 27 August 1927, 94 LNTS 57.

[2] *Case concerning Armed Activities on the Territory of the Congo* (Democratic Republic of the Congo *v* Uganda) *Judgment of 19 December 2005* [hereafter *Armed Activities (Uganda)*], para. 148.

[3] The principal pronouncements of the International Court of Justice on the use of armed force in self-defence and the relationship between Article 2 (4) and Article 51 of the Charter are: *Military and Paramilitary Activities in and against Nicaragua* (Merits) case (Nicaragua *v* U.S.A.), ICJ Reports 1986, p. 14, 98 (paras. 187 ff.), *Oil Platforms* case (Iran *v* U.S.A.), ICJ Reports 2001, p. 161, 183 (paras. 43 ff.); *Legal Consequences of the Construction of a Wall in the Occupied Palestinian Territory* advisory opinion, ICJ Reports 2004, pp. 136, 194 (paras.

A.C.G.M. Eyffinger, A. Stephens and A.S. Muller (eds.), Self-Defence as a Fundamental Principle

However, the use of armed force is not the only way in which a State can exercise its right to defend itself as a reaction to an unexpected illegal situation that contains elements of risk and danger to persons or property and which requires remedial or preventive action involving the use of armed force, frequently, in fact usually, as a matter of urgency. In international law these remedial actions, which now go under the generic name of circumstances precluding wrongfulness in the recently codified law of the responsibility of States for internationally wrongful acts, are given designations such as *force majeure*, distress, necessity, and the like.[4] These remedial acts are often, though not invariably, acts that are themselves unlawful or bordering on the unlawful and certainly unfriendly – reprisals and retorsion. There is also the vast area, so far as I know largely unexplored in legal scholarship, of economic self-defence, that is the use of economic measures in self-defence against other illegal acts of whatever kind, such as the United States' acts of economic compulsion directed against the illegal detention of American nationals in the U.S. Embassy in Tehran. Recent events seem to be pointing to the emergence of another situation which may force States and other societies to act in self-defence – cyber-crime, daily becoming more urgent and even potentially a threat to world peace.

In international law and relations, self-defence in the sense just described is often treated today as though Article 51 of the United Nations Charter is the be-all and end-all of the matter. There is high authority for looking at the topic in this way. In so far as the International Court of Justice has had to consider issues of self-defence it seems to have approached the matter through the prism of Article 51.

Before going further into the substance of the matter, we should note one of the practical implications of the Charter's prohibition on the use of force recently made by the United Nations Secretariat in a communication to the International Law Commission in its fifty-seventh session in 2005:

---

138 ff.); *Armed Activities (Uganda)* case, paras. 106 ff. There is sharp criticism of some of these passages in different opinions attached to those judicial pronouncements.

[4] International Law Commission, Report for 2001, GAOR, 56th session, *Official Records*, Sup. 10 (A/56/10) ch. V. And see General Assembly resolutions 56/83, 12 December 2001 and 59/35, 2 December 2004. For the current status of those draft articles, frequently cited by the International Court, see Sh. Rosenne, 'State Responsibility – *Festina Lente*', 74 *British Year Book of International Law*, p. 363 (2004).

> 'As a result of the prohibition on the use of force in Article 2, paragraph 4, of the Charter of the United Nations, States have moved away from formalised war in the traditional sense towards armed conflicts under the guise of police actions, limited acts of self-defence or humanitarian intervention'.[5]

This is something which should be kept in mind in any consideration of self-defence in modern international law. The Charter has engendered new forms of violence for the attainment of political aims, especially the use of armed force by non-State entities claiming to be exercising the right of self-determination; those new forms of violence requiring new forms of self-protection. On the one hand, that passage gives expression to the reality of contemporary globalisation of interests, of the individual and equally of the State. On the other hand it is a warning to be alert to possible false claims to be acting in self-defence. This means that we must look more closely at the conception of self-defence in any legal order, as a general principle of law within the meaning of Article 38, paragraph 1, of the Statute of the International Court of Justice, before pursuing more closely the nature of the concept of self-defence, this rule and this exception all in one in today's international law. So one should start by asking: What *is* self-defence?

Human societies, however organised, have been faced with the problem of self-protection since the earliest of times, and as far as concerns international law the evolution of the modern sovereign nation-State has passed the problem on to the State. Furthermore, the matter has become more complicated since the Charter was negotiated in 1945, over sixty years ago. New types of hostile and aggressive action involving the illegal use of armed force and requiring a given society to react in self-defence have come to the fore, classed under the general name of terrorism. This is almost invariably performed by what can be known generically as 'non-State actors' or, as the *Armed Activities (Uganda)* Judgment repeatedly calls them in the circumstances of that case, 'irregulars'. Whatever term is used, it carries the implication that the acts cannot be attributed to any State, normally an essential element of an internationally wrongful act and the only kind of internationally wrongful act that comes within the scope of the International Law Commission's draft articles of 2001.

---

[5] *The effect of armed conflict on treaties: an examination of practice and doctrine: Memorandum by the Secretariat* (A/CN.4/550 + Corr.1) para. 3 (2005).

One of the principal characteristics of terrorism is its indiscriminate acts of violence with weapons (such as nail-filled bombs or booby traps set off by remote control devices, such as cellular phones) banned in the *jus in bello* or to give it its current designation, international humanitarian law, directed against society at large and not against any specific identified and genuine military objective. One of the most deadly forms of terrorism is the appearance of the 'suicide bomber', a man, a woman, or even a child – civilians who under the normal rules of international humanitarian law are supposedly protected persons themselves immune from direct attack and harm. These kinds of acts often – indeed usually – require quick and effective riposte in circumstances in which calm and careful assessment of the legalities of the situation, including such over-generalised matters as necessity, reasonableness or proportionality in the scope of the reaction, is neither possible nor practical. In that respect there is a certain naivety in what the International Committee of the Red Cross (ICRC) calls Rule 141 in its rules of customary international humanitarian law, taken from Additional Protocol I of 1974. Under that rule, each State must make legal advisers available, when necessary, to advise military commanders at the appropriate level on the application of international humanitarian law.[6] Desirable – certainly. Feasible – doubtful. Self-defence, in its very nature, operates in a general situation of illegality. It is a legal consequence of an illegal act, and its urgency is to be taken for granted. It is worthy of notice that the Security Council, after the tragic outrages of the attacks on American cities on 11 September 2001, acting under Chapter VII of the Charter (that is, finding itself faced with the necessity of taking action with respect to threats to the peace, breaches of the peace, and acts of aggression), adopted a series of binding resolutions directed against acts of terrorism and their perpetrators in its efforts to deal with them.

Chapter VII (which includes Article 51) sets out the powers and duties of the Security Council regarding action with respect to threats to the peace, breaches of the peace and acts of aggression. It empowers the Security Council to prescribe measures to deal with the situation, including measures involving the use of armed force. Decisions taken under Chapter VII are binding on

---

[6] J-M. Henckaerts and L. Doswald-Beck, *Customary International Humanitarian Law: Volume I: Rules* 500 (2005). The authors state that this is a norm of customary international law for State armed forces. This is doubtful. The rule is copied from Article 82 of Additional Protocol I of 1974, 1125 UNTS 3.

all members of the United Nations and indeed, given the changing structure of international society one could argue, following Article 2, paragraph 6, of the Charter, on all entities active on the international scene so far as may be necessary for the maintenance of international peace and security. This would include non-State entities. In resolution 1373 (2001) of 28 September 2001 on threats to international peace and security caused by terrorist acts, the Security Council reaffirmed the inherent right of individual or collective self-defence 'as recognised by the Charter', but without any reference to Article 51. A little later, in resolution 1377 (2001) of 12 November 2001, the Security Council adopted another resolution on the matter. Here it declared that acts of terrorism constitute one of the most serious threats to international peace and security and a challenge to all States and to humanity. Once more the Security Council made no allusion to Article 51 of the Charter. The Security Council continues its efforts to develop a universal response to the growing threats of terrorism, notably through specialised working groups and committees, for instance under resolution 1540 (2004), 25 April 2004 and later in the same year, under resolution 1566 (2004), 8 October 2004. This shows that even if, as the International Court has said, Article 51 recognises the existence of an inherent right of self-defence in the case of armed attack by one State against another State, but apparently not when the attack is not imputable to a foreign State,[7] the Security Council has gone further and accepts the position that the Charter does not in any way limit the concept of self-defence to attacks organised by a foreign State. In that respect, when the attack is not attributable to a State the right of self-defence becomes separated from the principle of the non-use of force, which has little if any relevance in that type of situation. The Court has left open the qualification of an armed attack that does not meet that requirement.[8]

In those and other resolutions the Security Council placed heavy emphasis on acts of terrorism, not on the motives of those who perpetrate them or their legal status. This approach is characteristic of all the prolonged negotiations that have taken place and are still taking place within a United Nations context, and which has so far prevented a general definition of the term 'terrorism'. What is notable is that not one of those resolutions (each one of

---

[7] *Construction of a Wall* advisory opinion (fn. 3 *supra*) at p. 194, para. 139. See on this the separate opinion of Judge Higgins at p. 215 (para. 33), of Judge Kooijmans at p. 230 (para. 35), of Judge Buergenthal at p. 242 (para. 6).

[8] *Armed Activities (Uganda)* case, para. 147.

which was carefully negotiated in the modern practice of conducting those negotiations in 'informal' meetings not open to the public) did the Security Council make any mention of Article 51. Their recognition that a State that is the victim of indiscriminate acts of terrorism may exercise its inherent right of self-defence without recourse to the Security Council is an important application of the Charter by the organ that bears the primary responsibility for the maintenance of international peace and security.

It is to be presumed that the International Court of Justice was aware of the series of Security Council resolutions when it formulated its recent pronouncements on self-defence and that its refusal to refer to them was deliberate. Nevertheless, many see in the Court's unwillingness to take them directly into consideration in formulating its observations on self-defence, and in forcing its pronouncements on self-defence into the confines of a narrow interpretation of Article 51, an unhelpful input to the international society's ongoing work, under the auspices of the Security Council, to contain and suppress international terrorism as a factor so disturbing to the maintenance of international peace and security.

The general rule on self-defence is now paralleled by Article 21 of the draft articles on the international responsibility of States for internationally wrongful acts adopted by the International Law Commission in 2001. That reads: 'The wrongfulness of an act of a State is precluded if the act constitutes a lawful measure of self-defence in conformity with the Charter of the United Nations.'[9]

One can note the general formulation of this principle without any direct reference to Article 51 of the Charter. In its commentary on that draft article the Commission saw the existence of a general principle admitting self-defence as an exception to the prohibition against the use of force in international relations, and regarded Article 51 of the Charter as 'part of the obligation to refrain from the use of force laid down in Article 2 (4)'.[10] However, this is not enough. The concept of self-defence has to be given a much wider scope than a bare exception to another provision of the Charter. This takes us back to some words of that great Roman philosopher and orator Cicero. In his defence on behalf of Milo he wrote:

> 'And if there is any occasion (and there are many such) when homicide is justifiable, it is surely not merely justifiable but even inevitable when the offer of vio-

[9] See above, fn. 1.
[10] Commentary to draft Article 21, para. (1).

> lence is repelled by violence ... There does exist therefore, gentlemen, a law which is a law not of the statute-book, but of nature; a law which we possess not by instruction, tradition or reading, but which we have caught, imbibed, and sucked in at Nature's own breast; a law which comes to us not by education but by constitution, not by training but by intuition – the law, I mean, that, should our life have fallen into a snare, into the violence and the weapons of robbers or foes, every method of winning a way to safety would be morally justifiable. When arms speak, the laws are silent;–that is the famous *inter enim arma silent leges* – they bid none to await their word, since he who chooses to await it must pay an undeserved penalty ere he can exact a deserved one. And yet most wisely, and, in a way, tacitly, the law itself authorises self-defence ...'.[11]

It seems that this is what the authors of the UN Charter had in mind when they spoke in Article 51 about the 'inherent right of self-defence if an armed attack occurs'; the sages of the Talmud told us: 'if one is coming to kill you, get in first and kill him.'[12] Maimonides codified this more clearly and more emphatically in his *Laws of Kings and their Wars,* when he defined a war for religious duty (*Milhemet Mitzvah*) as a war 'to deliver Israel from the enemy attacking him'.[13] To this we may add the Quran which proclaims that if a person does help and defend himself after a wrong is done to him, against such there is no cause of blame.[14] Self-defence is a natural inherent right of every human being, and of every human society. Indeed I would say that self-defence is the rule because the threat or use of force or any act of violence otherwise than when permitted by the law is itself unlawful. That is equally the position in international law under the Charter of the United Nations and under general international law independently of the Charter. The right of self-defence is a natural and inherent right recognised under any legal, religious or philosophical approach to international law.

There is one further aspect of the Court's approach to the principle of the non-use of force that should be noted, since if a claim that force was used in

[11] Cicero, *Pro T. Annio Milone* iv:11; *Cicero: The Speeches with an English Translation by N.H. Watts*, p. 15 (1931). For comment by Grotius, see *De jure belli ac pacis* ii.1.7: 'The killing of a man under such circumstances is ... a justifiable defence ...'. Kelsey translation in the Classics of International Law at p. 175.

[12] Babylonian Talmud, Sanhedrin 72A.

[13] Maimonides, *Code*, Book xiv, *The Book of Judges,* Treatise Five, *Kings and their Wars* ch. 5 (trans. M. Hershman, Yale Judaica Series, vol. III, 1949). Further on this see Sh. Rosenne, 'The Influence of Judaism on the Development of International Law', *An International Law Miscellany* pp. 509, 538 fn. 60 (1993).

[14] Surat al-Shura (42), pp. 39, 41.

self-defence is not accepted, that use of force may be found to be illegal. The Court has demonstrated a tendency to measure the legality of a use of force by reference either to the definition of aggression adopted by the General Assembly in its resolution 3314 (XXIX), 14 December 1974, or to the Declaration of Principles of International Law concerning Friendly Relations and Co-operation among States in accordance with the Charter of the United Nations, adopted by the General Assembly in its resolution 2625 (XXV).[15] Grading an instance of the use of force in that way has led the Court to find in a particular case that the use of force reached the level of a 'grave breach' of the principle expressed in Article 2, paragraph 4, of the Charter. The international law of State responsibility for breach of a treaty as it stands at present does not include the concept of punitive damages, and accordingly this qualification of the breach as 'grave' does not have practical consequences for the legal relations of the two States concerned. The Court has recognised that in any later proceedings for the determination of the reparation due for that breach, the injured State has to 'demonstrate and prove the exact injury that was suffered as a result of specific actions' of the other State 'constituting internationally wrongful acts for which that State was responsible'.[16]

Since this volume is devoted to fundamental principles of the concept and not to detailed consideration of the particular rules of self-defence in the international law of today, one should say more about what Grotius expounded on the philosophical level concerning the right to self-defence. Grotius

---

[15] 24 October 1970.

[16] The qualification of the internationally wrongful acts as constituting a 'grave breach' of the Charter may have implications should international criminal charges be preferred against the nationals of that State in the International Criminal Court. In the particular case, the Prosecutor of the International Criminal Court has opened proceedings in that Court in connection with actions of Uganda, a fact which was considered by the International Court in its deliberations in the *Armed Activities (Uganda)* case; see the Separate Opinion of Judge Parra-Aranguren at para. 22 and the Dissenting Opinion of Judge ad hoc Kateka at para. 29. Another instance of the grading of the use of force appears in the decisions of the Ethiopia-Eritrea Claims Commission. In para. 11 of its Partial Award of 19 December 2005 in the *Jus ad Bellum – Ethiopia's Claims 1-8* case, that Commission stated: 'As the text of Article 51 of the Charter makes clear, the predicate for a valid claim of self-defense under the Charter is that the party resorting to force has been subjected to armed attack. Localised border encounters between small infantry units, even those involving loss of life, do not constitute armed attack for the purposes of the Charter.' This passage must be treated with reserve: at most it only applies where the attack is attributed to a foreign State, following the interpretation of Article 51 given by the International Court.

devotes a large part of Book II of *De jure belli ac pacis* to explaining the significance of self-defence in his conception of the law of nations and the law of nature. One major reference to what he wrote neatly sums it all up:

> 'The right of self-defence ... has its origin directly, and chiefly, in the fact that nature commits to each his own protection ... it is enough that I am not under obligation to suffer what ... an assailant attempts, any more than I should be if attacked by an animal belonging to another'.[17]

It is submitted that this was fully recognised by the International Court of Justice in its advisory opinion on the construction of Israel's defensive fence in the light of the repeated Palestinian attacks on Israeli civilian targets. In that advisory opinion the Court said:

> 'The fact remains that Israel has to face numerous indiscriminate and deadly acts of violence against its civilian population. It has the right, and indeed the duty, to respond in order to protect the life of its citizens'.[18]

It is worth repeating: *the right, and indeed even the duty, to respond in order to protect the life of its citizens*. What is this, if not self-defence merely re-worded? All States have that right. All States have that duty. Here the International Court has used language that is much stronger and much more to the point than the vague reference to an inherent right of self-defence which appears in Article 51 of the Charter of the United Nations. A few years earlier the Court itself in a rather curious passage reaffirmed 'the fundamental right of every State to survival, and thus to resort to self-defence when its survival is at stake'.[19] Does the State's right to survival require any judicial reaffirmation? Is it not THE one fundamental precept of all international law?

Before going further into the field of international law, we should dispose of an argument about Article 51 of the Charter that has sometimes befuddled clear thinking since 1945 on the right of self-defence, both generally and particularly under the regime of the UN Charter. Current international legal thinking on this cardinal aspect of the law has become confused by two quite separate matters which collide when the natural and inherent right of self-

[17] *De jure belli ac pacis*, II.1.3; Kelsey translation p. 172 (see above, fn. 11).

[18] *Legal Consequences* advisory opinion, see fn. 3, at p. 195 (para. 142).

[19] *Legality of the Threat or Use of Nuclear Weapons* advisory opinion, International Court of Justice Reports 1996-II, pp. 226, 263 (para. 96).

defence is invoked – on the assumption that there is some difference between a natural right and an inherent right, although it could be doubted whether there is and whether, in this respect, there is any difference of substance between the English and the French texts of Article 51 of the United Nations Charter. The English text speaks of 'the inherent right of … self-defence if an armed attack occurs', and the French text speaks of 'droit naturel de légitime défense … dans le cas où un Membre des Nations Unies est l'objet d'une agression armée'.[20] My contention is that there is no difference of substance between the English and French versions of the Charter. There may be shades of superficial difference in appearance. These are due to the genius of each language, not to any other reason, and they do not lead to any difference of meaning or require any intellectual effort to reconcile them. To recall the wise observation of Maimonides to his translator Samuel Ibn Tibbon:

> 'The translator should first try to grasp the sense of the subject thoroughly and then state the theme with perfect clearness in the other language. This, however, cannot be done without changing the order of the words, putting many words for one word or vice versa, and adding or taking away words, so that the subject be perfectly intelligible in the language into which he translates'.[21]

That is what was done here. That is why the French may look and sound different from the English. There is no difference in substance and both texts say the same thing.

The implication of the Charter rule is that if an armed attack constitutes a violation of the principle of the non-use of force it is inherently an illegal act, and the use of force to ward off that inherently unlawful act is completely legitimate and is the inevitable legal consequence. One could go further – and here is where the collision just mentioned begins to come in. In the same way that an individual always has a *right* of self-defence whenever that individual with reason suspects that he or she is under a threat of actual or impending illegal assault on person or property, so does the State in international law have the right to take whatever remedial or preventive action it finds appropriate, whether or not involving the use of armed force in its reaction to

[20] The French word *agression* means both *attaque non provoquée* and *attaque violente contre une personne*. Micro-Robert *ad. loc.* In the *Armed Activities (Uganda)* judgment (para. 142), of which the English text is authoritative, the Court found no difference between the two language versions of Article 51.

[21] Taken from http://www.sacred–texts.com/jud.mhl/mhl19/htm accessed on 16 June 2005.

such threats. Here it is quite immaterial who or what is at the origin of the impending illegal act. If the threat comes from a State, Article 51 of the Charter applies and the use of force in exercise of the right of self-defence is later to be integrated into whatever action the Security Council decides to adopt. If that other party is not a State – and let us recall that the United Nations has its own conception of what is a State – then, in the words of the International Court, Article 51 of the Charter has no relevance.[22] And if the State has that right, then every individual within the State is entitled to expect the State to exercise that right and to afford him or her all necessary protection if anyone outside the State (and inside it too) comes to inflict some irreparable harm on that individual, and the State that acts in that way suffers no cause of blame. This means that in international law, for a State, self-defence is something more than a right. It also has elements of a duty owed to all persons within its borders or otherwise under its protection and which the State is obliged to observe in appropriate cases. It may even owe that duty to the international community at large.

During the twentieth century major developments have taken place in the concept of the State, in its rights and duties, and in the rights and duties of the State towards its individuals and of these individuals towards the State. The nineteenth century concepts of the State, derived directly from the aristocratic societies of that period and a laissez-faire approach to social and economic issues, have given way to a democratic approach by which all citizens have – or should have – some sort of say in the solution of society's internal problems, and an increasing say in its foreign policy, accompanied by increasing State interest and interference in social and economic issues broadly conceived. These developments are marked in the evolution of what in the West is called the 'welfare State', largely inspired by President Roosevelt's New Deal to take the United States out of the depression of the 1930s. In a different social and political form it exists also in the evolution of the Marxist workers' State under the influence of the Russian Revolution, although in many respects that evolution came about independently of Soviet Communism.

Both these approaches imply that the State as such has obligations to ensure a minimum standard of life, a minimum quality of life, for all its citizens and that every citizen has corresponding rights against the State.

---

[22] See above, fn. 7.

However, they differ both in their conceptions of what that minimum standard is or should be, and on how to achieve it. The State accordingly also has the obligation to do its utmost to preserve the security and welfare of its citizens and all others within its borders and under its protection. That explains why the International Court of Justice, in the passage from the *Fence* case quoted earlier, recalled the *duty* of the State to respond in order to protect the life – that includes the quality of life – of its citizens. The Universal Declaration of Human Rights proclaims the right to life in broad terms – 'Everyone has the right to life, liberty and security of person' (Article 2). Nevertheless, there is an extraordinary and unexplained omission from the Universal Declaration which contains no mention of the right of every individual to live in peace and security. Yet the right of the individual to live in peace and security must be the most fundamental of all human rights. In the Mishna we are told: 'The world stands on three things: truth, law, and peace'.[23] As Rashi said in commenting on the verse in Leviticus xxvi:6: 'And I will give peace in the land' – 'Peace outweighs all else'.

The Court has interpreted Article 1 of the Charter as pointing to the goal of international peace and security and friendly relations.

> '... The primary place ascribed to international peace and security is natural, since the fulfilment of the other purposes will be dependent upon the attainment of that basic condition'.[24]

The right to live in peace and security is implicit in the concept of the right of self-defence as it has developed in the different legal systems of the world. The right of self-defence is the other side of the coin of the right to live in peace. However, it was not until 1984 that the General Assembly remedied the omission from the Universal Declaration. In its 39th session the General Assembly adopted a Declaration on the Right of Peoples to Peace.[25] That Declaration commences with a preamble in which the General Assembly affirmed its conviction that life without war serves as the primary international prerequisite for the material well-being, development and progress of

---

[23] *The Mishna* (trans. H. Danby), Ethics of the Fathers, i:18 (1933).

[24] *Certain Expenses of the United Nations* advisory opinion, International Court of Justice Reports [1962], pp. 151, 168.

[25] General Assembly Resolution 39/11, 12 November 1984.

countries, and for the full implementation of the rights and fundamental human freedoms proclaimed by the United Nations. The Declaration then continues:

> 'The peoples of our planet have a sacred right to peace – [a *sacred* right].
> The preservation of the right of peoples to peace and the promotion of its implementation constitute a fundamental obligation of each State – [here the Declaration gives expression to the duty of the State].
> Ensuring the exercise of the right of peoples to peace demands that the policies of States be directed towards the renunciation of the use of force in international relations and the settlement of international disputes by peaceful means on the basis of the Charter of the United Nations'.

True, this does little more than reiterate the Charter doctrine of the renunciation of the use of force in international relations. It does not give adequate recognition to the Charter principle of the promotion and encouragement of respect for human rights and fundamental freedoms, including freedom from fear which, as President Roosevelt once said, was the only thing we have to fear. In the present state of international relations, with the virtual bankruptcy and marginalisation of the United Nations General Assembly as a significant factor in international relations, this may be seen as a platitude. Nevertheless, it is proper that the right of all peoples to peace should be recognised, and we may express the hope that one day the major precept of that Declaration will become not merely a binding and applied precept of international law, but be accepted as a norm of *jus cogens* protecting a right of *jus cogens.* What this means in our context is that the right of self-defence through the right to peace and security is inextricably linked to basic human rights, and has to be interpreted and applied in that framework.

The cardinal feature of the exercise of the right of self-defence and the performance of the duty of self-defence, using armed force in exercise of the right and in performance of the duty of self-defence, is that the occasion for it is always that it is provoked by an act that is itself illegal, whether by internal law or by international law, or indeed by both. The different passages quoted above, from the Roman Stoic philosopher Cicero, from the Talmud, from Maimonides, from the Quran, and from the father of European international law Hugo Grotius, all mention this, each in its own way. What is more, the illustrations such as those given by Cicero and Grotius all carry with them an element of urgency, of the need for an immediate reaction to an actual or impending illegal act of serious consequences leaving little time for any cold examination of the overall situation.

Many commentators on the UN Charter appear to have lost sight of this double element of the right of self-defence. How else can one explain the Court's approach in the *Nicaragua* case of 1986, that under customary international law appraisal of the actions taken in purported exercise of the right of self-defence must be made in relation to the criteria of necessity and proportionality?[26] If there is urgency in the situation, who at the time is capable of calmly weighing delicate issues of proportionality or of reasonableness or of necessity? The necessity is certainly present, otherwise the requirement to act in self-defence would not have arisen. And if issues such as proportionality and reasonableness are relevant criteria and can be evaluated in legal terms or through legal mechanisms, the decision to use force in self-defence and the acts of self-defence have to be assessed in light of the information available to the decision maker at the time, not months or even years later in light of other and fuller information that has become available in the meantime and which is being appraised in the relative distance and tranquillity of a deliberating chamber, and not in a military command post or in an emergency session of a Government.[27]

Another question is: To what does the right and duty of self-defence extend? What is it that the State is under the duty to defend? The answer is quite simple: the national way of life as embodied and personified in the State and its institutions.

Given the provision of Article 2, paragraph 4, of the Charter, obviously first and foremost it is the State itself as it is, its territorial integrity and political independence, that has pride of place. There is no question about that. The modern concept of a state embraces its ideological hue, whether we like it or not and whether we agree with it or not. The capitalist state is entitled to exercise its right of self-defence to preserve its character as a capitalist state. Likewise the socialist state and the communist state. The same applies to the Muslim State[28] and to the Jewish State and so on. Not

---

[26] *Military and Paramilitary Activities in and against Nicaragua* (Merits) case, International Court of Justice Reports [1986], pp. 14, 122 (para. 237).

[27] The Court's interpretations have all been adopted after a considerable lapse of time and following pleadings and careful deliberation, unlike the decisions to use armed force in self-defence, taken under the impact of a sense of immediate danger.

[28] Note the official name of Iran – the Islamic Republic of Iran.

merely the United Nations but the whole of modern international law has as its basic element the sovereign equality of States, regardless of their political or economic inequality, or in different international organisations, including the United Nations, their procedural inequality.

But developments since 1945 show us that there is much more to it than that. We have to take into account the modern practices involving the improper use of armed force by entities that are not states in any sense of the word. The passage from the *Fence* advisory opinion cited earlier mentions in a general way the State's duty 'to protect the life of its citizens'. It does not matter where those citizens are. If they are threatened because they are citizens of the State, that State is entitled, and may be under a duty, to exercise its right of self-defence to protect them. As an official publication of the British Government has put it: 'Self-defence may include the rescue of nationals where the territorial state is unable or unwilling to do so'.[29] That publication says nothing about where those nationals might be or how they got there. If they have been hijacked they simply have the right to be rescued if that is possible, and their State has the right to attempt their rescue should the territorial state be unable or unwilling to do so itself. This is obviously a conclusion drawn from the Entebbe rescue of Israelis from a hijacked foreign aircraft in 1976 and the proceedings in the Security Council that followed it.[30]

Another, quite different, use of the right of self-defence is the right of any organ of the state that is abroad to defend itself from any form of unlawful attack. In that type of situation (all too common today) Article 51 of the Charter has no relevance. Let us consider two examples. A national warship on the high seas which in good faith has reason to believe that it is being attacked or is about to be attacked may certainly take all measures at its disposal to defend itself and to ward off any suspected attack.[31] Likewise an

---

[29] Ministry of Defence, *The Manual of the Law of Armed Conflict* at 2 (Rule 1.5) (2004).

[30] See Security Council, S/PV.1939 to S/PV.1943 and relevant documentation, 31 SCOR, Sup. for July, August and September 1976; and L.C. Green, 'Rescue at Entebbe – Legal Aspects', 6 *Israel Yearbook on Human Rights* p. 312 (1976).

[31] This was the central issue in the *Aerial Incident of 3 July 1988* case brought by Iran against the United States following the shooting down by an American warship of an Iranian civil air liner during the time of the war between Iran and Iraq in the 1980s. The warship and its competent personnel, with only a few seconds within which to reach any decision on the matter, thought that the airliner was a military plane about to attack it, and shot it down with heavy loss of life. Only afterwards was the mistake discovered. This case was settled out of court, but what there is of the pleadings is a useful illustration of this aspect of self-defence. Although made in a specific context, that remark is of general application.

Embassy or a Consulate is certainly entitled to take all measures in its defence should it become clear or should it have good reason to suspect that it is going to be attacked.

Then we have the individual acting as an organ of the State or whose actions can be attributed to a State, where that person's personal safety may be at stake. As an individual that person is certainly entitled to take whatever action is appropriate and possible in self-defence, regardless of whether the act attributed to the State in which that individual took part was lawful or not. Personal self-defence is always an individual and independent right. The Rome Statute of the International Criminal Court recognises this type of self-defence of the individual.[32] Article 31, on grounds for excluding criminal responsibility, in paragraph 1 (c) removes the criminality from a person who acts reasonably to defend himself or herself or another person or, in the case of war crimes, property which is essential for the survival of the person or another person or property which is essential for accomplishing a military mission, against an imminent and unlawful use of force, in a manner proportionate to the degree of danger to the person or the other person or property protected. Such a person shall not be criminally responsible if at the time of that person's conduct the person was acting in self-defence in that manner. It remains to be seen how the International Criminal Court will apply this difficult provision.

* * *

Self-defence is an independent, self-standing, principle of law and as such also a general principle of international law. It is applicable in many different circumstances and takes many different forms, some involving the use of armed force and others involving some other action but without the use of armed force by the victim State. Under the regime of the Charter of the United Nations, if the self-defence against another State involves the use of armed force, the conditions of Article 51 apply, and the use of armed force in an act of self-defence may be seen as an exception to the general prohibition on the use of force laid down in Article 2, paragraph 4, of the Charter. If the situation requiring the urgent use of armed force is not in response to an attack from another State on the territorial integrity or the political independence of

[32] 2187 UNTS 3.

the victim State, as is frequently the position in present-day instances of indiscriminate terrorism, Article 51, in the words of the International Court of Justice and following the practice of the Security Council, is not relevant, leaving untouched the inherent or natural right of self-defence of the victim State.

SELF-DEFENCE AND TERRORISM

Paul Cliteur*

This Chapter sets out to analyse the dangers threatening international peace in the new, post-ideological age that began in 1989. With the Fall of the Berlin Wall, expectations that major ideological conflict would be a thing of the past seemed justified. The man who succeeded in defining this mood most pithily was the American political analyst Francis Fukuyama. Fukuyama argued in 1989 that since liberalism had won the great ideological battle against communism and fascism, this would result in a world where boredom reigned.

What Fukuyama failed to appreciate, however, was that in this very same year a death sentence was issued against a Western writer, Salman Rushdie, which gave us an insight into a brand new kind of threat to the Western world: radical Islam.

Later, radical Islam was to manifest itself in the attacks in the United States on 11 September 2001, the attacks in Madrid on 11 March 2004, the attacks in the London underground on 7 July 2005, the murder of the writer Theo van Gogh on 2 November 2004, and, more recently, in the calls for the murder of the cartoonists who had depicted the Prophet Muhammad by the Jamaat-e-Islami party from Pakistan, among others.

Some people believe that we are witnessing a divide between the ideology of the West, led by the United States, and at least a part of the Islamic world. Others believe that this is a tendentious representation of the facts, which may even be dangerous as a 'self-fulfilling prophesy'.

---

* Prof. Paul B. Cliteur, Ph.D. is professor at the Universities of Leiden and Delft, The Netherlands.

A.C.G.M. Eyffinger, A. Stephens and A.S. Muller (eds.), Self-Defence as a Fundamental Principle

This conflict raises countless questions. First: how should we define it? Is it a 'Clash of Civilizations', to use Samuel Huntington's well-known phrase?[1] Is it a 'religious' divide (or is it unrelated to religion)? Is it a problem that we should take seriously (or would it be better not to pay too much attention to it)? The most important question, however, is the following: can the problem be solved?

The justification for raising this problem in a book on 'self-defence' is that on both sides – the Western world as well as the Islamic world – people characterize their own response as a form of 'self-defence'. Both parties believe that they actually respond to the other's aggression. As far as that is concerned, the National Security Strategy of the United States of America of 20 September 2002[2] is not different from Ayatollah Khomeini's fatwa in which he rejects Rushdie's *The Satanic Verses*.[3] The Americans claim the right to defend themselves against attacks by religiously motivated international terrorists by means of 'pre-emptive strikes'. Radical Muslims[4] in Islamic countries and in the West – or at least some of them – view cartoons (*Jyllands Posten*), films (*Submission*) and novels (*Satanic Verses*) that are insulting (or that they regard as insulting) to the Prophet or Islam as an unjustified attack to which they must respond, if necessary by using force.

Because the right of self-defence is an important ground recognized in international law for ignoring the prohibition against the use of force, this may well give rise to further conflict, and in the most pessimistic scenario, pose a threat to world peace.

What should happen? Following Roger Scruton and – in part – Francis Fukuyama, it is argued in this Chapter that the situation is serious and, in all

---

[1] Huntington, Samuel, 'The Clash of Civilizations?', in *Foreign Affairs,* Summer 1993, pp. 22-49; Huntington, Samuel, *The Clash of Civilizations and the Remaking of World Order,* Simon & Schuster, New York 1996.

[2] http://www.whitehouse.gov./nsc/nss/html.

[3] Included in Pipes, Daniel, *The Rushdie Affair.* The Novel, the Ayatollah, and the West, Second Edition with a postscript by Koenraad Elst, Transaction Publishers, New Brunswick (USA) and London (UK) 2003, p. 27.

[4] I will refer to Islamic believers who take the view that the use of violence, for example, in response to cartoons about holy figures in Islam is permitted as 'radical Muslims', 'Muslim terrorists', 'Islamists' or 'supporters of political Islam'. In this way I hope to make it clear that I am not generalising about 'all Muslims' or about 'Islam as a whole'. I will not deal with the relationship between political Islam and 'ordinary Islam'. For the purposes of this Chapter, it is sufficient to note that certain people legitimize violence by invoking their religion. I will not address the question of whether they are right in doing so.

likelihood, insoluble in the short term. Perhaps we should not rule out that we are entering a phase that could last as long as the Cold War.[5] During this phase, two world views will be opposed to each other: that of the West and that of religious fundamentalism. In this process – as the French Islam expert Gilles Kepel has pointed out – *either* Europe will get Islamized *or* Islam will get Europeanized.[6]

Fortunately, there are signs suggesting that the latter may happen. This means the rise of liberal Islam (or European Islam).[7] Even so, we should not be blind to the fact that religious fundamentalism is gaining ground. And that means that the Western liberal democracies are no longer threatened by secular political ideologies such as communism and Nazism (as Fukuyama rightly pointed out), but by religious fundamentalism (to which Fukuyama paid too little attention).[8]

Due to its universalist nature (Islamic law prevails over democratic legislation) and its claim to absolute truth, religious fundamentalism is essentially incompatible with the principles of a liberal constitutional order. In the years to come, Western democratic states under the rule of law will have to do their utmost to develop a strong national identity that is acceptable to all citizens and is perceived as the primary focus of loyalty. In this context, it is particularly important to strengthen the principle of territorial jurisdiction. This, however, presupposes building on national identity and the integration of religious minorities in secular democracies. It is not easy to say how this should be done. It is possible, however, to say one thing that has received insufficient attention for a long time: religion, in particular religion in its fundamentalist form, is a factor that impedes the development of national identity and state formation. Authors such as Francis Fukuyama and Fareed

[5] For a pessimistic opinion, see Dalrymple, Theodore, 'When Islam breaks down', (2004), in Theodore Dalrymple, *Our Culture, What's Left of It*, Ivan R. Dee, Chicago 2005, pp. 283-296, p. 295: 'To be sure, fundamentalist Islam will be very dangerous for some time to come, and all of us, after all, live only in the short term; but ultimately the fate of the Church of England awaits it.'

[6] Kepel, Gilles, *Fitna.* Guerre au coeur de l'islam, Gallimard, Paris 2004; Kepel, Gilles, *Jihad.* Expansion et déclin de l'islamisme, Gallimard, Paris 2000.

[7] This is advocated, *inter alia*, by Tibi, Bassam, *Im Schatten Allahs.* Der Islam und die Menschenrechte, Ullstein, Düsseldorf 2003.

[8] And which Huntington understood better. A radical approach to this perspective is to be found in Harris, Sam, *The End of Faith.* Religion, Terror, and the Future of Reason, The Free Press, London 2005.

Zakaria do not pay sufficient attention to this point.[9] For this reason, it would be a good thing if religion became more of a private matter (*laïcité*) rather than a part of the nation's public morality (as rightly argued by Roger Scruton and, by implication, by Todorov). There are no signs, however, suggesting that this will be the case within the foreseeable future (as Sam Harris en Theodore Dalrymple rightly argue).

1. Fukuyama and the End of History in 1989

In 1989, a neoconservative magazine, *The National Interest*, published an article by the American political analyst Francis Fukuyama. The title was *The End of History*. Fukuyama's main thesis was that in his lifetime liberal democracy had defeated all its enemies (communism, fascism, socialism). We were living in a new age. This age witnessed the triumph of the West, of the Western *idea*. All the systematic alternatives to Western liberalism had been defeated. What we were witnessing was not only the end of the Cold War, but the end of history as such: that is, the end point of mankind's ideological evolution and the universalisation of Western liberal democracy as the final form of human government. 'The state that emerges at the end of history is liberal insofar as it recognizes and protects through a system of law man's universal right to freedom, and democratic insofar as it exists only with the consent of the governed.'[10]

Right at the end of his essay, there is a telling sentence, however, that shows that Fukuyama was slightly uneasy about something. It is not too difficult to imagine this uneasiness. In 1979, the Iranian Revolution overthrew the reign of the Shah and installed an Islamic government. What did Fukuyama have to say about that? In a famous sentence he implicitly refers to it as follows: 'Our task is not to answer exhaustively the challenges to liberalism promoted by every crackpot messiah around the world, but only those that are embodied in important social or political movements, and which

[9] Zakaria, Fareed, 'The Islamic Exception', in Fareed Zakaria, *The Future of Freedom.* Illiberal Democracy at Home and Abroad, W.W. Norton & Company, New York, London 2003, pp. 119-159.

[10] Fukuyama, Francis, 'The End of History?', in *The National Interest,* No. 16, Summer 1989, pp. 3-18, and in Paul Schumaker, Dwight C. Kiel, Thomas W. Heilke, eds., *Ideological Voices.* An Anthology in Modern Political Ideas, The McGraw-Hill Companies, Inc., New York etc. 1997, pp. 409-417, p. 411.

are therefore part of world history.'[11] Fukuyama also explains his statement. He says that for our purposes, 'it matters very little what strange thoughts occur to people in Albania or Burkina Faso, for we are interested in what one could in some sense call the common ideological heritage of mankind.'[12]

These are strange examples. Nobody was talking about Albania. And nobody would claim that Burkina Faso posed a threat to the United States of America and its Western allies. Why does Fukuyama not say more about this 'crackpot messiah'? By using the word 'messiah', Fukuyama seems to indicate that he has a person with religious authority in mind, but by adding the word 'crackpot', he also suggests that he does not take this spiritual authority seriously at all.

Back in 1989 this was not very strange. International terrorism, Bin Laden, Al-Qaeda: these were matters insiders concerned themselves with. It is true that the Iranian Revolution took place in 1979, but this was considered for the most part a relatively isolated event. This is why it is understandable up to a certain point that Fukuyama failed to appreciate the importance of religion as a factor of political tensions.

This failure to appreciate the significance of religion may also be related to secularisation. Charles Seelengut described in detail how Western, secularized intellectuals have developed a blind spot for the influence of religion.[13] In the Western world, religion has been privatized to a great extent. Many Westerners do not base their morality exclusively on their religion, but have come to regard this as such a matter of course that they forget that this is quite different in other parts of the world and in other cultures. In other parts of the world, secularisation has not progressed as much as in the West. Some people are of the opinion that it is even non-existent in the Islamic world.

In 1991, the philosopher and cultural anthropologist Ernest Gellner shocked many by putting this as follows. 'I think it is fair to say that no secularisation

[11] Fukuyama, *supra*, fn 10, p. 413.

[12] Idem.

[13] On this subject, see Seelengut, Charles, *Sacred Fury.* Understanding Religious Violence, Rowman & Littlefield Publishers, Walnut Creek, Lanham, New York, Toronto, Oxford 2003. A similar point was made in Nelson-Pallmeyer, Jack, *Is Religion Killing Us?* Violence in the Bible and the Quran, Trinity Press International, Harrisburg 2003; Röhrlich, Wilfried, *Die Macht der Religionen.* Glaubenskonflikte in der Weltpolitik, Verlag C.H. Beck, München 2004; Haught, James, *Holy Hatred.* Religious Conflicts of the '90s, Prometheus Books, Amherst, New York 1995.

has taken place in the world of Islam: that the hold of Islam over its believers is as strong, and in some ways stronger, now than it was 100 years ago. Somehow or other, Islam is secularisation-resistant, and the very striking thing is that this remains true under a whole range of political regimes.'[14]

Three years later Gellner repeated this point when he said that, compared to other world religions, Islam was different in this respect.[15] For all world religions, it is true that the gradual process of industrialisation that many societies have gone through has weakened the position of religion. This secularisation thesis is roughly correct: 'It would be difficult to deny the overall trend towards secularisation', writes Gellner. But the position of Islam is an exception to that. The position of Islam has not weakened in the past one hundred years; on the contrary, one may even claim that its position has become stronger.

The hold of Islam over the populations of the lands in which it is the main religion has in no way diminished in the course of the last hundred years. In some ways it has been markedly strengthened.[16]

The American Arabist Bernard Lewis has made similar observations.[17]

It was a long time before scholars began to recognize the correctness of this view and many have still not done so. Many still consider it more or less a matter of course that Islam will go through (or has already gone through) the same development as Christianity. This means a development of increasing liberalism, a development towards ever increasing secularisation.[18] This explains why Fukuyama was still able to believe in 1989 that with the disappearance of the classical ideologies, the most important cause of tensions between the states on the world stage would disappear too. The latter has proved to be a serious flaw in his analysis. Fukuyama's essay ended with a curious passage. After the writer had sung the praises of the triumph of liberal democracy and liberalism, he predicted that the new era without ideologies that we were about to enter would be a sad time:

---

[14] Gellner, Ernest, 'Islam and Marxism: Some Comparisons', in *International Affairs,* Vol. 67, No. 1, January 1991, pp. 1-6, p. 2.

[15] Gellner, Ernest, *Conditions of Liberty.* Civil Society and Its Rivals, Hamish Hamilton, London 1994, p. 15.

[16] Gellner, Ibid., p. 15.

[17] Lewis, Bernard, 'The Return of Islam', in *Commentary,* January 1976, pp. 39-49, revised and recast in Lewis, Bernard, *Islam and the West,* Oxford University Press, New York, Oxford 1993, pp. 133-155.

[18] In a way, this is also the position taken by Sorman, Guy, *Les Enfants de Rifaa.* Musulmans et modernes, Fayard, Paris 2003.

> 'The end of history will be a very sad time. The struggle for recognition, the willingness to risk one's life for a purely abstract goal, the worldwide ideological struggle that called forth daring, courage, imagination, and idealism, will be replaced by economic calculation, the endless solving of technical problems, environmental concerns, and the satisfaction of sophisticated consumer demands. In the post-historical period there will be neither art nor philosophy, just the perpetual caretaking of the museum of human history. I can feel myself, and see in others around me, a powerful nostalgia for the time when history existed. Such nostalgia, in fact, will continue to fuel competition and conflict even in the post-historical world for some time to come. I have the most ambivalent feelings for the civilisation that has been created in Europe since 1945, with its north Atlantic and Asian offshoots. Perhaps this very prospect of centuries of boredom at the end of history will serve to get history started again.'[19]

This is an interesting passage that includes – partly unintended perhaps – some elements that were later found to be correct but also some elements that show that Fukuyama was wide of the mark.

2. Criticism of Fukuyama

Let us start with the latter point. It will have escaped nobody's attention that these 'centuries of boredom at the end of history' have turned out quite different from what Fukuyama expected and predicted. Ideological tensions in the world have run high. But are these in any way related to ideology? Fukuyama would undoubtedly object. That depends on how one defines 'ideology'. One thing is clear: these are not the familiar ideologies we associate with the 1930s or those that manifested themselves in the battle of ideas during the Cold War. But that does not mean that nowadays people no longer devote their heart and soul to specific views for which they are prepared to literally go through fire and water. It is certainly ironic that Fukuyama refers to the unwillingness to 'risk one's life for a purely abstract goal'. What the new world of international religious terrorism has confronted us with is people who are *pre-eminently* willing to risk their lives for abstract goals. Present-day suicide terrorism is characterised by immense willingness to sacrifice. This willingness to sacrifice is greater than anything we have witnessed in

[19] See Fukuyama, *supra*, fn. 10, p. 417.

previous centuries.[20] This is what makes terrorism so difficult to grasp: all classical functions of criminal law and all classical theories about deterrence in international traffic fail to have any effect on religious terrorists.

As is well-known, we have undergone many traumatic experiences with religion as a factor in social tension and strife in Europe. In the 16th and 17th centuries, Europe was the scene of battle during the conflicts between Catholics and Protestants, a battle that was pacified with the rise of national states and the development of such principles as freedom of conscience, freedom of religion and freedom of speech. It is not inconceivable, however, that a new social contract of this kind will again have to be sought.

The 1990s were characterised by what has been called 'The Return of the Sacred' or '*La Revanche de Dieu*' (Gilles Kepel), and in particular, as mentioned above, 'The Return of Islam'.[21] The challenge facing Western democracies in the years to come is to integrate religion into the liberal constitutional order.

3. Does Political Islam Pose a Threat to the West?

As we have seen, Fukuyama devoted hardly any attention to religion in 1989. As a matter of fact, this has not changed subsequently, which may explain why Fukuyama has paid so little attention to political Islam. He considers political Islam a movement that will not pose a challenge to the West, because political Islam is probably not a viable alternative to liberalism. Socialism and fascism were such alternatives. Fukuyama himself makes it clear that he is concerned with challenges to liberalism that manifest themselves 'in important social or political movements, and which are therefore part of world history.'[22] Does political Islam satisfy this criterion? Fukuyama thinks not. This was his view not only in 1989 but also in 2004. In that year, he wrote: 'Al-Qaeda and other radical Islamist groups aspire to be existential threats to American civilisation but do not currently have anything like the

---

[20] See Cook, David, 'The Implications of 'Martyrdom Operations' For Contemporary Islam', in *Journal of Religious Ethics,* 2004 (32), pp. 129-151; Cook, David, *Understanding Jihad,* University of California Press, Berkeley, Los Angeles and London 2005; Broom, Mia, *Dying to Kill.* The Allure of Suicide Terror, Columbia University Press, New York 2005.

[21] See Lewis, Bernard, *supra*, fn. 17, pp. 133-155.

[22] See Fukuyama, *supra*, fn. 10, p. 413.

capacity to actualize their vision: They are extremely dangerous totalitarians, but pose threats primarily to regimes in the Middle East.'[23]

The theory Fukuyama presents here is frequently advocated by those who point out that Islamic fundamentalism actually testifies to the failure of political Islam rather than its success. Nowhere – except in Iran – have the political Islamists been able to install Islamic theocracies. This has exasperated the Islamists so much that they resort to violence. This violence takes the form of terrorism, but this terrorism does not show the power of political Islam, but its impotence. Fukuyama defines this theory as follows: 'The global Nazi and communist threats were existential both because their banner was carried by a great power, and because ideologically there were many people in the United States and throughout the Western world seduced by their vision. The Islamist threat has no such appeal (...)'.[24]

To be sure, communism and fascism represent a kind of threat to Western states that is *different* from the threat posed by Islamism. For example, Islamic states like Iran do not constitute a threat to the hated United States in the sense that tensions could result in a classical form of warfare that is potentially threatening to the United States. As Sadik Al-Azm puts it: the Islamic states are not in the same league as the West.[25] But those who are 'not in the same league' in the traditional sense of the word may still constitute a considerable threat in an entirely new sense.

Fukuyama thinks too much in the classical terms of danger and threat and perhaps also too much in terms of large numbers, because it may be true that the radicalism of political Islam is able to mobilize only few people in terms of *quantity*, but it seems that this small number of supporters is amply compensated by the fanaticism of the few who are inspired by it. The words spoken in this context by the American Arabist Bernard Lewis seem to be more sensible: 'Terrorism requires only a few. Obviously, the West must defend itself by whatever means will be effective. But in devising means to fight the terrorists, it would surely be useful to understand the forces that drive them.'[26] This is a penetrating observation: 'Terrorism requires only a few'.

[23] Fukuyama, Francis, 'The Neoconservative Moment', in *National Interest,* July 1, 2004.

[24] See Fukuyama, *supra*, fn. 10, p. 413.

[25] On the occasion of the presentation of the Erasmus Prize. Here quoted in: Ede Botje, Harm, 'De voorgangers van Van Gogh', in *Vrij Nederland*, 27 November 2004.

[26] Lewis, *The Crisis of Islam,* p. xxviii.

Incidentally, the flawed nature of Fukuyama's analysis relating to political Islam is also shown by the continuation of the passage quoted above. After Fukuyama has said 'the Islamist threat has no such appeal', he continues as follows: 'except perhaps in countries like France that have permitted high levels of immigration from Muslim countries.'

This is not an unimportant addition. After 11 September, after the murder of Theo van Gogh, after many other incidents, such as the attacks in London, which involved religiously motivated terrorists, this seems to be the concession to the power of religion Fukuyama is prepared to make. At this juncture, in 2004, he indicated that his optimistic assessment of the danger of Islamism was based on immigration figures and demographic relations in the United States. But in European countries, such as France – countries with a considerable Muslim population – this 'may be different'.

Accordingly, it seems perfectly justified to give some further thought to the challenge posed by political Islam to the Western countries – even on the basis of what Fukuyama *himself* writes about it.

4. Rushdie's Death Sentence

The year 1989 saw not only the publication of Fukuyama's article and the Fall of the Berlin Wall, which had defined the ideological differences between the East and the West since the end of the Second World War, but also the emergence of a new actor on the stage of world history. This was the very 'crackpot messiah' about whom Fukuyama had spoken in such slighting but also soothing terms. One of the most striking letters in recent political history written by one head of state to another was sent in that very year of 1989. The letter was sent by Ayatollah Khomeini to Michael Gorbachev. In this letter of January 1989, Khomeini commented on the failure of Marxism ('henceforth communism should be found in the museums of world political history'). That should not drive Gorbachev in the hands of liberalism, Khomeini argued. He should not look to the West for spiritual renewal, but to the South. 'I strongly urge that in breaking down the walls of Marxist fantasies, you do not fall into the prison of the West and the Great Satan', the Iranian leader wrote to his disillusioned colleague. 'I call upon you seriously to study and conduct research into Islam (…). I openly announce that the Islamic Republic of Iran, as the greatest and most powerful base of the

Islamic world, can easily help fill up the ideological vacuum of your system.'[27]

This letter breathes enormous self-confidence, which is also expressed in the pretensions of the fatwa Khomeini issued against Rushdie. Since 1570, when Pope Pius V issued the bull *Regnans in excelsis*, in which he called on the population to resist the British Queen Elizabeth I, no spiritual leader had addressed the British secular authorities in this manner. The pretensions of this kind of fatwa are far-reaching, as we are gradually beginning to realise. How can an Iranian spiritual leader claim jurisdiction over a *British* writer?

In a way, this is related to the specific nature of Islam, but also to the conditions under which we live nowadays. This specific nature of Islam means that Muslims believe in the revealed Word of God, whose Will has been written in a Holy Book, which prescribes rules of life that may under no circumstances be violated.

Of course, this was not a new theory. It is not even a theory that needs to result in insuperable problems under conditions other than those under which we live today. Khomeini's theory, for example, would not be too great a problem in a homogeneous society in which people sharing the territory of the state believe in one and the same god. That is no longer the case, however, in the world in which we live. We live in a globalising world, in which people with the most different religious views live more-or-less next to each other. This 'living next to each other' may actually mean living physically next to each other, but it may also concern a situation in which the modern means of communication inform us about what happens in other parts of the world at amazing speed. It is a cliché, but the world has become smaller. Anyone who publishes a book in Britain may deeply insult a person in Iran or Pakistan with it (as actually happened with Rushdie's book). In the new global world, everybody feels 'vulnerable'. Everybody is aware that he or she is directly confronted with a world that remained hidden from him or her in the past or about which it was extremely difficult to gain any knowledge.

This vulnerability means that people feel that they have to 'defend' themselves. And the act of defending oneself may be accompanied by 'force'.

Terrorist violence manifests itself in two ways. First of all, in the attacks in London, Madrid and the United States of America, a group of terrorists place a bomb on an underground train, in a train station or another place

[27] Quoted in Pipes, Daniel, *supra*, fn. 3, p. 192.

where many people are gathered. The victims are random strangers, or at least their only involvement in the 'conflict' is that they are part of the culture that is rejected by pious believers or that they have tolerated the wrong government (in democracies nobody is innocent, terrorists tend to say, because the citizens in a democracy tolerate their governments). A second kind of attack is the targeted killing of people the radicals accuse of insulting Islam. Examples of the latter include the fatwa against Rushdie, the murder of Dr. Farag Foda on 8 June 1992, the attack on Egypt's Nobel laureate writer Naguib Mahfuz, who 'was stabbed in order to silence and intimidate outspoken critics of fundamentalists' in 1994,[28] the murder of Theo van Gogh on 2 November 2004[29] because he had insulted the Prophet, and the calls for the killing of cartoonists who satirised the Prophet Muhammad in February 2006.

With the murder of Theo van Gogh, a new chapter in the history of political-religious terrorism on European soil was written. Before the murder of Van Gogh, religious terrorism had been confined to collective attacks. With the murder of van Gogh, the practice of murdering individuals, such as Farag Foda in Egypt, had come to Europe.

Present-day religious terrorism is different from traditional terrorism in yet another respect: the use of violence against people because of their ideological views or the opinions they express. Pim Fortuyn had become a prominent politician in the Netherlands, van Gogh was only a writer and film-maker.

This means that the ambitions of modern religious terrorists are different from those of the terrorists of the past. They attempt to hit Western societies in the heart of their existence. This heart is the free discussion of political views, scientific views and religious views.

The latest conflict is relatively recent and, by way of illustration, it will be dealt with in somewhat greater detail.[30]

5. The Danish Cartoon Affair

In September 2005, the Danish newspaper *Jyllands Posten* published a series of 12 cartoons about the Prophet Muhammad, which triggered a great

---

[28] Esposito, John L., *Unholy War.* Terror in the Name of Islam, Oxford University Press, New York 2002, p. 92.

[29] See Jansen, Johannes, *The Dual Nature of Islamic Fundamentalism,* Cornell University Press, Ithaca, New York 1997, p. 113.

[30] See 'Woede over cartoons raast voort', in *Trouw*, 1 February 2006.

many protests, death threats, mass demonstrations, and diplomatic boycotts. Initially, only Danish Muslims were angry about the cartoons, but after some time it escalated into an international row.

For example, when the interior ministers of the Arab League gathered in Tunis on 31 January 2006, they opened the attack on what they perceived as the Western principle of freedom of speech and requested the Danish Government to punish the relevant cartoonists 'severely'.

On 31 January 2006, the editorial office of *Jyllands Posten* in Aarhus was evacuated following a bomb alert. The Pakistani Jamaat-e-Islami offered a reward of 8000 dollars to anyone who managed to murder one of the cartoonists. This meant that once again a reward was offered for murdering people because of their views. This time it did not concern views expressed in a novel but views expressed in cartoons.

Throughout the world, there was a storm of protest against the cartoons, and supporters and opponents were at each other's throats, which claimed several victims.

In this respect, there seems to be a contrast between the predominant opinion in the Western world and the predominant opinion in Islamic countries. Muslims – and perhaps not just radical Muslims – think that insulting the Prophet constitutes an absolute limit to what can be tolerated in the name of the freedom of speech. The writer Theo van Gogh was killed because he had insulted the Prophet. Of course, many Muslims reject this kind of murder, but the cartoon affair shows that insulting the Prophet is a very sensitive issue in the Islamic world, and not just among religious fanatics.

It is often said that the issue should be resolved by considering each other's sensitivity, by refraining from hurting each other's feelings. In fact, the Danish cartoons affair is a repeat of the Rushdie affair. The Iranians could not understand in 1989 why the British Government did not take disciplinary action against the writer Rushdie, who had insulted the Prophet in his book *The Satanic Verses*. The British had made it clear that they were not happy with the book either, had they not? The British made it clear that they did not want to insult Muslims. Why was the book not banned? Why was the book not withdrawn from the market?

These are obvious demands from the perspective of a dictatorial regime. Any failure to meet these demands cannot but be regarded as hypocrisy on the part of the Western states.

When viewed from a Western perspective, on the other hand, it is virtually impossible to punish a writer for what the characters in his novel say. There are similar problems when it comes to prohibiting cartoons. Any artist faced with a statutory ban against making cartoons could challenge this statute immediately on account of its inconsistency with the Constitution or with a provision from one of the human rights conventions.

In addition, it is virtually impossible for any government in a Western state under the rule of law, to control all manifestations the new means of communication allow (the Internet, for example). This means that those who want to prohibit cartoons and novels place high demands from a legal perspective and their demands are also technically impossible. It may sound far-fetched, but it seems justified to conclude that prohibiting simple cartoons or novels would require a Western open society to transform itself into a dictatorship.

It does not seem to be overly pessimistic to claim that there is a fundamental clash between the predominant opinion in the Western world and the predominant opinion in Islamic states in relation to matters such as freedom of speech, freedom of religion,[31] equality before the law between men and women, and sexual freedom.[32] In all likelihood, this clash will continue to be a source of conflicts[33] between population groups sharing territory in one and the same state, but also between states and, above all, between terrorist and fundamentalist religious groups on the one hand and Western states on the other, whereby terrorists will use the ultimate instrument (murder) to destabilize and intimidate Western societies.

We should not forget that many of the attacks committed by religious terrorists are connected with what may well be regarded from the Western perspective as the core principle of Western freedom: the freedom of speech and the freedom of religion.[34] When viewed from the Islamic perspective,

---

[31] See Warraq, Ibn, ed., *Leaving Islam.* Apostates Speak Out, Prometheus Books, Amherst, New York, 2003.

[32] Howland, Courtney, ed., *Religious Fundamentalism and the Human Rights of Women,* Palgrave, New York 2001.

[33] On the introduction of parts of Sharia in Western legal systems, among other issues, see Marshall, Paul, ed., *Radical Islam's Rules.* The Worldwide Spread of Extreme *Shari'a* Law, Rowman & Littlefied Publishers, Inc., Lanham etc. 2005.

[34] The basis for the other fundamental rights. On this subject, see Jellinek, George, *Die Erklärung der Menschen- und Bürgerrechte,* Vierte Auflage, in Dritter Auflage bearbeitet von Walter Jellinek, Duncker & Humblot, München und Leipzig 1927.

these attacks are connected with the holiest of the holiest: God and the Prophet.

6. The Context of Globalisation Sharpens the Differences

Naturally, the question to be addressed is whether we are facing a problem of radical Islam,[35] Islam,[36] monotheism,[37] religion, or fanaticism?[38] It lies outside the scope of this Chapter to deal with this question, but the point we can make is that conflicts that did not exist or were only of local significance in the past have a much greater impact in this day and age. This was already shown by the conflict about the publication of Rushdie's *The Satanic Verses*, but is also clear from the Danish cartoons affair. It was a *Pakistani* organisation that offered a reward for the murder of cartoonists in *Denmark*. It was *Iraqi* terrorists who took *French* tourists hostage because they wanted to exert influence on French legislation.[39] After the *Dutch* Member of Parliament Hirsi Ali had made some remarks about the Prophet Muhammad, representatives of the *international* Organisation of Islamic Conference reported to the Chairman of the parliamentary party of the Dutch Liberals (*VVD*) in order to complain about the discourteous treatment of the Prophet by a Liberal Member of Parliament.[40] A *Danish* imam informed Al-Jazeera about the cartoons

---

[35] This is the opinion of Tibi, Bassam, *Der neue Totalitarismus.* Heiliger Krieg und westliche Sicherheit, Primus Verlag, Darmstadt 2004.

[36] This is the opinion of Spencer, Robert, *Islam Unveiled.* Disturbing Questions About the World's Fastest-Growing Faith, Encounter Books, San Francisco 2002; Spencer, Robert, *On ward Muslim Soldiers.* How Jihad Still Threatens America and the West, Regnery Publishing, Inc., Washington 2003; Raddatz, Hans-Peter, *Allahs Frauen.* Djihad zwischen Scharia und Demokratie, Herbig, München 2005.

[37] Kirsch, Jonathan, *God against the Gods.* The History of the War between Monotheism and Polytheism, Viking Compass, New York 2004.

[38] As is argued by Laqueur, Walter, *Krieg dem Westen.* Terrorismus im 21. Jahrhundert, Propyläen, München 2003.

[39] 'Headscarf, the reason for kidnapping', in *De Telegraaf,* 30 August 2004: In August 2004, two French journalists were kidnapped by Iraq Muslim terrorists. The journalists involved were Christian Chesnot from *Radio France International* and George Malbrunot from *Le Figaro*. They were kidnapped by the Islamic Army, which killed the Italian journalist Baldoni on 26 August 2004. The terrorists threatened to behead the journalists if France did not immediately lift the headscarf ban in French schools.

[40] On 26 February 2003, a letter was sent to the Chairman of the parliamentary party of the VVD, Gerrit Zalm. The letter was sent by 21 members of an Islamic organisation known

affair, as a result of which the conflict took an *international* dimension. And so on and so forth. In this context, globalisation presents an important problem: the national borders seem to crumble.

Because different parties rely on the concept of 'self-defence', it is important to reflect on its nature, as it forms a second core concept of the argument advanced in this Chapter.

7. The Concept of Self-Defence

Self-defence is considered to be a fundamental principle of law. It is an inherent right that, according to the great Roman lawyer, philosopher and statesman Cicero has the status of a natural law principle: 'There exists a law, not written down anywhere but inborn in our hearts; a law that comes to us not by training or reading but from nature itself (...) that if our lives are endangered, any and every method of protecting ourselves is morally right.'[41]

According to contemporary standards relating to rights and morals, this formulation is much too broad. Numerous questions of interpretation present themselves. Is it true that the right to self-defence is a natural law principle? Is it really inborn in our hearts and not acquired by training? Is really *every* method of protecting ourselves morally right if our lives are endangered? Or should we even then restrain ourselves to proportional violence?

We can also formulate interesting questions regarding the interpretation of the word 'lives'. 'If our lives are endangered, any and every method of protecting ourselves is morally right.' What does that mean? Is 'lives' only our biological lives? That would mean that self-defence would not be allowed if I am attacked for the purpose of being sold as a slave (it is not my life that is in danger, but my freedom). Is self-defence possible only if my *own life* is attacked or also the lives of my relatives, my friends and compatriots?

---

as the 'Organisation of the Islamic Conference' (OIC). The signatories of the letter complained about the 'insulting comments made against the Prophet Muhammad by a newly elected Member of Parliament, Ms. Ayaan Hirsi Ali' in the newspaper *Trouw* of 25 January 2003. Hirsi Ali had called Muhammad a 'perverse man', because he was married to a nine-year-old girl: Aïsja.

[41] The Second Amendment: America's First Freedom, by Charlton Heston, Fall 1999 *Human Rights Magazine*.

And finally: who decides what is my 'self'? Can I define my 'self' as my 'honour', my ethnic and religious pride? And, most important, perhaps, can I define my 'self' with reference to the Prophet, so that I am justified in defending my 'self', when the Prophet is insulted?

On this particular point, there seems to be a great difference of opinion between the Western world on the one hand and some parts of Islamic culture on the other, as the row over the Danish cartoons has demonstrated. In Islamic culture there seems to be not only a different conception of 'self', but also a different conception of 'violence' and 'attack'. Self-defence is considered to be justified not only in the case of an *armed* attack on the *physical integrity* of the state, but also when the Prophet's honour is violated or when 'Islam' is threatened by means of speech and even drawings.

In Lucknow, the capital of the Indian state of Uttar Pradesh, an Islamic court issued a death sentence against the 12 cartoonists of the Danish Muhammad cartoons on 20 February 2006. This also took the form of a fatwa, a religious ruling. The religious head of the court, Maulana Mufti Abul Irfan, declared: 'Death is the only sentence for the sacrilege of the cartoons.'[42] Irfan claimed that the court's opinion was binding on all Muslims, wherever they were.[43]

Some questions that can be posed in the footsteps of Cicero's formulation of self-defence have been answered by courts dealing with cases in which these questions were relevant.

As would be expected, self-defence has a place in national penal law, but also in international law. According to the law of nations, the *state* is an entity that is allowed to defend itself. And what the state is allowed to defend is its *territorial integrity*. Some writers infer this from the concept of a sovereign state. 'A sovereign state is entitled to defend itself, that is, to protect its territorial integrity.'[44] According to Wheaton, the right to self-preservation is an absolute right, lying at the foundation of all the other rights of states.[45] A state's right of self-defence is nowadays recognized in Article 51 of the United Nations Charter: 'Nothing in the present Charter shall impair the inher-

---

42 'Iran, too, wants to soothe the cartoons affair', in: *NRC Handelsblad*, 21 January 2006.

43 'Islamic court in India issues death sentence to cartoonists', in *Agence France Press*, 20 February 2006.

44 Janis, Mark W., *An Introduction to International Law,* Second Edition, Little Brown and Company, Boston etc. 1993, p. 179.

45 Cited in Janis, *supra*, fn. 44, p. 178.

ent right of individual or collective self-defence if an armed attack occurs against a Member of the United Nations (...).' Concomitant with Article 51's right to self-defence is Article 2(4)'s prohibition against 'the threat or use of force against the territorial integrity or political independence of any state.'

The classic definition of the right of self-defence in customary international law was formulated in the *Caroline* case. As a result of this case, the American Secretary of State laid down the essentials of self-defence that made history. There had to exist 'a necessity of self-defence, instant, overwhelming, leaving no choice of means, and no moment for deliberation.'[46]

The history of the case goes back to the middle of the 19th century. In 1837, the British tried to crush a rebellion in Upper Canada. The United States was unwilling to antagonize the British by giving direct support to the rebels, but did not prevent the formation of private militias in New York. The volunteers used a steamboat, the *Caroline,* to transport arms and men to the rebel headquarters of Navy Island, on the Canadian side of the Niagara River. The British responded with a night raid. They captured the boat, as it docked at Fort Schlosser, New York, set it on fire and sent it over Niagara Falls. Two men were killed as they fled the steamer.[47]

The incident meant that the British had intervened on US territory. The British justified their action by saying that the destruction of the *Caroline* was an act of 'necessary self-defence'.

In 1842 the incident was discussed again when the two parties tried to settle the case amicably. On this occasion, the American Secretary of State, Daniel Webster, presented his famous definition of self-defence. He conceded that the use of self-defence could be justified in some circumstances. He said:

> 'Undoubtedly it is just, that, while it is admitted that exceptions growing out of the great law of self-defence do exist, those exceptions should be confined to cases in which the necessity of that self-defence is instant, overwhelming, leaving no choice of means, and no moment for deliberation'.[48]

Webster added that nothing 'unreasonable or excessive' could be done in self-defence. Since then these parameters of customary international law have

---

[46] Cited in Shaw, Malcolm, *International Law,* Third Edition, Grotius Publications, England 1991, p. 692.

[47] Byers, Michael, *War Law.* International Law and Armed Conflict, Atlantic Books, London 2005, p. 53.

[48] Cited in Byers, *supra*, fn. 47, p. 54.

been accepted by other governments: 'necessity' and 'proportionality' were the keywords. Force used in self-defence must be 'necessary' and 'proportional' to the seriousness of the armed attack.[49]

Although much effort has been made to present a viable concept of justified self-defence, the content of Article 51 is very much rooted in customary international law.[50]

First, there is the question of territory. The attack that gives rise to the right of self-defence need not necessarily be directed against a state's territory. Article 6 of the North Atlantic Treaty 1949 provided for collective self-defence against 'an armed attack on the territory of any of the parties in Europe or North America (....), on the occupation forces of any of the parties in the North Atlantic area (...) or on the vessels or aircrafts in this area of any of the parties'.[51] In the *Corfu Channel* case, the International Court of Justice held that British warships under attack in foreign territorial waters were entitled to return fire.

Another question is whether the right to self-defence can be invoked when a state's citizens are attacked. Can the right to self-defence also be invoked when a state's nationals resident abroad are attacked? Most writers do not think so.[52]

There are also some important questions concerning the notion of 'armed attack'. What is the precise extent of the right of self-defence? Can it be resorted to only 'if an armed attack occurs' or also in other circumstances? And what is 'armed attack'? The Court noted that this includes not only action by regular armed forces across an international border, but also other activities similar to an armed attack.

8. Can the Americans Invoke Self-Defence in the War on Terror?

Naturally, international law may adhere to a limited conception of self-defence. In that case self-defence could be justified if

---

[49] Nicaragua *v* USA, *ICJ Reports,* 1986, pp. 14, 94 and pp. 122-123.

[50] This is the opinion of Byers, see above, fn. 47, p. 56.

[51] Akehurst, Michael, *A Modern Introduction to International Law,* Sixth Edition, Harper Collins Academic, London 1991 (1970), p. 264.

[52] Idem.

- a state (and not a group of people);
- is physically attacked (i.e. by military means, not by words);
- by another state;
- and the Security Council has authorized this.

The United States were not attacked by a state, but by an organisation (Al-Qaeda), perhaps backed by one or more states.[53]

About one year after 11 September 2001, the Bush administration presented a new national security plan: The National Security Strategy of the United States of America (2002).[54] The Bush administration does not deny that the events of 9/11 were a major factor in its drafting. 'The events of September 11, 2001, fundamentally changed the context for relations between the United States and other main centres of global power', the plan states.[55] And another passage reads: 'The major institutions of American national security were designed in a different era to meet different requirements. All of them must be transformed.'[56] It is hard to deny that the American administration presented a very controversial plan, but it cannot be denied either that it is based on a consistent idea. In fact, the guiding ideas are mentioned in the introduction and are elaborated in the succeeding chapters. One could characterize the plan or the memorandum on the basis of five pillars or themes. The plan itself does not distinguish these very clearly, but it may clarify matters to present it in this way.

First pillar: communism defeated. The first pillar of the plan comprises an historical assertion, and one which is not particularly controversial. It means that the world has fundamentally changed as a result of the disappearance of the Soviet Union as a world power and the disappearance of communism as the ideology that poses a challenge to the Western world. 'The great struggle of the twentieth century between liberty and totalitarianism ended with the victory of the forces of freedom', the Bush administration writes.[57]

---

[53] See Franck, Thomas M., 'Terrorism and the Right of Self-Defense', in *The American Journal of International Law,* Vol. 95, No. 4 (Oct., 2001), pp. 839-843, who criticizes the grounds for the European condemnation of the US.

[54] http://www.whitehouse.gov./nsc/nss/html.

[55] *The National Security Strategy of the United States of America,* p. 28.

[56] Ibid., p. 29.

[57] Ibid., introduction.

Second pillar: rejection of cultural relativism. The second policy pillar is defined less explicitly and certainly not in the terms I will now use, yet it constitutes an unmistakable element of the United States' new security strategy and the underlying world view. This second pillar is the rejection of cultural relativism.

Cultural relativism is the conviction that every culture has its own values and standards that cannot be traced to another culture.[58] Morality is always local morality. Politics is always local politics. Any idea that there is such a thing as universal morality, values and standards that apply to all people is an illusion. The American policy memorandum rejects this cultural relativism and argues in favour of universality.

People everywhere want to be able to speak freely; choose who will govern them; worship as they please; and enjoy the fruits of their labour. These values of freedom, the plan continues, are 'right and true for every person, in every society'.[59]

In this way the Bush administration does not comment on the time in which we live (as with the first pillar), but it commits itself to a philosophical position. It embraces the universalist position of the natural-law doctrine or of universal morality. It rejects the principles of cultural relativism that indicate that values and standards are a matter of local customs without any claim to universality. A phrase that is sometimes used in this context is that certain values 'are non-negotiable'. The strategy plan defines it as follows: 'America must stand firmly for the non-negotiable demands of human dignity: the rule of law; limits on the absolute power of the state; free speech; freedom of worship; equal justice; respect for women; religious and ethnic tolerance and respect for property.'[60] In the same way that Cicero bases the right of self-defence on a universal human nature, other values may be derived from this human nature.[61] The US also indicates that it wants to propa-

---

58 Scc Rachels, James, 'The challenge of cultural relativism', in *The Elements of Moral Philosophy,* Fourth edition, McGraw-Hill Inc., New York etc. 2003 (1986), pp. 61-31, p. 18/19; Donnelly, Jack, 'Cultural Relativism and Universal Human Rights', in *Human Rights Quarterly,* 6 (1984), pp. 400-419; Gensler, Harry, 'Cultural Relativism', in *Ethics,* Routledge, London & New York 1998, pp. 11-20.

59 *The National Security Strategy of the United States of America,* introduction.

60 Ibid., p. 3.

61 With respect to human nature as the basis for natural law, see Gardner, Martin, 'Beyond Cultural Relativism', in Gardner, Martin, *The Night is Large.* Collected Essays 1938-1995, Penguin Books, London 1996, pp. 149-161.

gate these values across the world: 'the United States will use this moment of opportunity to extend the benefits of freedom across the globe.'[62]

Third pillar: American supremacy. The third pillar is in fact the military-strategic counterpart of the first pillar. The third pillar means that the United States of America is the only superpower left. This position entails certain obligations, the Americans argue.

Today, the United States enjoys a position of unparalleled military strength and great economic and political influence.[63]

Fourth pillar: all the same, the world has not become a safer place. It could be argued that the fourth observation is the most innovative. It is an idea fostered by 9/11: in spite of the first three points, the world has not become a safer place for Americans, or for others.

In this modern world, however, the threats to freedom are different from those of the Cold War. The threats are no longer posed by large states, but by 'shadowy networks of individuals' that may cause considerable damage. These networks 'can bring great chaos and suffering to our shores' for less than the cost of purchasing a single tank.[64] The biggest threat, according to the Bush administration, lies 'at the crossroads of radicalism and technology.'[65] For example, the opponents of the US claim that they are attempting to develop or have already developed weapons of mass destruction.

Another way of putting it is as follows. The danger is no longer posed by strong states but by weak states, because the latter states often provide the space within which terrorist organisations can develop. What 11 September 2001 has taught us, the Bush administration writes, is 'that weak states, like Afghanistan, can pose as great a danger to our national interests as strong states.'[66] 'America', it writes, 'is now threatened less by conquering states than we are by failing ones. We are menaced less by fleets and armies than by catastrophic technologies in the hands of the embittered few.'[67]

Incidentally, this part of American thinking about defence is broadly supported, even by some critics of American policy. For example, Fukuyama writes: 'The fact is that the chief threats to us and to world order come today

[62] *The National Security Strategy of the United States of America,* introduction.
[63] Ibid., introduction.
[64] Idem.
[65] Idem.
[66] Idem.
[67] Ibid., p. 1.

from weak, collapsed, or failed states. (...) Before 9/11 the United States felt it could safely ignore chaos in a far-off place like Afghanistan; but the intersection of religious terrorism and weapons of mass destruction has meant that formerly peripheral areas are now of central concern.'[68]

The danger is also called 'terrorism'. According to the plan, the United States of America 'is fighting a war against terrorists of global reach. The enemy is not a single political regime or person or religion or ideology. The enemy is terrorism – premeditated, politically motivated violence perpetrated against innocents.'[69] Poverty alone does not cause terrorism, the plan claims, but poverty in combination with weak institutions, a corrupt state and terrorist networks constitutes a deadly danger.[70]

Besides terrorism, the plan refers to 'rogue states' as a big threat to the US.

Fifth pillar: The US must defend itself. So far the plan has not legitimized regime change, humanitarian interventions or pre-emptive strikes in self-defence. It is perfectly possible to take the view (a) that communism has been defeated; (b) that the time has come in which all people, all over the world, should be entitled to the same rights; (c) that US military supremacy is firmly established and (d) that the world has not become a safer place in spite of the earlier processes; it is possible to endorse all four points (in other words, the first four pillars) and *still* maintain that the United States does not have the right to preserve order in the world as the unipolar[71] superpower or take defensive action against foreign attacks without the explicit support of the Security Council of the United Nations.[72]

---

[68] Fukuyama, Francis, 'Nation-building', in *The Atlantic Monthly,* 293 (1), pp. 159-162. See also Fukuyama, Francis, *State-Building.* Governance and World Order in the Twenty-First Century, Profile Books, London 2004, preface.

[69] *The National Security Strategy of the United States of America,* p. 5.

[70] This idea is also expressed in Pipes, Daniel, 'God and Mammon: Does Poverty Cause Militant Islam?', in *National Interest,* Winter 2002, and also at www.danielpipes.org/article/104.

[71] This term was introduced by Charles Krauthammer. See Krauthammer, Charles, *Democratic Realism: An American Foreign Policy for a A Unipolar World,* The 2004 Irving Kristol Lecture, the American Enterprise Institute, Washington, DC. 'The unipolar moment has become the unipolar era', said Krauthammer in the years 1990-1991. This view was shared by intellectuals who had gathered round the journal *The National Interest,* people such as Irving Kristol, Bill Kristol, Samuel Huntington, Paul Wolfowitz, Norman Podhoretz and Daniel Pipes.

[72] As a substantial proportion of the commentaries indicate. See, for example: Charney, Jonathan, 'The Use of Force against Terrorism and International Law', in *The American Jour-*

But that is not the conviction of the Bush administration. As presented in September 2002, the plan has a fifth pillar. The Bush administration infers a fifth point from the preceding four points, namely that the United States must defend itself: 'To defeat this threat, we must make use of every tool in our arsenal – military power, better homeland defences, law enforcement, intelligence, and vigorous efforts to cut off terrorist financing.'[73]

The passages in which the Bush administration indicates that it wants to confront the dangers differently from in the past are undoubtedly the most important part of the document. It does not want to wait passively until disaster strikes but to intervene before the danger has fully materialized: 'America will act against such emerging threats before they are fully formed.'[74] And another passage reads: 'Nations that enjoy freedom must actively fight terror.'[75] The word 'prevention' is used regularly in the plan. The United States of America will 'prevent our enemies from threatening us'.[76]

The policy memorandum also invokes the notion of 'self-defence'. It is noted that the US will do everything possible to maintain alliances with others, but if this is not successful, it will have to act alone. 'While the United States will constantly strive to enlist the support of the international community, we will not hesitate to act alone, if necessary, to exercise our right of self-defence by acting pre-emptively against such terrorists, to prevent them from doing harm against our people and our country.'[77] And a little later we find the following passage: 'To forestall or prevent such hostile acts by our adversaries, the United States will, if necessary, act pre-emptively.'[78]

It justifies this new approach by claiming that the traditional concepts of deterrence will not work in the new situation. 'Traditional concepts of deterrence will not work against a terrorist enemy whose avowed tactics are wanton destruction and the targeting of innocents; whose so-called soldiers seek martyrdom in death and whose most potent protection is statelessness.'[79]

---

nal of International Law, Vol. 95, No. 4 (Oct., 2001), pp. 835-839. This was criticised by Franck, Thomas, 'Terrorism and the Right of Self-Defense', in *The American Journal of International Law,* Vol. 95, No. 4 (Oct., 2001), pp. 839-843.

[73] *The National Security Strategy of the United States of America,* introduction.

[74] Ibid., introduction.

[75] Idem.

[76] Ibid., p. 1.

[77] Ibid., p. 6.

[78] Ibid., p. 15.

[79] Idem.

The last passage quoted above allows us to catch a glimpse of the nature of the terrorist danger that the US fears: it concerns a kind of terrorism whose 'soldiers' seek martyrdom. This is the only reference to the nature of the terrorist danger. It concerns religious terrorism and – it is safe to assume – primarily the terrorism that is created by Islamic groups and persons. The Bush administration is deliberately very cautious, however, in referring to the religious background of the threat. The latter finds expression only in the reference to 'martyrs'.

9. Criticism and the New Policy in the USA

The new defence policy of the US has aroused a storm of criticism. According to Jonathan Charney, the new US policy is disastrous.[80] Actions in self-defence under Article 51 of the Charter, uses of force against the territorial integrity or political independence of another state, must be authorized by the Security Council under Chapter VII. Article 2(4) prohibits both the conduct of a just war and forceful reprisals.[81] The use of force in self-defence is limited to situations where the state is truly required to defend itself from serious attack. 'In such situations, the state must carry the burden of presenting evidence to support its actions, normally before these irreversible and irreparable measures are taken. The United States should have disclosed the factual bases for its claim of self-defence against the terrorist attacks before engaging in military action.'[82] Over the long term, the interests of the United States and the international community will be best served by the Charter-based system of world order. 'If international terrorists have a coherent goal, it is to undermine this system – an objective the United States is perhaps unwittingly promoting by its actions.'[83]

The French philosopher Tzvetan Todorov is another opponent of this American defence policy. Todorov believes that the policy is guided by an entirely new view on humans and society. According to this view, there are no limits to the extent to which government action can transform society. This is also called neo-conservatism, but, in Todorov's opinion, this is not

---

[80] Charney, see above, fn. 72, pp. 835-839.
[81] Ibid., p. 835.
[82] Ibid., p. 836.
[83] Ibid., p. 838.

quite correct. It could also be called 'neo-fundamentalism'. The architects of the new security policy are 'fundamentalists', as they use the concept of Absolute Goodness as a guideline they wish to prescribe to everyone in a binding manner. It is called 'neo', because it is not dictated by God but by the values of liberal democracy. '*Les fondamentalistes croient aux valeurs absolues, ils rejettent donc le relativisme ambiant, les excuses données aux entorses de la démocratie par les multiculturalistes, la langue de bois du 'politiquement correct'*.'[84] The idea that government action can transform society is predominant. That is why it is hardly surprising that most neo-conservatives used to be Trotskyists or Maoists.[85]

This is not the strongest part of Todorov's criticism, however, because the neo-conservatives would, perhaps, not deny that they still believe in the idea that government action can transform society.

An interesting point in Todorov's criticism of the American intervention in Iraq and other areas is that a democracy should never impose its values on others. Todorov puts it as follows: '*Dans une démocratie, il n'a pas le droit d'imposer son propre mode de vie aux autres par la force*.'[86] Anyone who does do so is called a 'fundamentalist'.

This is, of course, a rather tendentious representation of the facts. As if it concerned the imposition of a 'mode de vie'. Legitimisation of military intervention may be based on humanitarian considerations (in other countries fundamental rights are violated on such an enormous scale that it would be irresponsible to stand by and watch)[87] and considerations of self-defence (to which we will confine ourselves in this Chapter). Naturally, it is never about imposing another way of life!

A second issue concerns Todorov's suggestion that a democracy should never be allowed to impose its values *by force*. This would mean that democ-

---

[84] Todorov, Tzvetan, *Le Nouveau Désordre mondial.* Reflexions d'un Européen, Préface de Stanley Hoffmann, Robert Laffont, Paris 2003, p. 36. Todorov's view bears some resemblance to the view of those who believe that both the United States of America and its fundamentalist opponents in the Middle East are guided by a form of fundamentalism. This view is expressed by Ali, Tariq, *The Clash of Fundamentalisms.* Crusades, Jihads and Modernity, Verso, London and New York 2002, and Sim, Stuart, *Fundamentalist World.* The New Dark Age of Dogma, Icon Books UK, Totem Books USA 2004.

[85] Todorov, see above, fn. 84, p. 36.

[86] Ibid., p. 39.

[87] On this subject, see Cushman, Thomas, ed., *A Matter of Principle.* Humanitarian Arguments for War in Iraq, University of California Press, Berkeley, Los Angeles, London 2005.

racies should, by the nature of things, be pacifist. This is a far-reaching claim, which raises the question whether Todorov confuses the *internal functioning* of democracy with the question whether democracy *may be created through military intervention.* It is true that a democracy is characterized by the fact that political elites succeed each other without the use of force. But this does not mean that democracies have to be pacifist *in their relations with the outside world.* Nor does it rule out that democracies may be established by force. One may oppose such developments, but it is highly questionable whether this opposition can be legitimized on the basis of any reflection on the nature of the ideal of 'democracy', as Todorov suggests.

Todorov thinks that democracy means that every people is sovereign and that it has the right to define itself what it considers to be good. ('*La démocratie signifie que chaque peuple est souverain, qu'il a donc aussi le droit de définir pour lui-même le Bien, plutôt que de se le voir imposer du dehors.*') But here Todorov is mistaken in the sense that a specific people's decisions command respect only if this people reaches a decision through a democratic process. In other words: a people must *first* achieve a democracy *before* it earns respect for its own choices.

If we take this argument to its logical conclusion, this naturally leads to the position that only democracies should not have to fear interventions by foreign states, whereas dictators can be overthrown with impunity by powers that are democracies themselves. Is this correct?

This may be morally correct, even though it is arguably undesirable from a pragmatic perspective, because it puts the world's security at too much risk.

This latter consideration seems to be decisive in Francis Fukuyama's criticism of the Bush administration. As a matter of fact, Fukuyama's analysis of the state of the world resembles that of the neo-conservatives (to which he belongs, according to some people) and that of the Bush administration in many respects. Nevertheless, he makes some critical comments on the new defence policy of the United States in the light of the great ambitions that may not be achieved.[88] Fukuyama also criticizes the Americans' 'voluntarism': the optimistic idea that it is possible to establish democracies everywhere, independently of tradition and context. And like Todorov, Fukuyama considers the neo-conservatives to be the architects of the new policy. For

---

[88] Fukuyama, Francis, 'The Neoconservative Moment', in *National Interest,* July 1, 2004.

example, Fukuyama comments on Charles Krauthammer's opinion on American unipolarity.[89]

His criticism is, however, mainly based on his assessment that the United States of America overestimates its power. If considered in terms of the various pillars of the American strategy plan of 2002, one may well argue that Fukuyama agrees with the first pillar (the defeat of communism), the second pillar (rejection of cultural relativism), the fourth pillar (the world has not become a safer place), but that he questions the third pillar (American supremacy) and fifth pillar (we must defend ourselves militarily).

As we have seen above, Fukuyama's diagnosis is poor where it concerns the analysis of the causes of the current threats posed to social cohesion in Western states. Political Islam constitutes this threat. This political Islam cannot yet organise traditional armies, as the Soviet Union could, but it is widely supported in 'weak states' and it appeals to the rootless in the Western world.

The problem that seems to occur in this context is that Western multicultural states now have a population of which a proportion trust the traditional institutions that have taken shape since the 17th and 18th centuries and that can be referred to briefly as: democracy, state under the rule of law, and human rights (which are ultimately defined in the Universal Declaration of Human Rights of 1948). On the other hand, a proportion of the population feels alienated from society and seeks refuge in a form of radical religiosity, in particular, that of radical Islam. Roger Scruton defines it as follows: 'Western civilisation has left behind its religious belief and its sacred text, to place its trust not in religious certainties but in open discussion, trial and error, and the ubiquitousness of doubt.'[90] A considerable group of radical Islamists, however, experience this rational discussion, this trial and error and the 'ubiquitousness of doubt' as an enormous attack on their faith, against which they may defend themselves, in their opinion, by using all means, even violent ones, with a plea based on the right of self-defence.

---

[89] Other books and articles in which the neo-conservative view is clearly expressed include Frum, David, & Perle, Richard, *An End to Evil.* How to Win the War on Terror, Ballantine Books, New York 2003; 'Part II, Neoconservatives and Foreign Policy with Some Comments by Friendly Dissenters', in: Stelzer, Irwin, ed., *Neoconservatism,* Atlantic Books, London 2004, pp. 53-141; and for the older neo-conservatism: 'Security and Freedom: Making the World Safe with Ronald Reagan', in Gerson, Mark, ed., *The Essential Neoconservative Reader,* Addison-Wesly Publishing Company, Inc., Reading Massachusetts 1996, pp. 161-207.

[90] Scruton, *The West and the Rest,* p. xi.

Scruton defines the dilemma very clearly when he writes: 'Territorial jurisdictions sit uneasily upon credal communities, which tend to recognize the validity of no law other than the divine command that shapes their identity.'[91] This is of great significance to Islam. 'For the true Muslim, no law is validated merely by deriving it from the customary law or sovereign edicts that establish a territorial jurisdiction. Laws can warrant our obedience only if they are divinely sanctioned; this means that their validity is established only if they can be derived from the *shari'a* – the revealed will of God.'[92]

Naturally, this does not apply to all Muslims. Islam, too, includes secularized and modernized groups. Nevertheless, Gellner and Lewis rightly state that it seems that, of the three monotheistic religions, Islam is the most immune to secularisation.[93] It is hard to reconcile the idea of territorial jurisdiction with the political culture that is predominant in Muslim countries. These countries have tried to achieve a kind of loyalty to territorial jurisdiction with the philosophy of Arabic nationalism. The territorially defined nation (*qawm*) was supposed to replace the Islamic *umma* as the 'focus of loyalty'.[94]

According to Scruton, we have to do everything possible for this reason to revitalise specific ideas that may otherwise be lost: 'territorial concepts of sovereignty of law, and secular ideas of citizenship'.[95] If we do not succeed, we will be faced with a period of chaos, both in a national and in an international context.

10. Neutral Ground

It is argued here that it is Scruton who has written the most sensible things about this subject. His suggestions deserve to be translated into concrete policy, but how could this be done? It would seem that it could be achieved only if citizenship were based on a neutral footing, meaning: independent of religious affiliation. However, there is little enthusiasm for this kind of citi-

---

[91] Ibid., p. 25.

[92] Ibid., p. 26.

[93] Nevertheless, the other theistic religions have radical forms as well. On this subject, see Fourest, Caroline, & Venner, Fiametta, *Tirs Croisés. La laïcité à l'épreuve des intégrismes juif, chrétien et musulman*, Calmann-Lévy, Paris 2003 en Ruthven, Malise, *Fundamentalism.* The Search for Meaning, Oxford University Press, Oxford 2004.

[94] Scruton, see above, fn. 90, p. 32.

[95] Ibid., p. 46.

zenship because of the influence of postmodernism and multiculturalism.[96] This applies not only to the Islamic world, but also to the United States of America. For example, the present Bush administration has wandered from the original ideal of the American founding fathers, who, in Jefferson's memorable words, envisaged a 'Wall of Separation': a separation between church and state.[97] On various occasions, the American President expresses his own religious conviction. In doing so, he creates the impression in the Islamic world that there is a clash between Christianity and Islam. Every criticism and certainly every military intervention is then perceived as religiously motivated: the crusaders that want to conquer (or liberate) the Holy Land.

Susan Jacoby, author of a book in the American secularist tradition, writes how President George W. Bush presided over an ecumenical prayer service in Washington's National Cathedral. 'Delivering an address indistinguishable from a sermon, replacing the language of civic virtue with the language of faith, the nation's chief executive might as well have been the Reverend Bush.'[98]

From the perspective of an unbeliever and someone with another religion than the president, this is not the kind of language that fosters social cohesion within a pluralist community. Bush felt free to ignore Americans who do not adhere to any religious faith, whose outlook is predominantly secular, and who interpret history as the work of man rather than God. The Jewish-American lawyer Alan Dershowitz, one of Bush's vehement critics in this field, has this to say about it: 'The very first act of the new Bush administration was to have a Protestant Evangelist minister officially dedicate the inauguration to Jesus Christ, whom he declared to be 'our Savior.' Invoking 'the Father, the Son, the Lord Jesus Christ' and 'the Holy Spirit,' Billy Graham's son, the man selected by President George W. Bush to bless his presidency, excluded the tens of millions of Americans who are Muslims, Jews, Buddhists, Shintoists, Unitarians, agnostics, and atheists from his blessing by his particularistic and parochial language.'[99]

---

[96] For an analysis of these concepts, see Gellner, Ernest, *Postmodernism, Reason, and Religion,* Routledge, London and New York 1992.

[97] On this topic, see Howse, Brannon, *One Nation under Man?* The worldview war between Christians and the Secular Left, Broadman & Holman Publishers, Nashville, Tennessee 2005.

[98] Jacoby, Susan, *Freethinkers.* A History of American Secularism, Henry Holt and Company, New York 2004, p. 2.

[99] Dershowitz, Alan, 'Bush Starts Off by Defying the Constitution', in *Los Angeles Times*, January 24, 2001; Dershowitz, Alan, *Shouting Fire.* Civil Liberties in a turbulent Age, Little, Brown and Company, Boston / New York / London 2002, p. 201.

The plain message conveyed by the new administration was that George W. Bush's America was a Christian nation. Non-Christians were welcome in the tent so long as they agreed to accept their status as a tolerated minority rather than as fully equal citizens, Dershowitz wrote.

Another critic of Bush in this regard is the philosopher Peter Singer. Singer formulates the problem with this confusion of evangelizing and politics thus: 'The Islamic militant who believes he is doing the will of God when he flies a plane full of passengers into the World Trade Center is just as much a person of faith as the Christian who believes she is doing the will of God when she spends her days picketing a clinic that offers abortions.'[100] Also the philosopher Sam Harris explains why all this 'God-talk' does not help us in the struggle with international terrorism. Harris's diagnosis is alarming. There seems to be a problem with some of our most cherished beliefs about the world, he tells us. 'They are leading us, inexorably, to kill one another. A glance at history, or at the pages of any newspaper, reveals that ideas which divide one group of human beings from another, only to unite them in slaughter generally have their roots in religion.'[101] According to Harris, it seems that if our species ever eradicates itself through war, it will not be because it was written in the stars but because it was written in our books: 'It is what we do with words like 'God' and 'paradise' and 'sin' in the present that will determine our future.'[102] A nuclear war between India and Pakistan seems 'almost inevitable, given what most Indians and Pakistanis believe about the afterlife.'[103] Many people say that 'extremists' should be taken to task only for what they do. Harris does not think so. He contends it is important to specify the dimension in which some terrorists are deemed to be extreme. They are extreme in their *faith*. 'They are extreme in their devotion to the literal word of the Koran and the hadith (...) and *this* leads them to be extreme in the degree to which they believe that modernity and secular culture are incompatible with moral and spiritual health.'[104] Certain beliefs are *intrinsically* dangerous.[105] We are killing ourselves over ancient literature.[106]

---

[100] Singer, Peter, *The President of Good and Evil.* Taking George W. Bush seriously, Granta Books, London 2004, p. 104.

[101] Harris, *The End of Faith*, see above, fn. 9, p. 12.

[102] Ibid., p. 12.

[103] Ibid., p. 27.

[104] Ibid., p. 29.

[105] Ibid., p. 44.

[106] Ibid., p. 73.

Some people say that radicals put a wrong interpretation on the sacred texts. This may be true, but does that help us? Does it help us to say that people 'misuse' their religion? According to the Pope, Luther 'misused' his religion. According to Luther, the Pope 'misused' his religion. According to Sayyid Qutb, the source of inspiration for Osama Bin Laden and other religious terrorists, liberal Muslims 'misuse' their religion. According to liberal Muslims, Qutb 'misuses' their religion.[107]

We do not have to hold a theological debate here,[108] but an axiomatic contention that every reference to violence cannot be sincerely 'religious' is premature and not very fruitful. We have to deal with the social reality of religion, and this social reality confronts us with radical interpretations that do not shun violence. It is contended that James Gow is right when he writes: 'One of the biggest challenges to stability for the West concerns social cohesion. The impact of violent Islamist action in one Western state, above all within the EU, would have undoubted impact on others, including the prospect of further terrorist activity. One point of this, from the perspective of the Islamist terrorist, would be to mobilize support among co-religionists, no matter what their ethnic, cultural or political background otherwise, and to foster international tensions.'[109]

What can be done to avoid the Clash of Civilizations? One thing is clear: silencing those who point out the problems is not a solution. When Huntington presented his thesis, commentators warned the public against this 'dangerous idea'. They assumed that Huntington proposed that we should allow civilisations to clash. As if the American political analyst *wanted* a clash or took the risk that a clash of this kind might occur by using such misleading statements. But, of course, Huntington was not proposing anything of that sort; he was *describing* what he saw that had happened in the social world.

---

[107] On Qutb, Ibn Taymiyya and other ideological sources of contemporary religious terrorism, see Esposito, John, *Unholy War.* Terror in the Name of Islam, Oxford University Press, New York 2002, pp. 30-31; Jansen, Johannes, *The Dual Nature of Islamic Fundamentalism,* Cornell University Press, Ithaca, New York 1997, pp. 47-54.

[108] See Krauthammer, Charles, 'Violence and Islam', in *The Washington Post,* December 6, 2002, who, when asked the question 'is Islam an inherently violent religion?' answers: 'The question is not just unanswerable, it is irrelevant'. What counts are the 'actions of actual Muslims in the world today'. And then we cannot deny that 'some of the worst, most hate-driven violence in the world today is perpetrated by Muslims and in the name of Islam.'

[109] Gow, James, *Defending the West,* Polity Press, Malden / Cambridge 2005, p. 12.

And in this respect his essay was prophetic, in the same way that Fukuyama's essay was prophetic, at least in part, in 1989.

So what can be done?

11. A Secular State Identity Based on Shared Values

The first solution (or direction of a solution) would be to foster loyalty to a state that can been seen as a neutral arbiter in the eyes of all citizens. That means that all attempts to place the focus of political loyalty on a religiously oriented state or on sacred law, are futile. European countries have to make a tremendous effort to integrate their religious minorities. A necessary feature of the integration process is to relinquish the idea that the primary focus of loyalty should be on the heavenly state and that holy law has priority over secular law.

Todorov clearly defines the values that should play a vital role. He mentions six core values.

Rationality. In this context, rationality does not mean that Europeans always act rationally, but that they assume that the world can be understood by rational means. Even the most curious and mysterious deeds can be understood by the power of reason.[110] This assumption also forms the basis for Western science.

Justice. Private acts are based on the idea of justice.

Democracy. A third value Todorov presents as being constitutive of the European tradition is democracy. He calls it an invention of the Greeks. It is true that all kinds of groups were excluded in Ancient Greece: women, slaves, aliens. But this does not alter the fact that they expressed an idea.

Individual freedom. Protagoras' statement that man is the measure of all things indicates that man is central in this mode of thinking. And this is positive. It will eventually result in a greater degree of freedom.[111]

Laïcité. It is remarkable that Todorov presents laïcité as part of an explicitly European heritage. He refers to its Christian roots. It is based on a saying of

[110] Todorov, see above, fn. 84, p. 120.
[111] Ibid., p. 126.

Jesus in Matthew 22:21 that we should give to the emperor the things that are the emperor's, and to God the things that are God's. One can also refer to a saying of Jesus in John (18:36) that his kingdom is not of this world. This is the reason why, in the Christian tradition, there is a contrast between heaven and earth, between the theological and the political. '*La laïcité désigne, non l'absence ou le rejet du religieux mais cette séparation même, et donc le refur d'imposer les valeurs chrétiennes par le glaive.*'

In contradistinction to a regime that recognizes laïcité, Todorov uses the term 'ideocracy'. This is a collective name for theocracy and totalitarianism.[112]

Tolerance. Todorov refers to tolerance as a sixth value.

The Return of Britishness

It will also be necessary to foster a sense of solidarity with the nation-state people live in. It seems that the United Kingdom, the most multicultural country in the West,[113] is reconsidering the double loyalties of multiculturalism. On 14 January 2006, Prime Minister Gordon Brown, then Chancellor of the Exchequer, made a speech at the Fabian New Year Conference in London. He asked the following question: 'Should we do more to define a positive sense of Britishness?'[114] And his answer was: yes.

Once again, it had been terrorist acts that had given the British – like the Americans – food for thought. Since 7 July 2005, the balance between diversity and integration had to be reconsidered. According to Brown, you had to have a clear view of what being British meant, what you valued about being British and what gave the British purpose as a nation. Brown argued that British values demanded a new constitutional settlement and renewed civic patriotism.

Brown also gave a warning. When people were insecure, he said, there was always a risk that they would retreat into more exclusive identities rooted in 19th-century conception of blood, race and territory. What people tended to forget was that they should celebrate a British identity which was bigger

---

112 Ibid., p. 130.

113 On this subject, see Thomas, Dominique, *Le Londonistan. Le djihad au Coeur de l'Europe,* Éditions Michalon, 2005.

114 Speech by the Rt Hon Gordon Brown MP, Chancellor of the Exchequer, at the Fabian New Year Conference, London, 14/01/2006.

than the sum of its parts and that a union was strong because of its shared values. Race and ethnicity were no basis for a common British identity. Although the British response to the events of 7 July had been magnificent, they had to face the uncomfortable facts that there were British citizens, British born, apparently integrated into the British community, who were prepared to 'maim and kill fellow British citizens, irrespective of their religion.' That meant that the British had to be 'far more ambitious in defining for our time the responsibilities of citizenship'. If they did not promote Britishness, they ran a real risk of having a divided society. 'And this British patriotism is, in my view, founded not on ethnicity nor race, not just on institutions we share and respect, but on enduring ideals which shape our view of ourselves and our communities – values which in turn influence the way our institutions evolve.'

What then are these values that Brown defines? He summarizes these as follows: 'Liberty for all, responsibility by all and fairness to all.'

These are important values. But are they specifically British? Perhaps that is only partly the case. Brown carried it off by pointing out that even before America had made these values its own, Britain could lay claim to the idea of liberty. 'Out of the necessity of finding a way to live together in a multicultural state came the practice of toleration and then the pursuit of liberty.'

It can be argued that Brown confuses historical genesis with the claim to validity. It may be true that the British were the first to discover the idea of political liberty in the Western world and include such an idea in their constitution. Voltaire was right when he indicated that Britain had given to the world the idea of liberty. But the question of which nation has discovered an idea is less important than the question of its universal validity. And it cannot be denied that the value of political liberty has universal appeal. This is the true core of the American defence plan. The idea of a 'government accountable to the people' was also first developed in the United Kingdom, but is in fact a universal idea.

* * *

The Berlin Wall fell in 1989. The general expectation was that the world we live in would be characterized by great ideological consensus. This expectation turned out to be unrealistic. It is correct to state that the primary focus of political loyalty is no longer ideological, as Fukuyama has argued. This should be a hopeful sign, but unfortunately, ideology has been replaced by something else that continues to divide people: religion. Western states have multicultural populations and a proportion of these populations is loyal primarily to religion. This does not apply to all members of religious minorities, but is applies to some of them.

Moreover, members of religious minorities feel out of touch with Western society and its standards. One of these standards is a far-reaching freedom of speech on religious matters. It is perhaps not an exaggeration to say that European states have their roots in religious criticism.[115] This means that it is hardly conceivable to consider any concessions in this standard for the sake of pacifying radical Muslims. At the same time, members of religious minorities regard this religious criticism as a violation of the integrity of their world view and as senseless mockery of all that is sacred to them. They defend themselves against it by various means, including violence. Part of international religious terrorism is a response to views and opinions expressed by Western authors. The United Kingdom was the first Western country to be confronted with this international religious terrorism, at the time of the fatwa against Rushdie. In 2004, the Netherlands followed with the murder of Theo van Gogh. This confronts Western countries with a very specific form of religious terrorism, which countries in the Middle East have been dealing with for a longer time (Farag Foda).

Another source of tension concerns the universalist efforts of the United States and other Western states to export Western or universal values to parts of the world referred to as 'failed states' or 'rogue states'. This ambition is justified partly by invoking the universality of the values at issue, partly by invoking self-defence.

It is of crucial importance to world peace and social cohesion within the states of the world community that these tensions are relieved. This necessitates consensus about a new constitutional order, which should be neutral and – consequently – secular. The idea of territorial jurisdiction will have to be strengthened and accompanied by a new kind of focus on citizenship and even patriotism.

---

[115] On the value of the freedom of religion, see Jellinek, George, *Die Erklärung der Menschen- und Bürgerrechte,* Vierte Auflage, in Dritter Auflage bearbeitet von Walter Jellinek, Duncker & Humblot, München und Leipzig 1927.

SELF-DEFENCE OR THE MEANDERINGS OF A PROTEAN PRINCIPLE

Arthur Eyffinger*

1. The Sport of Opportunism

If elasticity were the hallmark of vitality, self-defence would have to figure as a paragon of the resilience of international law. If in our day and age, the province and reach of the principle have been intellectually explored and politically stretched to the utter limit, there is nothing new here. Throughout history, the principle has been prone to endless reinterpretation and has been tossed around infinitely.[1] In the process, it has proven to be eminently protean. Unfortunately, elasticity is a rather ambiguous quality in the legal sphere, and a positively dubious one when a 'general principle' is being considered. In short, there is definitely a shady side to the current acclaim by the commonwealth of nations for a principle which, in their heydays of uncontested sovereignty, they never thought worth their while to consider.

Now why, one may wonder, with the world venturing upon its first faltering steps on the thorny path towards a collective security system, would the nations embrace this 'atavism' of self-help and unilateral action? Why, to be more precise, would they eagerly rally to the 'exception' [Art. 51] of their

* Arthur Eyffinger is director of JUDICAP, The Hague, The Netherlands. www.judicap.com

[1] Overviews of the history of the principle of self-defence in Bowett 1958, Brownlie 1963, Delivanis 1971, Cassese [ed.] 1986, Dinstein 1988. [For full titles see the *Bibliography* at the end of this volume.] Two recent and fairly comprehensive historical surveys of the issues can be found in Alexandrov, *Self-Defense Against the Use of Force* in *International Law*, The Hague 1996 [hereinafter Alexandrov 1996] and Neff, *War and the Law of Nations; A General History*, Cambridge 2005 [hereinafter Neff 2005].

A.C.G.M. Eyffinger, A. Stephens and A.S. Muller (eds.), Self-Defence as a Fundamental Principle

own Charter's stern rule [Art. 2(4)]?[2] But then again, why would a principle which the alleged Legislator of Mankind, Hugo Grotius, once hailed as man's First Law[3] reflecting the very *ektupos* of human nature and prompted by man's innate urge for self-preservation,[4] enter the Charter as if by the back door and in this rather 'negative' way of exception?[5] The more so, if this right is being invoked in the Charter's Article 51 with reference to a so-called 'inherent right' or, even more puzzlingly, 'droit naturel', as the French version reads, in a phraseology which, otherwise alien to the Charter's vocabulary, precisely recalls those scorned legal concepts which seemed long buried by the unstoppable march of positivist thought? For, to be sure, if self-defence, as the natural expression of self-love, is indeed to be identified along Grotian lines as the fulfilment of His Will, then, by virtue of its very origin, it is clearly superior to all positive, human law[6] and no issues of hierarchy can possibly arise.

---

[2] The positioning of Art. 51 *vis-à-vis* Art. 2 (4) somehow keeps puzzling commentators, both with regards to substance and hierarchy. Apart from the comprehensive commentaries on the Charter (Goodrich / Hambo / Simons; Cot / Pellet; Simma), see for specific comments on Article 51: Ezdi 1974, Holman 1982, Baker 1987, Visser 1987, Greig 1991, Plofchan 1992, Constantinou 2000, King 2003, Stahn 2004, Papisca 2005. On Article 2(4) see notably Dörr 2004, Bothe 2005.

[3] The reference is, of course, to Hugo Grotius' Nine Rules and Thirteen Laws as first stated in his *De jure praedae* [hereinafter DJP] of 1604-5. The First Law reads: 'It shall be permissible to defend [one's own] life and to shun that which threatens to prove injurious.' See *Classics of International Law* No. 22, ed. J.B. Williams, Oxford/London 1950, at pp. [369]-370 (Appendix A).

[4] In the opening paragraphs of DJP Grotius maintains that self-defence is a fundamental precept of God and of the Law of Nature. Indeed, he readily falls in with Homer [*Il.* 12.243] that 'There is no act more noble than defence of one's own land upon the battlefield' (ed. Scott, p. 3) and cites instances from the Bible where leaders later on came to regret their reluctance to do so (*Num.* 31.1-19; *Deut.* 7.2; *I Sam.* 15 a.o.). For its philosophical underpinning he relied on tenets as advanced *e.g.* by Cicero (*Acad.* I.22-23; *De Fin.* 4.25) that 'since God fashioned creation and willed its existence, every individual part thereof has received from Him certain natural properties whereby that existence may be preserved and each part may be guided for its own good, in conformity, one might say, with the fundamental law inherent in its origin.' Consequently, he avows that 'love, whose primary force and action are directed to self-interest, is the first principle of the whole natural order' and, with reference to Plato and Aristotle, that 'the just man's highest concern is for himself'. (ed. Scott, p. 9). Twenty years later, in his *De jure belli ac pacis* of 1625, Grotius presented a systematic treatment of the issue of self-defence (DJBP II.1 1-18).

[5] On the interpretation of Article 51 and the appreciation of self-defence as an 'exception' by commentators see generally Alexandrov 1996, pp. 93-120.

[6] Cf. Grotius DJP II.13 (ed. Williams, p. 29): 'For, from the standpoint of origin, the divine law is superior to human law, and the latter to civil law. From the standpoint of pur-

Indeed, if the claim rings true which Grotius echoed from Cicero,[7] i.e., that the true love of oneself does not need to be carved in marble or chiselled in brass tablets, in as much as it is carved in our very hearts, then why would this 'inherent' right need codifying in the first place? Still, if in 1945 this need was felt, why then did the masters of legal parlance who first drafted the Charter construe the articles 2(4) and 51, which were meant to be the flipsides of a coin that were to secure a watertight presentation, in such veiled, elusive phraseology and in seemingly contradictory and open-ended terms?[8] And what should one think of the recent definition by the International Law Commission which precludes wrongfulness if an Act of State constitutes 'a lawful measure of self-defence taken in conformity with' the UN Charter.[9] Or, to raise yet another *non liquet*, why would the International Court of Justice, in its recent case law, keep harping on the concept's narrowest interpretation – as befitting an 'exception'?[10]

Obviously, putting the question is begging the answer. In defining man's first faculty, i.e. self-preservation, in such veiled phraseology, the founding fathers of the Charter did not quite belie that other unique faculty of man, to wit, sound reason.[11] They rather bespoke wisdom in acknowledging the harsh reality that, in human understandings over the centuries, the concept of self-defence had invariably proved to be the sport of opportunism.

---

pose, that which concerns one's own good is preferred to that which concerns another's good; the greater good to the lesser, and the removal of a major evil to the promotion of a minor good. If, for example, your life is imperilled in the wilderness as the result of an attack from some individual, under circumstances of time and place that do not permit of recourse to a judge, you will rightly defend yourself, disregarding the Ninth Law, relative to judicial procedure. For that matter, not even the Third Law, which forbids you to injure another, will be an obstacle to such righteous self-defence; for otherwise you would not be able to exercise your right under the First Law, which commends your own life to your care.'

[7] Cic. *Pro Mil.* 10-11, referred to by Grotius in DJP (ed. Scott, p. 6) *inter alia*. On the prominent role of the concept throughout Grotius' oeuvre see Eyffinger, 'The Third Man', in Blom/Winkel 2004.

[8] These issues will be discussed in more detail later on.

[9] Responsibility of States for Internationally Wrongful Acts, Article 21. ILC Rep. 2001 (A/56/10). GA Res. 56/83 (2001) and 59/35 (2004). On its genesis Malanczuk 1983, 1987; Alland 1983, Jagota 1985, Lowe 1999.

[10] Major statements on self-defence by the ICJ are to be found in *Military and Paramilitary Activities* (ICJ Rep. 1986 pp. 14ff. pp. 102ff.); *Legality of the Threat* (ICJ Rep. 1996 pp. 226ff., pp. 266ff.); *Oil Platforms* (ICJ Rep. 2003 pp.161ff., pp. 183ff.); *Legal Consequences* (ICJ Rep. 2004 pp. 136ff., pp. 194ff.); *Armed Activities* (ICJ Rep. 2005).

[11] Grotius DJBP Prolegomena 9.

2. The 'Catharina'

Self-defence – the implementation of the human urge for self-preservation – figures high both as an instinctive reaction of man and a basic, inalienable human right. However, given man's social nature (*appetitus societatis*),[12] the idea (still according to Grotius) branched out in two parts: not just the egoistic part [desire] but an altruistic part as well [solidarity].[13] In advancing his thesis, Grotius – needless to recall – was inspired, first and foremost by the notion of that Great Brotherhood of Man as commanded by God Himself[14] and by the magnanimous Stoic concept of *oikeioosis*.[15] Grotius for one felt no qualms in expanding this right which up to then had been reserved for the individual to that 'natural entity' which eminently embodied solidarity and social commitment and which could therefore pose as the *perfectissima societas*, this being the State. Actually, with the State proudly heralding the protection of its citizens as its paramount *raison d'être,* the principle which on the individual plane constituted a mere *right* on the level of States assumed the status of positive *duty*.

This at least was the theory the way Grotius saw it. In practice, however, the concept of self-defence proved all too liable to all sorts of distortion and mishandling at the hands of State officials. Ironically, Grotius himself may be the best case in point. If his impressive theses on the relationship of Right and Might were mostly developed in 1625, in his capacity as the 'New Justinian' of his age,[16] the nucleus of his thesis on self-defence was advanced a full two decades earlier, in a different capacity and context altogether. Featuring as the first of the Seven Laws and Thirteen Rules elaborated in his *De Iure Praedae* of 1605, the thesis was first conceived by Grotius in his capac-

[12] Grotius DJBP Prolegomena para. 6,

[13] Grotius DJP II.6 (ed. Williams, p. 11): 'Love, then, is twofold: love for oneself, and love for others. In the former aspect, it is known as "desire"; in the latter, as "friendliness".'

[14] Grotius DJBP II.6 (ed. Williams, p. 11): 'But God judged [...] that all might be linked in mutual harmony as if by an everlasting covenant.'

[15] The idea, best known from DJBP Prol. 6, is also found in DJP II. 7 (ed. Scott, p. 13), where Grotius states, with reference to Seneca: '"Security must be obtained by offering security in exchange." Herein lies that brotherhood of man, that world state, commended to us so frequently by the ancient philosophers and particularly by the Stoics, whose view Cicero adopts.'

[16] It was the Louvain and Leiden scholar Justus Lipsius, who had proclaimed that his age needed a new Justinian.

ity of Counsel to the VOC (the Dutch East India Company), in what at core was a rather bellicose plea by the young, smart barrister in defence of an utterly questionable seizure by a Dutch captain (who happened to be an uncle of his) of a Portuguese vessel, the [*Santa*] *Catharina*.[17] So much for our paradigm of altruism!

3. A Distant Echo

Still, foremost among the claims advanced by Grotius as the logical consequence of the 'inherent' nature of self-defence was its universal application. In recent decades the world of diplomacy, be this for want of better or prompted by more cynical motives, has only too willingly paid lip-service to this claim which, otherwise, would seem to stem from a period and legal philosophy long overhauled by the Age of Enlightenment. Now, a swift glance around soon reveals the quicksand underlying Grotius' claim, both in theory and practice, and whether it was advanced as the product of observation or speculation.[18]

Buddhist tradition, for one, has always entertained quite different views. When one day the Buddha, by the evil doing of the monk Devadatta, found himself charged by an intoxicated elephant, he reputedly countered the attack by his universal, overwhelming compassion for the animal.[19] The incident is not without its parallels. In short, from the Buddhist perspective, compassion, *not* self-defence – empathy, not confrontation – has always been the paramount yardstick. In its philosophy, self-restraint is looked upon as the first step towards self-purification, in that it inspires the mind to take

[17] On *De jure praedae* see Haggenmacher 1983 at pp. 51-444; Roelofsen in *Grotius Reader* (Roelofsen/van Holk eds.; The Hague 1983) at pp. 5-15.

[18] Cf. Jenks, *Common Law of Mankind* 1956 at pp. 139ff.

[19] From the life of the Buddha: 'Devadatta's third attempt to kill the Blessed One was to make the fierce man-killer elephant, Nalagiri, drunk with liquor. When Nalagiri saw the Buddha coming at a distance, it raised its ears, tail and trunk and charged at him. As the elephant came close, the Buddha radiated his loving-kindness (metta) towards the elephant. So vast and deep was the Buddha's love that as the elephant reached the Buddha, it stopped, became quiet and stood before the Master. The Buddha then stroked Nalagiri on the trunk and spoke softly. Respectfully, the elephant removed the dust at the master's feet with its trunk, and scattered the dust over its own head. Then it retreated, with its head facing the Buddha, as far as the stable, and remained fully tamed. Usually elephants are tamed with whips and weapons, but the Blessed One tamed the elephant with the power of his loving-kindness.'

prevalence over matter. As is advanced by Buddhism, a mind poisoned by greed, hatred or delusion poses a far more acute danger to oneself than any challenge from external agents.

Somehow, as the echo of distant rumblings, the above-sketched incident has a ring of familiarity to Western man. Was it not it the Christ himself who, entering a world of tit-for-tat, insisted on turning 'the other cheek'? And was this not part and parcel of the Covenant he introduced, of the 'good news' (*evangelium*) he spread to link humanity worldwide (*katholikon*)? So how universal indeed, let alone Christian, is this alleged 'inherent right' to self-defence? And how did Grotius' claim come about in the first place? It is with the above dilemma in mind, and at that precise juncture of time (the opening of the Christian Era) that we best start our survey of the meanderings of a heralded 'general principle' of law through the centuries.

4. The Perfect Chameleon

To anticipate our conclusions, time definitely proved Grotius right to the extent that, more than anything else, it is human nature, in all its devious ways, that has dictated the application of the principle and presents the key to its interpretation. Our tale will readily show us that, in the uneasy alliance of doctrine and practice, now moulded by speculative thought then again by purely utilitarian power politics, the principle of self-defence, while nimbly taking the hurdles separating the private and public spheres and debonairly skipping the barriers of national and international domains, has presented itself as the perfect chameleon to serve man's ever varying ends.

How else to explain that a notion which, for a full millennium, was cherished by European lawyers as precisely the counterpart of war and of all military contest at any level surmounting the strictly personal and individual plane, came to be upgraded by later generations to become part and parcel of natural law war doctrine? And, that, still in that same capacity, the principle was perfectly ignored by the nations the moment war itself was upgraded into a regular 'institution' of public international law? Finally, that the moment war was being outlawed and proscribed from international society as a distinct atavism (first and in a faltering way by the Paris Pact, then more explicitly by the UN Charter) self-defence was promptly embraced by the nations (and notably the most powerful ones) in perfect analogy of natural law's just war tradition. *Cui bono* reads the riddle as ever facing the lawyer.

5. The Stoic Legacy[20]

European or, in a wider sense, Western Civilisation is the merger of two venerable mainstreams, the Greco-Roman and Judaeo-Christian traditions. Unlikely bedfellows as they proved in many respects during the early days of their marriage of convenience, the legacy they shared at the philosophical, religious and legal levels was impressive. For our purposes, the most high social notions that were inherited from the Hellenistic world by early Christianity were embedded in the afore-mentioned Stoic 'cosmopolitan' approach as advocated in Rome by Cicero and Seneca, to mention just two familiar names. The Stoa looked upon mankind as a single society knitted together by one single law, the universally applicable 'law of nature'.

In its historical context, Stoic philosophy of *oikeioosis*, or the Brotherhood of Man, whatever its ultimate source, was a major asset of civilisation. It embodied distinct social progress in comparison to the Roman sway at 'gunpoint', to African tribal feud or to prevailing concepts in the Islamic world, which strictly separated its own confine from the Dar al-Harb,[21] indeed in a quite similar way to the 'classical' Greek world which, for all its internal strife, distinctly set apart its own commonwealth from that of the 'barbaroi'.[22] Any broader-minded notions comparable to Stoic doctrine (that is, a normative approach to global society) can only be found in the leaps and bounds of Chinese civilisation as spurred by Confucian thought[23] and, if less prevalent, in the Indian subcontinent.[24] Paramount for our purposes, it was Stoic thought that – in spite of its mostly speculative, indeed unworldly approach – paved the way for the acceptance of the *katholikon* formula as advanced by Christian apologists, from there to spread with time into the authoritative source of the European natural law tradition.

With that other major ingredient of the Mediterranean cauldron, to wit, Hebrew religion and philosophy, the classical Greco-Roman world shared

[20] For a recent survey of the notion of *oikeioosis* through the centuries see Blom/Winkel 2004.

[21] For the development of the concept through the ages see Khadduri 1955, Charnay 1986, Johnson 1990, Kelsay 1991, Firestone 1999, Fadl 2001, Esposito 2002.

[22] See Coleman Philipson 1911, Bickerman 1950, Nussbaum 1962, Alexandrov 1996.

[23] See Britton in 29 *AJIL* 1935, p. 616, Chen in 35 *AJIL* 1941, p. 648, Lewis 1990, Alexandrow 1996, p. 1, Neff 2005, pp. 31-34.

[24] As exemplified by *The Code of Manu*, ed. Doniger/Smith 1991. See Viswanatha 1925, Basham 1967, Bhatia 1977.

Antiquity's mentality of tit-for-tat. This attitude on the individual plane was neatly paralleled by its approach to war.[25] If, admittedly, in Deuteronomy wars were forked into wars of *conquest* and wars waged at Jahweh's orders and by *divine law*, even these latter readily ran into genocide (witness the wars waged against the Palestinian tribes), as if to show that Jahweh's commands were adjusted so as to run true to the spirit of the times.[26] To Rome, likewise, war was the natural state of affairs and the closure of the doors of Janus' temple, if idealised,[27] was an all too rare phenomenon. *Pax* was merely the positive conclusion of a temporally well-defined and, in most cases, exclusively bilateral agreement [*pactum*] between specific political actors, an *act* to formally end, or rather interrupt, the 'normal' *state* of affairs.[28]

There could be no greater contrast with Stoic philosophy. From the Stoic perspective, which deemed brotherhood the natural *condition*, and consequently peace the natural *state* of man, any act of aggression, most of all war, required explicit justification. And this justification could only be found in strictly defensive action with the sole objective to uphold the fabric and norms of the Commonwealth of Man and to enforce the Rule of Law.[29]

6. The Other Cheek

Now, if Stoa and early Christianity readily agreed on advocating peace as the natural state of man, the two ideologies differed in the extreme with respect to the justification of aggression. It was therefore in their response to

---

[25] See Ferguson 1977, Craigie 1978, Harris 1979, Good 1985, Thürlemann 1985, Von Rad 1991, Niditch 1995.

[26] *Deuteronomy* 20 seems to be representative in this respect. Once peace proposals were rejected, the barrier was raised to indiscriminate plunder and massacre: 'But of the cities of these people, which the Lord thy God doth give thee for an inheritance, thou shalt save alive nothing that breatheth; but thou shalt utterly destroy them; namely the Hittites, and the Amorites, the Canaanites, and the Perizzites, the Hivites, and the Jebusites, as the Lord thy God hath commanded thee;' (*Deut*. 20.16-17).

[27] As eminently in Virgil *Aen*. 7.6-7-15. See Garlan 1976.

[28] On the various aspects of theory and practice see Phillipson 1911, Hausmaniger 1961, Bengtson 1969-78, Ballis 1973, Zampaglione 1973, Garlan 1976, Bari 1980, Ziegler 1985, 1989, Arend/Beck 1993, Rich 1993, Watson 1993, Alexandrov 1996, Dawson 1996, Ferrill 1997, Partner 1997, Bederman 2001, Price 2001, Bobbitt 2002.

[29] For recent historical surveys of Stoic concepts see Inwood (ed.) The *Cambridge Companion to the Stoics*, 2003; Blom/Winkel (eds.) *Grotius and the Stoa*, 2004.

violence that the Pagan and early Christian commonwealths were bound to clash.

According to the radical pacifist doctrine that was advanced in the Gospels *any* use of violence, for whatever purposes, was ruled out indiscriminately and in most apodictic terms.[30] Christians, consequently, were not supposed to endorse the idea of a military, let alone join the ranks. Much of the speculation of Christian apologists during the span of time we like to call the Middle Ages was involved precisely in gradually modifying this absolute doctrine to ultimately come to terms with the pragmatics of acute social demands and worldly affairs.[31]

This goal was achieved notably with reference to Stoic precepts, the closest philosophical parallel at hand.[32] Stoic doctrine emphasised the positive notions of the military in salvaging community interests from the onslaught of barbarism. Some critics have called this process of coming to terms with reality, 'the Coming of Age of Christianity', others its 'Loss of Innocence'. Be this as it may, the military, gradually, came to be looked upon as a profession eminently suited to nurture civic virtues and promote community interests. The *miles christianus*, it was advanced, in securing discipline and observance of the law, aspired to the same goals its legal counterpart sought, though by different, more compulsive means. In short, the use of force (and war) came to be appreciated in a relative manner, that is, depending on their purpose. Defensive wars were legitimised, wars of aggression invariably proscribed.[33]

Once this vexed issue had been dealt with, by the time of St. Augustine,[34] it took Christian apologists close to a full millennium to construe that impressive doctrinal underpinning in the justification of specific types of war that reached its *summa summarum* in Aquinas' full-fledged just-war theory.[35]

---

[30] See Cadoux 1919, Bainton 1946, Ferguson 1977, Childress 1984, Helgeland a.o. 1985.

[31] As encapsulated in the gradual shift of opinion from Ambrose's *De Officiis* or Tertullian's *Apology* to St. Augustine's *City of God.*

[32] See Rist, *Stoic philosophy*, 1969; Pohlenz, *Die Stoa: Geschichte einer geistigen Bewegung*, 1978; Inwood, *Ethics and human action in early Stoicism*, 1985; Colish, *The Stoic tradition from antiquity to the early Middle Ages*, 1990; Engberg-Pedersen, *Paul and the Stoics*, 2000.

[33] For an overview of this process see Neff 2005, pp. 45-54.

[34] On St. Augustine's views see Regout 1935, Wehberg in 78 RCDI 1951-I, Hartigan 1966, Langan 1984.

[35] On the evolution of Christian theology with respect to the *just war* doctrine see De la Brière 1938; François in 66 RCDI 1938-IV, Wehberg in 78 RCDI 1951-I.

To fully appreciate this achievement, it must be stipulated that, ironically enough, the political context and concomitant of this doctrine was the Church Militant.

7. Medieval Just War Theory

True to the society it was to serve, Aquinas' comprehensive doctrine which stipulated self-defence, redress and punishment as proper titles to waging war[36] was the happy outcome of joint efforts from the legal and theological spheres, as can easily be distilled from its normative, moral approach. Medieval just-war theory aimed far higher than merely defining the *formal* requisites for temporarily frustrating the highest bond of mankind, such as the need for a proper authority, a professional war machine, and a well-defined goal. It insisted not just on an objectively verifiable *justa causa* and the strictest adherence to the key elements of *proportionality*[37] and *necessity*[38] (that notion full of ambiguity that prompted licence as readily as moderation), which were the unmistakable domains of the lawyer. It also emphatically insisted on a *justa intentio*, and stressed the substantive and objective criteria of justice – clearly the acknowledged domains of the theologian.[39]

In short, medieval just war doctrine – not, to be sure, mirrored by harsh reality[40] – stood out as a bulwark of justice and moral integrity.[41] Being considered the ultimate means of law enforcement, war, by definition, was a matter of crime and punishment, trespassing and sanction. War was to be waged exclusively in defence of man's common ideal, the world's social fabric. Consequently, *just* wars were, by definition, wars of *defence*. This concept of war, by its very nature, excluded any notion of equal moral stand-

---

[36] Tooke 1965, Russell 1975, Johnson 1981, Haggenmacher 1983, Dinstein 1988, Bacot 1989, Kelsay 1991.

[37] On the principle of proportionality in this context see Cannizzaro 2001, Bonafede 2002, Parker 2003, Carmola 2005, Dinstein 2005, Gardam 2005.

[38] On the concept of necessity see Linnan 1991, McCoubrey 1991, Gardam 2004, Laursen 2004.

[39] Alexandrov 1996, p. 3; Cf. Kunz'well-known distinction between *bellum justum* and *bellum legale*; see Kunz in 45 *AJIL* 1951 at p. 528.

[40] See Brownlie 1981, McKay-Scott 1983.

[41] See Keen 1965, Johnson 1975, 1990, 1997; Russell 1975, Wright 1976, Contamine 1984, Kaeuper 1999, Neff 2005.

ing of the antagonists, as little as it allowed latitude for such a notion as 'neutrality' on the part of 'third parties'. With the identification of 'right and wrong' never in doubt and the ultimate stakes paramount, the moral obligations imposed on all were inescapable – and unequivocal.

The endless ransacking of church-fathers and theologians by Vitorio, Suarez, Gentili, Ayalez and Grotius while developing their theses eminently bespeaks the paramount relevance of this achievement of centuries of interdisciplinary learning for our understanding of modern legal conceptions.[42] Still, no question about it, rather than moral theology, it was precisely the Stoic natural law component, with its uncompromising aspiration to embrace the whole of humanity and its insistence on reason rather than revelation which, at the breakdown point of the *Una Sancta* in the unprecedented intellectual crisis of the late 16th century, enabled lawyers to remould medieval doctrine into the perfect vehicle to underpin the new, secularised world – even if before long this world was to be compartmentalised into State units whose philosophy and interests would prove to be diametrically opposed to the very idea of an undivided humanity.

For all its lofty notions, the idealistic just war doctrine of Aquinas' days, far from dictating contemporary military practice, more often than not fell short of even being taken into serious consideration in the grim reality of, say, the Hundred Years War.[43] The growing perception from which the works of Grotius *c.s.* emanated, *viz.*, that the relations of modern State-entities were regulated by specific rules all of their own, indeed of their own *making*, did much to bridge this gap. The newly emerging Law of Nations, instead of being handed down by Heaven or dictated by Nature, was acknowledged to steadily grow on the spur of the interests of the international actors, out of their own conscious will, in a volitional process, indeed as the positive expression of their will and, ideally, mutual consent. It was a *secular* concept and a strictly *legal* concept at that.[44]

---

[42] See Scott 1934, Tooke 1965, Johnson 1975, 1981; Russell 1975, Haggenmacher 1983, Anderson 1988, Onuma 1993, Alexandrov 1996, Tuck 1999, Neff 2005. Major source references are Gentili DJB 1612 at 1.4.48 (ed. Rolfe 1933, p. 31); Ayala DJOB 1.2.12 and 34 (ed. Bate 1912 , p. 12, 23); Grotius DJBP 1625 2.23.13.2 and 3.4.4 (ed. Kelsey 1925, p. 565, 644); Vittoria DIJB 1696 SR429.13 (ed. Bate 1917, p. 170); Suarez Selections 1621 13.4.3.2 (ed. Williams 1944, pp. 816-817).

[43] See Meron 1998 passim.

[44] A general description in Neff 2005, pp. 95ff.

8. The Notion of Self-Defence

What status had the concept of self-defence in the idealistic Medieval fabric of just-war theory? Intriguingly enough, it had none, in the early stages at least. The reason for this is that, initially, *self*-defence was taken to the letter, that is, viewed exclusively in terms of the *individual* and his exercise of the inherent right of *self*-preservation. To forestall self-defence from ever being considered 'war' in the technical sense, let alone 'just war', the concept was deficient both in formal terms and with regard to motive and objective. It did not just lack the proper authority and so on, but, more than this, the right intention. It was, in all respects, 'selfish'. It implied waging a 'personal war', that is, not with a view to upholding community ends but to securing individual ends. In fact, in salvaging or vindicating one's *own* interests in the face of presumably wrongful attacks, self-defence, more often than not, militarised at the cost of 'higher' social interests. To that extent, the very notion of self-defence ran counter to the concept of just war.

On top of this, self-defence militated against official Church doctrine and what was invariably deemed the eminent Christian value of 'the other cheek'. An act of self-defence, in short, could at best be *excused* as the exercise of that inherent, inalienable right of the individual, that 'relic' from a pre-social, pre-Christian era, to be exercised in a state of emergency, for lack of better means. Self-defence was therefore *tolerated* or *condoned*, be this within perimeters well-defined both in time and substance, precisely so as not to durably disrupt the higher social fabric. If, to be sure, one was entitled to spontaneous, *impromptu* defence so as to fend off a surprise attack either on one's person or one's property, by the same token either *pre-emptive* action (so as to forestall an anticipated assault) or *remedial* reaction (punitive action in the sphere of reprisal and retaliation) were strictly proscribed and reserved exclusively to formal authorities.[45]

To sum up, up to the 'early modern' period, and on logically compelling grounds, the very essence of just war, to wit, universal law enforcement, was deemed to be entirely absent from the plane of the individual. Indeed, as an instrument, self-defence recalled primitive society and the 'natural' state of man as seen in terms later to be identified as Hobbesian. For that very reason, self-defence required no just cause, but neither could any moral evalua-

[45] Neff 2005, pp. 60-62.

tion in terms of right and wrong be applied to it. And this, needless to say, proved a two-edged sword.

9. Defensive War

Such were the birth-pangs of the concept of self-defence in the European law tradition. However, in much the same way as the notion of reprisals – which, though endemic in Germanic law, had been alien to Roman legal traditions[46] – was by analogy applied to States (from there finally to become a corner-stone of the just-war theory), the concept of self-defence was gradually conveyed towards the public sphere.[47] While in its strict and narrow sense still invariably applied to the individual, with time and by extrapolation it was to emerge in international law under the title of 'defensive war'.

However, given the fundamentally different nature and state of development of these two domains of the law – personal feud with its ample means of legal redress in the domestic sphere on the one hand, and State aggression within the only nascent public international legal order on the other – this transfer, as inevitably as it was presumably unintentionally, involved a quite distinct change of perception, a different perspective and an altogether new conception of the notion of self-defence. In view of the undisciplined, decentralised character of international society in-the-making, and the absence of both a proper authority and adequate means to efficiently deal with crises, far more latitude had to be given to international actors so as to effectively protect their lives, or 'vital interests' as they were to be called in time, by rightful defensive action. By its very nature, 'defensive' at this level was almost inevitably pre-emptive, anticipatory action, only too liable to be confused with 'offensive' action. Again, in its ultimate objective to forestall recurrence, this action often bore a punitive character and, besides, was not by definition proportionate either.

It was at this stage that Grotius and the lawyers we call our modern 'classics' first came to think of self-defence as a legitimate cause of action for the State in its own right, to be clearly distinguished from redress or punish-

46 Neff 2005, p. 77.

47 On reprisals in relation to self-defence see Taulbee 1973, 1984; Friedlander 1978, Levenfeld 1982, Maccredie 1987, Roberts 1987, O'Brien 1990, Politakis 1994, Kelly 2003.

ment.[48] This was a major juncture in the history of the principle. Gentili was probably the first to suggest self-defence as a *natural* reason for war, as duly reflecting the instinct for self-preservation implanted in all living beings.[49] As Grotius would put it, Nature commits to each his own protection; self-defence, consequently, was a natural, *inherent* right, not one that was merely triggered by the wrongdoing of an aggressor.[50] This perception became the prevailing one up to the days of Vattel.[51] In fact, as was pointed out by Gentili and Suarez most incisively,[52] what had always been considered a *right* at the level of the individual, became a positive *duty* on the plane of the State *vis-à-vis* its subjects, whose protection and well-being were its very *raison d'être*.[53]

However, given the precarious and nascent status of international relations, and because of the lack of an undisputed, centralised legal authority, there was a definite dark side clinging to the concept. In the absence of proper legal redress, States from early on tended to grant themselves ample latitude in their interpretation of the element of 'necessity'. Grotius *c.s.* were eminently aware of this and vainly struggled, not to pierce the veil, but to counter it by effective legal redress. Thus, Grotius' insistence on the formal requirements of 'clear and imminent danger', and on the concept of 'fault' on the part of the actual assailant stand out as veritable beacons at sea.[54] Likewise, his insistence on *necessity*, rather than *advantage* as the criterion for validity of the concept,[55] and his conditioning of the justification of any pre-emptive strike to the ruling out of the slightest trace of doubt with respect to the effective *power* of the alleged assailant and his actual *intention* to attack, are valuable standards for all times.[56] They were readily backed by succeeding generations of lawyers as is eminently exemplified by Vattel.[57]

Still, as stipulated above, the drawbacks of this just war theory and of the above interpretation of self-defence were plain to see: the absence of objec-

---

48 Alexandrov 1996, p. 5.

49 Gentili DJB I.5.45; I.13.94 (ed. Rolfe 1933, pp. 28, 59)

50 Grotius DJBP 2.1.2-3 (ed. Kelsey 1925, pp. 171ff.). Lauterpacht in 13 BYIL 1946, pp. 1ff.

51 Ayala DJOB I.2.11.10 (ed. Bate 1912, p. 10); Suarez SEL. 2.17.6 (ed. Williams 1944, p. 329).

52 Gentili DJB I.9-10; I.13-25; Suarez SEL.13.4.1

53 Alexandrov 1996, p. 6.

54 Grotius DJBP 2.1.5; cf. 2.1.16-17.

55 Grotius DJBP 2.1.2.1; 2.22.5-6.

56 Cf. Bowett 1958, p. 6.

57 Vattel LN 1758 3.3.3 (ed. Fenwick 1916, p. 244); cf. *ibid.* 2.4.49 (p. 130)

tive criteria to decide on justified and unjustified uses of force, and the lack of an impartial authority to objectively decide as to who was actually on the defence and who the aggressor.[58] And there was something else: if war was, in Grotius' conception, the enforcement of rights by other means,[59] the outcome of this 'alternative lawsuit' was definitely not decided by legal or moral norms but by dint of arms and the fortunes of war – a contest in which the aggressor might easily get the upper hand.

The aspirations of these first international lawyers to curb the unlimited ambitions of potentates by a full-fledged doctrine, their explicit formulation of a legal framework to comprehensively cover the areas of just war, self-defence and reprisal were precious enough assets in their days. Still, their speculative reliance on morals and *interna justitia* constituted too weak a line of defence to successfully counter Machiavellian *raison d'état* running loose. It was their fundamental incapacity to adequately deal with the complexities and urgencies of inter-State relations and restrain violence which, over time, made jurists – if not perhaps dismiss the ethical norms of natural law theory as such, still – abandon its application for practical purposes. Gradually, the criterion of just cause (*bellum justum*), which kept defying man, was left alone and legal aspirations were focused on a different norm: that of the legality of means: *bellum legale*.[60] In other words, focus was shifted from *ius ad bellum* to *ius in bello*.

10. The Law of Nations

A handmaiden to natural law on the philosophical level, the pragmatic value of the new, 'positivist' approach to the law soon became paramount. State counsel, while in matters of morals or conscience comfortably relying on the higher legal echelon, and while leaving the thorny issues of *justa causa* and substantive justice to the domain of natural law, now first and foremost addressed the *formal* requirements to the proper *conduct* of war. In dropping all moral qualms, they were bound to focus primarily, and with time virtually exclusively, on pragmatics and strictly utilitarian aspects as dictated by State interest. In an altogether natural process, therefore, the quickening pace of

[58] Grotius insisted on a legal cause for war, verifiable by a court of law (DJBP 2.22.16).
[59] Grotius DJBP 2.1.2.1.
[60] Alexandrov 1996, p. 9.

interrelations between these nation-States and the ever growing corpus of treaties available to reflect State practice and the expression of their (collective) will gradually shifted the balance to the point were *natural* law gave way to *cultural* law, morals to utility, speculation to applied science.

Stepping down from idealism, international law, while dropping all concern for morality, became an integrated part of the anarchic Hobbesian society of sovereign nation-States in which each actor jealously protected his territory, political integrity and economic independence from all forms of external intrusion.[61] War, in this cauldron, was no longer the instrument of law enforcement and overall social ends, but the pursuit of cabinet policy by more drastic means. The system of the *Trutina*, or the maintenance of the Balance of Power,[62] stands out as probably the best-known veil, endemic in European power play, to cover unblemished State interest. The law was no longer deemed the guardian-angel of community interests, but was turned into the smart handmaiden of undisguised *raison d'état*. War was identified as the virtually inevitable periodical clash of rival powers, a recurrent incident and a means of power politics applied 'for a good reason, a bad reason, or no reason at all', as Briggs[63] once put it, and which was of no particular concern to third parties. Indeed, to strictly define what was expected from third parties, a full-fledged law of neutrality was now being developed.[64] Clearly, the need for any such law was never felt by previous generations who, theoretically at least, rallied to war exclusively for the sake of law enforcement in the interest of *all*.

All this tells us how fundamentally the tables had been turned. To add just one more example, the notion of humanitarian intervention,[65] almost a sacred duty from the natural law perspective and a 'justa causa' *par excellence* for war, was now frowned upon with utmost suspicion and unveiled hostility. Contrarily, on the ebb and flow of inter-State society, and depending on the measure of consensus between the rivalling nations, the rules and regula-

---

[61] As elaborated by Thomas Hobbes in his *De Cive* and *Leviathan*. See Sorell (ed.) 1996 passim, Tuck 1993, p. 279-345; Tuck 1999, pp. 109-139; Neff 2005, pp. 133-137.

[62] On the concept see Dupuis 1909, Vagts-Vagts 1979, Holsti 1991, Anderson 1988, Sheehan 1995.

[63] Briggs 1952 at p. 976.

[64] On the evolution of the concept of neutrality see Neff 2000 passim; Neff 2005 at pp. 75-76, pp. 151-155, pp. 191-194.

[65] Neff 2005 at pp. 223-225 and see Lillich 1973, Tesón 1987. On the further development of the concept see below, p. 115 and fn. 129.

tions of the 'proper' conduct of war – or its 'laws and customs' as they were now coined – grew into a highly formalistic ritual. By the 19th century, war had become a perfectly legitimate instrument of national, 'cabinet' policy, irrespective of its intention or objectives and wholly devoid of any moral appreciation. No longer was peace deemed the normal condition of international society. War was looked upon as an equally acceptable state of affairs. More than this, war had become a generally accepted, indeed highly respected *institution* of international law, with *just war* measured by purely formal, legalistic criteria.[66]

11. THE AFFAIR OF THE 'CAROLINE'

With war neatly stripped of all its moral complexities and the just war doctrine of medieval and humanist times obsolete, how was self-defence looked upon? As an act of necessity, to ward off a blow, and prompted by that deeply ingrained human sense of self-preservation, the concept was, as before, felt to be perfectly legitimate. In fact, politicians or lawyers could not have cared less about its niceties. On this one condition and one all too typical of the nation-State's preoccupation: that no trespassing of borderlines took place, in as much as this would automatically bring the action within the realm of belligerency.

If therefore the history of the concept of self-defence in the 19th century is quite uneventful as far as theory goes, one single political incident sufficed to prove its status in State practice.[67] This incident occurred in 1837, and was the well-known *Caroline* affair.[68] As Jennings once put it, this incident changed self-defence 'from a political excuse to a legal doctrine'.[69] It was triggered by a pre-emptive strike on American soil by British forces so as to seize a ship used by Canadian insurgents to raid the coast. If the British action should perhaps rather be defined as a form of reprisals to counter previous wrongdoing, the raid was justified by British authorities, not convincingly perhaps, as strictly preventive.

66 Neff 2005, pp. 89-93, pp. 177-178.

67 Other notable 19th-century incidents are singled out by Alexandrov 1996, pp. 20-22: the seizure of the Danish fleet by the British in 1807; the case of Amelia Island in 1817, and the *Virginius* case of 1873.

68 Stevens 1989, Alexandrov 1996, pp. 19ff.

69 Jennings 32 *AJIL* 1938, p. 82.

The action triggered a somewhat hot-headed reaction by US President Van Buren, who categorically denounced the British raid (which otherwise had fairly limited scope and a clear-cut objective) as a 'hostile though temporary invasion of our Territory',[70] before relations were smoothed and customary law canalised by Secretary of State Daniel Webster's clear-cut definition of the prerequisites of self-defence in a formula that has become canonical: *clear and absolute necessity and instant, overwhelming danger, leaving no choice of means and no moment for deliberation.*[71] Incidentally, it should be observed that, in the *Caroline* case, as generally throughout the 19th century, and contrary to modern legal parlance, the concept of self-defence was still viewed, in the best of natural law traditions, as interchangeable with – because identical, if not subsidiary to – the primordial right of self-preservation.[72]

Now, the latitude granted by States in the application of self-defence has traditionally depended largely on whether they were the party that inflicted or the one that received the blow – and the appraisal of the principle by the USA over the past two centuries is no exception to this rule, indeed it is perhaps its best documented proof.[73] The same can be concluded from the appraisal of that other kind of trans-boundary military operation born out of necessity, indeed one that is more amply recorded over the period and apparently also enjoyed greater credit, namely that undertaken with the intent to rescue nationals imperilled abroad. This formula is probably best exemplified by the joint military action of Western powers to relieve diplomats during the Boxer Revolt in 1900.[74] US Secretary of State Elihu Root for one felt no qualms over that matter.[75]

---

[70] 26 BFSP 1372-73 [1838]

[71] 29 BFSP 1127-38 [1841], 30 BFSP 195 [1841]

[72] Jennings 1938, p. 92. On the clear distinction between the two concepts maintained by modern scholarship see Alexandrov, 1996, pp. 23ff. While 'self-defence presupposes an attack, self-preservation has no such limitation' and could 'serve to cloak with an appearance of legality almost any unwarranted act of violence on the part of a state.' (Jennings 1938, p. 91).

[73] See e.g. DUSPIL 1975, p. 17.

[74] Grob 1949, pp. 64-79; Neff 2005, pp. 244-245.

[75] Neff 2005, p. 245. On 20 Century American practice see below, fn. 132-135.

12. INTERNATIONALISM ON THE RISE

It is only fair to say that, as the 19th century advanced, unbridled positivism in support of adamant Hobbesian lines of State policy was increasingly challenged from various angles. The *levée en masse* and conscription armies of the Napolleonic wars, and the resulting massacres, gave birth, on both sides of the Atlantic, to a peace movement. Again, the wars of the mid-19th century, notably the Crimean War and American Civil War, engendered the first truly humanitarian codes. Finally, the Franco-Prussian contest of 1869-70 revealed to the world at large some of the gloomy side-effects of that generation's foremost boast, the technology of the Industrial Revolution.[76] Increasingly, an odium became attached to war.[77]

It was at this juncture that the diplomacy of *laissez faire* was first seriously challenged by nascent 'internationalist thought'. The economic imperatives of rapidly expanding markets and (means of) communication led parliamentarians and lawyers into creating the IPU and the *Institut*, in quest of some model of consensus to defy this Iron Age of confrontation. The mostly abortive debate of the Hague Peace Conferences probably best illustrates the ideological stalemate that ensued, and the quickly widening gap between the new normative aspirations of lawyers and prevailing diplomatic practice.[78]

Small surprise if, with legal parameters shifting, the principle of self-defence once more surfaced as a bone of contention. Minister Beernaert's plea in The Hague, on behalf of the small and, by treaty, neutrality-bound State of Belgium, in support of his citizenry's rightful claim to self-defence in the eventuality of a surprise invasion, not only challenged the regulations proposed in The Hague, but actually touched the very sore of the prevailing regime: its perfect moral indifference. Current debate on the position of 'irregulars' can still draw some wise lessons from that debate at the Huis ten Bosch a full century ago.[79] In the end, to break the deadlock, the Martens Clause, to the repugnance of die-hard positivists, sought refuge in the alleged legal atavism of 'inherent rights'. It was the first crack in the solid icy

[76] Grossi 1994; Eyffinger 1999, pp. 41-68.
[77] Alexandrov 1996, pp. 14-15.
[78] Dülffer 1981; Eyffinger 1999, pp. 203-254.
[79] Eyffinger 1999, pp. 296ff.

surface of positivism. Meanwhile, Belgium's qualms would prove all too real, and the Martens Clause more than just an incident.[80]

13. Interbellum Fallacies

The society that first acknowledged the dilemma saw its fabric torn to pieces in the disillusioning cataclysm of the First World War. A repenting world recanted: the legal world, that is. 'Grotius' once more took a firm stand against 'Richelieu'. If the aspirations of the generation of inter-bellum lawyers have perhaps all too readily been labelled as a return to natural law traditions and the just war doctrine, these decades of growing despair and depression *did* aspire to impose norms, indeed 'The Rule of Law', on troubled international society. Its intended panacea, the League of Nations, *was* meant, along all too familiar Stoic lines, to constitute '*Humankind Inc.*'[81]

Brandishing a Covenant and boasting a standing international judiciary, lawyers and diplomats in the 1920s gallantly explored ways to turn the tables of inter-State relations overnight. Their quest for a 'new international order' (if not exactly innovative, the call for a *Novus Rerum Ordo* being raised twice every century) *did* once again presuppose peace as the normal state of affairs and demanded positive justification for resort to war and the ripping apart of the precious social fabric. In Articles 12-15 of the Covenant at least a partial renunciation of war was imposed.[82] For one thing, its legality was made dependent on the previous exhaustion of the brand new mechanisms[83] for the peaceful settlement of disputes (a new criterion altogether!), and its justification found precisely in the enforcement of the law. Amidst lively debate of a world emergency police force and a League Navy patrolling the oceans,[84] economic reprisals were hailed as a panacea to curb obstinate trespassers of the new world order. In 1928, in Paris, League Member-States

---

[80] On the Martens Clause see Pustogarov in 1 *JHIL* (1999) pp. 125-135; Cassese in 11 *EJIL* (2000) pp. 187-216; Meron in 94 *AJIL* (2000) pp. 78-89; Schircks, *Die Martens'sche Klausel; Rezeption und Rechtqualität*, 2001.

[81] On the League and its Covenant see Bassett 1930, Walters 1952, Dexter 1967, Alexandrov 1996, pp. 29-49.

[82] Alexandrov 1996, pp. 32-34.

[83] Notably the PCA (1899) and PCIJ (1923) in The Hague.

[84] As advocated in the Netherlands by the Leiden professor Van Vollenhoven. See *Verspreide Geschriften*, 3 vols., 1934, vol. 2 , pp. 210ff.

trapped themselves, almost unaware it would seem, into formally abandoning war as an instrument of their national policy.[85] Or did they?

Miracles are more readily believed than performed, as Ethiopia would soon tell the world. From the best intentions often the highest ideals are born, but rarely sober rationale. The lofty ideals were not advanced in the void – and well established State interests are rarely by-passed by with impunity. Within a decade, internationalists in Geneva found their aspirations wrecked on the sturdy cliffs of steadfast Westphalians; it was a rude awakening. With hindsight, one may wonder at that generation's optimism of overthrowing the diplomatic practice of centuries.

If in political terms the League proved a perfect failure, a precious miscalculation which would take a new global war to mend, then what about its aspirations with respect to the Rule of Law?[86] Ominously, the League's paramount institutional boast in the domain, the Permanent Court of International Justice, found itself saddled with a curious dual role.[87] If its advisory capacity made it pose as the handmaiden of the nascent world constituency (in a role widely felt to be puzzlingly at odds with the proper province of a court of law), the purely consensual basis of its adjudicative role dragged it back into the Westphalian cauldron. Judges soon found The Hague situated somewhere halfway between Geneva and Munster.

But, worst of all, the victory over the moloch of war, proudly announced in 1928, soon proved to be a Pyrrhic one. While still busily putting the thumbscrews on politicians, lawyers, standing agape, saw glib diplomats adroitly slip through their fingers. By merely changing the direction of policy, politicians cunningly overturned all previous conceptions of war *and* the use of force as such. Perhaps the single most dramatic outcome of events was their complete reappraisal of the principle of self-defence.[88] For this, there was ample ground. As long as States needed no legal justification to start a war, self-defence had no role to play in that arena, its relevance being neatly restricted to the area of State responsibility for forcible measures undertaken in peacetime. Or, as it was once put more pointedly: up to that juncture 'self-defence was not a legal concept but merely a political excuse for the use of

[85] Paris Pact 1928; 94 LNTS 57, pp. 285ff. As Neff observes (at p. 294), in 1928 the Pact was widely understood to render resorting to war unlawful rather than impossible.

[86] See notably Zimmern 1939.

[87] Fachiri 1932 [repr. 1980]; Schenk von Staufenberg 1934; Hudson 1943 [repr. 1972].

[88] Bowett 1958, pp. 120-131; Neff 2005, pp. 303-307.

force'.[89] All this was now about to change. With the 'use or threat of force' now being branded as delict, sanction or self-defence, the concept was to assume a brand new status – and one with distinct juridical overtones.[90]

14. Kellogg vs. Briand

Lawyers soon found out that the task set apart for them was a Herculean one. In having duly cut the head of the Hydra, they saw no less than three new heads emerge.[91] In complacently focussing on regulating war, rather than proscribing the use of force *tout court,* they had somewhat inadvertently overlooked those other forms of inter-State coercion, the so-called 'measures short of war',[92] these being forcible reprisals,[93] intervention[94] and self-defence as an act of necessity. In tackling one of these measures at a time, they were faced with ever new varieties of the others. In other words – the heads kept multiplying. And, great irony of fate, and something that seemed to elude lawyers at the time, it was precisely their constraining efforts, their coercive zeal that called the new forms, indeed a new phase of inter-State relations, into being. Seen from the perspective of the self-focused *Leviathan*, the States' increasing reliance on self-defence (and, consequently, the growing international status of the principle) may actually be called an act of self-defence in itself. Stripped of their foremost instrument of conflict settlement, the military machinery, they felt positively crippled. Cornered by lawyers they felt as if 'provoked' into addressing other options.

The rise of the principle of self-defence, to reflect changing political circumstance, can be readily traced back over the inter-bellum period. The Covenant of the League itself did not even mention the concept. Being considered

---

[89] Jiménez de Aréchaga in 159 RCDI 1978-I, p. 96.

[90] Bowett 1958, p. 120.

[91] The reference, of course, is to Hercules' fighting the hydra or Lernean water-serpent, one of his twelve labours, a 'labour in vain', as two heads sprung up for every one that was cut off. (See Hesiod. *Th.* 313).

[92] All of them means of 'self-help' acknowledged as such since the days of Clausewitz. See Alexandrov 1996, pp. 11-18, Neff 2005, pp. 164-165, 215-216.

[93] The idea of reprisals harks back to ancient and medieval times. See Alexandrov, 1996 at pp. 15ff. and the wealth of references there.

[94] On the history of the concept see Briggs 1952, p. 960; Winfield in 3 *BYBIL* 1922-23, p. 130, and in 5 *BYBIL* 1924, p. 149.

an 'inherent right', explicit reference to the concept was deemed superfluous.[95] Meanwhile, as appears from the Assembly Reports, there is no doubt that is was implicitly acknowledged.[96] Neither did the Paris Pact contain any such reference.[97] But by that time, in 1928, its omission was no longer a matter of coincidence. At that juncture, quite a number of bilateral treaties did contain explicit reference to the principle as a legitimate exception to the general proscription of the use of force, thus to counter unprovoked, illegitimate aggression.[98] In multilateral treaty law, the concept was first introduced in Locarno in 1925.[99] However, three years later, in Paris, it was Kellogg himself who countered the proposition made by Briand to include specific reference to the principle in the Pact named after them both. As the USA argued on that occasion, both concepts – aggression and self-defence – were rather elusive titles, extremely hard to catch in watertight definitions.[100] The truth of this statement was to be confirmed only too painfully by subsequent attempts of scholars prior to, say, 1974.[101] By the same token, however, the US delegation in Paris asserted that there was no urgent need for any such specific reference. Self-defence was generally acknowledged to be a natural right inherent to every sovereign State, to be invoked at its full discretion and irrespective of any treaty provisions.[102]

Unfortunately, by then, practice had proven distinctly less reassuring. Already in 1923, in the Corfu incident between Italy and Greece – as for that matter in the dispute between Paraguay and Bolivia – the 'gaps' in the Covenant and League machinery when faced with measures short of war were laid bare for all to see, and to the embarrassment of the world.[103] It would prove a mere prelude. In the early 1930s Japan, in its conflict with China

---

[95] Bowett 1958, p. 124.

[96] Witness the 1931 Report of the First Committee to the Assembly, cited in Alexandrov 1996, p. 37.

[97] 94 LNTS 57. On the Paris Pact see Miller 1928, Shotwell 1929, Ferrell 1968. Alexandrov 1996, pp. 51-76.

[98] Alexandrov 1996, pp. 45-49. Neff 2005, p. 304.

[99] 54 LNTS 289.

[100] Bowett 1958, pp. 132-138, Alexandrov 1996, pp. 53-68, Neff 2005, pp. 303-307. For later attempts, proposed by the USSR in 1934, and by the Allied Powers at Nuremberg, see Alexandrov, 1996, pp. 72-76.

[101] The 1974 definition of 'aggression' in UN GA Res. 3314 (XXIX).

[102] Although the 'self-judging' aspects of self-defence constituted a bone of discontent. See Alexandrov 1996, pp. 60ff.

[103] Alexandrov, 1996, p. 35 and p. 70 respectively.

over Manchuria, which in 1937 would constitute a forcible invasion, stretched the application of the principle to questionable dimensions, thus putting the legal conscience of the world community to the test.[104] In 1935, Italy invaded Ethiopia in blatant violation of both Covenant and Pact.[105] On both occasions, reaction by the assembled League Members (in firmly rejecting the first claim and trying to curb the other by economic sanctions) proved ominously ineffective. It merely resulted in putting the trespassers beyond the pale – with impunity, that is.[106]

Accordingly, it should come as no surprise that the legal luminaries of the inter-bellum period, for all their efforts, never really got the upper hand in their hide-and-seek game with politicians called *Right vs. Might*. Their half-hearted efforts at proscribing war, but not aggression as such, never produced the intended effects. *Ure et Seca* of all forms of aggression would have been the only proper remedy. However, to achieve this, there was just one tiny obstacle. As good old Archimedes once put it: 'Give me a place to stand, and I will turn the world over.' Who in the decentralised international order would muster the standing and embody the authority to enforce this ideal of peace? It had to be left to the next post-war generation to try and solve that riddle.

15. Towards a Collective Security System

There is no doubt that the founding fathers of the UN Charter availed themselves to the full of the depressing experience of the League.[107] Having learned their lessons well, lawyers, diplomats and politicians now drew their ambit wider to encompass not just 'war' but all forms of the 'use of force' in their deliberations.[108] For the first time ever, a general and categorical ban on the use of force by all actors other than the World Organisation itself was proclaimed, with self-defence being the only 'atavism' left pardonable as an

---

[104] See Willoughby 1935; Alexandrov, 1996, pp. 68-70.

[105] Generally Wright in 30 *AJIL* 1936, p. 45, Mandelstam 1937, Rousseau 1938.

[106] Neff 2005, pp. 304-307. Alexandrov, 1996, p. 70. On Russia's reliance on self-defence to justify its invasion of Poland in 1939 see Ginsburg in 52 *AJIL* 1958, pp. 69ff. On the issue of self-defence and aggression at Nuremberg see Bowett 1958, pp. 263-268.

[107] For the Dumbarton Oaks proposals see Stettinius 1945, Hilderbrand 1990; for the San Francisco Conference see the UNCIOO Documents.

[108] *Travaux préparatoires* in UNCIOO vol. 6.

impromptu response to deceit and surprise attack. More than this, to steer the New World Order, an expert enforcement organ was created within the new UN Organisation to monitor, indeed impose the maintenance of international peace and security. This 'Security Council', as was truly expected by many, would before long render even the last relic of self-help redundant. By effective community policing of a collective security system, it would soon condemn the very idea of self-defence to oblivion. Heir to the 19th-century 'Concert', the Organ was to curb war and its many derivates back into… the venerable just war formula of law enforcement for the benefit of mankind.

History should have warned idealists that, in linking State policy to the law, they were creating uneasy bedfellows. Still, as it was, the union-to-be was never even seriously tested. The world's proud new Ship of State was grounded on its maiden trip by the clash of ideology of its putative pilots. It took a full four decades to float her again. By then, the many wreckers of this world, the natural self-help experts, had long stripped it of most of its attributes, to the point of questioning its seaworthiness.

16. THE HEYDAY OF SELF-DEFENCE

Ironically, it is precisely due to the above unfortunate state of affairs of the Cold War era that the time-honoured concept of self-defence gained a new lease of life, becoming even the fondling of politicians. The paramount normative passage of the UN Charter, Article 2(4), left no doubt whatsoever that any use of force, in order to be legitimate, must take place at the initiative and under the auspices of the UN – in a collective defence action of the world community tantamount to the law enforcement formula of the medieval just war era.[109] In that era, self-defence – as we have seen – had a perfectly legitimate status, for the individual that is. This holds true, unimpaired, to the present day, also witness Article 31[c] of the 1998 Rome Statute of the International Criminal Court, which spells out among the grounds for excluding criminal responsibility a 'reasonable' action of defence of oneself or another person 'against an imminent and unlawful use of force in a manner proportionate to the degree of danger'.[110]

---

[109] On the interpretation of Art. 2(4) see Kelsen 1950, Goodrich a.o. 1969³, Cot/Pellet 1985, Simma 1991. See also Dörr 2004, Bothe 2005.

[110] 2187 UNTS 3.

As was discussed above, by the 17th century, the principle of self-defence had by analogy been 'upgraded' to the status of 'inherent right' of sovereign States. If this status had been accepted tacitly and implicitly by the League Covenant and, albeit with some qualifications, by the Paris Pact, the same held true at the 1944 Dumbarton Oak talks. So much so indeed, that its Proposals to the 1945 UN Conference, to all intents and purposes, contained no reference to the principle, let alone expressed reservation of the right. At Washington, to be on the safe side, the Chinese delegation explicitly double-checked the validity of the right, which was confirmed.[111] If, less than a year later, at San Francisco, the issue was raised anew, this was prompted by a very particular reason, *viz.*, to bring the draft of the proposed UN Charter in line with existing regional arrangements.[112] It is here that the origin of Article 51 must be sought, being the outcome of the prolonged debate between globalists and regionalists and the compromise resulting from a wide range of amendments.[113]

Prevailing regional arrangements, notably in Latin-America, also lay at the base of that other puzzling novelty first introduced at San Francisco and which at first sight seems in such blatant contrast to that Conference's stringent policy of restricting all forms of self-help. The reference, of course, is to its actual *expansion* of the notion of self-defence by its introduction of the concept of '*collective* self-defence'. This formula (by analogy to the private sphere) granted States the positive right to come to the help of allies in distress – the rather puzzling 'self-defence of others'.[114] If, over the past decades, commentators have justly criticised the many perplexing loopholes in the rather ambiguous phraseology of Art. 2(4) and Art. 51, it is precisely the expansion of the concept first introduced here which leaves one puzzled about the philosophy of the Charter.[115]

Be this as it may, we are bound to conclude, that it was, if anything, due to the competing aspirations of global and regional security that the concept of self-defence was upgraded from an implicit reservation to an explicitly recognised right, and was invested with an unprecedented status, that is, not

---

111 Alexandrov 1996, p. 79.

112 Within Committee III/4; Alexandrov 1996, p. 81.

113 Alexandrov 1996, pp. 85-90.

114 Ibid., pp. 90-93.

115 On the genesis and role of the concept of 'collective self-defence' see Kelsen 1964, Barns 1983, Linnan 1991, Bowett 1995, Delbrück 2002, Papastavridis 2002, Leurdijk 2003, Delcourt *a.o.* 1994, Nanda 2004, Tsagourias 2004, Brock 2005.

just to cover the possible interlude between surprise attack and UN response, but precisely to constitute a safeguard against the eventual malfunctioning of the nascent UN machinery – or the breakdown of the all too ambitious collective security system itself. Regional machineries, it was argued, could then get into gear, so as to forestall unilateral self-help. Still, as was widely rumoured, under the umbrella of Article 51, distinctly higher ambitions and less lofty aims had found refuge together: the assessment of regional authorities in keen competition with UN efforts and, if needs be, blatant defiance of Security Council vetoes. Whatever the hidden agendas, the long and short of it was that self-defence, for the first time in history, had reached the charmed status of 'just war'.

All this is not to say that this form of 'self-help-writ-large' was deemed to be on an equal footing with the machinery of collective law enforcement. Actually, it was readily appreciated from early on that abuse lurked around every corner. The restriction of its perimeters of application to 'armed attack' neatly reflect this widely felt concern. A concern which was only confirmed by the subsequent debate over the exact definition of that latter notion. This is precisely why most commentators insist on the 'narrow' interpretation of Article 51 as a mere 'exception to the rule'.[116] Obviously, there is much to support this view. For one thing, both the General Assembly (through its resolutions)[117] and the ICJ (in successive judgments)[118] invariably have insisted on this strict interpretation of the principle, along the classical lines of Webster's definition in the *Caroline* affair. Again, by emphasizing 'prompt notification' to the Security Council as a prerequisite to any act of self-defence,[119] the Charter itself quite intentionally limits the role of self-defence, again in perfect analogy to the origin of the concept, to a first *impromptu* response, with the effective salvaging of rights to be handed over at the first possible instance to the appropriate executive organ of the world community.

---

[116] On the various interpretations of Art. 51 see the literature in nt. 2 and Alexandrov 1996, pp. 77-120.

[117] UN GA/Res 1373 and 1377]

[118] See the discussion of the Corfu Channel and Nicaragua cases in Alexandrov 1996, pp. 122ff, pp. 135ff.

[119] The English text reads: 'Nothing ... shall impair the inherent right ... until the Security Council has taken measures ... Measures taken by Members ... shall be immediately reported to the Security Council. And shall not in any way affect the authority and responsibility of the Security Council ...'

Still, other interpretations have been advanced and not accidentally so, one must say.[120] The phraseology of Article 51 remains intriguingly puzzling. For one thing, if the right of self-defence we are speaking of is still the same good old right of natural law, this right was not just established well before the drafting of the Charter but, if taken as such, is of necessity independent of treaty law and indeed of a superior hierarchy. So why the explicit statement, contrary to League practice, that this right is not impaired by Charter provisions? Or should the text rather be read as referring to a right of customary law, now basically supplanted by the positive law of the Charter and left extant only in its rudimentary form, in eventualities not provided for by the Charter or where Security Council measures might prove (temporarily) wanting? Again, was the term 'armed attack' merely meant to substitute the term 'aggression' of the League period, for want of a proper definition of that latter notion, or was it, to all intents and purposes, meant to circumscribe very specific forms of attack?[121] But then again, would any such interpretation not of necessity preclude any pre-emptive strike in the best tradition of the Caroline?[122] Again, what about the definition of 'collective defence', and what about the right of self-defence with respect to attacks directed against *non*-UN Member States?[123]

Clearly, this is not the place to try and disentangle the many loopholes of the Charter, or to add to the wealth of comments provoked by a text which already posed huge problems in San Francisco. What should be emphasised, though, is that the ambiguity of the Articles 2(4) and 51 did not just invite endless academic debate but, more than just that, decades of State practice have served precisely as a ready excuse to delude and belie the very purpose of the Charter, that is, to replace all self-help and unilateral use of force with a collective security system.

17. War Bypassed

It has often been advanced that, as the outcome of the Charter, inter-State war in the UN-era has been reduced to an all time minimum. In formal terms

[120] A detailed analysis and full references in Alexandrov, 1996, pp. 93-120.
[121] Alexandrov 1996, pp. 105-120.
[122] Ibid., pp. 95-99, and notably Schwebel in 136 RCDI 1972-II 411, p. 479.
[123] Alexandrov 1996 , pp. 103-104.

and as far as statistics go, this observation may be correct. However, if one takes into consideration the explosion of *sub*-State conflicts, one cannot but wonder whether one should rather speak of formal war having been 'deviated' or 'devolved'.[124] For decades on end, the ready excuse of nations for their recurrent recourse to unilateral self-help under the guise of self-defence was, predictably enough, the ideological stalemate of the Cold War Era, which effectively paralyzed the Security Council. Obviously, this unfortunate circumstance did much to activate self-help. Inasmuch as the two kinds of redress are linked to each other as communicating vessels, the vacuum left by the one mechanism was automatically filled by the other.

Still, in the opening years of the UN Era, even the great powers showed themselves fairly hesitant to rely on the principle. The Suez and Cuban missile crisis are cases in point.[125] Some early instances of the use of force in self-defence were defended on the ground of self-determination.[126] Over the decades, however, the argument was advanced with ever greater audacity. The scope of the concept gradually widened in time, space, and substance,[127] finally to be turned into its current state of ready receptacle for tailor-made application of any kind of force, and virtually covering all forms of anticipatory action,[128] political or humanitarian intervention,[129] or reprisal.[130] In re-

[124] Neff 2005, pp. 314ff.

[125] In 1951 Egypt vainly invoked the right of self-defence with respect to passage through the Suez canal. In the Suez crisis of 1956 both Great Britain and France presented their military action as a peace-keeping intervention and police-action rather than as spurred by self-defence. In similar vein, in 1962, in the Cuban missile crisis, the USA presented its quarantine policy of foreign ships as an enforcement measure. On these issues see Neff 2005, pp. 328-334.

[126] Notable instances are Palestine 1948, India/Pakistan 1948; see Alexandrov 1996, pp. 125-129.

[127] The Israeli attack in 1967 being a notable example of pre-emptive strike, British action in the Falklands in 1982 being a case of postponed action.

[128] 'Anticipatory' self-defence is a case in point. Instances that come to mind are the Sinai and Suez Canal crisis of 1956, the 1962 Cuban missile crisis, the 1967 Six Day War, the 1968 Beirut Raid, Israel vs. Jordan and Lebanon 1966-74, the Israeli actions against Lebanon in 1975, 1981, 1982, and finally the 1981 Israeli strike against the Iraqi nuclear reactor. See Alexandrov 1996, pp. 149-179.

[129] As exemplified by the Indian intervention in East Pakistan in 1971, Vietnam's occupation of Cambodia in 1978, and the Tanzanian invasion of Uganda in 1979.

[130] As in the case of the US air attack on Libya in 1986 or Turkish action against Kurdish guerillas in 1995. Earlier instances are Tunisia (1958, 1961), Yemen (1964), Gulf of Tonkin (1964), Portugal/Guinea 1969.

cent decades, instances of self-defence have literally exploded,[131] varieties growing countless, and byways to circumvent the proper channels of the collective security system proving legion. To that extent, self-defence in the face of terrorism is only the latest variety.[132]

Predictably, not the last to use the veil were not the least of powers, those self-imposed watchdogs of the collective security system. In this, perhaps the most alarming aspect of all was their blatant reference to 'vital interests'[133] or 'the protection of nationals abroad'[134] as ready excuses for military action. 'Grenada' and 'Panama' stand out as two instances of US military intervention in complete defiance of the stern judgment rendered at that time by the ICJ with respect to US military and paramilitary actions in Nicaragua.[135] The offhand dismissal of a World Court verdict tells us that power politics, having comfortably taken all legal hurdles posed by the Charter, once more feel 'at their ease'. The quickly widening gap between legal norms and State practice no longer gave rise to any qualms on the part of diplomats.

The above tells us that, for all the growth of legal doctrine, and in spite of the wealth of jurisprudence in the international arena, the progress of *implementation* in the decentralised international legal order has not been all that impressive over the past century. This impression is corroborated by many other signals. There is little room for doubt nowadays that the celebrated *trouvaille* of the 1920s, the *optional clause*, whatever its actual status, has missed the point and will never fulfil its promise. Its magical spell clearly failed to charm the austere world of high politics.[136]

The ICJ itself, while justly boasting an unprecedented caseload, may at times wonder whether, with the above-mentioned fundamental change of

---

[131] Two notable instances being the Falklands war (1982) and Bosnia (1991-93)

[132] Starting with the US bombing of Libya in 1986 and its missile attacks on Baghdad in 1993.

[133] As in US President Carter's reference to protecting American vital interests in the Persian Gulf in 1980, or the Israeli attack on an Iraqi nuclear reactor in 1981.

[134] As exemplified by the Israeli action at Entebbe in 1976 and the similar American attempt in Tehran in 1980. Earlier examples are the British intervention in Suez in 1956, Belgian intervention in the Congo in 1960, US intervention in the Dominican Republic in 1965, the US attack in the *Mayaguez* crisis in Cambodia in 1975.

[135] Protection of its nationals was the trump card of American policy in justifying its intervention in Grenada in 1983 and in Panama in 1989-90 in the face of the ICJ judgment in the Nicaragua case, ICJ Rep. 1986, *Military and Paramilitary Actions*, para. 195.

[136] See e.g. Merrills in 50 *BYIL* (1979), pp. 87-116.

patterns of dispute, its rigid mandate will not in the end effectively frustrate its impressive intellectual potential and its patron role as true World Relief Court. By the same token, as we speak, the Court's advisory role is no less in peril of being drawn into troubled political waters as was its predecessor in the days of the *Zoll Union*.[137] Held by many observers to be a questionable formula from day one, most requests from New York clearly reflect the realm of hidden agendas of States. While the ICJ, in recent cases as in earlier ones, duly observed all judicial restraint without refraining from firmly restating the law, there is ample ground for questioning the rationale, and social relevance, of the formula.[138]

18. Law Bypassed

Far more alarming than the lame but ready excuses advanced by States up to 1988, has been the ways they have relied on self-defence over the past fifteen years, with the Berlin Wall no longer obstructing their view and the Security Council 'back in business'. More than anything else, this tells us that the concept advanced in 1945 seems to be an unworkable proposition.

Confronted by ever more severe attacks from non-State actors, the USA, on the spur of 9/11, announced that the frequency and intensity of the terrorist challenge it was facing had effectively created a state of armed conflict. It declared war on terrorism, a war which it declared justified on the grounds of self-defence.[139] In legal terms there could indeed be no closer parallel to the British action against the *Caroline*. However, it soon became clear that the then US Secretary of State did not consider himself to be bound by the formula of his 19th century predecessor, let alone by that corollary of self-defence, proportionality,[140] or otherwise to be bound to stop short of deterrence and reprisal. Reaching far beyond the boundaries of self-defence *stricto sensu*, the fight against terrorism was soon heralded as a struggle between good and

[137] German-Austrian customs union. PCIJ A/B 41 (1931).

[138] On the Advisory Role of the ICJ see Greig in 15 ICLQ (1966), pp. 325-368; Keith 1971, Pratap 1972, Pomerance 1973, Waldock 1976, Olivares 1992.

[139] 40 *ILM* (2001) p. 1281; 41 *ILM* (2002) pp. 252ff.; 97 *AJIL* (2003) pp. 203ff. On this so-called Bush doctrine see Beres 2002, Gray 2002, Gardner 2003, Pérez González 2003, Anghie 2004, Bradford 2004, Brimmer 2004, Heisbourg 2004, Jervis 2004, Henderson 2004, Paul 2004, Rezac 2004, Satkunathan 2004, Wall 2004, Dunn 2005.

[140] On the concept see *supra*, fn. 37.

evil, in which no quarter would be given, not even to the neutrality of third parties.[141] In other words: the war on terrorism was acclaimed as a *just war* in the fullest sense, a crusade on behalf of and for the sake of humanity – and one in which hostile States and non-State actors would be treated indiscriminately. Soon the spheres of criminal law enforcement and belligerent strategy were blurred, deemed interchangeable, and ignored or applied *ad libidem*.

The consequences of this sidelining of all established legal distinctions revealed themselves most perplexingly in the treatment of the prisoners of (this new type of) war. These were denied qualification as lawful combatants under the 1907 Hague Rules[142] or as POWs in terms of the 1949 Geneva Convention.[143] But neither were they deemed entitled to the standard human rights procedures of criminal law. Not considered civilians nor lawful combatants, they were labelled, in highly unorthodox and rather questionable terms, as 'unlawful' combatants to whom 'different' (unspecified) rules applied.[144]

Whatever else may be said on the matter, clearly the appropriate answer to the challenges posed to humanity by terrorism, unprecedented as they may be, should not be sought in abandoning the international legal order altogether or in creating a whole new range of legal entanglements, but rather in strengthening this world's all too precious legal fabric. Again, in our day and age, a just war in defence of civilisation should not be construed as self-help-writ-large and waged unilaterally, with the application of duress so as to persuade third parties to join the banners, but clearly under the auspices of the world's appropriate organs. Still, as we speak, the same country that spearheads the Coalition of the Willing in Baghdad, is rallying a Coalition of the Unwilling in The Hague – bending the law to bring one villain down, while blocking the law that stops others from rising. It would seem that, for all their apparent lip-service to the law, even the greatest powers in this world, to the present day, rely on pre-emptive strike rather than on peremptory norms.

* * *

---

[141] 96 *AJIL* (2002) p. 237. See Neff 2005, pp. 388ff.
[142] 205 CTS p. 277.
[143] 75 UNTS p. 135, art. 5. See 96 *AJIL* (2002) pp. 475ff.
[144] Neff 2005, pp. 390-394.

Let us try and tie up the many loose ends, with a view to properly evaluating the current state of affairs and the position of the law. Obviously, in recent decades, the highly-tuned 'general principle' of self-defence has exploded in its application and, as a corollary, imploded in its meaning. In the day-to-day practice of inter-State relations it seems to have degenerated into an all too ready palliative. But what does all this tell us about the relations of States and the Law?

Clearly, the natural tension between Right and Might is put under particular pressure once States feel their position imperilled by hostile actors that do not respect the rules of the law and mock the niceties of their once exclusive game. Feeling backstabbed by these 'irregulars' – terrorists, *guerrilleros*, insurgents and the like – States will first turn to the law for answers as to how best to protect their subjects, rights and vital interests. Wherever the laws fall silent – *bellum incipit*, as the old adage reads. Now, the question is of course to what extent current State policy can be excused from – and the present state of affairs actually deemed to have been provoked by – the legal regime, *in casu*, the silence or inapplicability of the laws.

From our survey it can easily be concluded that the current state of the law with respect to the issues discussed in this paper is far from satisfactory. The vivid, critical debate among internationalists, both on the philosophical level and in their review of State practice and case law tells a hard tale, however encouraging the debate in itself may be.[145]

The paramount yardstick to review State practice is the definition of self-defence found in the UN Charter. The reference in this authoritative text to the principle of self-defence as an 'inherent right', that is, as a right which can be invoked on grounds of wider ambit, or should one say at a philosophically higher level than the Charter itself (however vague the sources and contours of that right), bespeaks rather of impotence than of a clearly charted, normative regime. It may be suggested in this context that, in focussing on mirroring Art. 51 to Art. 2(4), critics have perhaps somewhat overlooked the much wider implications of the former article's first words: '*Nothing in this Charter*'. Words that definitely suggest a clear-cut hierarchy and the precedence, at all times, of 'inherent rights' over Charter provisions. This, in turn, would suggest the greatest latitude in the application of the principle of self-defence, which in turn makes its clear definition all the more imperative.

---

[145] As the bibliography in this volume amply shows, recent literature is overwhelming, albeit not always very conducive to the philosophical or doctrinal debate of the concept.

But then again, why was this overruling principle not stipulated in the Preamble of the Charter, but instead hidden as a kind of afterthought or *obiter dictum*. It is rather perplexing to find an 'inherent right', which in all respects recalls Cicero's *dictum*[146] or, for that matter, the position of the USA in the 1928 debate,[147] presented as an *exception* to a specific rule. Indeed, if one takes the phraseology of the Charter to the letter, one wonders why its appreciation of self-defence as an 'inherent right' should not be extrapolated to all three categories specified by Grotius and his contemporaries, so as to include recovery and, more intriguingly, punishment, i.e., reprisals. In other words, neither the source, the definition, nor the substance of these 'inherent rights' seem to have been adequately identified so far.

If one turns to the most authoritative Judicial Organ of the UN, one is struck with similar perplexity. While, on the one hand, in order to counter abuse, the ICJ has repeatedly insisted on the narrow interpretation of the principle of self-defence, the Court, by the same token – so as to bridge the gap between the constructionist interpretation of the 'use of force' in its relation to 'military attack' – has extrapolated the latter to also include the 'indirect' use of irregulars, and thus virtually identified this with regular 'use of force' in all respects but scale. Now this would not exactly seem a reassuring definition (let alone criterion) given its potentially momentous implications for the invocation of such a protean principle as self-defence.[148]

Quite another observation touches upon the position of 'irregulars' or 'unlawful combatants' whose omnipresent threat has triggered much of the current debate and perplexities. As highlighted above, the legal complexities involved here were first worded in no uncertain terms, and including all moral and social implications, at The Hague in 1899 by Beernaert, Martens and Asser. Why should we depreciate their answer as 'Pie in the Sky', while betraying ourselves unable, to the present day, to come up with better answers?[149]

---

[146] See *supra*, fn. 7. Grotius, in DJP (ed. Williams, p. 96), readily falls in with Cicero in *Pro Mil.* 11 that public wars may often originate in a defect of judicial recourse in much the same manner as private wars: 'this [justification for extra-legal warfare] exists whenever he who chooses to wait [for legal authorisation] will be obliged to pay an unjust penalty before he can exact a just penalty; and, in a general sense, it exists whenever matters do not admit of delay. Thus it is obvious that a just war can be waged in return, without recourse to judicial procedure, against an opponent who has begun an unjust war.'

[147] See *supra*, fn. 85.

[148] Cf. R. Higgins, *Problems and Process: International Law and How we Use it* (1997).

[149] Cassese in 11 *EJIL* (2000) pp. 187-216.

Back in 1945, the drafting committee of the UN Charter, in its (with hindsight) all too confident and virtually exclusive reliance on the world's latest *trouvaille*, the collective security system, never made any systematic provisions for dealings with sub-State actors and unilateral self-help. In the past sixty years, during which the collective security system proved abortive most of the time, the world has changed beyond recognition. This, however, has hardly prompted any anticipatory (or should one say 'pre-emptive') legislative 'strike' on the part of the nations with respect to the issues at stake here. By the same token, this circumstance never stopped these same High Defenders of the Charter from readily availing themselves of the loopholes in the law to recruit 'irregulars' so as to infiltrate or topple foreign regimes, for reasons varying from purely selfish ends to exclusively humanitarian aims. In other words, in conveniently slipping the meshes of the law (with legal luminaries protesting a *non liquet*) the nations may themselves inadvertently have opened Pandora's box and called into being the imminent undoing of their own prerogatives with respect to the use of force. Having first *eroded* the law, State-entities now, more often than not, seem set on a ram-course to virtually *erase* the law for its lack of pragmatic pertinence and to rely exclusively on self-help.

And what of the international law discipline? Having all too passively tolerated the former situation, the erosion of its norms, it is now confronted with the latter, their imminent erasure. This time it is not just International Law that finds itself in the predicament of gradually losing its political credibility and social relevance. The once impregnable nation-State itself is in peril of awakening, one day soon, to find its time-honoured trump-card of sovereignty eroded of all meaning. Small comfort indeed that Grotius, for one, foresaw this eventuality with eerie precision from his vantage-point at the other end of the Westphalian equation, and at the very dawn of that self-seeking and, for all appearances, self-sufficient *Leviathan*.[150]

The indiscriminate contempt of terrorists for Right *and* Might, their indifference towards legal norms and political sovereignty alike, may perhaps suggest a renewed attempt at a marriage of convenience of these traditionally quarrelsome bed-fellows, politics and the law, who so often before were driven into each other's arms by force of circumstance. The critical evaluation of the present situation of emergency for both entities may suggest that,

[150] Grotius DJBP Prolegomena pp. 18, 21, 22.

rather than gratuitously paying lip-service to lofty notions in Crusader-like, bellicose terms, the Powers may indeed do best to turn to the law for effective shelter, to follow good-old Solon's wise advice in 'putting right and might under one yoke'[151] and, harnessed this way, start making earnest in upholding that precious fabric that was first defined by the Stoics and towards whose preservation the General Principles of International Law were formulated in the first place.

[151] Plutarch *Solon* 15.2; cf. Grotius DJBP Prolegomena 19.

Part II

SELF-DEFENCE IN HISTORICAL CONTEXT *A BIBLIOGRAPHY*

Arthur Eyffinger

1. Just War

1.1. Sources

Ambrose of Milan, *De Officiis*, Ivor J. Davidson, ed./transl. (2001)
Aquinas, Thomas, *Summa theologiae* (Alba and Rome 1962)
Aquinas, Thomas, *On Law, Morality, and Politics*, William P. Baumgarth and Richard J. Regan, eds./transl. (1988)
Aquinas, Thomas, *The Treatise on Law*, R.J. Henle, ed./transl. (1993)
Augustine of Hippo, *Concerning the City of God Against the Pagans*, Henry Bettenson, ed./transl. (1972)
Augustine of Hippo, *The Political Writings of St Augustine*, Henri Paolucci, ed./transl. (1962).
Ayala, Balthasar, *De Jure et officiis bellicis et disciplina militari*, John P. Bate, ed./transl. (1912). (1st edn. 1582)
Azorius, Ioannes, *Institutiones morales* (Brixen 1622)
Bañez, Domingo, *De fide, spe, et charitate* (Salamanca 1584)
Bartolus de Saxoferrato, *Prima super Digesto veteri* (Lyon 1533)
Belli, Pierino, *A Treatise on Military Matters and Warfare*, Herbert C. Nutting, ed./transl. (1936). (1st edn. 1563)
Blackstone, William, *Commentaries on the Laws of England* (Oxford 1765-1769)
Bonet, Honoré de, *The Tree of Battles of Honoré Bonet*, G.W. Coopland, ed./transl. (1949). (1st edn. c. 1386)
Calvinus, Iohannes, *Lexicon iuridicum iuris caesarei simul, et canonici, feudalis item, civilis, criminalis* (Geneva 1670).
Cicero, Marcus Tullius, *On Duties*, E.M. Atkins and M.T. Griffin, eds./transl. (1991).
Cicero, Marcus Tullius, *The Republic and the Laws*, Niall Rudd, ed./transl. (1998).
Cicero, Marcus Tullius, *Pro Milone*, A.B. Poynton, ed., 2nd edn. (Oxford 1902).
Cicéron, M.T., *Discours*, t. XVII (Paris, Société d'édition "Les Belles Lettres" 1967).
Decretum divi Gratiani ... una cum glossis, Lyon 1554.
Domat, Jean-Baptiste, *Loix civiles dans leur ordre naturel* (1689/1697) (Paris 1777).
Doniger, Wendy, and Brian K. Smith, ed./transl., *The Laws of Manu* (1991).
Gentili, Alberico, *On the Law of War*, John C. Rolfe, ed./transl. (1933). (1st edn. 1598).
Gentilis, Albericus, *De iure belli libri tres* (1598) (Hanau 1612).
Gentilis, Albericus, *De legationibus libri tres* (1585) (Hanau 1594).
Grotius, Hugo, *De iure belli ac pacis libri tres* (1625) (Aalen 1993).
Grotius, Hugo, *De jure Praedae*, H.C. Hamaker, ed. (Leiden 1868).

Grotius, Hugo, *De jure Praedae*, James Brown Scott, ed., G.L. Williams and W.H. Zeydel, transl., 2 vols. (1950).
Grotius, Hugo, *On the Law of War and Peace*, Francis W. Kelsey, ed./transl. (1925).
Grotius, Hugo, *The Rights of War and Peace*, Richard Tuck, ed./transl. (2005).
Hobbes, Thomas, *Leviathan* (1651), W.C. Pogson Smith, ed. (Oxford 1909).
Isidorus Hispalensis, *Etymologiarum sive originum libri viginti*, Lindsay, ed. (Oxford 1911).
Kant, Immanuel, *Metaphysik der Sitten, Rechtslehre* (1707).
Klüber, Johann L., *Droit des gens moderne de l'Europe* (1819), M.A. Ott, ed. (Paris 1861).
Legnano, John of, *Tractatus de Bello, de Represaliis et de Duello*, T.E. Holland, ed., J.L. Brierly, transl. (1917). (1st edn. 1360).
Lessius, Leonardus, *De iustitia et iure caeterisque virtutibus cardinalibus libri quatuor* (1605) (Milan 1618).
Lignano, Iohannes de, *De bello, repraesaliis et duello*, T.E. Holland, ed., *The Classics of International Law* (Washington 1917).
Locke, John, *Two Treatises of Government*, T.L. Cook, ed. (New York 1947).
Martens, Georg F., *Précis de droit des gens moderne de l'Europe* (1788/1802/1821), Ch. Vergé, ed. (Paris 1864).
Meister, F.G., *Principia iuris criminalis Germaniae communis* (1755) (Goettingen 1780).
Molina, Ludovicus, *De iustitia et iure* (Geneva 1733).
Monaldus de Capo d' Istria, *Summa perutilis* (Lyon 1516).
Penãfort, Raymundus de, *Summa de poenitentia et matrimonio* (Rome 1603).
Pufendorff, Samuel von, *De jure naturae et gentium libri octo* (1672) (Amsterdam 1688).
Pufendorff, Samuel von, *De officio hominis & civis juxta legem naturalem libri duo* (1673) (Cambridge 1682).
Pufendorff, Samuel von, *Elementorum jurisprudentiae universalis libri duo* (1660), 2nd edn. (Cambridge 1672), in *Classics of International Law* 15 (Oxford/London 1931).
Soto, Domingo de, *De iustitia et iure* (Salamanca 1556).
Stooss, Carl, *Die schweizerischen Strafgesetzbücher zur Vergleichung zusammengestellt* (Basel and Geneva 1890).
Suárez, Francisco, *A Work on the Three Theological Virtues: Faith, Hope and Charity*, G.L. Williams, ed./transl. (1944). (1st edn. 1612).
Suárez, Franciscus, *Opus de triplici virtute theologica, fide, spe, et charitate* (Coimbra 1621).
Sylvester de Prierio, *Summae Sylvestrinae quae summa summarum merito nuncupatur*, pars prima (Antwerp 1581).
Valentia, Gregorius de, *Commentariorum theologicorum tomus tertius* (1595) (Lyon 1619).
Vattel, Emer de, *Le droit des gens* (London 1758).
Vattel, Emmerich de, *The Law of Nations; or The Principles of Natural Law Applied to the Conduct and to the Affairs of Nations and Sovereigns*, Charles G. Fenwick, ed./transl. (1916). (1st edn. 1758).
Vitoria, Francisco de, *De Indis et De iure belli relectiones* (1917).
Vitoria, Francisco de, *On the Law of War*, in *Political Writings*, A. Pagden and J. Lawrance, eds./transl. (1991). (1st edn. 1557).
Vitoria, Francisco de, *Relecciones teológicas*, T. Urdánoz, ed. (Madrid 1960).
Wheaton, Henry, *Elements of International Law* (1836), R.H. Dana, ed. (Boston 1866).
Wolff, Christian von, *Institutions du droit de la nature et des gens*, E. Luzac, ed. (Leiden 1772).
Wolff, Christian von, *Jus naturae methodo scientifica pertractatum*, pars prima (Francfort and Leipzig 1740).

1.2 History

Albrecht-Carrié, René, ed., *The Concert of Europe* (1968).
Alexandrov, Stanmir A., *Self-defence Against the Use of Force in International Law* (1996).
Allen, Nick, 'Just War in the Mahabharata', in Richard Sorabji and David Rodin, eds., *The Ethics of War: Shared Problems in Different Traditions* (2006).
Allgemeines Landrecht für die Preussischen Staaten, Neue Ausgabe (Berlin 1817).
Anderson, M.S., *War and Society in Europe of the Old Regime 1618-1789* (1988).
Aquinas, Thomas, 'Just War and Sins against Peace', in Gregory M. Reichberg, Henrik Syse, and Endre Begby, eds., *The Ethics of War: Classic and Contemporary* (2006).
Augustine, 'Just War in the Service of Peace', in Gregory M. Reichberg, Henrik Syse, and Endre Begby, eds., *The Ethics of War: Classic and Contemporary* (2006).
Bacot, Guillaume, *La doctrine de la guerre juste* (1989).
Bainton, Ronald, 'The Early Church and War', 39 *Harvard Theological Review* (1946) pp. 189-212.
Ballis, William, *The Legal Position of War: Changes in its Practice and Theory from Plato to Vattel* (1973).
Bartlett, Ruhl J., ed., *The Record of American Diplomacy: Documents and Readings in the History of American Foreign Relation* (1964).
Basdevant, Jules, 'Étude sur quelques pratiques du droit des gens à la fin du XVIe siècle et au commencement du XVIIe siècle, d'après les "Annales" et "Histoires" de Grotius', 10 *Revue Générale de Droit International Public* (1903) pp. 619-650.
Basham, A.L., *The Wonder That Was India: A Survey of the History and Culture of the Indian Sub-Continent before the Coming of the Moslims* (1967).
Bederman, David J., *International Law in Antiquity* (2001).
Best, Geoffrey, *Humanity in Warfare*: *The Modern History of the International Law of Armed Conflict* (1980).
Bhatia, H.S., ed., *International Law and Practice in Ancient India* (1977).
Blom, Hans W., and Laurens C. Winkel, eds., *Grotius and the Stoa* (2004).
Bobbitt, Philip, *The Shield of Achilles: War, Peace and the Course of History* (2002).
Bowett, Derek W., *Self-defence in International Law* (1958).
Boyle, Joseph, 'Traditional Just War Theory and Humanitarian Intervention', in Terry Nardin and Melissa W. Williams, eds., *Humanitarian Intervention* (2006).
Bozeman, Adda B., *Politics and Culture in International History* (1960).
Brownlie, Ian, *International Law and the Use of Force by States* (1963).
Cadoux, C. John, *The Early Christian Attitude to War: A Contribution to the History of Christian Ethics* (1919).
Cassese, Antonio, 'The Martens Clause: half a loaf or simply pie in the sky?', *European Journal of International Law* (2000) pp. 187-216.
Castrén, Erik, *The Present Law of War and Neutrality* (1954).
Chaliand, Gerard, ed., *The Art of War in World History*: *From Antiquity to the Nuclear Age* (1994).
Charles, J. Daryl, *Between pacifism and Jihad: just war and Christian tradition* (2005).
Charnay, Jean-Paul, *L'Islam et la guerre: De la guerre juste à la révolution sainte* (1986).
Cheng, Bin, *General Principles of Law as applied by International Courts and Tribunals* (London 1953).
Childress, James F., 'Moral Discourse about War in the Early Church', 12 *Journal of Religious Ethics* (1984) pp. 2-18.
Cicero, *The Speeches*. With an English translation (1964).
Colish, Marcia L, *The Stoic tradition from antiquity to the early Middle Ages* (1990).

Contamine, Philippe, *War in the Middle Ages*, Michael Jones, transl. (1984).
Cox, Richard, *Locke on War and Peace* (Oxford 1960).
Craigie, Peter C., *The Problem of War in the Old Testament* (1978).
Dahm, Georg, *Das Strafrecht Italiens im ausgehenden Mittelalter* (Berlin and Leipzig 1931).
Dawson, Doyne, *The Origins of Western Warfare: Militarism and Morality in the Ancient World* (1996).
Delaney, Carol, 'Sacrificial Heroics: the Story of Abraham and its Use in the Justification of War', in Joseph Hoffmann, ed., *The Just War and Jihad: Violence in Judaism, Christianity, and Islam* (2006).
Delivanis, J., *La légitime défense en droit International public moderne: Le droit International face à ses limites* (1971).
Detter Delupis, Ingrid, *The Law of War* (2000).
Dinstein, Yoram, 'The Dinstinction between Unlawful Combatants and War Criminals', in Yoram Dinstein and Mala Tabory, eds., *International Law at a Time of Perplexity: Essays in Honour of Shabtai Rosenne* (1989).
Dinstein, Yoram, *War, aggression and self-defence* (2005).
Doniger, W., and B.K. Smith, eds., *The Code of Manu* (1991).
Dülffer, Jost, *Regeln gegen den Krieg*? (1981).
Dupuis, Charles, *Le principe d'équilibre et le concert européen de la Paix de Westphalie à l'Acte d'Algésiras* (1909).
Dupuis, Charles, 'Les théories anglaises sur le droit de la guerre en général', 5 *Revue Générale du Droit International Public* (1898) pp. 35-56.
Ehrlich, Ludwig, 'Guillaume de Rennes et les origines de la science du droit de la guerre', in *Mélanges G. Gidel* (Paris 1961) pp. 215-227.
Elbe, Joachim von, 'The Evolution of the Concept of the Just War in International Law', 33 *American Journal of International Law* (1939) pp. 665-688.
Engberg-Pedersen, Troels, *Paul and the Stoics* (2000).
Esposito, John L., *Unholy War: Terror in the name of the Islam* (2002).
Eyffinger, Arthur, *The 1899 Hague Peace Conference: The Parliament of Man, the Federation of the World* (1999).
Fadl, Khaled Abou El., *Rebellion and Violence in Islamic Law* (2001).
Fanck, Thomas C., *Recourse to Force: State Action against Threats and Armed Attacks* (2002).
Ferguson, John, *War and Peace in the World's Religions* (1977).
Ferril, Arther, *The Origins of War: From the Stone Age to Alexander the Great* (1997).
Finkelstein, Claire, ed., *Hobbes on law* (2005).
Firestone, Reuven, *Jihad: The Origin of Holy War in Islam* (1999).
Forsyth, William, *Life of Marcus Tullius Cicero*, 2nd edn. (London 1867).
Fulgosius, Raphael, 'Just War reduced to Public War', in Gregory M. Reichberg, Henrik Syse, and Endre Begby, eds., *The Ethics of War: Classic and Contemporary* (2006).
Garlan, Yvon, *War in the Ancient World: A Social History* (1976).
Good, Robert M., 'The Just War in Ancient Israel', 104 *Journal of Biblical Literature* (1985) pp. 385-400.
Green, L.C., *The Contemporary Law of Armed Conflict* (1993).
Green, L.C., 'The Nature of the "War" in Korea', 4 *International and Comparative Law Quarterly* (1951) pp. 462-468.
Grewe, Wilhelm, *Epochs of International Law*, Michael Byers, transl. (2000).
Grob, Fritz, *The Relativity of War and Peace: A Study of Law, History and Politics* (1949).
Grotius, Hugo, 'The Theory of Just War systematized', in Gregory M. Reichberg, Henrik Syse, and Endre Begby, eds., *The Ethics of War: Classic and Contemporary* (2006).
Hafter, Ernst, *Lehrbuch des schweizerischen Strafrechts*, Allgemeiner Teil (Berlin 1926).

Haggenmacher, P., *Grotius et la doctrine de la guerre juste* (1983).
Haggenmacher, P., 'Droits subjectifs et système juridique chez Grotius', in L. Foisneau, ed., *Politique, droit et théologie chez Bodin, Grotius et Hobbes* (Paris 1997) pp. 73-130.
Haleem, Harfiyah Abdel, ed., *The Crescent and the Cross: Muslim and Christian Approaches to War and Peace* (1998).
Harris, W.V., *War and Imperialism in Republican Rome 327-70 BC* (1979).
Hartigan, Richard Shelly, *Lieber's Code and the Law of War* (1983).
Hartigan, Richard Shelly, 'Saint Augustine on War and Killing: The Problem of the Innocent', 27 *Journal of the History of Ideas* (1966) pp. 195-204.
Helgeland, John, Robert J. Daly and J. Patout Burns, *Christians and the Military: The Early Experience* (1985).
Hoffmann, R. Joseph, 'Just War and Jihad: Positioning the Question of Religious Violence', in Joseph Hoffmann, ed., *The Just War and Jihad: Violence in Judaism, Christianity, and Islam* (2006).
Holbraad, C., *The Concept of Europe: A Study in German and British International Theory, 1815-1914* (1970).
Holk, L.E. van, en Roelofsen, C.G., eds., *Grotius Reader* (The Hague 1983).
Holsti, Kalevi J., *Peace and War: Armed Conflicts and International Order 1648-1989* (1991).
Inwood, Brad, *Ethics and human action in early Stoicism* (1985).
Inwood, Brad, ed., *The Cambridge Companion to the Stoics* (2003).
Jenks, C.W., *Common Law of Mankind* (1956).
Jinks, David, 'September 11 and the Laws of War', 28 *Yale Journal of International Law* (2003) pp. 1-49.
Johnson, James Turner, and John Kelsay, eds., *Cross, Crescent, and Sword: The Justification and Limitation of War in Western and Islamic Tradition* (1990).
Johnson, James Turner, *Ideology, Reason and the Limitation of War: Religious and Secular Concepts 1200-1740* (1975).
Johnson, James Turner, *Just War Tradition and the Restraint of War: A Moral and Historical Inquiry* (1981).
Johnson, James Turner, *The Holy War in Western and Islamic Traditions* (1997).
Kaeuper, Richard W., *Chivalry and Violence in Medieval Europe* (1999).
Kaikobad, Kaiyam Homi, 'Self-defence, Enforcement Action and the Gulf Wars, 1980-88 and 1990-91', *British Year Book of International Law*, Vol. 63 (1992) pp. 299-366.
Keen, Maurice, *The Laws of War in the Late Middle Ages* (1965).
Kelsay, John, and James Turner Johnson, eds., *Just War and Jihad: Historical and Theoretical Perspectives on War and Peace in Western and Islamic Traditions* (1991).
Kelsen, Hans, 'Collective Security and Collective Self-Defence under the Charter of the United Nations', 42 *American Journal of International Law* (1948) pp. 783-796.
Khadduri, M., *War and Peace in the Law of Islam* (1955).
Kuttner, St., *Die kanonistische Schuldlehre von Gratian bis auf die Dekretalen Gregors IX.* (Vatican City 1935).
Kuttner, St., 'Zur Entstehungsgeschichte der Summa de casibus poenitentiae des hl. Raymond von Penyafort', *Zeitschrift der Savigny-Stiftung für Rechtsgeschichte*, kan. Abt., 70 (1953) pp. 419-434.
Laiou, Angeliki, 'The Just War of Eastern Christians and the Holy War of the Crusaders', in Richard Sorabji and David Rodin, eds., *The Ethics of War: Shared Problems in Different Traditions* (2006).
Landrecht des Schwabenspiegels, Das, Wilhelm Wackernagel, ed. (Zurich and Frauenfeld 1840).
Langan, John, 'The Elements of St Augustine's Just War Theory', 12 *Journal of Religious Ethics* (1984) pp. 19-38.

Lauterpacht, Sir Hersch, *Private Law Sources and Analogies of International Law* (London 1927).
Lichtenberg, Judith, 'Some Central Problems in Just War Theory', in Joseph Hoffmann, ed., *The Just War and Jihad: Violence in Judaism, Christianity, and Islam* (2006).
Locke, John, 'The Rights of Man and the Limits of Just Warfare', in Gregory M. Reichberg, Henrik Syse, and Endre Begby, eds., *The Ethics of War: Classic and Contemporary* (2006).
Logoz, Paul, *Commentaire du Code pénal suisse*, 2nd edn. (Neuchâtel and Paris 1976) pp. 168-174.
Lysen, A., ed., *Le Pacte Kellogg. Documents concernant le traité multilatéral contre la guerre signé à Paris le 27 août 1928* (Leiden 1928).
Machiavelli, Niccolò, 'War is just to whom it is Necessary', in Gregory M. Reichberg, Henrik Syse, and Endre Begby, eds., *The Ethics of War: Classic and Contemporary* (2006).
Mallison, W. Thomas, and Sally V. Mallison, 'The Juridical Status of Irregular Combatants under the International Humanitarian Law of Armed Conflict', 9 *Case Western Reserve Journal of International Law* (1977) pp. 39-78.
Mattox, John Mark, *Saint Augustine and the theory of just war* (2006).
May, Larry, Eric Rovie, and Steve Viner, eds., *The Morality of War: classical and contemporary readings* (2006).
McKay, Derek, and H.M. Scott, *The Rise of the Great Powers 1648-1815* (1983).
Mérignhac, Alexandre, *Les Lois et coutumes de la guerre sur terre d'après le droit International moderne et la codification de la Conférence de la Haye de 1899* (1903).
Meron, Theodor, *Bloody Constraint: War and Chivalry in Shakespeare* (1998).
Meron, Theodor, 'The Martens Clause, Principles of Humanity, and Dictates of Public Conscience', 94 *American Journal of International Law* (2000) pp. 78-89.
Moir, Lindsay, *The Law of Internal Armed Conflict*(2002).
Mommsen, Theodor, *Römisches Strafrecht* (1899) (Graz 1955).
Neff, Stephen C., 'The Prerogatives of Violence – In Search of the Conceptual Foundations of Belligerents' Rights', *German Yearbook of International Law*, Vol. 38, 1995, pp. 41-72.
Neff, Stephen C., *The Rights and Duties of Neutrals: A General History* (2000).
Neff, Stephen C., *War and the Law of Nations; A General History* (Cambridge 2005).
Niditch, Susan, *War in the Hebrew Bible: A Study in the Ethics of Violence* (1995).
Nisbet, R.G.M., 'The Speeches', in T.A. Dorey, ed., *Cicero* (London 1965).
Olivelle, Patrick, ed., *The law code of Manu* (2004).
Onuma, Yasuaki, *A Normative Approach to War: Peace, War, and Justice in Hugo Grotius* (1993).
Orend, Brian, 'Kant's Just War Theory', in B. Sharon Byrd and Joachim Hruschka, eds., *Kant and Law* (2006).
Ostwald, Martin, 'Peace and War in Plato and Aristotle', *Scripta Classica Israelica* 15 (1996) pp. 102-118.
Partner, Peter, *God of Battles: Holy Wars of Christianity and Islam* (1997).
Phillipson, C., *The International Law and Customs of Ancient Greece and Rome* (1911).
Pillitu, Paola A., *Lo stato di necessità nel diritto internazionale* (Perugia 1891).
Pohlenz, Max, *Die Stoa: Geschichte einer geistigen Bewegung* (1978).
Price, Jonathan J., *Thucydides and Internal War* (2001).
Przetacznik, Frank, *The Philosophical and Legal Concept of War* (1994).
Purdy, Laura, 'Vitoria's Just War Theory: still relevant today?', in Joseph Hoffmann, ed., *The Just War and Jihad: Violence in Judaism, Christianity, and Islam* (2006).
Pustogarov, V.V., 'The Martens clause in international law', 1 *Journal of the History of International Law* (1999) pp. 125-135.
Rad, Gerhard von, *Holy War in Ancient Israel*, Marva J. Dawn, ed./trans. (1991).

Regout, Robert, *La doctrine de la guerre juste de Saint Augustin à nos jours, d'après les théologiens et les canonistes catholiques* (1935).
Reichberg, Gregory M., et al., eds., *The Ethics of War: Classic and Contemporary Readings* (Oxford 2006).
Rich, John, and Graham Shipley, eds., *War and Society in the Roman World* (1993).
Rist, John M., *Stoic philosophy* (1969).
Ronzitti, Natalino, *Rescuing Nationals Abroad through Military Coercion and Intervention on Grounds of Humanity* (1985).
Root, Elihu, 'The Basis of Protection to Citizens Residing Abroad', 4 *American Journal of International Law* (1910) pp. 517-528.
Russell, Frederick H., *The Just War in the Middle Ages* (1975).
Rutgers, V.H., 'La mise en harmonie du Pacte de la Société des Nations avec le Pacte de Paris', 38 *Recueil des Cours* (1931) pp. 1-123.
Salisbury, J.E., '"In vain have I smitten your Children": Augustine defines Just War', in Joseph Hoffmann, ed., *The Just War and Jihad: Violence in Judaism, Christianity, and Islam* (2006).
Saxoferrato, Bartolus of, 'Roman War within Christendom', in Gregory M. Reichberg, Henrik Syse, and Endre Begby, eds., *The Ethics of War: Classic and Contemporary Readings* (2006).
Schilling, Bernard N., *Dryden and the conservative myth: a reading of Absalom and Achitophel* (Yale 1961).
Schircks, Rhea, *Die Martens'sche Klausel; Rezeption und Rechtqualität* (2001).
Scott, James Brown, ed., *Resolutions of the Institute of International Law Dealing with the Law of Nations* (1916).
Scott, James Brown, ed., *The Proceedings of the Hague Peace Conferences* (1920-21).
Scott, James Brown, ed., *The Reports to the Hague Conferences of 1899 and 1907* (1917).
Sheehan, Michael, *The Balance of Power: History and Theory* (1995).
Shotwell, James T., *War as an Instrument of National Policy and Its Renunciation in the Pact of Paris* (1929).
Sicilianos, Linos-Alexandre, *Les réactions décentralisées à l'illicité: Des contremesures à la légitime défence* (1990).
Sorabji, Richard, 'Just War from Ancient Origins to the Conquistadors Debate and its Modern Relevance', in Richard Sorabji and David Rodin, eds., *The Ethics of War: Shared Problems in Different Traditions* (2006).
Teichman, Jenny, 'The Just War I: Christian Philosophers & Jurists in the Middle Ages', in Jenny Teichman, ed., *The Philosophy of War and Peace* (2006).
Tesón, Fernando R., *Humanitarian Intervention: An Inquiry into Law and Morality* (1997).
Tooke, Joan Doreen, *The Just War in Aquinas and Grotius* (1965).
Tuck, Richard, *Natural rights theories: their origin and development* (1979).
Tuck, Richard, *The rights of war and peace: political thought and the international order from Grotius to Kant* (1999).
Tucker, Robert W., 'The Interpretation of War under Present International Law', 4 *International Law Quarterly* (1951) pp. 11-33.
Tucker, Robert W., *The Just War: A Study in Contemporary American Doctrine* (1960).
Tucker, Robert W., *The Law of War and Neutrality at Sea* (1957).
Vagts, Alfred, and Detlev F. Vagts, 'The Balance of Power in International Law: A History of an Idea', 73 *American Journal of International Law* (1979) pp. 555-580.
Vidal, G., *Cours de droit criminel et de science pénentiaire*, 6ème éd., par J. Magnol (Paris 1921).
Viswanatha, S.V., *International Law in Ancient India* (1925).

Vitoria, Francisco de, 'Just War in the Age of Discovery', in Gregory M. Reichberg, Henrik Syse, and Endre Begby, eds., *The Ethics of War: Classic and Contemporary* (2006).
Vollenhoven, C. Van, *Verspreide Geschriften*, 3 vols. (1934).
Walzer, Michael, *Just and Unjust Wars: A Moral Argument with Historical Illustrations* (1992).
Watson, Alan, *International Law in Archaic Rome: War and Religion* (1993).
Wehberg, Hans, *The Outlawry of War* (1931).
Welch, David A., *Justice and the Genesis of War*, 1993.
Winfield, P.H., 'The History of Intervention in International Law', *British Year Book of International Law*, Vol. 3 (1922-3) pp. 130-149.
Wright, N.A.R., 'The Tree of Battles of Honoré Bouvet and the Laws of War', in C.T. Allmand. ed., *War, Literature, and Politics in the Late Middle Ages* (1976).
Zampaglione, Gerardo, *The Idea of Peace in Antiquity* (1973).
Ziegler, Karl-Heinz, 'Friedensverträge im römischen Altertum', 27 *Archiv des Völkerrechts* (1989) pp. 45-61.

1.3 **Theory**

'21st Annual Scholarly Programs: the Future of Force: Waging War in the 21st Century', 27 *Hastings International and Comparative Law Review* (2004) pp. 421-510.
Akehurst, Michael, *A Modern Introduction to International Law* (1991).
Allan, Pierre, 'Measuring International Ethics: a Moral Scale of War, Peace, Justice, and Global Care', in Pierre Allan and Alexis Keller, eds., *What is a Just Peace?* (2006).
Anghie, Antony, 'On Critique and the Other', in Anne Orford, ed., *International Law and its Others* (2006).
Avalos, Hector, 'Rethinking Religious Violence: Fighting over Nothing', in Joseph Hoffmann, ed., *The Just War and Jihad: Violence in Judaism, Christianity, and Islam* (2006).
Bellinger, Charles K., 'Understanding Violence: the New Copernican Revolution, in Joseph Hoffmann', ed., *The Just War and Jihad: Violence in Judaism, Christianity, and Islam* (2006).
Boyle, Joseph M., 'Just War Doctrine and the Military Response to Terrorism: (2003)', in Larry May, Eric Rovie, and Steve Viner, eds., *The Morality of War: Classical and Contemporary Readings* (2006).
'*Caroline Case* – Daniel Webster, Secretary of State, Letter to Lord Ashburton, British Plenipotentiary (August 6, 1842)', in John Basset Moore, ed., *A Digest of International Law*, Vol. 2 (1906) pp. 412ff.
Casanovas, Oriol, 'Nouvelles questions sur le principe de l'interdiction du recours à la force', 6 *Baltic Yearbook of International Law* (2006) pp. 143-156.
Corstens, Geert and Jean Pradel, *European Criminal Law* (2002).
Dais, Eugene E., 'Just War Theory Post-9/11: Perfect Terrorism and Superpower Defense', in Steven P. Lee, ed., *Intervention, Terrorism, and Torture: Contemporary Challenges to Just War* (2007).
DiMeglio, Richard P., 'The Evolution of the Just War Tradition: Defining Jus Post Bellum', 186 *Military Law Review* (2006) pp. 116-163.
Duquette, David, 'From Rights to Realism: Incoherence in Walzer's Conception of Jus in Bello', in Steven P. Lee, ed., *Intervention, Terrorism, and Torture: Contemporary Challenges to Just War* (2007).
Evans, Mark, *Just War Theory: A Reappraisal* (2005).
Firestone, Reuven, 'Who broke their Vow first?: the "three Vows" and Contemporary Thinking about Jewish Holy War', in Joseph Hoffmann, ed., *The Just War and Jihad: Violence in Judaism, Christianity, and Islam* (2006).

Gazzini, Tarcisio, *The changing rules on the use of force in international law* (2006).
Gray, Christine, 'The Use of Force and the International Legal Order', in Malcolm D. Evans, ed., *International Law*, Vol. 3 (2006).
Green L.C., 'Rescue at Entebbe – Legal Aspects', *Israel Yearbook of Human Rights*, Vol. 6 (1976) pp. 312ff.
Higgins, Rosalyn and Danesh Sarooshi, 'Institutional Modes of Conflict Management', in John Norton Moore and Robert Turner, eds., *National Security Law* (2005) pp. 267-289.
Higgins, Rosalyn, *Problems and Process: International Law and How We Use It* (1994).
Hubbard, Patrick, 'A Realist Response to Walzer's Just and Unjust Wars', in Steven P. Lee, ed., *Intervention, Terrorism, and Torture: Contemporary Challenges to Just War* (2007).
Hulu, J.D., *Materieel Strafrecht* (2003).
Janis, Mark W., *An introduction to International Law* (1993).
Jellinek, Georg, *Die Erklarung der Menschen- und Bürgerrechte* (1927).
Johnson, James Turner, 'Contemporary Just War', in Gregory M. Reichberg, Henrik Syse, and Endre Begby, eds., *The Ethics of War: Classic and Contemporary* (2006).
Johnson, James Turner, 'The Just War Idea: the State of the Question', in Ellen Frankel Paul, Fred D. Miller, Jr., and Jeffrey Paul, eds., *Justice and Global Politics* (2006).
Johnson, James Turner, *The war to oust Saddam Hussein: just war and the new face of conflict* (2005).
Lee, Steven P., *Intervention, terrorism, and torture: contemporary challenges to just war theory* (2007).
Linn, Alexander C., 'The Just War Doctrine and State Liability For Paramilitary War Crimes', 34 *Georgia Journal of International and Comparative Law* (2006) pp. 619-656.
Lucas, George R., 'From "Jus ad bellum" to "Jus ad pacem": Rethinking Just-War Criteria for the Use of Military Force for Humanitarian Ends: (2003)', in Larry May, Eric Rovie, and Steve Viner, eds., *The Morality of War: Classical and Contemporary Readings* (2006).
Martin, Rex, 'Walzer and Rawls on Just Wars and Humanitarian Interventions', in Steven P. Lee, ed., *Intervention, Terrorism, and Torture: Contemporary Challenges to Just War* (2007).
McDougal, Myres S., 'The Soviet Cuban Quarantine and Self Defense', 57 *American Journal of International Law* (1963) pp. 597ff.
Murnion, William E., 'A Postmodern View of Just War', in Steven P. Lee, ed., *Intervention, Terrorism, and Torture: Contemporary Challenges to Just War* (2007).
O'Connell, Mary Ellen, 'Crying War', in Thomas J. Biersteker, ed., *International Law and International Relations: Bridging Theory and Practice* (2007).
Olusanya, Olaoluwa, *Identifying the aggressor under International Law: a principles approach* (2006).
Otis, Pauletta, 'Religious Warfare on the Global Battlefield', in Joseph Hoffmann, ed., *The Just War and Jihad: Violence in Judaism, Christianity, and Islam* (2006).
Ovey, Clare, and Robin White, eds., *Jacobs and White, The European Convention on Human Rights* (2002).
Palmer-Fernandez, Gabriel, 'Religion and Violence: War, Tyrannicide, Terrorism', in Joseph Hoffmann, ed., *The Just War and Jihad: Violence in Judaism, Christianity, and Islam* (2006).
Patterson, Eric, 'Just War in the 21st Century: reconceptualizing Just War Theory after September 11', 42 *International Politics* (2005) pp. 116-134.
Peñafort, Raymond and William Rennes, 'The Conditions of Just War, Self-defense and their Legal Consequences under Penitential Jurisdiction', in Gregory M. Reichberg, Henrik Syse, and Endre Begby, eds., *The Ethics of War: Classic and Contemporary* (2006).

Pettiti, L.E., Decaux, E., Imbert, P.H., eds., *La Convention Européenne des Droits de l'Homme* (1995).
Reisman, W. Michael, 'Assessing claims to revise the laws of war', 97 *American Journal of International Law* (2003) pp. 82-90.
Rosenne, S., *An International Law Miscellany* (1993).
Rosenne, S., 'State Responsibility – Festina Lente', *British Year Book of International Law*, Vol. 74 (2004) pp. 363-371.
Scholz, Sally J., 'War Rape's Challenge to Just War Theory', in Steven P. Lee, ed., *Intervention, Terrorism, and Torture: Contemporary Challenges to Just War* (2007).
Schwartz, Regina M., 'Holy Terror', in Joseph Hoffmann, ed., *The Just War and Jihad: Violence in Judaism, Christianity, and Islam* (2006).
Shaw, Malcolm N., *International Law*, 1991.
Simma, Brunno, 'NATO, the UN and the Use of Force: Legal Aspects', 10 *European Journal of International Law* (1999) pp. 1ff.
Tapp, Robert B., 'Critics of Just War Theories: Charles E. Raven and A.J. Muste', in Joseph Hoffmann, ed., *The Just War and Jihad: Violence in Judaism, Christianity, and Islam* (2006).
Teichman, Jenny, 'The Just War II: Philosophers & Clergy in the twentieth Century', in Jenny Teichman, ed., *The Philosophy of War and Peace* (2006).
Walzer, Michael, 'Just and Unjust Wars: (1977)', in Larry May, Eric Rovie, and Steve Viner, eds., *The Morality of War: Classical and Contemporary Readings* (2006).
Weiner, Allen S., 'Law, Just War and the International Fight against Terrorism: is it War?', in Steven P. Lee, ed., *Intervention, Terrorism, and Torture: Contemporary Challenges to Just War* (2007).
Yoder, John Howard, 'When War is Unjust: being Honest in Just-War Thinking (1984)', in Larry May, Eric Rovie, and Steve Viner, eds., *The Morality of War: Classical and Contemporary Readings* (2006).

2. Self-Defence

2.1 **Philosophy and History**

Byers, Michael, 'Der Irak und der Fall Caroline: Präventivkrieg und Selbstverteidigung im Völkerrecht', in Kai Ambos, Jörg Arnold, eds., *Der Irak-Krieg und das Völkerrecht* (2004).
Byers, Michael, 'Terror and the future of International law', *Worlds in collision* (2002).
Ceulemans, Carl, 'Just Cause', in Bruno Coppieters and Nick Fotion, eds., *Moral Constraints on War: Principles and Cases* (2002).
Corthay, Eric, 'Le régime juridique du recours à la force tel qu'interprété par les Etats membres de l'Organisation de la Conférence islamique', 7 *Journal of the History of International Law* (2005) pp. 211-253.
Dekker, Ige F., 'De bijna-oorlog en het Internationaal Recht', in André W.M. Gerrits & Jaap H. de Wilde, eds., *Aan het slagveld ontsnapt: over oorlogen die niet plaatsvonden*; *Een Liber Amicorum Voor Hylke Tromp* (2000).
Fassbender, Bardo, 'Die Gegenwartskrise des völkerrechtlichen Gewaltverbotes vor dem Hintergrung der geschichtlichen Entwicklung', 31 *Europäische Grundrechte Zeitschrift* (2004) pp. 241-256.
Finkelstein, Claire, 'A Puzzle about Hobbes on Self-defense', in *Hobbes on Law*, Claire Finkelstein, ed. (2005).

Harry, Debra, 'Acts of Self-Determination and Self-Defense: Indigenous Peoples' Responses to Biocolonialism', in Sheldon Krimsky and Peter Shorett, eds., *Rights and Liberties in the Biotech Age: why we need a Genetic Bill of Rights* (2005).

Kahgan, Carin, 'Jus cogens and the inherent right to self defense', 3 *ILSA Journal of International & Comparative Law* (1997) pp. 767-827.

Kaufmann, Matthias, 'Gewalt zur Beherrschung der Gewalt: über Möglichkeiten und Grenzen der Legitimierbarkeit von Gewalt aus rechtsphiliosophischer Sicht', in Ludger Kühnhardt, Mamoru Takayama, eds., *Menschenrechte, Kulturen und Gewalt: Ansätze einer interkulturellen Ethik* (2005).

Kelly, Michael J., 'Time warp to 1945: resurrection of the reprisal and anticipatory self-defense doctrines in International law', 13 *Journal of Transnational Law and Policy* (2003) pp. 1-39.

Khalid, Mohd, 'Right of self-defence or right to exist in International law', 39 *Civil & military Law Journal* (2003) pp. 157-160.

Kopel, David B., 'The Torah and Self-Defense', 109 *Penn State Law Review* (2004) pp.17-42.

Lillich, R.B., 'Forcible self-help under International law', *Readings in International law from the Naval War College Review 1947-1977*, Vol. 2: *The use of force, human rights and general International legal issues* (1980).

MacHugh, J.J., 'Forcible self-help in International law', *Readings in International law from the Naval War College Review 1947-1977*, Vol. 2: *The use of force, human rights and general International legal issues* (1980).

Magenis, Sean D., 'Natural Law as the Customary International Law of Self-defense', 20 *Boston University International Law Journal* (2002) pp. 413-435.

Müllerson, Rein, 'The Law of Use of Force at the Turn of the Millennia', *Baltic Yearbook of International Law*, Vol. 3 (2003) pp. 191-228.

Nabati, Mikael, 'International Law at a Crossroads: Self-Defense, global Terrorism, and Preemption: a call to rethink the Self-Defense normative Framework', 13 *Transnational Law & Contemporary Problems* (2003) pp. 771-802.

Noll, Gregor, 'Force, partisanship, dislocation: an essay on International law in the state of the exceptional', in Jarna Petman & Jan Klabbers, eds., *Nordic cosmopolitanism* (2003).

Reisman, W. Michael, 'In defense of world public order', 95 *American Journal of International Law* (2001) pp. 833-835.

Rubin, Alfred P., 'Jus ad bellum and jus cogens: is immorality illegal?', in A.J.M. Delissen and G.J. Tanja, eds., *Humanitarian Law of armed conflict challenges ahead* (1991).

Seidel, Gerd, 'Quo vadis Völkerrecht?', 41 *Archiv des Völkerrechts* (2003) pp. 449-483.

Trindade, Antônio Augusto Cançado, El primado del derecho sobre la fuerza como imperativo del "jus cogens": post scriptum', 2 *Doctrina latinoamericana del derecho internacional* (2003).

2.2 In Reports of the International Law Comission

Ago, Roberto, in *Annuaire de la Commission du Droit International*, Vol. II, 2nd part (1980) pp. 33-59.

Alland, D., 'La légitime défense et les contre-mesures dans la codification du droit International de la responsabilité', 110 *Journal du Droit International* (1983) pp. 728-762.

Badr, G.M., 'The exulpatory effect of self-defense in state responsibility', 10 *Georgia Journal of International and Comparative Law* (1980) pp. 1-28.

Barboza, Julio, 'Contramedidas en la reciente codificación de las responsabilidad de los Estados: fronteras con la legítima defensa y el Estado de necesidad', *Anuario argentino de derecho internacional*, Vol. 12 (2003) pp. 15-47.

Battaglini, Giovanni, 'War against Terrorism extra moenia, Self-defence and Responsibility: A Pure Juridical Approach', in Maurizio Ragazzi, ed., *Responsibility today: Essays in Memory of Oscar Schachter* (2005).
Linnan, David K., 'Iran Air Flight 655 and Beyond: Free Passage, Mistaken Self-defence, and State Responsibility', 16 *Yale Journal of International Law* (1991) pp. 245-389.
Malanczuk, P., 'Countermeasures and Self-Defence as Circumstances Precluding Wrongfulness in the International Law Commission's Draft Articles on State Responsibility', 43 *Zeitschrift für ausländisches öffentliches Recht und Völkerrecht* (1983) pp. 705-812.

2.3 **General**

Alexandrov, Stanimir A., *Self-defense against the use of force in International Law* (1996).
Amann, Diane Marie, 'Unipolar Disorder: A European Perspective on U.S. Security Strategy', 27 *Hastings International and Comparative Law Review* (2004) pp. 447-456.
Arai-Takahashi, Yutaka, 'Shifting boundaries of the right of self-defence: appraising the impact of the September 11 attacks on jus ad bellum', 36 *The International Lawyer* (2002) pp. 1081-1102.
Barnes, J., 'Self-defence and collective security', 36 *Studia Diplomatica* (1983) pp. 521-532.
Beaumont, John S., 'Self-defence as a justification for disregarding diplomatic immunity', *The Canadian Yearbook of International Law*, Vol. 29 (1992) pp. 391-402.
Benvinisti, Eyal, 'The US and the Use of Force: Double-edged Hegemony and the Management of Global Emergencies', 15 *European Journal of International Law* (2004) pp. 677-700.
Bowett, Derk W., 'Collective security and collective self-defence: the errors and risks in identification', in Manuel Rama-Montaldo, ed., *El derecho internacional en un mundo en transformacion*, Vol. 1 (1995).
Brock, Lothar, 'The Use of Force in the Post-Cold War Era: from Collective Action back to Pre-Charter Self-defense?', in Michael Bothe, et al., eds., *Redefining Sovereignty: the Use of Force after the Cold War* (2005).
Bruha, Thomas, 'Gewaltverbot und humanitäres Völkerrecht nach dem 11. September 2001', 40 *Archiv des Völkerrechts* (2002) pp. 383-421.
Butler, W.E., *The non-use of force in International Law* (1989).
Byers, Michael, 'The shifting foundations of International law: a decade of forceful measures against Iraq', 13 *European Journal of International Law* (2002) pp. 21-41.
Byers, Michael, *War Law: International Law and Armed Conflict* (2005).
Ceausu, D., 'Quelques considérations relatives à l'interdiction de l'emploi de la force dans les relations Internationales et le droit de légitime défense', 15 *Revue Roumaine d'Études Internationales* (1981) pp. 123-132.
Christakis, Théodore, & Bannelier, Karine, 'Volenti Non Fit Injuria?: les effets du consentement à l'intervention militaire', *Annuaire Français de Droit International*, Vol. 50 (2005) pp. 102-137.
Cockburn, Alexander, *Imperial crusades: Iraq, Afghanistan and Yugoslavia: a diary of three wars* (2004).
Craven, Matthew, 'We are Teachers of Internatioanl Law', 17 *Leiden Journal of International Law* (2004) pp. 363-374.
Delcourt, Barbara, 'De la sécurité collective à la sécurité sélective: les dommages collatéraux de la stratégie américaine', in Barbara Delcourt, Denis Duez & Éric Remacle, eds., *La guerre d'Irak: prélude d'un nouvel ordre International?* (2004).
Delivanis, Jean, *La légitime défense en droit International public moderne: (le droit International face à ses limites)* (1971).

Dinstein, Yoram, 'The right of self-defence against armed attacks', in Magnus D. Sandbu and Peter Nordbeck, eds., *International terrorism: Report from a Seminar arranged by The European Law Students' Association 1987* (1989).
Dinstein, Yoram, *War, aggression and self-defence* (2005).
Dittmar, Falko, *Angriffe auf Computernetzwerke: ius ad bellum und ius in bello* (2005).
Doebbler, Curtis F., 'How can we really protect national security?', 9 *ILSA Journal of International and Comparative Law* (2003) pp. 399-405.
Ecobescu, N., & E. Glaser, 'La légitime défense individuelle – institution de base de la légalité Internationale contemporaine', 8 *Revue Roumaine d'Études Internationales* (1971) pp. 131-142.
Estrada y de Miguel, E., 'Agresion y legitima defensa', *Estudios de derecho internacional público y privado: homenaje al profesor Luis Sela Sampil*' Vol. 2 (1970).
Evans, Mark, 'Moral Theory and the Idea of a Just War', in Mark Evans, ed., *Just War Theory: a Reappraisal* (2005).
Feinstein, B., 'Self-defence and Israel in International law: a reappraisal', 11 *Israel Law Review* (1976) pp. 517-562.
Fernandez Flores, J.L., 'El uso de la fuerza y la defensa', 51 *Revista Española de Derecho Militar* (1988) pp. 145-158.
Franck, Thomas M., '"In extremis": are there legal principles applicable to the illegal use of force?', in Lal Chand Vohrah, et al., eds., *Man's inhumanity to man* (2003).
Frowein, Jochen Abr., 'Is Public International Law dead?', *German Yearbook of International Law*, Vol. 46 (2004) pp. 9-16.
Gaddis, John Lewis, *Surprise, security, and the American experience* (2004).
Garcia, Th., 'De la transgression du droit International par la recours à la force', 82 *Revue de Droit International et de Droit Comparé* (2005) pp. 52-67.
Genoni, Maurizio A.M., *Die Notwehr im Völkerrecht* (1987).
Genugten, Willem van, 'Nederlandse troepen ter zelfverdediging naar Afghanistan?', 80 *Nederlands juristenblad* (2005) pp. 790-791.
Gill, T.D., 'The forcible protection, affirmation and exercise of rights by states under contemporary International law', *Netherlands Yearbook of International Law*, Vol. 23 (1993) pp. 105-173.
Gioia, Andrea, 'The End of the Conflict and Post-conflict Peace-building', in Michael Bothe, et al., eds., *Redefining Sovereignty: the Use of Force after the Cold War* (2005).
Giraud, Emile, 'La théorie de la légitime défense', 49 *Recueil des cours* (1935).
Global Governance: Reports and Discussions of a Symposium held in Trier on October 9th and 10th, 2003 (2004).
Golash, Dierdre, 'Torture and Self-defense', in Steven P. Lee, ed., *Intervention, Terrorism, and Torture: Contemporary Challenges to Just War Theory* (2007).
Gramm, Christof, 'Die Aufgaben der Bundeswehr und ihre Grenzen in der Verfassung', 47 *Neue Zeitschrift für Wehrrecht* (2005) pp. 133-146.
Gramsch, Werner, *Abrüstung, das Problem der völkerrechtlichen Notwehr: ein Schrift von Werner Gramsch* (1935).
Greenwood, Christopher, 'Self-defence and conduct of International armed conflict', in Y. Dinstein, ed., *International law at a time of perplexity: essays in honour of Shabtai Rosenne* (1989).
Hargrove, John Lawrence, 'Force, a culture of law, and American interests', in Jonathan I. Charney, Donald K. Anton and Mary Ellen O'Connell, eds., *Politics, values and functions* (1997).
Higginbotham, F. Michael, 'International law, the use of force in self-defense, and Southern African conflict', 25 *Columbia Journal of Transnational Law* (1987) pp. 529-592.

Higgins, R., *Problems and Process: International Law and How we Use it* (1997).
Hillgenberg, Hartmut, 'Gewaltverbot: was gilt noch?', in Jochen Abr. Frowein, et al., eds., *Verhandeln für den Frieden* (2003).
Hortatos, Constantine P., *The self-defense of the states under the current International legal status* (1966).
Hoyer, Werner, 'Völkerrecht reformieren, um es zu bewahren: auf die neuen Bedrohungen muss reagiert werden', 59 *Internationale Politik* (2004) pp. 63-66.
International Terrorism: Report from a Seminar arranged by The European Law Students' Association 1987 (1989).
Islam, M. Rafiqul, 'The use of force in International relations: the Indian invasion of East Pakistan', 2 *Lawasia* (1983) pp. 171-193.
Jahn, Matthias, *Das Strafrecht des Staatsnotstandes: die strafrechtlichen Rechtfertigungsgründe und ihr Verhältnis zu Eingriff und Intervention im Verfassungs- und Völkerrecht der Gegenwart* (2004).
Kates, Don B., 'Genocide, Self Defense and the Right to Arms', 29 *Hamline Law Review* (2006) pp. 501-517.
Kolb, Robert, 'Quelques réflexions sur le droit relatif au maintien de la paix au début du XXieme siècle', *African Yearbook of International Law*, Vol. 11 (2005) pp. 193-215.
Krift, T.R., 'Self-defense and self-help: the Israeli raid on Entebbe', 4 *Brooklyn Journal of International Law* (1977) pp. 43-62.
Krisch, Nico, *Selbstverteidigung und kollektive Sicherheit* (2001).
Kritsiotis, Dino, 'Arguments of mass confusion', 15 *European Journal of International Law* (2004) pp. 233-278.
La guerra: profili di diritto internazionale e diritto interno; lezione congiunta dei corsi di diritto internazionale e di istituzioni di diritto pubblico, Teramo, 11 gennaio 2002 (2002).
Lamberti Zanardi, Pierluigi, *La legittima difensa nel diritto internazionale* (1972).
Lewan, K.M., 'Justifications for the opening hostilities in the Middle East', 26 *Revue Egyptienne de Droit International* (1970) pp. 88-105.
Lhommeau, Géraldine, *Le droit International à l'épreuve de la puissance américaine* (2005).
Linnan, David K., 'Self-defense, necessity and U.N. collective security: United States and other views', 1 *Duke Journal of Comparative & International Law* (1991) pp. 57-123.
López-Pina, Antonio, 'Die verstärkte Zusammenarbeit als europäische Regierungsform', in Alexander Blankenagel, Ingolf Pernice und Helmuth Schulze-Fielitz, eds., *Verfassung im Diskurs der Welt: liber amicorum Peter Häberle* (2004).
MacCormack, Timothy L.H., *Self-defense in International Law: the Israeli raid on the Iraqi nuclear reactor* (1996).
Mandel, Michael, 'Rounding up the Usual Suspects while America gets away with Murder', in Hélène Dumont et Anne-Marie Boisvert, eds., *La voie vers la Cour Pénale Internationale: tous les chemins mènent à Rome* (2004).
Maxwell, Mark David, 'Individual self-defense and the rules of engagement: are the two mutually exclusive?, 41 *Revue de Droit Militaire et de Droit de la Guerre* (2002) pp. 39-53.
Mayer, Franz C., 'Angriffskrieg und europäisches Verfassungsrecht', 41 *Archiv des Völkerrechts* (2003) pp. 394-418.
Mezillas, Glodel, 'La régulation de la force en droit International', 24 *La Chronique judiciaire d'Haiti* (2004) pp. 6-13.
Mikulka, V., 'K pojetí sebeobrany v nauce mezinárodního právo', 115 *Právník* (1976) pp. 1044-1058.
Mrazek, Josef, 'Prohibition of the use and threat of force: self-defence and self-help in International law', *The Canadian Yearbook of International Law*, Vol. 27 (1990) pp. 81-111.

Müllerson, Rein, 'Jus ad bellum: plus ça change (le monde), plus c'est la même chose (le droit)?', 7 *Journal of Conflict and Security Law* (2002) pp. 149-189.

Nabers, Dirk, *Kollektive Selbstverteidigung in Japans Sicherheitsstrategie* (Institut für Asienkunde 2000).

Nawaz, M.K., 'Limits of self-defense: legitimacy of use of force against economic strangulation', 16 *Indian Journal of International Law* (1976) pp. 252-266.

Nolte, Georg, *Le droit International face au défi américain* (2005).

Ochoa-Ruiz, Natalie, & Salamanca-Aguado, Esther, 'Exploring the Limits of International Law Relating to the Use of Force in Self-defence', 16 *European Journal of International Law* (2005) pp. 499-524.

O'Connell, Mary Ellen, & Hall, B. Welling, 'Report from Columbus: Discussions on the Future of Law and Institutions on the Use of Force in a one Superpower World', in Michael Bothe, et al., eds., *Redefining Sovereignty: the Use of Force after the Cold War* (2005).

Ortega Carcelén, Martin C., *La legitima defensa del territorio del estado: requisitos para su ejercicio* (1991).

Ouma, Stephen, '"Operation Iron Fist" and the Conflict in Northern Uganda: the Legal Regulation of the Use of Force in Extra-territorial Law Enforcement', 10 *East African Journal of Peace & Human Rights* (2004) pp. 325-330.

Peters, Anne, 'The Growth of International Law between Globalization and the Great Power', 8 *Austrian Review of International and European Law* (2005) pp. 109-140.

Plofchan, Thomas K., 'A concept of International law: protecting systematic values', 33 *Virginia Journal of International Law* (1992) pp. 197-238.

PoKempner, Dinah, 'Bending the Rules: Laws of War', 59 *World Today* (2003) pp.14-15.

Posner, Eric A., & Sykes, Alan O., 'Optimal War and Jus Ad Bellum', 93 *The Georgetown Law Journal* (2005) pp. 993-1022.

Quigley, John, 'The United Nations' Response to Israel's Seizure of the Gaza Strip and West Bank', *Palestine Yearbook of International Law*, Vol. 12, 2005, pp. 145-164.

Ramsey, Paul, 'Nuclear Weapons and Legitimate Defense', in Gregory M. Reichberg, Henrik Syse, and Endre Begby, eds., *The Ethics of War: Classic and Contemporary Readings* (2006).

Rehrl, Jochen, 'Beistandsgarantie und Solidaritätsklausel: völker- und verfassungsrechtliche Herausforderungen für Österreich durch den neuen EU-Verfassungsvertrag', 60 *Zeitschrift für öffentliches Recht* (2005) pp. 31-53.

Reisman, W. Michael, 'Assessing claims to revise the laws of war', 97 *American Journal of International Law* (2003) pp. 82-90.

Ripol Carulla, Santiago, 'La nueva doctrina global de defensa preventiva: consideraciones sobre su caracterización y fundamento', in Caterina García Segura, Angel J. Rodrigo Hernández, eds., *El imperio inviable: el orden internacional tras el confícto de Irak* (2004).

Rivkin, David B., and Casey, Lee A., 'Using Force Lawfully in the Twenty-first Century', *Israel Yearbook on Human Rights*, Vol. 35 (2005) pp. 15-32.

Robin, David/Pearson Prentice Hall, 'War and Self-Defense:(2002)', in Larry May, Eric Rovie, and Steve Viner, eds., *The Morality of War: Classical and Contemporary Readings* (2006).

Rodin, David, *War and self-defense* (2002).

Rohlik, J., 'Some remarks on self-defense and intervention: a reaction to reading law and civil war in the modern world', 6 *Georgia Journal of International and Comparative Law* (1976) pp. 395-435.

Schachter, Oscar, 'Self-defense and the rule of law', 8 *American Journal of International Law* (1989) pp. 259-277.

Schmidt-Jortzig, Edzard, 'Die Verallgemeinerung des Außergewöhnlichen', in Jürgen Bröhmer, et al., eds., *Internationale Gemeinschaft und Menschenrechte: Festschrift Georg Ress* (2005).

Schröder, Meinhard, 'The Status of Public International Law seen from a European Perspective', in Bernd von Hoffmann, ed., *Global Governance: Reports and Discussions of a Symposium held in Trier on October 9th and 10th, 2003* (2004).

Schwebel, S.M., 'Aggression, intervention and self-defence in modern International law', 136 *Recueil des cours* (1973).

Schweisfurth, Theodor, 'Aggression', in Kai Ambos, Jörg Arnold, eds., *Der Irak-Krieg und das Völkerrecht* (2004).

Shapira, A., 'The six-day war and the right of self-defense', *The Arab-Israeli conflict*, Vol. 2 (1974) pp. 205-220.

Sicilianos, Linos-Alexandre, *Les réactions décentralisées á l'illicite: des contre-mesures à la légitime défense* (1990).

Singh, Jai Narain, *Use of force under International Law* (1984).

Skopets, Michael, 'Battered Nation Syndrom: Relaxing the Imminence Requirement of Self-Defense in International Law', 55 *The American University Law Review* (2006) pp. 753-783.

Staden, A. van, 'Effectief multilateralisme: van retoriek naar daadkracht', 58 *Internationale Spectator* (2004) pp. 343-349.

Symonides, Janusz, 'A few Remarks about the Foundations of International Security and Order under International Law', in Hans-Joachim Giessmann, Roman Kúzniar, Zdzislaw Lachowski, eds., *International Security in a Time of Change: Threats, Concepts, Institutions: Festschrift Adam Daniel Rotfeld* (2004).

Talmon, Stefan, 'Changing Views on the Use of Force: the German Position', *Baltic Yearbook of International Law*, Vol. 5 (2005) pp. 41-76.

Taoka, R., *The right of self-defence in International Law* (Osaka University of Economics and Law 1978).

Tchanile, Ali Tchakoly, *Israel et la légitime défense* (Université de Nice, Institut du Droit de la Paix et du Développement 1985).

Toope, Stephen J., 'The Measure of International Law: Canada's Role after September 11th, 2001', in *The Measure of International Law: Effectiveness, Fairness and Validity; Proceedings of the 31st Annual Conference of the Canadian Council on International Law, Ottawa, October 24-26, 2002* (2004).

Tsagourias, Nicholas, 'Irrational Governance: the Use of Force', in Wybo P. Heere, ed., *The Growing Impact of Non-state Actors on the International and European Legal System: Proceedings Sixth Hague Joint Conference, the Netherlands, 3-5 July 2003* (2004).

Tuzmukhamedov, Bakhtiyar, 'Keeping Pace with the Times?', 8 *Austrian Review of International and European Law* (2005) pp. 205-209.

Valki, Lászlő, 'Merely the Notion of Self-defence is Changing', 8 *Austrian Review of International and European Law* (2005) pp. 211-219.

Verhoeven, Joe, 'Les "étirement" de la légitime défense", *Annuaire Français de Droit International*, Vol. 48 (2003) pp. 49-80.

Volk, Daniel, *Die Begrenzung kriegerischer Konflikte durch das moderne Völkerrecht* (2005).

Waldock, C.H.M., 'The regulation of the Use of Force by Individual States in International Law', 81(2) *Receuil des Cours* (1952) pp. 451-517.

Watts, Arthur, 'Physical Barriers to Armed Infiltration: Self-defence and Israel's Wall in the Occupied Palestinian Territories', in Vesna Crníc-Grotíc, Miomir Matulovíc, eds., *International Law and the Use of Force at the Turn of Centuries: Essays in Honour of V. Degan* (2005).

Weckel, Philippe, 'Nouvelles pratiques américaines en matière de légitime défense?', *Annuaire Français de Relations Internationales*, Vol. 6 (2005) pp. 128-137.

Wedgwood, Ruth, 'The use of armed force in International affairs: self-defense and the Panama invasion', 29 *Columbia Journal of Transnational Law* (1991) pp. 609-628.

Wortley, B.A., 'Some jurisprudential reflections on human rights and self-defence', *Um Recht und Freiheit: Festschrift Friedrich August Freiherr von der Heydte* (1977).

Yamamoto, Ryo, 'Legal Issues concerning Japan's Participation in United Nations Peace-Keeping Operations', *The Japanese Annual of International Law,* Vol. 47 (2005) pp. 136-167.

Zourek, J., 'La notion de légitime défense en droit International', *Annuaire de l'Institut de Droit International*, Vol. 56 (1975) pp. 1-79.

2.4 **Maritime Self-Defence**

Barry, Ian Patrick, 'The Right of Visit, Search and Seizure of Foreign Flagged Vessels on the High Seas Pursuant to Customary International Law: a Defense of the Proliferation Security Initiative', 33 *Hofstra Law Review* (2004) pp. 299-330.

Byers, Michael, 'Gunboat diplomacy: policing the seas and skies', 59 *World Today* (2003) pp. 14-15.

Byers, Michael, 'Policing the high Seas: the Proliferation Security Initiative', 98 *American Journal of International Law* (2004) pp. 526-545.

Heintschel von Heinegg, Wolff, 'Legality of Maritime Interception Operations within the Framework of Operation of Enduring Freedom', in Michael Bothe, et al., eds., *Redefining Sovereignty: the Use of Force after the Cold War* (2005).

Heintschel von Heinegg, Wolff, 'The Legality of Maritime Interception Operations Within the Framework of Operation Enduring Freedom', in Wybo P. Heere, ed., *Terrorism and the Military: International Legal Implications* (2003).

Kinley, Geoffrey, 'The law of self-defense, contemporary naval operations, and the United Nations Conventions on the Law of the Sea', *The UN Convention on the Law of the Sea,* Vol. 19 (1987) pp. 10-40.

Ronzitti, N., 'The right of self-defense at sea and its impact on the law of naval warfare', *Thesaurus Acroasium*, Vol. 17 (1991) pp. 261-294.

Ronzitti, Natalino, 'The right of self-defense and the law of naval warfare', 14 *Syracuse Journal of International Law and Commerce* (1988) pp. 571-579.

3. NECESSITY AND PROPORTIONALITY

3.1 **Necessity**

Barboza, Julio, 'Contramedidas en la reciente codificacíon de la responsabilidad de los Estados: fronteras con la legítima defensa y el Estado de Necesidad', *Anuario argentino de derecho internacional*, Vol. 12 (2003) pp. 15-47.

Dworkin, Anthony, 'Military Necessity and Due Process: the Place of Human Rights in the War on Terror', in David Wippman & Matthew Evangelista, eds., *New Wars, New Laws?: Applying the Laws of War in 21st Century Conflicts* (2005).

Gardam, Judith, *Necessity, Proportionality and the Use of Force by States* (2004).

Ghanayim, Khalid, 'Excused Necessity in Western Legal Philosophy', 19 *The Canadian Journal of Law and Jurisprudence* (2006) pp. 31-65.

Gutierrez, Espada, *El estado de necesidad y el uso de la fuerza en derecho internacional: reflexiones sobre la interpretación y consecuencias que pueden derivarse, en tal materia, de la aceptación por la CDI del estado de necesidad* (1987).

Gutteridge, Chris, 'R v. Jones and Others: the Justiciability of UK Aggression Against Iraq and its Relevance to the Domestic Criminal Defences of Prevention of Crime, Lawful

Excuse and Necessity or Duress of Circumstances', *The Global Community*, 1 (2006) pp. 263-280.

Heiskanen, Veijo, 'Virtue out of Necessity: International Mass Claims and New Uses of Information Technology', in *Redressing Injustices through Mass Claims Processes: Innovative Responses to Unique Challenges* (International Bureau Permanent Court of Arbitration 2006).

Johnstone, Ian, 'The Plea of "Necessity" in International Legal Discourse: Humanitarian Intervention and Counter-terrorism', 43 *Columbia Journal of Transnational Law* (2005) pp. 337-388.

Laursen, Andreas, 'The use of force and (the state of) necessity', 37 *Vanderbilt Journal of Transnational Law* (2004) pp. 485-526.

Linnan, David K., 'Self-defense, necessity and U.N. collective security: United States and other views, 1 *Duke Journal of Comparative & International Law* (1991) pp. 57-123.

McCoubrey, H., 'The nature of the modern doctrine of military necessity', 30 *Revue de Droit Militaire et de Droit de la Guerre* (1991) pp. 215-252.

Raymond, Gregory A., 'Military Necessity and the War against Global Terrorism', in Howard M. Hensel, *Law of Armed Conflict: Constraints on the Contemporary Use of Military Force* (2005).

3.2 **Proportionality**

Bonafede, Michael C., 'Here, there, and everywhere: assessing the proportionality doctrine and U.S. uses of force in response to terrorism after the September 11 attacks', 88 *Cornell Law Review* (2002) pp. 155-214.

Cannizzaro, Enzo, 'The role of proportionality in the law of International countermeasures', 12 *European Journal of International Law* (2001) pp. 889-916.

Carmola, Kateri, 'The Concept of Proportionality: Old Questions and New Ambiguities', in Mark Evans, ed., *Just War Theory: a Reappraisal* (2005).

Cohen-Eliya, Moshe, 'The Formal and the Substantive Meanings of Proportionality in the Supreme Court's Decision regarding the Security Fence', 38 *Israel Law Review* (2005) pp. 262-291.

Dinstein, Yoram, 'Collateral Damage and the Principle of Proportionality', in David Wippman & Matthew Evangelista, eds., *New Wars, New Laws?: Applying the Laws of War in 21st Century Conflicts* (2005).

Gardam, Judith G., 'A Role for Proportionality in the War on Terror', 74 *Nordic Journal of International Law* (2005) pp. 3-25.

Parker, Tom, 'The proportionality principle in the war on terror', *Hague Yearbook of International Law*, Vol. 15 (2003) pp. 3-15.

Tridimas, Takis, 'The Rule of Reason and its Relation to Proportionality and Subsidiarity', in Annette Schrauwen, ed., *Rule of Reason: Rethinking another Classic of European Legal Doctrine* (2005).

4. Collective Self-Defence

Barnes, J., 'Self-defence and collective security', 36 *Studia diplomatica* (1983) pp. 521-532.

Bowett, Derk W., 'Collective security and collective self-defence: the errors and risks in identification', in Manuel Rama-Montaldo, ed., *El derecho internacional en un mundo en transformacion*, Vol. 1 (1995).

Delbrück, Jost, 'The fight against global terrorism: self-defense or collective security as International police action?: some comments on the International legal implications of the

"war against terrorism"', *German Yearbook of International Law*, Vol. 44 (2002) pp. 9-24.
Delcourt, Barbara, 'De la sécurité collective à la sécurité sélective: les dommages collatéraux de la stratégie américaine', in Barbara Delcourt, Denis Duez & Éric Remacle, eds., *La guerre d'Irak: prélude d'un nouvel ordre International?* (2004).
Krisch, Nico, *Selbstverteidigung und kollektive Sicherheit* (2001).
Leurdijk, Dick, 'The US after 9/11: the Exercise of its Inherent Right of Individual and Collective Self-Defence', in Alfred van Staden, Jan Rood, Hans Labohm, eds., *Cannons and Canons: Clingendael Views of Global and Regional Politics* (2003).
Linnan, David K., 'Self-defense, necessity and U.N. collective security: United States and other views', 1 *Duke Journal of Comparative & International Law* (1991) pp. 57-123.
McCoubrey, H., 'The nature of the modern doctrine of military necessity', 30 *Revue de Droit Militaire et de Droit de la Guerre* (1991) pp. 215-252.
Modabber, Zia, 'Collective Self-Defense: Nicaragua *v.* United States", 10 *Loyola of Los Angeles International and Comparative Law Journal* (1988) pp. 449-468.
Nabers, Dirk, *Kollektive Selbstverteidigung in Japans Sicherheitsstrategie* (Institut für Asienkunde 2000).
Nanda, Ved P., 'Preemptive and Preventive Use of Force, Collective Security, and Human Security', 33 *Denver Journal of International Law and Policy* (2004) pp. 7-15.
Nanda, Ved P., 'Preemptive and Preventive Use of Force, Collective Security, and Human Security', 47 *Neue Zeitschrift für Wehrrecht* (2005) pp. 45-58.
Papastavridis, Efthymios, 'Security Council Resolutions 1368/2001 and 1373/2001: collective security or the right of self-defence?', 55 *Revue Hellénique de Droit International* (2002) pp. 501-512.
Schaller, Christian, 'Das Friedenssicherungsrecht im Kampf gegen den Terrorismus: Gewaltverbot, kollektive Sicherheit, Selbstverteidigung und Präemption' (Stiftung Wissenschaft und Politik, Deutsches Institut für Internationale Politik und Sicherheit 2004).
Tsagourias, Nicholas, 'The Shifting Laws on the Use of Force and the Trivialization of the UN Collective Security System: the Need to Reconstitute it', *Netherlands Yearbook of International Law*, Vol. 34 (2004) pp. 55-87.

5. The Role of the UN

5.1 United Nations

Dörr, Oliver, 'Das völkerrechtliche Gewaltverbot und die Vereinten Nationen', in Johannes Varwick, Andreas Zimmermann, eds., *Die Reform der Vereinten Nationen: Bilanz und Perspektiven* (2006).
Evans, Gareth, 'Völkerrecht und Vereinte Nationen: zum Einsatz militärischer Gewalt', in *Die Zukunft des Völkerrechts in einer globalisierten Welt* (Heinrich-Böll-Stiftung 2006).
Fernandez Sanchez, Pablo Antonio, 'Operaciones de las Naciones Unidas para el mantenimiento de la paz', in Pablo Antonio Fernandez Sanchez, ed., *Analisis juridico de las operaciones de las Naciones Unidas para el mantenimiento de la paz* (1998) pp. 317-358.
Franck, Thomas M., 'The Role of International Law and the UN after Iraq', *Proceedings ASIL Annual Meeting*, Vol. 98 (2004) pp. 266-269.
Genugten, W.J.M. van, 'De oorlog in Irak als bijdrage aan het hervormingsdebat binnen de VN', 97 *Militair rechtelijk tijdschrift* (2004) pp. 185-191.
Hilpold, Peter, 'Die Vereinten Nationen und das Gewaltverbot', 53 *Vereinte Nationen* (2005) pp. 81-88.

Kress, Claus, *Gewaltverbot und Selbstverteidigungsrecht nach der Satzung der Vereinten Nationen bei staatlicher Verwicklung in Gewaltakte Privater* (1995).
Leurdijk, Dick A., 'Kofi Annans pleidooi voor "radicale hervormingen" van de VN', 58 *Internationale Spectator* (2004) pp. 84-89.
Linnan, David K., 'Self-defense, necessity and U.N. collective security: United States and other views', 1 *Duke Journal of Comparative & International Law* (1991) pp. 57-123.
Murphy, Ray, 'United Nations Peacekeeping in Lebanon and Somalia, and the Use of Force', 8 *Journal of Conflict and Security Law* (2003) pp. 71-99.
Pemmaraju, Sreenivasa Rao, 'International organizations and use of force', in *Liber amicorum judge Shigeru Oda*, Vol. 2 (2002).
Penna, David R., 'The right to self-defense in the post-cold war era: the role of the United Nations', 20 *Denver Journal of International Law and Policy* (1991) pp. 41-54.
Quigley, John, 'The United Nations action against Iraq: a precedent for Israel's Arab territories?', 2 *Duke Journal of Comparative & International law* (1992) pp. 195-228.
Thomas, F., 'VN "Rules of Engagement": een strafrechtelijke benadering', in G.J.M. Corstens en M.S. Groenhuijsen, eds., *Rede en recht: opstellen ter gelegenheid van het afscheid van Prof. mr. N. Keijzer van de Katholieke Universiteit Brabant* (2000).
Tomuschat, Christian, 'Das Völkerrecht und die Rolle der Vereinten Nationen', in Helmut König, Manfred Sicking, eds., *Der Irak-Krieg und die Zukunft Europas* (2004).
Tsagourias, Nicholas, 'The Shifting Laws on the Use of Force and the Trivialization of the UN Collective Security System: the Need to Reconstitute it', *Netherlands Yearbook of International Law*, Vol. 34 (2004) pp. 55-87.
Vitucci, Maria Chiara, 'Has Pandora's Box Been Closed?: the Decisions on the Legality of Use of Force Cases in Relation to the Status of the Federal Republic of Yugoslavia (Serbia and Montenegro) within the United Nations', 19 *Leiden Journal of International Law* (2006) pp. 105-127.
Weller, Marc, 'The United Nations and the jus ad bellum', in Peter Rowe, ed., *The Gulf War 1990-91 in International and English Law* (1993).

5.2 UN Charter: Article 2(4) and Article (51)

Baker, Mark B., 'Terrorism and the inherent right of self-defense: a call to amend article 51 of the United Nations Charter', 10 *Houston Journal of International Law* (1987) pp. 25-49.
Ben Achour, Rafaa, 'Les opérations de maintien de la paix', in J.P. Coet and A. Pellet, eds., *La Charte des Nations Unies* (2005) pp. 265-286.
Bothe, Michael, 'Has Article 2(4) survived the Iraq War?', in Michael Bothe, et al., eds., *Redefining Sovereignty: the Use of Force after the Cold War* (2005).
Cassese, A., 'Commentaire de l'article 51 de la Charte', in J.P. Cot and A. Pellet, eds., *La Charte des Nations Unies* (2005) pp. 1335-1336.
Constantinou, Avra, *The right of self-defence under customary International law and article 51 of the United Nations Charter* (2000).
Cot, Jean-Pierre, *La Charte des Nations Unies: commentaire article par article*, 3rd edn., 2005.
Dörr, Oliver, 'Das völkerrechtliche Gewaltverbot am Beginn des 21. Jahrhunderts – Was bleibt von Art. 2(4) UN-Charta?', in Oliver Dörr, ed., *Ein Rechtslehrer in Berlin: Symposium für Albrecht Randelzhofer* (2004).
Elliott, Kathryn S., 'The new world order and the right of self-defense in the United Nations Charter', 15 *Hastings International and Comparative Law Review* (1991) pp. 55-81.
Ezdi, A., 'Self defence and article 51 of the United Nations charter: a critical analysis', 27 *Pakistan Horizon* (1974) pp. 29-51.

Goodrich, Leland M., Hambro, E., *Charter of the United Nations: commentary and documents,* 3rd edn. (1969).
Greig, D.W., 'Self-defense and the Security Council: what does Article 51 require?', 40 *The International and Comparative Law quarterly* (1991) pp. 366-402.
Grzeszick, Bernd, 'Die Staatsgewalt in der UN-Charta zwischen Gewaltverbot und Selbstverteidigungsrecht', 41 *Archiv des Völkerrechts* (2003) pp. 484-505.
Hilderbrand, Robert C., *Dumbarton Oaks: the origins of the United Nations and the search for postwar security* (1990).
Holman, O., 'De volkenrechtelijke implikaties van de militaire operatie van de Verenigde Staten in Iran: (zelfverdediging volgens artikel 51 van het Handvest der Verenigde Naties of onrechtmatige daad?)', 31 *Ars Aequi* (1982) pp. 576-580.
Kammerhofer, Jörg, 'Uncertainties of the Law on Self-defence in the United Nations Charter', *Netherlands Yearbook of International Law*, Vol. 35 (2004) pp. 143-204.
Kearley, Timothy, 'Regulation of preventive and preemptive force in the United Nations Charter: a search for original intent', 3 *Wyoming Law Review* (2003) pp. 663-733.
King, Matthew Scott, 'The legality of the United States war on terror: is Article 51 a legitimate vehicle for the war in Afghanistan or just a blanket to cover-up International war crimes', 9 *ILSA Journal of International and Comparative Law* (2003) pp. 457-472.
MacCormack, Timothy L.H., 'Anticipatory self-defence in the legislative history of the United Nations charter', 25 *Israeli Law Review* (1991) pp. 1-42.
Papisca, Antonio, 'Article 51 of the United Nations Charter: Exception or General Rule?: the Nightmare of the Easy War', 2 *Pace Diritti Umani* (2005) pp. 13-28.
Plofchan, Thomas K., 'Article 51: limits on self-defense?', 13 *Michigan Journal of International Law* (1992) pp. 336-373.
Preiser, Simone, '"Operation enduring freedom" and the UN Charter: the terrorist attack of 11 September 2001 and the subsequent military response', *International Peacekeeping*, Vol. 8 (2004) pp. 213-240.
Roberts, Guy B., 'The UN Charter paradigm on the brink: the legal and Policy predicates for use of force against Iraq', 42 *Revue de Droit Militaire et de Droit de la Guerre* (2003) pp. 441-458.
Rowles, James P., '"Secret Wars", Self-Defense and the Charter – A Reply to Professor Moore', 80 *American Journal of International Law* (1986) pp. 568-583.
Simma, Bruno, *The charter of the United Nations: a commentary*, 2nd edn. (2002).
Stahn, Carsten, '"Nicaragua is dead, long live Nicaragua": the Right to Self-defence under Art. 51 UN Charter and International Terrorism', in Christian Walter, et al., eds., *Terrorism as a Challenge for national and International Law: Security versus Liberty?* (2004).
Stettinius, Edward R. Jr., *Charter of the United Nations: report to the President on the results of the San Francisco conference by the chairman of the United States delegation, the Secretary of State [June 26, 1945]* (1945).
Visser, Aukje W., *The right of self-defence against terrorism based upon article 51 of the United Nations Charter* (1987).

5.3 **Security Council**

Brunnée, Jutta, 'The Security Council and Self-Defence: which Way to Global Security?', in Niels Blokker & Nico Schrijver, eds., *The Security Council and the Use of Force: Theory and Reality: a Need for Change?* (2005).
Cronin-Furman, Kathleen Renée, 'The International Court of Justice and the United Nations Security Council: Rethinking a Complicated Relationship', 106 *Columbia Law Review* (2006) pp. 435-463.

Fassbender, Bardo, 'The UN Security Council and International Terrorism', in Andrea Bianchi, ed., *Enforcing International Law Norms against Terrorism* (2004).
Future Implications of the Iraq Conflict (American Society of International Law 2004).
Gardner, Richard N., 'The Fall of Saddam Hussein: Security Council Mandates and Preemptive Self-Defense', in *Future Implications of the Iraq Conflict* (American Society of International Law 2004).
Higgins, Rosalyn, 'The UN Security Council and the individual state', in Hazel Fox, ed., *The changing constitution of the United Nations* (1997).
MacLaughlin, Rob, 'An Assessment of the Authority for Australia to Use Force under United Nations Security Council Resolutions concerning Iraq', 51 *Naval Law Review* (2005) pp. 252-288.
Oellers-Frahm, Karin, 'The International Court of Justice and Article 51 of the UN Charter', in Klaus Dicke, et al., eds., *Weltinnenrecht: liber amicorum Jost Delbrück* (2005).
Papastavridis, Efthymios, 'Security Council Resolutions 1368/2001 and 1373/2001: collective security or the right of self-defence?', 55 *Revue Hellénique de Droit International* (2002) pp. 501-512.
Pedigo, Jason, 'Rogue states, weapons of mass destruction, and terrorism: was Security Council approval necessary for the invasion of Iraq?', 32 *Georgia Journal of International and Comparative Law* (2004) pp. 199-229.
Piotrowicz, Ryszard, 'The Easter Bunny, the Tooth Fairy, Santa Claus and the Security Council: a Heart of Darkness at the ICJ in Democratic Republic of Congo v. Uganda', 80 *Australian Law Journal* (2006) pp. 162-166.
Tomuschat, Christian, 'Der Sicherheitsrat ist gestärkt', in Kai Ambos, Jörg Arnold, eds., *Der Irak-Krieg und das Völkerrecht* (2004).
White, Nigel D., 'Self-Defence, Security Council Authority and Iraq', in Richard Burchill, Nigel D. White and Justin Morris, eds., *International Conflict and Security Law: Essays in Memory of Hilaire McCoubrey* (2005).

5.4 ICJ Case Law

Andaluz, Horacio, *Coercive international action, a task for the International Court of Justice: the case of the attack on Iraq* (2003).
Andaluz, Horacio, *La acción coercitiva internacional, una tarea para la Corte Internacional de Justicia: a propósito de la agresión a Iraq* (2003).
Bekker, Peter H.F., 'Oil Platforms (Iran v. United States), Preliminary Objection, Judgment. International Court of Justice, December 12, 1996', 91 *American Journal of International Law* (1997) pp. 518-523.
Carlowitz, Leopold von, 'The "Oil Platforms" Case Before the International Court of Justice: a Contribution to the Present Debate on Self-Defense', 15(2) *Schweizerische Zeitschrift für Internationales und europäisches Recht* (2005) pp. 245-280.
Carnerero Castilla, Rubén, 'Libertad de comercio, uso de la fuerza y legítima defensa: la sentencia de la Corte Internacuional de Justicia de 6 de noviembre de 2003 en el asunto de la plataformas petrolíferas (República Islámica de Irán c. Estados Unidos de América)', 2 *Cuadernos de jurisprudencia internacional* (2005) pp. 45-69.
Cronin-Furman, Kathleen Renée, 'The International Court of Justice and the United Nations Security Council: Rethinking a Complicated Relationship', 106 *Columbia Law Review* (2006) pp. 435-463.
Foster, Caroline E., 'The Oil Platforms Case and the Use of Force in International Law', 17 *Singapore Journal of International & Comparative Law* (2003) pp. 579-588.
Foster, Caroline E., *The Oil Platforms Case and the Use of Force in International Law* (2003).

García Rico, Elena, 'La legítima defensa en el Derecho internacional contemporáneo: ¿algo nuevo bajo el sol tras la Sentencia de la CIJ sobre el asunto de las plataformas petrolíferas?", 55 *Revista Española de Derecho Internacional* (2004) pp. 819-838.

Gattini, Andrea, 'La legittima difensa nel nuovo secolo: la sentenza della Corte internazionale di giustizia nell'affare delle piatforme petrolifere', 87 *Rivista di Diritto Internazionale* (2004) pp. 147-170.

Kammerhofer, Jörg, 'Oil's Well that Ends Well?: Critical Comments on the Merits Judgement in the Oil Platform Case', 17 *Leiden Journal of International Law* (2004) pp. 695-718.

Kaye, David, 'Adjudicating Self-Defense', 22 *Merkourios*, special edn. (no. 59) (2004), pp. 55-63.

Kelly, Michael J., 'Critical Analysis of the International Court of Justice Ruling on Israel's Security Barrier', 28 *Fordham International Law Journal* (2005) pp. 181-228.

Kooijmans, P.H., 'De rol van recht en rechtspraak in een roerige wereld', 57 *Internationale Spectator* (2003) pp. 59-63.

Kritsiotis, Dino, 'Case concerning oil platforms (Islamic Republic of Iran v. United States of America)', 8 *International Journal of marine and coastal Law* (1993) pp. 507-509.

Kwiatkowska, Barbara, 'Case concerning Oil Platforms (Islamic Republic of Iran v. United States of America)', *Hague Yearbook of International Law*, Vol. 9 (1996) pp. 55-75.

Laursen, Andreas, 'The Judgment by the International Court of Justice in the Oil Platforms Case', 73 *Nordic Journal of International Law* (2004) pp. 135-160.

Linnan, David K., 'Iran Air Flight 655 and Beyond: Free Passage, Mistaken Self-defence, and State Responsibility', 16 *Yale Journal of International Law* (1991) pp. 245-389.

McKinnon, Fiona, 'Reprisals as a Method of Enforcing International Law', 4 *Leiden Journal of International Law* (1991) pp. 221-248.

Modabber, Zia, 'Collective Self-Defense: Nicaragua *v.* United States', 10 *Loyola of Los Angeles International and Comparative Law Journal* (1988) pp. 449-468.

Murphy, Sean D., 'Self-Defense and the Israeli Wall Advisory Opinion: an IPSE Dixit from the ICJ?', 99 *American Journal of International Law* (2005) pp. 62-76.

Oellers-Frahm, Karin, 'The International Court of Justice and Article 51 of the UN Charter', in Klaus Dicke, et al., eds., *Weltinnenrecht: liber amicorum Jost Delbrück* (2005).

Piotrowicz, Ryszard, 'The Easter Bunny, the Tooth Fairy, Santa Claus and the Security Council: a Heart of Darkness at the ICJ in Democratic Republic of Congo v. Uganda', 80 *Australian Law Journal* (2006) pp. 162-166.

Pogany, Istvan, 'Nuclear weapons and self-defence in International law', *Nuclear weapons and International Law* (1987).

Raab, Dominic, '"Armed Attack" after the Oil Platforms Case', 17 *Leiden Journal of International Law* (2004) pp. 719-735.

Rishikof, Harvey, 'When naked came the Doctrine of "Self-Defense": what is the proper Role of the International Court of Justice', 29 *The Yale Journal of International Law* (2004) pp. 331-342.

Rostow, Eugene V., 'Disputes involving the inherent right of self-defense', *The International Court of Justice at a crossroads* (1987).

Rostow, Nicholas, 'Nicaragua and the Law of Self-Defense Revisited', 11 *The Yale Journal of International Law* (1986) pp. 437-461.

Scobbie, Iain, 'Words my Mother never taught me: "In Defense of the International Court"', 99 *American Journal of International Law* (2005) pp. 76-88.

Sohn, Louis B., 'The International Court of Justice and the scope of the right of self-defence and the duty of non-intervention', in Y. Dinstein, ed., *International Law at a time of perplexity: essays in honour of Shabtai Rosenne* (1989).

Taft, William H., 'Self-Defense and the "Oil Platforms" Decision', 29 *The Yale Journal of International Law* (2004) pp. 295-306.

Vitucci, Maria Chiara, 'Has Pandora's Box Been Closed?: the Decisions on the Legality of Use of Force Cases in Relation to the Status of the Federal Republic of Yugoslavia (Serbia and Montenegro) within the United Nations', 19 *Leiden Journal of International Law* (2006) pp. 105-127.

Young, Stewart M., 'Destruction of Property (on an International Scale): the Recent Oil Platforms Case and the International Court of Justice's Inconsistent Commentary on the Use of Force by the United States', 30 *North Carolina Journal of International Law and Commercial Regulation* (2004) pp. 335-377.

6. Non-State Entities

6.1 Private Actors

Kress, Claus, *Gewaltverbot und Selbstverteidigungsrecht nach der Satzung der Vereinten Nationen bei staatlicher Verwicklung in Gewaltakte Privater* (1995).

Ruys, Tom, & Verhoeven, Sten, 'Attacks by Private Actors and the Right of Self-Defence', 10 *Journal of Conflict and Security Law* (2005) pp. 239-320.

Sicilianos, Linos-Alexandre, 'L'invocation de la légitime défense face aux activités d'entités non-étatiques', *Hague Yearbook of International Law*, Vol. 2 (1989) pp. 147-168.

6.2 Terrorism

Abraham, Garth, & Hopkins, Kevin, 'Bombing for humanity: the American response to the 11 September attacks and the plea of self-defence', 119 *The South African Law Journal* (2002) pp. 783-801.

Abu Rashid, Mansour, 'A Practioner's Thoughts about Terrorism', in Samuel Peleg and Wilhelm Kempf, eds., *Fighting Terrorism in the Liberal State: an Integrated Model of Research, Intelligence and International Law* (2006).

Addicott, Jeffrey F., 'Proposal for a new executive order on assassination', 37 *University of Richmond Law Review* (2003) pp. 751-785.

Addicott, Jeffrey F., *Terrorism Law: the rule of law and the war on terror* (2004).

Aldrich, George H., 'The Taliban, Al Qaeda, and the Determination of Illegal Combatants', 96 *American Journal of International Law* (2002) pp. 891-898.

Anghie, Antony, 'The War on Terror and Iraq in Historical Perspective', 43 *Osgoode Hall Law Journal* (2005) pp. 45-66.

Arai-Takahashi, Yutaka, 'Shifting boundaries of the right of self-defence: appraising the impact of the September 11 attacks on jus ad bellum', 36 *The International Lawyer* (2002) pp. 1081-1102.

Baker, Mark B., 'Terrorism and the inherent right of self-defense: a call to amend article 51 of the United Nations Charter', 10 *Houston Journal of International Law* (1987) pp. 25-49.

Banks, William C., & Raven-Hansen, Peter, 'Targeted killing and assassination: the U.S. legal framework', 37 *University of Richmond Law Review* (2003) pp. 667-749,

Battaglini, Giovanni, 'War against Terrorism extra moenia, Self-defence and Responsibility: a Pure Juridical Approach, in Maurizio Ragazzi', ed., *Responsibility today: Essays in Memory of Oscar Schachter* (2005).

Baufeld, Stefan, *Der 11. September 2001 als Herausforderung für das Völkerrecht* (2005).

Baxi, Upendra, 'The "War on Terror" and the "War of Terror": Nomadic Multitudes, Aggressive Incumbents, and the "New" International Law', 43 *Osgoode Hall Law Journal* (2005) pp. 7-43.

Beres, Louis R., 'The permissibility of state-sponsored assassination during peace and war', 5 *Temple International and Comparative Law Journal* (1991) pp. 231-249.
Beres, Louis René, 'After the Scud attacks: Israel, "Palestine", and anticipatory self-defense', 6 *Emory International Law Review* (1992) pp. 71-104.
Besser-Jones, Lorraine, 'Just War Theory, Legitimate Authority and the "War" on Terror', in Timothy Shahanan, ed., *Philosophy 9/11: Thinking about the War on Terrorism* (2005).
Bonafede, Michael C., 'Here, there, and everywhere: assessing the proportionality doctrine and U.S. uses of force in response to terrorism after the September 11 attacks', 88 *Cornell Law Review* (2002) pp. 155-214.
Bothe, Michael, 'Terrorism and the legality of pre-emptive force', 14 *European Journal of International Law* (2003) pp. 227-240.
Boyle, Francis A., 'The Outstanding crisis between the United States and Libya over International terrorism', in H. Köchler, ed., *Terrorism and national liberation* (1988).
Broom, Mia, *Dying to Kill. The Allure of Suicide Terror* (2005).
Bruha, Thomas, & Tams, Christian J., 'Self-Defence against Terrorist Attacks: Considerations in the Light of the ICJ's "Israeli Wall" Opinion', in Klaus Dicke, et al., eds., *Weltinnenrecht: liber amicorum Jost Delbrück* (2005).
Brunnée, Jutta, & Toope, Stephen J., 'The Use of Force: International Law After Iraq', 53 *The International and Comparative Law Quarterly* (2004) pp. 785-806.
Byers, Michael, 'Terrorism, the use of force and International law after 11 September 2001', 51 *The International and Comparative Law quarterly* (2002) pp. 401-414.
Canestaro, Nathan, 'American law and Policy on assassinations of foreign leaders: the practicality of maintaining the status quo', 26 *Boston College International and Comparative Law Review* (2003) pp. 1-34.
Canor, Iris, 'When Jus ad Bellum Meets Jus in Bello: the Occupier's Right of Self-Defence Against Terrorism Stemming from Occupied Territories', 19 *Leiden Journal of International Law* (2006) pp.129-149.
Carpenter, G., 'The south African raid on terrorist bases in Lesotho', *South African Yearbook of International Law*, Vol. 8 (1982) pp. 154-161.
Charney, Jonathan I., 'The use of force against terrorism and International law', 95 *American Journal of International Law* (2001) pp. 835-839.
Cohan, John Alan, 'Formulation of a state's response to terrorism and state-sponsored terrorism", 14 *Pace International Law Review* (2002) pp. 77-119.
Dahinden, Erwin, 'Terrorism: military and legal challenges', *International Peacekeeping*, Vol. 8 (2004) pp. 315-331.
Dederer, Hans-Georg, 'Krieg gegen Terror', 59 *Juristenzeitung* (2004) pp. 421-431.
Delbrück, Jost, 'The fight against global terrorism: self-defense or collective security as International police action?: some comments on the International legal implications of the "war against terrorism"', *German Yearbook of International Law*, Vol. 44 (2002) pp. 9-24.
Dinstein, Yoram, 'Ius ad bellum Aspects of the "War on Terrorism"', in Wybo P. Heere, ed., *Terrorism and the Military: International Legal Implications* (2003).
Downes, Chris, '"Targeted Killings" in an Age of Terror: the Legality of the Yemen Strike', 9 *Journal of Conflict and Security Law* (2004) pp. 277-294.
Drumbl, Mark, 'Self-defense in an age of terrorism', Proceedings ASIL annual meeting, Vol. 97 (2003) pp. 141-152.
Dunlap, Ben N., 'State Failure and the Use of Force in the Age of Global Terror', 27 *Boston College International and Comparative Law Review* (2004) pp. 453-475.
Dunn, David Hastings, 'Bush, 11 September and the Conflicting Strategies of the "War on Terrorism"', 16 *Irish Studies in International Affairs* (2005) pp. 11-33.

Eisemann, Pierre Michel, 'Attaques du 11 septembre et exercise d'un droit naturel de légitime défense', in Karine Banneier, et al., eds., *Le droit International face au terrorisme* (2003).
Fassbender, Bardo, 'The UN Security Council and International Terrorism', in Andrea Bianchi, ed., *Enforcing International Law Norms against Terrorism* (2004).
Feinstein, Barry A., 'A Paradigm for the Analysis of the Legality of the Use of Armed Force Against Terrorist and States that Aid and Abet Them', 17 *The Transnational Lawyer* (2004) pp. 51-81.
Feinstein, Barry A., 'Combating Terrorism through International Law', in Samuel Peleg and Wilhelm Kempf, eds., *Fighting Terrorism in the Liberal State: an Integrated Model of Research, Intelligence and International Law* (2006).
Feinstein, Barry A., 'Operation Enduring Freedom: legal dimensions of an infinitely just operation', 11 *Journal of Transnational Law and Policy* (2002) pp. 201-295.
Fernández Tomás, Antonio Francisco, 'El recurso al artículo del Tratado de Washington tras los acontecimientos del 11 septiembre: mucho ruido y pocas nueces', 53 *Revista Española de Derecho Internacional* (2001) pp. 205-226.
Fitzpatrick, Joan, 'Speaking law to power: the war against terrorism and human rights', 14 *European Journal of International Law* (2003) pp. 241-264.
Franck, Thomas M., *Recourse to force: state action against threats and armed attacks* (2002).
Franck, Thomas M., 'Terrorism and the right of self-defense', 95 *American Journal of International Law* (2001) pp. 839-843.
Frigessi di Rattalma, Marco, 'War in Afghanistan, Self Defence and Questions of Attribution of the September 11 Attacks to the Afghan-Taliban Regime', *The Italian Yearbook of International Law*, Vol. 13 (2005) pp. 59-75.
Frun, David and Richard Perle, *An End to Evil. How to Win the War on Terror* (2003).
Futterman, Stanley N., 'Law and Justice in the Response to 9/11', in Yassin El-Ayouty, ed., *Perspectives on 9/11* (2004).
Gardner, Hall, *American global strategy and the "war on terrorism"* (2005).
Gill, T.D., *The 11th of September and the International law of military operations* (2002).
Gill, T.D., 'The Eleventh of September and the Right of Self-Defense', in Wybo P. Heere, ed., *Terrorism and the Military: International Legal Implications* (2003).
González Vega, Javier A., 'Los atentados del 11 de septiembre, la operación "Libertad Duradera" y el derecho de legítima defensa', 53 *Revista Española de Derecho Internacional* (2001) pp. 247-271.
Gray, Christine, 'A New War for a New Century?: the Use of Force against Terrorism after Septemeber 11, 2001', in Paul Eden and Thérèse O'Donnell, eds., *September 11, 2001: a Turning Point in International and Domestic Law* (2005).
Greenwood, Christopher, 'International law and the "war against terrorism"', 78 *International affairs* (2002) pp. 301-317.
Greenwood, Christopher, *War, terrorism and International Law* (2003).
Gross, Emanuel, 'The laws of war waged between democratic states and terrorist organizations: real or illusive', 15 *Florida Journal of International Law* (2003) pp. 389-480.
Gross, Emanuel, 'Thwarting terrorist acts by attacking the perpetrators or their commanders as an act of self-defense: human rights versus the state's duty to protect its citizens', 15 *Temple International and Comparative Law Journal* (2001) pp. 195-246.
Guiora, Amos, 'Targeted Killing as Active Self-Defense', 36 *Case Western Reserve Journal of International Law* (2004) pp. 319-334.
Haer, Roger Cooling, 'The Gulf of Sidra', 24 *San Diego Law Review* (1987) pp. 751-767.
Halberstam, Malvina, 'The U.S. Right to use Force in Response to the Attacks on the Pentagon and the World Trade Center', in Yassin El-Ayouty, ed., *Perspectives on 9/11* (2004).
Hannikainen, Lauri, 'The world after 11 September 2001: is the prohibition of the use of force disintegrating?', in Jarna Petman & Jan Klabbers, eds., *Nordic cosmopolitanism* (2003).

'Headscarf, the reason for kidnapping', *De Telegraaf* (30.8.2004).
Heintschel von Heinegg, Wolff, 'The Legality of Maritime Interception Operations Within the Framework of Operation Enduring Freedom', in Wybo P. Heere, ed., *Terrorism and the Military: International Legal Implications* (2003).
Heisbourg, François, Odile Jacob, *Hyperterrorisme: la nouvelle guerre* (2001).
Holcomb, M. Scott, 'Operation Enduring Freedom: the use of force in self-defense against Al Qaida and the Taliban', 10 *Houston Journal of International Law* (1987) pp. 25-49.
Hovell, Devika, 'Chinks in the Armour: International Law, Terrorism and the Use of Force', 27 *University of New South Wales Law Journal* (2004) pp. 398-427.
Ibáñez Muñoz, Josep, 'El desafío a la Pax Americana desde el 11 de septiembre de 2001', in Caterina García Segura, Angel J. Rodrigo Hernández, eds., *El imperio inviable: el orden internacional tras el conficto de Irak* (2004).
Janse, Daniel, 'International Terrorism and Self-Defense', *Israel Yearbook on Human Rights*, Vol. 36 (2006) pp. 149-180.
Kegley, Charles W., & Raymond, Gregory A., 'Global terrorism and military preemption: Policy problems and normative perils', 41 *International Politics* (2004) pp. 37-49.
Khan, Rahmatullah, 'The War on Terrorism', 45 *Indian Journal of International Law* (2005) pp. 1-16.
King, Matthew Scott, 'The legality of the United States war on terror: is Article 51 a legitimate vehicle for the war in Afghanistan or just a blanket to cover-up International war crimes', 9 *ILSA Journal of International and Comparative Law* (2003) pp. 457-472.
Kotzur, Markus, '"Krieg gegen den Terrorismus": politische Rhetorik oder neue Konturen des "Kriegsbegriffs" im Völkerrecht?', 40 *Archiv des Völkerrechts* (2002) pp. 454-479.
Kretzmer, David, 'Targeted Killing of Suspected Terrorists: Extra-Judicial Executions or Legitimate Means of Defence?', 16 *European Journal of International Law* (2005) pp. 171-212.
Kühn, T.M., 'Terrorism and the right of self-defence', *South African Yearbook of International Law*, Vol. 6 (1980) pp. 42-52.
Lee, Win-Chiat, 'Terrorism and Universal Jurisdiction', in Steven P. Lee, ed., *Intervention, Terrorism, and Torture: Contemporary Challenges to Just War* (2007).
Leffler, Melvyn P., '9/11 and the past and future of American foreign Policy', 79 *International Affairs* (2003) pp. 1045-1063.
Leurdijk, Dick A., 'NATO's Shifting Priorities: From Peace Support Operations to Counter-Terrorism', in Thierry Tardy, ed., *Peace Operations After 11 September 2001* (2004).
Leurdijk, Dick, 'The US after 9/11: the Exercise of its Inherent Right of Individual and Collective Self-Defence', in Alfred van Staden, Jan Rood, Hans Labohm, eds., *Cannons and Canons: Clingendael Views of Global and Regional Politics* (2003).
Lietzau, William K., 'Old Laws, New Wars: Jus ad Bellum in an Age of Terrorism', *Max Planck Yearbook of United Nations Law*, Vol. 8 (2005) pp. 383-455.
Lohr, Michael Franklin, 'Legal analysis of U.S. military responses to state-sponsored international terrorism, 34 *Naval Law Review* (1985) pp. 1-48.
MacCredie, Jeffrey Allen, 'The April 14, 1986 bombing of Libya: act of self-defense or reprisal?', 19 *Case Western Reserve Journal of International Law* (1987) pp. 215-242.
Macleod, Alistair M., 'The War against Terrorism and the "War" against Terrorism', in Steven P. Lee, ed., *Intervention, Terrorism, and Torture: Contemporary Challenges to Just War* (2007).
MacWhinney, Edward, *The September 11 terrorist attacks and the invasion of Iraq in contemporary International law: opinions on the emerging new world order system* (2004).
Mahmoudi, Said, 'Self-Defence and International Terrorism', *Scandinavian Studies in Law* Vol. 48 (2005) pp. 203-213.

Maogoto, Jackson Nyamuya, *Battling terrorism: legal perspectives on the use of force and the war on terror* (2005).

Margulies, Peter, 'Making "Regime Change" multilateral: the War on Terror and Transitions to Democracy', 32 *Denver Journal of International Law and Policy* (2004) pp. 389-420.

May, Larry, 'Humanity, Prisoners of War and Torture', in Steven P. Lee, ed., *Intervention, Terrorism, and Torture: Contemporary Challenges to Just War* (2007).

McWhinney, Edward, 'International law-based responses to the September 11 International terrorist attacks', 1 *Chinese Journal of International Law/Chinese Society of International Law* (2002) pp. 280-286.

Miller, Rory, 'From 11 September 2001 to the War in Iraq: Irish Responses to the Global "War on Terrorism"', 16 *Irish Studies in International Affairs* (2005) pp. 155-174.

Motshabi, Khanya, 'International law and the United States raid on Libya', 104 *The South African Law Journal* (1987) pp. 669-683.

Moyano Bonilla, César, 'La represión del terrorismo mediante el derecho internacional', 102 *Universitas* (2001) pp. 107-161.

Müllerson, Rein, 'Jus ad bellum and International terrorism', *Israel Yearbook on Human Rights*, Vol. 32 (2003) pp. 1-51.

Naert, Frederik, 'The Impact of the Fight against International Terrorism on the Ius ad Bellum after "11 September"', 43 *Revue de Droit Militaire et de Droit de la Guerre*, Vol. 43, 2004, pp. 55-107.

Nathanson, Stephen, 'Terrorism and the Ethics of War', in Steven P. Lee, ed., *Intervention, Terrorism, and Torture: Contemporary Challenges to Just War* (2007).

O'Brien, William V, 'Reprisals, deterrence and self-defense in counterterror operations', 30 *Virginia Journal of International Law* (1990) pp. 421-478.

O'Connell, Mary Ellen, 'Lawful and Unlawful Wars against Terrorism', in Ved P. Nanda, ed., *Law in the War on International Terrorism* (2005).

O'Connell, Mary Ellen, 'Lawful self-defense to terrorism', 63 *University of Pittsburgh Law Review* (2002) pp. 889-908.

Oeter, Stefan, 'Terrorismus und Menschenrechte', 40 *Archiv des Völkerrechts* (2002) pp. 422-453.

Paasche, Franz W., 'The use of force in combatting terrorism', 25 *Columbia Journal of Transnational Law* (1987) pp. 377-402.

Pearson, Frederic, 'A global declaration of war on terrorism, building alliances and defining victory', 10 *Journal of International Law and practice* (2001) pp. 578-588.

Pedigo, Jason, 'Rogue states, weapons of mass destruction, and terrorism: was Security Council approval necessary for the invasion of Iraq?', 32 *Georgia Journal of International and Comparative Law* (2004) pp. 199-229.

Peleg, S., et al., eds., *Fighting Terrorism in the Liberal State: an Integrated Model of Research, Intelligence and International Law* (2006).

Ramón Chornet, Consuelo, 'La lucha contra el terrorismo internacional después del 11 de septiembre de 2001', 53 *Revista Española de Derecho Internacional* (2001) pp. 273-288.

Regourd, Serge, 'Raids anti-terroristes et développement récents des atteintes illicites au principe de non-intervention', *Annuaire Français de Droit International*, Vol. 32 (1987) pp. 79-103.

Remiro Brotóns, Antonio, 'Terrorismo, mantenimiento de la paz y nuevo orden', 53 *Revista Española de Derecho Internacional* (2001) pp. 125-171.

Rigoulet-Roze, David, 'Une notion problématique pour le droit International contemporain, celle de "guerre contre le terrorisme": la première guerre "mondialisée" du genre?', 45 *Droit et Cultures* (2003) pp. 213-240.

Roberts, Adam, 'The laws of war in the war on terror', *Israel Yearbook on Human Rights*, Vol. 32 (2003) pp. 193-245.
Roberts, Guy B., 'Self-help in combatting state-sponsored terrorism: self-defense and peacetime reprisals', 19 *Case Western Reserve Journal of International Law* (1987) pp. 243-293.
Ronzitti, Natalino, 'The Legality of Covert Operations against Terrorism in Foreign States', in Andrea Bianchi, ed., *Enforcing International Law Norms against Terrorism* (2004).
Roth, Brad R.,'Terrorism and the inherent right to self defense', 10 *Journal of International Law and Practice* (2001) pp. 542-551.
Schachter, Oscar, 'The lawful use of force by a state against terrorists in another country', in Henry H. Han, ed., *Terrorism & political violence* (1993).
Schachter, Oscar, 'The lawful use of force by a state against terrorists in another country', *Israel Yearbook on Human Rights*, Vol. 19 (1990) pp. 209-231.
Schaller, Christian, *Das Friedenssicherungsrecht im Kampf gegen den Terrorismus: Gewaltverbot, kollektive Sicherheit, Selbstverteidigung und Präemption* (Stiftung Wissenschaft und Politik, Deutsches Institut für Internationale Politik und Sicherheit 2004).
Schmitt, Michael N., 'Counter-terrorism and the use of force in International Law', *Israel Yearbook on Human Rights*, Vol. 32 (2003) pp. 53-116.
Scholz, Michael, *Staatliches Selbstverteidigungsrecht gegen terroristische Gewalt* (2006).
Schonsheck, Jonathan, 'Determining Moral Rectitude in Thwarting Suicide Terrorist Attacks: Moral Terra Incognita', in Steven P. Lee, ed., *Intervention, Terrorism, and Torture: Contemporary Challenges to Just War* (2007).
Schorlemer, Sabine von, 'Human rights: substantive and institutional implications of the war against terrorism', 14 *European Journal of International Law* (2003) pp. 265-282.
Schrijver, Nico J., 'Elf September en het Internationale recht', 80(32) *Nederlands juristenblad* (2005) pp. 1688-1692.
Schrijver, Nico, 'Responding to International Terrorism: Moving the Frontiers of International Law for "Enduring Freedom"?', *The Law on Terror: Terrorism and Human Rights* (2003).
Schrijver, Nico, 'September 11 and challenges to International law', in Jane Boulden and Thomas G. Weiss, eds., *Terrorism and the UN* (2004).
Schütz, Hans Joachim, *Der völkerrechtliche Rahmen zur Bekämpfung von Flugzeugentführungen und anderen Terrorakten gegen die Internationale Zivilluftfahrt* (1975).
Simon, Jeffrey D., *Misunderstanding terrorism* (Carnegie Endowment for International Peace 1987).
Stahn, Carsten, 'International law at a crossroads?: the impact of September 11', 62 *Zeitschrift für ausländisches öffentliches Recht und Völkerrecht* (2002) pp. 183-255.
Stahn, Carsten, '"Nicaragua is dead, long live Nicaragua": the Right to Self-defence under Art. 51 UN Charter and International Terrorism', in Christian Walter, et al., eds., *Terrorism as a Challenge for national and International Law: Security versus Liberty?* (2004).
Stein, Torsten, 'Preemption and Terrorism', *International Peacekeeping*, Vol. 9 (2005) pp. 155-171.
Tantawi, Mohamed Sayyed, 'Les attentats suicides sont de la légitime défense: (8 avril 1997)', in Gérard Chaliand et Arnaud Blin, eds., *Histoire du terrorisme: de l'Antiquité à Al Qaida* (2004).
Tomuschat, Christian, 'Der 11. September 2001 und seine rechtlichen Konsequenzen', 28 *Europäische Grundrechte-Zeitschrift* (2001) pp. 535-545.
Tomuschat, Christian, *Der 11. September 2001 und seine rechtlichen Konsequenzen* (Institut für Rechtspolitik an der Universität Trier 2002).
Torr, James D., *U. S. Policy toward rogue nations* (2004).

Turner, Robert F., 'It's not really "assassination": legal and moral implications of intentionally targeting terrorists and aggressor-state regime elites', 37 *University of Richmond Law Review* (2003) pp. 787-810.
Ulfstein, Geir, 'Terrorism and the use of force', 34 *Security dialogue* (2003) pp. 153-167.
Valki, Lászlό, 'The 11 September terrorist attacks and the rules of International law', 41 *Revue de Droit Militaire et de Droit de la Guerre* (2002) pp. 111-127.
Villani, Ugo, 'Legittima difesa e lotta al terrorismo nell'operazione enduring freedom', in *Studi di diritto internazionale in onore di Gaetano Arangio-Ruiz* (2003).
Visser, Aukje W., *The right of self-defence against terrorism based upon article 51 of the United Nations Charter* (1987).
Wandscher, Christiane, *Internationaler Terrorismus und Selbstverteidigungsrecht* (2006).
Warriner, Wallace F., 'The unilateral use of coercion under International law: a legal analysis of the United States raid on Libya on april 14, 1986', 37 *Naval Law Review* (1988) pp. 49-95.
Weber, Hermann, 'Gewalt, Gegengewalt, Gewaltverbot: der Internationale Terrorismus als Herausforderung der Vereinten Nationen', 35 *Vereinte Nationen* (1987) pp. 50-55.
Weckel, Philippe, 'Coordination entre la prohibition de l'emploi de la force et les exigences de la lutte contre le terrorisme', in Enzo Cannizzaro and Paolo Palchetti, eds., *Customary International Law on the Use of Force: a Methodological Approach* (2005).
Wedgwood, R., 'Al-Qaida, Military Commissions and American Self-defence', in C. Fijnaut, J. Wouters and F. Naert, eds., *Legal Instruments in the Fight against International Terrorism: a Transatlantic Dialogue* (2004).
Wedgwood, R., 'Al Qaeda, Military Commissions and American Self-Defense', in Demetrios James Caraley, ed., *September 11, Terrorist Attacks, and U. S. Foreign Policy* (2002).
Wedgwood, R., 'Al Qaeda, Military Commissions and American Self-defense', in Paul Eden and Thérèse O'Donnell, eds., *September 11, 2001: a Turning Point in International and Domestic Law* (2005).
Wolfrum, Rüdiger. 'The attack of September 11, 2001, the wars against the Taliban and Iraq: is there a need to reconsider International law on the recourse to force and the rules in armed conflict?', *Max Planck Yearbook of United Nations Law*, Vol. 7 (2004) pp. 1-78.
Yee, Sienho, 'The potential impact of the possible US responses to the 9-11 atrocities on the law regarding the use of force and self-defence', 1 *Chinese Journal of International Law/ Chinese Society of International Law* (2002) pp. 287-293.
Yoon, Joon Hyuk, *A critical overview of International law with regard to the problem of terrorism in the aftermath of the September 11, 2001 terrorist attacks* (2003).

6.3 **Afghanistan**

Empel, Hans-Michael, 'Ist der Krieg der USA gegen Afghanistan vom Selbstverteidigungsrecht gedeckt?', *Friedensgutachten*, Vol. 2002 (2002) pp. 158-166.
Frigessi di Rattalma, Marco, 'Qualche riflessione sull'azione bellica in Afghanistan e la legittima difesa', in Antonello Calore, ed., *Seminari di storia e di diritto*, Vol. 3 (2003).
Frigessi di Rattalma, Marco, 'Qualche riflessione sull'azione bellica in Afghanistan e la legittima difesa', *Studi di diritto internazionale in onore di Gaetano Arangio-Ruiz*, Vol. 3 (2003).
Hilaire, Max, 'The laws of armed conflict, the right to self-defense, and the United States military operation against terrorism in Afghanistan', 41(1-2) *Revue de Droit Militaire et de Droit de la Guerre* (2002) pp. 103-140.
Juan, Michelle, 'Testing the legality of the attack on Afghanistan', 47 *Ateneo Law Journal* (2002) pp. 499-551.

Krajewski, Markus, 'Terroranschläge in den USA und Krieg gegen Afghanistan: welche Antworten gibt das Völkerrecht?', 34 *Kritische Justiz* (2001) pp. 363-383.
Krauthammer, Charles, 'The United States Should Attack Afghanistan to Overthrow the Taliban', in *The Rise and Fall of the Taliban* (2005).
Miller, Judith, 'Comments on the use of force in Afghanistan', 35 *Cornell International law Journal* (2002) pp. 605-610.
Paust, Jordan J., 'Use of armed force against terrorists in Afghanistan, Iraq, and beyond', 35 *Cornell International Law Journal* (2002) pp. 533-557.
Perrin de Brichambaut, Marc, 'Le recours à la force et l'emploi de la force: le cas du Kosovo et celui de l'Afghanistan', in Marc Perrin de Brichambaut, Jean-François Dobelle, eds., *Leçons de droit international public* (2002).
Quénivet, Noëlle, 'The legality of the use of force by the United States and the United Kingdom against Afghanistan', 6 *Austrian Review of International and European Law* (2003) pp. 205-240.
Schmidt-Radefeldt, Roman, 'Enduring Freedom: Antiterrorkrieg für immer?: ein Beitrag zum Ius post bellum in Afghanistan', 18 *Humanitäres Völkerrecht* (2005) pp. 245-253.

6.4 **Iraq**

Aldrich, Richard J., 'Whitehall and the Iraq War: the UK's Four Intelligence Enquiries', 16 *Irish Studies in International Affairs* (2005) pp. 73-88.
Alexander of Weedon, 'Iraq: the Pax Americana and the Law', *Yearbook of Islamic and Middle Eastern Law*, Vol. 9 (2004) pp. 3-28.
Amitai Etzioni and Jason H. Marsh, 'This is not our war: a letter from United States citizens to friends in Europe', *Rights vs. public safety after 9/11* (2003).
Andaluz, Horacio, *Coercive international action, a task for the International Court of Justice: the case of the attack on Iraq* (2003).
Andaluz, Horacio, La acción coercitiva internacional, una tarea para la Corte Internacional de Justicia: a propósito de la agresión a Iraq (2003).
Antonopoulos, Constantino, 'Some thoughts on the NATO position in relation to the Iraqi crisis', 17 *Leiden Journal of International Law* (2004) pp. 177-183,
Baxi, Upendra, 'Operation enduring freedom: towards a new International law and order?', in Antony Anghie, et al., eds., *The Third World and International order* (2003).
Beres, Louis René, 'Prosecuting Iraqi crimes against Israel during the Gulf war: Jerusalem's rights under International law', 9 *Arizona Journal of International and Comparative Law* (1992) pp. 337-360.
Bothe, Michael, 'Der Irakkrieg und das Völkerrecht: Verstoß gegen die UN-Charta oder deren Weiterentwicklung?', in Bernd W. Kubbig, ed., *Brandherd Irak: US-Hegemonialanspruch, die UNO und die Rolle Europas* (2003).
Bothe, Michael, 'Der Irak-Krieg und das völkerrechtliche Gewaltverbot', 41 *Archiv des Völkerrechts* (2003) pp. 255-271.
Brunnée, Jutta, & Toope, Stephen J., 'The Use of Force: International Law After Iraq', 53 *The International and Comparative Law Quarterly* (2004) pp. 785-806.
Byers, Michael, 'Der Irak und der Fall Caroline: Präventivkrieg und Selbstverteidigung im Völkerrecht', in Kai Ambos, Jörg Arnold, eds., *Der Irak-Krieg und das Völkerrecht* (2004).
Byers, Michael, 'The shifting foundations of International law: a decade of forceful measures against Iraq', 13 *European Journal of International Law* (2002) pp. 21-41.
Condorelli, Luigi, 'A propos de l'attaque américaine contre l'Irak du 26 juin 1993: lettre d'un professeur désemparé aux lecteurs du JEDI', 5 *European Journal of International law* (1994) pp. 134-144.

DeMello, Kevin P., 'A Method of Direct Action: the Humanitarian Justification for Regime Change in Iraq', 38 *Suffolk University Law Review* (2005) pp. 789-809.
Dinstein, Yoram, 'The Gulf War, 1990-2004 (and still counting)', *Israel Yearbook on Human Rights*, Vol. 35 (2005) pp. 1-14.
Dörr, Oliver, 'Staats- und völkerrechtliche Aspekte des Irak-Krieges 2003', 16 *Humanitäres Völkerrecht* (2003) pp. 181-188.
Feinstein, Barry A., 'A Paradigm for the Analysis of the Legality of the Use of Armed Force Against Terrorist and States that Aid and Abet Them', 17 *The Transnational Lawyer* (2004) pp. 51-81.
Ferzan, Kimberly Kessler, 'Defending imminence: from battered women to Iraq', 46 *Arizona Law Review* (2004) pp. 213-262.
Flood, Patrick J., 'A Next Rwanda?: a Next Iraq?: Military Intervention in the 21st Century', 11 *ILSA Journal of International and Comparative Law* (2005) pp. 379-393.
Franck, Thomas M., 'Legitimacy after Kosovo and Iraq', in Vesna Crníc-Grotíc, Miomir Matulovíc, eds., *International Law and the Use of Force at the Turn of Centuries: Essays in Honour of V. Degan* (2005).
García Segura, Caterina, *El imperio inviable: el orden internacional tras el conficto de Irak* (2004).
Genugten, W.J.M. van, 'De oorlog in Irak als bijdrage aan het hervormingsdebat binnen de VN', 97 *Militair rechtelijk tijdschrift* (2004) pp. 185-191.
Gill, Terry D., 'The War in Iraq and the Contemporary Jus ad Bellum', 22 *Merkourios*, special edn. (no. 59) (2004) pp. 50-54.
Greenwood, Christopher, 'The Legality of the Use of Force: Iraq in 2003', in Michael Bothe, et al., eds., *Redifining Sovereignty: the Use of Force after the Cold War* (2005).
Häußler, Ulf, 'Irak-Krieg und Völkerrecht', 46 *Neue Zeitschrift für Wehrrecht* (2004) pp. 221-233.
Iovane, Massimo, & De Vittor, Francesca, 'La doctrine européenne et l'intervention en Iraq', *Annuaire Français de Droit International*, Vol. 49 (2004) pp. 17-31.
Johnstone, Ian, 'Jus ad Bellum: the Next Iraq', 11 *ILSA Journal of International and Comparative Law* (2005) pp. 395-401.
Kaikobad, Kaiyan Homi, 'Self-defence, enforcement action and the Gulf wars, 1980-1988 and 1990-91', *British Year Book of International Law*, Vol. 63 (1993) pp. 299-366.
Kohen, Marcelo G., 'The use of force by the United States after the end of the Cold War, and its impact on International law', in Michael Byers, Georg Nolte, eds., *United States hegemony and the foundations of International Law* (2003).
'Krieg dem Irak?: Fakten, Analyse, Alternativen: eine Stellungnahme aus dem IFSH', in Kai Ambos, Jörg Arnold, eds., Auszug BWV, *Der Irak-Krieg und das Völkerrecht* (2004).
Kritsiotis, Dino, 'On the jus ad bellum and jus in bello of Operation Enduring Freedom', *Proceedings of the ... annual meeting* (2002) pp. 35-41.
Kurt, Michael E., 'Der dritte Golfkrieg aus völkerrechtlicher Sicht', 36 *Zeitschrift für Rechtspolitik* (2003) pp. 195-198.
Latifulhayat, Atip, 'Perang Irak dan hukum internasional', 3 *Jurnal hukum internasional UNPAD* (2004) pp. 70-86.
Lawrence, Robert M., 'The Preventive/Preemptive War Doctrine cannot justify the Iraq War', 33 *Denver Journal of International Law and Policy* (2004) pp. 16-30.
MacWhinney, Edward, *The September 11 terrorist attacks and the invasion of Iraq in contemporary International law: opinions on the emerging new world order system* (2004).
Mandel, Michael, 'Illegal wars and International criminal law: opinion', in Antony Anghie, et al., eds., *The Third World and International order* (2003).
Nguyen-Rouault, Florence, 'L'intervention armée en Irak et son occupation au regard du droit International', 107 *Revue Générale de Droit International Public* (2003) pp. 835-864.

Noone, Michael, 'Legal lessons from operation enduring freedom', *International Peacekeeping*, Vol. 8 (2004) pp. 241-253.

O'Connell, Mary Ellen, 'La doctrine américaine et l'intervention en Iraq', *Annuaire Français de Droit International*, Vol. 49 (2004) pp. 3-16.

O'Halpin, Eunan, 'British Intelligence and the Case for Confronting Iraq: Evidence from the Butler and Hutton Reports', 16 *Irish Studies in International Affairs* (2005) pp. 89-102.

Pedigo, Jason, 'Rogue states, weapons of mass destruction, and terrorism: was Security Council approval necessary for the invasion of Iraq?', 32 *Georgia Journal of International and Comparative Law* (2004) pp. 199-229.

Permata, Rika Ratna, 'Suata tinjauan hukum terhadap pelanggaran Piagam PBB oleh invasi Amerika Serikat ke Irak', 2 *Jurnal hukum internasional UNPAD* (2003) pp. 152-160.

Pierson, Charles, 'Preemptive Self-Defense in an Age of Weapons of Mass Destruction: Operation Iraqi Freedom', 33 *Denver Journal of International Law and Policy* (2004) pp. 150-178.

Politakis, George P., 'From action stations to action: U.S. naval deployment, "non-belligerency", and "defensive reprisals" in the final year of the Iran-Iraq war', 25 *Ocean Development and International Law* (1994) pp. 31-60.

Pollack, Kenneth M., 'Next stop Baghdad?', 81 *Foreign Affairs* (2002) pp. 32-47.

Quigley, John, 'Missiles with a message: the legality of the United States raid on Iraq's Intelligence Headquarters', 17 *Hastings International and Comparative Law Review* (1994) pp. 241-274.

Ramírez, Jorge Alberto, 'Iraq war: anticipatory self-defense or unlawful unilateralism?', 34 *California Western International Law Journal* (2003) pp. 1-27.

Reisman, W. Michael, 'The raid on Baghdad: some reflections on its lawfulness and implications', 5 *European Journal of International Law* (1994) pp. 120-133.

Sapiro, Miriam, 'Iraq: the Shifting Sands of Preemptive Self-Defense (2003)', in Larry May, Eric Rovie, and Steve Viner, eds., *The Morality of War: Classical and Contemporary Readings* (2006).

Satkunanathan, Radhika, 'The US Invasion of Iraq: "Neoconned" into an Illegal War?. a Critical Evaluation of the Bush Doctrine', 16 *Sri Lanka Journal of International Law* (2004) pp. 65-82.

Schaller, Christian, 'Massenvernichtungswaffen und Präventivkrieg: Möglichkeiten der Rechtfertigung einer militärischen Intervention im Irak aus völkerrechtlicher Sicht', in Kai Ambos, Jörg Arnold, eds., *Der Irak-Krieg und das Völkerrecht* (2004).

Simma, Bruno, 'Gefährlicher Bumerang-Effekt', in Kai Ambos, Jörg Arnold, eds., *Der Irak-Krieg und das Völkerrecht* (2004).

Slaughter, Anne-Marie, 'The Use of Force in Iraq: Illegal and Illegitimate', *Proceedings ASIL Annual Meeting*, Vol. 98 (2004) pp. 262-263.

Spiliopoulouv Åkermark, Sia, 'Storms, Foxes, and Nebulous Legal Arguments: Twelve Years of Force Against Iraq, 1991-2003', 54 *The International and Comparative Law Quarterly* (2005) pp. 221-235.

Stein, Torsten, 'The war against Iraq and the "ius ad bellum"', 42 *Revue de Droit Militaire et de Droit de la Guerre* (2003) pp. 459-465.

Streinz, Rudolf, 'Wo steht das Gewaltverbot heute?: das Völkerrecht nach demk Irakkrieg', *Jahrbuch des öffentlichen Rechts der Gegenwart* (2004) pp. 219-243.

Stromseth, Jane E., 'Law and Force After Iraq: a Transitional Moment', in *Future Implications of the Iraq Conflict: January 2004* (American Society of International Law 2004).

Stromseth, Jane E., 'Law and force after Iraq: a transitional moment', 97 *American Journal of International Law* (2003) pp. 628-642.

Taft, William H., Buchwald, Todd F., 'Preemption, Iraq, and International Law', in *Future Implications of the Iraq Conflict: January 2004* (American Society of International Law 2004).
Taft, William H., Buchwald, Todd F., 'Preemption, Iraq and International law', 97 *American Journal of International Law* (2003) pp. 557-563.
Tomuschat, Christian, 'Der Sommerkrieg des Jahres 2006 im Nahen Osten: eine Skizze', 81 *Die Friedenswarte* (2006) pp. 179-190.
Tomuschat, Christian, 'Völkerrecht ist kein Zweiklassenrecht: der Irak-Krieg und seine Folgen', 51 *Vereinte Nationen* (2003) pp. 41-46.
Volk, Daniel/Hanns-Seidel-Stiftung, 'Friedenssicherung im 21. Jahrhundert: der Irak-Krieg und seine Folgen für die Internationale Friedensordnung', in Dieter Blumenwitz, Gerd Wehrer, eds., *Völkerrechtliche Fragen der Friedenssicherung* (2003) pp.167-188.
Walker, George K., 'The lawfulness of Operation Enduring Freedom's self-defense responses', 37 *Valparaiso University Law Review* (2003) pp. 489-540.
Walker, George K., *The tanker war, 1980-1988: law and Policy* (Naval War College 2000).
Wedgwood, Ruth, 'The fall of Saddam Hussein: Security Council mandates and preemptive self-defense', 97 *American Journal of International Law* (2003) pp. 576-585.
White, Nigel D., 'Self-Defence, Security Council Authority and Iraq', in Richard Burchill, Nigel D. White and Justin Morris, eds., *International Conflict and Security Law: Essays in Memory of Hilaire McCoubrey* (2005).
Wolfrum, Rüdiger, 'The attack of September 11, 2001, the wars against the Taliban and Iraq: is there a need to reconsider International law on the recourse to force and the rules in armed conflict?', *Max Planck Yearbook of United Nations Law*, Vol. 7 (2004) pp. 1-78.
Yoo, John, 'International law and the war in Iraq', 97 *American Journal of International Law* (2003) pp. 563-576.
Yoo, John, 'International Law and the War in Iraq', in *Future Implications of the Iraq Conflict: January 2004* (American Society of International Law 2004).

7. Anticipatory Self-Defence

7.1 **Preemption**

Anderson, Richard, 'The Moral Consequences of Preemptive Strikes and Preventive War', in Timothy Shahanan, ed,, *Philosophy 9/11: Thinking about the War on Terrorism* (2005).
Anghie, Antony, 'The Bush Administration Preemption Doctrine and the United Nations', *Proceedings ASIL Annual Meeting,* Vol. 98 (2004) pp. 326-331.
Arend, Anthony Clark, 'International Law and the Preemptive Use of Military Force', in Alexander T.J. Lennon and Camille Eiss, eds., *Reshaping Rogue States: Preemption, Regime Change, and U. S. Policy toward Iran, Iraq, and North Korea* (2004).
Barela, Steven J., 'Preemptive or Preventive War: a Discussion of Legal and Moral Standards', 33 *Denver Journal of International Law and Policy* (2004) pp. 31-42.
Baxi, Upendra, 'The "War on Terror" and the "War of Terror": Nomadic Multitudes, Aggressive Incumbents, and the "New" International Law', 43 *Osgoode Hall Law Journal* (2005) pp. 7-43.
Beres, Louis René, 'After the Gulf war: Israël, pre-emption and anticipatory self-defense', 13 *Houston Journal of International Law* (1991) pp. 259-280.
Beres, Louis René, 'Preserving the third temple: Israel's right of anticipatory self-defense under International law', 26 *Vanderbilt Journal of Transnational Law* (1993) pp. 111-148.
Berman, Franklin D., 'Preemption and Weapons of Mass Destruction', *International Peacekeeping*, Vol. 9 (2005) pp. 173-182.

Blankenhorn, David, et al., eds., *The Islam/West Debate: Documents from a Global Debate on Terrorism, U. S. Policy, and the Middle East* (2005).
Bothe, Michael, 'Terrorism and the legality of pre-emptive force', 14 *European Journal of International Law* (2003) pp. 227-240.
Bradford, William C., '"The Duty to Defend Them": a Natural Law Justification for the Bush Doctrine of Preventive War', 79 *Notre Dame Law Review* (2004) pp. 1365-1492.
Breitwieser, Thomas, 'Vorweggenommene Selbstverteidigung und das Völkerrecht', 47 *Neue Zeitschrift für Wehrrecht* (2005) pp. 45-58.
Brimmer, Esther, 'L'action préventive selon George W. Bush', *Annuaire Français de Relations Internationales*, Vol. 5 (2004) pp. 679-686.
Buttlar, Christian von, 'Rechtsstreit oder Glaubensstreit?: Anmerkungen zur Debatte um die präventive Selbstverteidigung im Völkerrecht', in Jürgen Bröhmer, et al., eds., *Internationale Gemeinschaft und Menschenrechte: Festschrift Georg Ress* (2005).
Byers, Michael, 'Der Irak und der Fall Caroline: Präventivkrieg und Selbstverteidigung im Völkerrecht', in Kai Ambos, Jörg Arnold, eds., *Der Irak-Krieg und das Völkerrecht* (2004).
Cannizzaro, Enzo, 'La dottrina della guerra preventiva e la disciplina internazionale sull'uso della forza', 86 *Rivista di Diritto Internazionale* (2003) pp. 171-174.
Caron, David D., 'The Rule-Outcome Paradox, Madness Cascades and the Fog of Preemption: Seeking the "Best Rule" for Use of Force', 27 *Hastings International and Comparative Law Review* (2004) pp. 481-496.
Christakis, Théodore, 'Vers une reconnaissance de la notion de guerre préventive', in Bannelier, Karin et al., *L'intervention en Irak et le droit international* (Paris, Pedone 2004) p. 20.
Cox, Stephen J., 'Confronting Threats Through Unconventional Means: Offensive Information Warfare as a Covert Alternative to Preemptive War', 42 *Houston Law Review* (2005) pp. 881-909.
Crawford, Neta C., 'The Justice of Preemption and Preventive War Doctrines', in Mark Evans, ed., *War Theory: a Reappraisal* (2005).
Darby, Joseph J., 'Self Defense in Public International Law: the Doctrine of Pre-emption and its Discontents', in Jürgen Bröhmer, et al., eds., *Internationale Gemeinschaft und Menschenrechte: Festschrift für Georg Ress zum 70. Geburtstag* (2005).
Dershowitz, Alan M., *Preemption: a knife that cuts both ways* (2006).
Dubuisson, François, & Lagerwall, Anne, 'Que signifie encore l'interdiction de recourir à la menace de la force?', in Karine Bannelier, et al., eds., *L'intervention en Irak et le droit International* (2004).
Eckert, Amy E., *Doctrine or Doctrinaire: the First Strike Doctrine and Preemptive Self-defense under International Law* (2004).
Eick, Christophe, '"Präemption", "Prävention" und die Weiterentwicklung des Völkerrechts', 37 *Zeitschrift für Rechtspolitik* (2004) pp. 200-203.
Feinstein, Lee, 'A Duty to Prevent', *Proceedings ASIL Annual Meeting*, Vol. 98 (2004) pp. 89-94.
Fischer, Horst, 'Zwischen autorisierter Gewaldanwendung und Präventivkrieg: der völkerrechtliche Kern der Debatte um ein militärisches Eingreifen gegen den Irak', 16 *Humanitäres Völkerrecht* (2003) pp. 4-7.
Franck, Thomas M., 'Preemption, Prevention and Anticipatory Self-Defense: New Law Regarding Recourse to Force?', 27 *Hastings International and Comparative Law Review* (2004) pp. 425-435.
Franke, Peter, 'A Pre-emptive Call to Arms: questioning the Legality & Effectiveness of Pre-emptive Self-defence as a Strategic Element of US National Security & Foreign Policy', 12 *Tilburg Foreign Law Review* (2004) pp. 232-254.

Freedman, Lawrence, 'Prevention, not Pre-emption', in Alexander Höse, Kai Opperman, eds., *Die Sicherheitsstrategien Europas und der USA: transatlantische Entwürfe für eine Weltordnungspolitik* (2005).

Freedman, Lawrence, 'Prevention, not Preemption', in Alexander T.J. Lennon and Camille Eiss, eds., *Reshaping Rogue States: Preemption, Regime Change, and U.S. Policy toward Iran, Iraq, and North Korea* (2004).

Galston, William, 'The Perils of Preemptive War: (2002)', in Larry May, Eric Rovie, and Steve Viner, eds., *The Morality of War: Classical and Contemporary Readings* (2006).

Gardner, Richard N., 'The Fall of Saddam Hussein: Security Council Mandates and Preemptive Self-Defense', in American Society of International Law, ed., *Future Implications of the Iraq Conflict: January 2004* (2004).

Garwood-Gowers, Andrew, 'Pre-emptive Self-Defence: a necessary Development or the Road to International Anarchy?', *Australian Year Book of International Law*, Vol. 23 (2004) pp. 51-72.

Gathii, James Thuo, 'Assessing Claims of a New Doctrine of Pre-emptive War under the Doctrine of Sources', 43 *Osgoode Hall Law Journal* (2005) pp. 67-103.

Gordon, Avishag, '"Purity of Arms", "Preemptive War", and "Selective Targeting" in the Context of terrorism: General, Conceptual, and Legal Analysis', 29 *Studies in Conflict and Terrorism* (2006) pp. 493-508.

Guoliang, Gu, 'Redefine Cooperative Security, not Preemption', in Alexander T.J. Lennon and Camille Eiss, eds., *Reshaping Rogue States: Preemption, Regime Change, and U.S. Policy toward Iran, Iraq, and North Korea* (2004).

Henderson, Christian, 'The Bush Doctrine: from Theory to Practice', 9 *Journal of Conflict and Security Law* (2004) pp. 3-24.

Inderfurth, Karl F., 'Preemption or Partnership?: the Future of International Security', in C. Uday Bhaskar, et al., eds., *United Nations: Multilateralism and International Security* (2005).

Jervis, Robert, 'Understanding the Bush Doctrine', in Demetrios James Caraley, ed., *American Hegemony: Preventive War, Iraq, and Imposing Democracy* (2004).

Kearley, Timothy, 'Regulation of preventive and preemptive force in the United Nations Charter: a search for original intent', 3 *Wyoming Law Review* (2003) pp. 663-733.

Kegley, Charles W., & Raymond, Gregory A., 'Global terrorism and military preemption: Policy problems and normative perils', 41 *International Politics* (2004) pp. 37-49.

Kolb, Robert, 'Self-Defense and preventive War at the Beginning of the Millennium', 59 *Zeitschrift für öffentliches Recht* (2004) pp. 111-134.

Kotzur, Markus, 'Die Weltgemeinschaft im Ausnahmezustand: Politische Einheitsbildung im Zeichen der Prävention: eine Skizze', 42 *Archiv des Völkerrechts* (2004) pp. 353-388.

Kristensen, Hans M., 'Le concept de "preemption" dans la Stratégie de sécurité nationale des États-Unis', 62 *Défense nationale* (2006) pp. 46-54.

Kröning, Volker, 'Prävention oder Präemption?', 16 *Humanitäres Völkerrecht* (2003) p. 82.

Lee, Steven P., 'Preventive Intervention', in Steven P. Lee, ed., *Intervention, Terrorism, and Torture: Contemporary Challenges to Just War Theory* (2007).

Lee, Thomas H., 'International Law, International Relations Theory, and Preemptive War: the Vitality of Sovereign Equality Today', 67 *Law and Contemporary Problems* (2004) pp. 147-167.

Lepel, Oskar Matthias von, 'Die präemptive Selbstverteidigung im Lichte des Völkerrechts', 16 *Humanitäres Völkerrecht* (2003) pp. 77-81.

Lichtenberg, Judith, 'Pre-emption and Exceptionalism in U.S. Foreign Policy: Precedent and Example in the International Arena', in Thomas G. Weiss, Margaret E. Crahan, and John Gering, eds., *Wars on Terrorism and Iraq: Human Rights, Unilateralism, and U. S. Foreign Policy* (2004).

MacClelland, Justin, 'Seminar A: Humanitarian Intervention and Preemption', *International Peacekeeping*, Vol. 9 (2005) pp. 229-232.

Mbao, Melvin L.M., 'Operation Shock and Awe: its Implications for the Future of Multilateralism and International Law', 37 *The Comparative and International Law Journal of Southern Africa* (2004) pp. 253-266.

Mitchell, John B., '"Preemptive war": is it constitutional?', 44 *Santa Clara Law Review* (2004) pp. 497-527.

Müller, Harald, '"Defensive Präemption" und Raketenabwehr: Unilateralismus als Weltordnungspolitik', in Bernd W. Kubbig, ed., *Brandherd Irak: US-Hegemonialanspruch, die UNO und die Rolle Europas* (2003).

Muravchik, Joshua, 'Preemptive War against Rogue Nations is Necessary for National Security', in James D. Torr, ed., *U.S. Policy toward Rogue Nations* (2004).

Murswiek, Dietrich, 'Die amerikanische Präventivkriegsstrategie und das Völkerrecht', 56 *Neue juristische Wochenschrift* (2003) pp. 1014-1020.

Murswiek, Dietrich, 'Die amerikanische Präventivkriegsstrategie und das Völkerrecht', in Kai Ambos, Jörg Arnold, eds., *Der Irak-Krieg und das Völkerrecht* (2004).

Murswiek, Dietrich, 'The American Strategy of Pre-emptive War and International Law', *The Finnish Yearbook of International Law*, Vol. 13 (2004) pp. 183-199.

Nanda, Ved P., 'Preemptive and Preventive Use of Force, Collective Security, and Human Security', 33 *Denver Journal of International Law and Policy* (2004) pp. 7-15.

Nanda, Ved P., 'Preemptive and Preventive Use of Force, Collective Security, and Human Security', 47 *Neue Zeitschrift für Wehrrecht* (2005) pp. 45-58.

Nolte, Georg, 'Vorbeugende Gewaltanwendung und gezielte Tötungen: der Weg in eine andere Rechtsordnung', in Kai Ambos, Jörg Arnold, eds., *Der Irak-Krieg und das Völkerrecht* (2004).

Nydell, M.S., 'Tensions between International law and strategic security: implications of Israel's preemptive raid on Iraq's nuclear reactor', 24 *Virginia Journal of International Law* (1984) pp. 459-492.

Patton, Ryan, 'Federal Preemption in an Age of Globalization', 37 *Case Western Reserve Journal of International Law* (2005) pp. 111-144.

Paul, Joel R., 'The Bush Doctrine: Making or Breaking Customary International Law', 27 *Hastings International and Comparative Law Review* (2004) pp. 457-479.

Pauly, Robert J., *Strategic preemption: US foreign policy and the second Iraq war* (2005).

Pierson, Charles, 'Preemptive Self-Defense in an Age of Weapons of Mass Destruction: Operation Iraqi Freedom', 33 *Denver Journal of International Law and Policy* (2004) pp. 150-178.

Rezac, David, 'President Bush's Security Strategy and its "Pre-emptive Strikes Doctrine"': a legal basis for the war in Iraq", 7 *Austrian Review of International and European Law* (2004) pp. 223-242.

Rezai, S., *An assessment of preemptive self-defense: a critical analysis of the Bush Doctrine of preemption* (2005).

Rockefeller, Mark L, 'The "Imminent Threat" Requirement for the Use of Preemptive Military Force: is it Time for a Non-Temporal Standard?', 33 *Denver Journal of International Law and Policy* (2004) pp. 131-149.

Rouillard, Louis-Philippe, 'The Caroline Case: Anticipatory Self-defence in Contemporary International Law', in Péter Kovacs, et al., eds., *L'histoire en droit international = History in International Law: historia ante portas* (2005).

Ruf, Werner, 'Präventifkrieg: zurück nach Anarchie?', *Jahrbuch Menschenrechte* (2003) pp. 131-137.

Sapiro, Miriam, 'Iraq: the Shifting Sands of Preemptive Self-Defense', in American Society of International Law, ed., *Future Implications of the Iraq Conflict: January 2004* (2004).

Sapiro, Miriam, 'Iraq: the Shifting Sands of Preemptive Self-Defense: (2003)', in Larry May, Eric Rovie, and Steve Viner, eds., *The Morality of War: Classical and Contemporary Readings* (2006).

Sapiro, Miriam, 'Iraq: the Shifting Sands or Preemptive Self-Defense', 97 *American Journal of International Law* (2003) pp. 599-607.

Sapiro, Miriam, 'Preempting Prevention: Lessons Learned', 37 *New York University Journal of International Law and Politics* (2005) pp. 357-371.

Satkunanathan, Radhika, 'The US Invasion of Iraq: "Neoconned" into an Illegal War?: a Critical Evaluation of the Bush Doctrine', 16 *Sri Lanka Journal of International Law* (2004) pp. 65-82.

Schaller, Christian, *Das Friedenssicherungsrecht im Kampf gegen den Terrorismus: Gewaltverbot, kollektive Sicherheit, Selbstverteidigung und Präemption* (Stiftung Wissenschaft und Politik, Deutsches Institut für Internationale Politik und Sicherheit 2004).

Schennink, Ben, 'Pre-emptieve oorlog of pre-emptieve vrede?: de Nationale Veiligheidsstrategie van de Verenigde Staten: een uitdaging voor de vredesbeweging', *Jaarboek vrede en veiligheid* (2003) pp. 118-130.

Schlesinger, Stephen, 'War Against Havens for Terrorism: Examining a New Presidential Doctrine', in John Tirman, ed., *The Maze of Fear: Security and Migration After 9/11* (2004).

Schmitt, Michael N., 'Preemptive strategies in International law', 24 *Michigan Journal of International Law* (2003) pp. 513-548.

Schütze, Robert, 'Supremacy without Pre-Emption?: the very slowly Emergent Doctrine of Community Pre-Emption', 43 *Common Market Law Review* (2006) pp. 1023-1048.

Sharma, Surya P., 'The American doctrine of "pre-emptive self-defence"', 43 *Indian Journal of International Law* (2003) pp. 215-230.

Simpson, Gerry, & Wheeler, Nicholas J., 'Preemption and Exception: International Law and the Revolutionary Power', in Thomas J. Biersteker, et al., eds., *International Law and International Relations: Bridging Theory and Practice* (2007).

Slocombe, Walter B., 'Force, Pre-emption and Legitimacy', 45 *Survival* (2003) pp. 117-130.

Sofaer, Abraham D., 'On the necessity of pre-emption', 14 *European Journal of International Law* (2003) pp. 209-226.

Sofaer, Abraham D., 'Professor Franck's Lament', 27 *Hastings International and Comparative Law Review* (2004) pp. 437-445.

Stein, Torsten, 'Preemption and Terrorism', *International Peacekeeping*, Vol. 9 (2005) pp. 155-171.

Taft, William H., 'Preemptive Action in Self-Defense', *Proceedings ASIL Meeting*, Vol. 98 (2004) pp. 331-333.

Taft, William H., & Buchwald, Todd F., 'Preemption, Iraq, and International Law', in American Society of International Law, ed., *Future Implications of the Iraq Conflict: January 2004* (2004).

Tomuschat, Christian, 'Präventivkrieg zur Bekämpfung des Internationalen Terrorismus?', *Jahrbuch Menschenrechte* (2003) pp. 121-130.

Van den Hole, Leo, 'Anticipatory self-defence under International law', 19 *American University International Law Review* (2003) pp. 69-106.

Wallack, Michael, 'From Compellence to Pre-emption: Kosovo and Iraq as US Responses to Contested Hegemony', in Osvaldo Croci & Amy Verdun, eds., *The Transatlantic Divide: Foreign and Security Policies in the Atlantic Aliance from Kosovo to Iraq* (2006).

Walt, Stephen M., 'La guerre préventive: une stratégie illogique', *Annuaire Français de Relations Internationales*, Vol. 6 (2005) pp. 138-139.

Walter, Christian, 'Zwischen Selbstverteidigung und Völkerstrafrecht: Bausteine für ein Internationales Recht der "präventiven Terrorismus-Bekämpfung"', in Dieter Fleck, ed.,

Rechtsfragen der Terrorismusbekämpfung durch Streitkräfte: legal issues of military counter-terrorist operations with English executive summary (2004).
Wiefelspütz, Dieter, 'Die Zulässigkeit der Anwendung präemptiver oder präventiver militärischer Gewalt', 19 *Humanitäres Völkerrecht* (2006) pp. 103-111.
Williams, Paul R., Scott R. Lyons, & Neuwirth, Tali, 'Preemption in the 21st Century: what are the Legal Parameters?', 10 *ILSA Journal of International and Comparative Law* (2004) pp. 353-366.
Zedalis, Rex J., 'Circumstances justifying Pre-Emptive Self-Defence: Thoughts prompted by the Military Action against Iraq', 74 *Nordic Journal of International Law* (2005) pp. 209-230.
Zedalis, Rex J., 'Preliminary thoughts on some unresolved questions involving the law of anticipatory self-defense', 19 *Case Western Reserve Journal of International Law* (1987) pp. 129-175.
Zoller, Elisabeth, 'The Law Applicable to the Preemption Doctrine', *Proceedings Annual Meeting*, Vol. 98 (2004) pp. 333-337.

7.2 Bush Doctrine

Anghie, Antony, 'The Bush Administration Preemption Doctrine and the United Nations', *Proceedings ASIL Annual Meeting*, Vol. 98 (2004) pp. 326-331.
Beres, Louis René, 'The newly expanded American doctrine of preemption: can it include assassination?', 31 *Denver Journal of International Law and Policy* (2002) pp. 157-177.
Blazyca, George, 'Poland and Central Europe', in Mary Buckley, Robert Singh, eds., *The Bush doctrine and the War on Terrorism: global responses, global consequences* (2006).
Bradford, William C., '"The Duty to Defend Them": a Natural Law Justification for the Bush Doctrine of Preventive War', 79 (2004) pp. 1365-1492.
Brimmer, Esther, 'L'action préventive selon George W. Bush', *Annuaire Français de Relations Internationales*, Vol. 5 (2004) pp. 679-686.
Buckley, Mary, 'Introduction', in Mary Buckley, Robert Singh, eds., *The Bush doctrine and the War on Terrorism: global responses, global consequences* (2006).
Buckley, Mary, 'Reactions in the Russian Federation and Security in Central Asia', in Mary Buckley, Robert Singh, eds., *The Bush doctrine and the War on Terrorism: global responses, global consequences* (2006).
Cannizzaro, Enzo, 'La dottrina della guerra preventiva e la disciplina internazionale sull'uso della forza', 86 *Rivista di Diritto Internazionale* (2003) pp. 171-174.
Cohan, John Alan, 'The Bush doctrine and the emerging norm of anticipatory self-defense in customary International law', 15 *Pace International Law Review* (2003).
Crawford, Neta C., 'The Justice of Preemption and Preventive War Doctrines', in Mark Evans, ed., *Just War Theory: a Reappraisal* (2005).
Cui, Zhiyuan, 'The Bush Doctrine and Neoconservatism: a Chinese Perspective', 46 *Harvard International Law Journal* (2005) pp. 403-410.
Darby, Joseph J., 'Self Defense in Public International Law: the Doctrine of Pre-emption and its Discontents', in Jürgen Bröhmer, et al., eds., *Internationale Gemeinschaft und Menschenrechte: Festschrift Georg Ress* (2005).
Dershowitz, Alan, 'Bush Starts Off by Defying the Constitution', *Los Angeles Times* 24.1.2001.
Dolan, Chris J., *In war we trust: the Bush doctrine and the pursuit of just war* (2005).
Dunn, David Hastings, 'Bush, 11 September and the Conflicting Strategies of the "War on Terrorism"', 16 *Irish Studies in International Affairs* (2005) pp. 11-33.
Eckert, Amy E., *Doctrine or Doctrinaire: the First Strike Doctrine and Preemptive Self-defense under International Law* (2004).

Ehteshami, Anoushiravan, 'The Middle East: between Ideology and Geo-Politics', in Mary Buckley, Robert Singh, eds., *The Bush doctrine and the War on Terrorism: global responses, global consequences* (2006).

Evans, Malcolm D., 'International Law and Human Rights in a Preemptive Era', in Mary Buckley, Robert Singh, eds., *The Bush doctrine and the War on Terrorism: global responses, global consequences* (2006).

Finlan, Alastair, 'International Security', in Mary Buckley, Robert Singh, eds., *The Bush doctrine and the War on Terrorism: global responses, global consequences* (2006).

Gardner, Richard N., 'Neither Bush nor the "jurisprudes"', 97 *American Journal of International Law* (2003) pp. 585-590.

Gathii, James Thuo, 'Assessing Claims of a New Doctrine of Pre-emptive War under the Doctrine of Sources', 43 *Osgoode Hall Law Journal* (2005) pp. 67-103.

Gray, Christine, 'The Bush Doctrine Revisited: the 2006 National Security Strategy of the USA', 5 *Chinese Journal of International Law* (2006) pp. 555-578.

Gray, Christine, 'The US National Security Strategy and the new "Bush doctrine" on preemptive self-defense', 1 *Chinese Journal of International Law/Chinese Society of International Law* (2002) pp. 437-447.

Grey, Robert D., 'Africa', in Mary Buckley, Robert Singh, eds., *The Bush doctrine and the War on Terrorism: global responses, global consequences* (2006).

Gurtov, Mel, 'The Bush Doctrine in Asia', in David P. Forsythe, Patrice McMahon and Andrew Hall Wedeman, eds., *American Foreign Policy in a Globalized World* (2006).

Hancock, M. Donald, 'Western Europe', in Mary Buckley, Robert Singh, eds., *The Bush doctrine and the War on Terrorism: global responses, global consequences* (2006).

Heisbourg, François, 'A Work in Progress: the Bush Doctrine and its Consequences', in Alexander T.J. Lennon and Camille Eiss, eds., *Reshaping Rogue States: Preemption, Regime Change, and U. S. Policy toward Iran, Iraq, and North Korea* (2004).

Henderson, Christian, 'The Bush Doctrine: from Theory to Practice, 9 *Journal of Conflict and Security Law* (2004) pp. 3-24.

Jervis, Robert, 'Understanding the Bush Doctrine', in Demetrios J. Caraley, ed., *American Hegemony: Preventive War, Iraq, and Imposing Democracy* (2004).

Jervis, Robert, 'Understanding the Bush Doctrine', in Thomas Jäger, Alexander Höse, Kai Opperman, eds., *Die Sicherheitsstrategien Europas und der USA: transatlantische Entwürfe für eine Weltordnungspolitik* (2005).

Josselin, Daphne, 'The Global Economy', in Mary Buckley, Robert Singh, eds., *The Bush doctrine and the War on Terrorism: global responses, global consequences* (2006).

Kelly, Michael J., 'Time warp to 1945: resurrection of the reprisal and anticipatory self-defense doctrines in International law', 13 *Journal of Transnational Law and Policy* (2003) pp. 1-39.

Lantis, Jeffrey S., & Moskowitz, Eric, 'The Return of the Imperial Presidency?: the Bush Doctrine and U. S. Intervention in Iraq', in Ralph G. Carter, ed., *Contemporary Cases in U.S. Foreign Policy: from Terrorism to Trade* (2005).

Lawrence, Robert M., 'The Preventive/Preemptive War Doctrine cannot justify the Iraq War', 33 *Denver Journal of International Law and Policy* (2004) pp. 16-30.

Li, Rex, 'North-East Asia', in Mary Buckley, Robert Singh, eds., *The Bush doctrine and the War on Terrorism: global responses, global consequences* (2006).

Mingst, Karen A., 'The Bush Doctrine and Multilateral Institutions', in David P. Forsythe, Patrice McMahon and Andrew Hall Wedeman, eds., *American Foreign Policy in a Globalized World* (2006).

Nagan, Winston P., & Hammer, Craig, 'The new Bush National Security Doctrine and the Rule of Law', 22 *Berkeley Journal of International Law* (2004) pp. 375-438.

Noël, Pierre, 'La "doctrine Bush" et la sécurité pétrolière', 71 *Politique étrangère* (2006) pp. 243-254.
O'Connell, Mary Ellen, 'La doctrine américaine et l'intervention en Iraq', *Annuaire Français de Droit International*, Vol. 49 (2004) pp. 3-16.
O'Connor, Brendon, 'Australasia, in Mary Buckley, Robert Singh, eds., *The Bush doctrine and the War on Terrorism: global responses, global consequences* (2006).
Paul, Joel R., 'The Bush Doctrine: Making or Breaking Customary International Law', 27 *Hastings International and Comparative Law Review* (2004) pp. 457-479.
Pérez González, Manuel, 'La legítima defensa puesta en su sitio: observaciones críticas sobre la doctrina Bush de la acción preventia', 55 *Revista Española de Derecho Internacional* (2003) pp. 187-204.
Record, Jeffrey, 'The Bush Doctrine and War with Iraq', in Thomas Jäger, Alexander Höse, Kai Opperman, eds., *Die Sicherheitsstrategien Europas und der USA: transatlantische Entwürfe für eine Weltordnungspolitik* (2005).
Rezac, David, 'President Bush's Security Strategy and its "Pre-emptive Strikes Doctrine": a legal basis for the war in Iraq', 7 *Austrian Review of International and European Law* (2004) pp. 223-242.
Rezai, S., *An assessment of preemptive self-defense: a critical analysis of the Bush Doctrine of preemption* (2005).
Ryan, Stephen, 'The United Nations', in Mary Buckley, Robert Singh, eds., *The Bush doctrine and the War on Terrorism: global responses, global consequences* (2006).
Satkunanathan, Radhika, 'The US Invasion of Iraq: "Neoconned" into an Illegal War?: a Critical Evaluation of the Bush Doctrine', 16 *Sri Lanka Journal of International Law* (2004) pp. 65-82.
Schlesinger, Stephen, 'War Against Havens for Terrorism: Examining a New Presidential Doctrine', John Tirman, ed., *The Maze of Fear: Security and Migration After 9/11* (2004).
Sharma, Surya P., 'The American doctrine of "pre-emptive self-defence"', 43 *Indian Journal of International Law* (2003) pp. 215-230.
Singer, Peter, *The President of Good and Evil – Taking George W. Bush Seriously* (2004).
Singh, Robert, 'The Bush Doctrine', in Mary Buckley, Robert Singh, eds., *The Bush doctrine and the War on Terrorism: global responses, global consequences* (2006).
Thies, Cameron G., 'From Containment to the Bush Doctrine: the Road to War with Iraq', in John Davis, ed., *Presidential Policies and the Road to the second Iraq War: from forty one to forty three* (2006).
Turner, Robert F., 'American Unilateralism and the Rule of Law', in Ronald St. John Macdonald and Douglas Johnston, eds., *Towards World Constitutionalism: Issues in the Legal Ordering of the World Community* (2005).
Wall, Andru E., 'International Law and the Bush Doctrine', *Israel Yearbook on Human Rights*, Vol. 34 (2004) pp. 193-229.
Western, Jon, 'American Security, the Use of Force, and the Limits of the Bush Doctrine', in David P. Forsythe, Patrice McMahon, and Andrew Hall Wedeman, eds., *American Foreign Policy in a Globalized World* (2006).
Yasmeen, Samina, 'India and Pakistan', in Mary Buckley, Robert Singh, eds., *The Bush doctrine and the War on Terrorism: global responses, global consequences* (2006).
Zoller, Elisabeth, 'The Law Applicable to the Preemption Doctrine', *Proceedings of ASIL Annual Meeting*, Vol. 98 (2004) pp. 333-337.

8. Reprisal/Retaliation

Bacevich, Andrew J., '"A Firm and Commensurate Response": U. S. Retaliation for the Bush Assassination Attempt', in Volker C. Franke, ed., *Terrorism and Peacekeeping: New Security Challenges* (2005).
Friedlander, R.A., 'Retaliation as an anti-terrorist weapon: the Israeli Lebanon incursion and International law', *Israel Yearbook on Human Rights,* Vol. 8 (1978) pp. 63-77.
Levenfeld, B., 'Israeli counter-Fedayeen tactics in Lebanon: self-defence and reprisal under modern International law, 21 *Columbia Journal of Transnational Law* (1982) pp. 1-48.
MacCredie, Jeffrey Allen, 'The April 14, 1986 bombing of Libya: act of self-defense or reprisal?', 19 *Case Western Reserve Journal of International Law* (1987) pp. 215-242.
O'Brien, William V., 'Reprisals, deterrence and self-defense in counterterror operations', 30 *Virginia Journal of International Law* (1990) pp. 421-478.
Roberts, Guy B., 'Self-help in combatting state-sponsored terrorism: self-defense and peacetime reprisals', 19 *Case Western Reserve Journal of International Law* (1987) pp. 243-293.
Taulbee, J.L., 'Retaliation and irregular warfare in contemporary International law', 7 *The International Lawyer* (1973) pp. 195-204.

9. Humanitarian Intervention

Abiew, Francis K., 'Kosovo, Iraq and the Evolution of the Theory and practice of Humanitarian Intervention', in Osvaldo Croci & Amy Verdun, eds., *The Transatlantic Divide: Foreign and Security Policies in the Atlantic Aliance from Kosovo to Iraq* (2006).
Bagaric, Mirko, & Morss, John R., 'Transforming Humanitarian Intervention from an Expedient Accident to a Categorical Imperative', 30 *Brooklyn Journal of International Law* (2005) pp. 421-452.
Bagnoli, Carla, 'Humanitarian Intervention as a Perfect Duty: a Kantian Argument', in Terry Nardin and Melissa W. Williams, eds., *Humanitarian Intervention* (2006).
Boyle, Joseph, 'Traditional Just War Theory and Humanitarian Intervention', in Terry Nardin and Melissa W. Williams, eds., *Humanitarian Intervention* (2006).
Breau, Susan, *Humanitarian intervention: the United Nations & collective responsibility* (2005).
Carment, David, & Rowlands, Dane, 'Twisting One Arm: the Effects of Biased Intervenors', in Natalie Mychajlyszyn and Timothy M. Shaw, eds., *Twisting Arms and Flexing Muscles: Humanitarian Intervention and Peacebuilding in Perspective* (2005).
Castro-Sánchez, Claribel de, 'From Kosovo to Iraq: a New Right of Pro-Human Rights Intervention?', in Pablo Antonio Fernández-Sánchez, ed., *The New Challenges of Humanitarian Law in Armed Conflicts: in Honour of Professor Juan Antonio Carrillo-Salcedo* (2005).
Coates, Anthony, 'Humanitarian Intervention: a Conflict of Traditions', in Terry Nardin and Melissa W. Williams, eds., *Humanitarian Intervention* (2006).
Cushman, Thomas, *A Matter of Principle- Humanitarian Arguments for War in Iraq* (2005).
DeMello, Kevin P., 'A Method of Direct Action: the Humanitarian Justification for Regime Change in Iraq', 38 *Suffolk University Law Review* (2005) pp. 789-809.
Evans, Gareth, 'The Responsibility to protect: Rethinking Humanitarian Intervention', in Sten Ask and Anna Mark-Jungkvist, eds., *The Adventure of Peace: Dag Hammarskjöld and the Future of the UN* (2006).
Flauss, Jean-François, 'La primauté des droits de la personne: licéité ou illicéité de l'intervention humanitaire?', *Kosovo and the International community* (2002).
Franck, Thomas, 'Legality and Legitimacy in Humanitarian Intervention', in Terry Nardin and Melissa W. Williams, eds., *Humanitarian Intervention* (2006).

Gill, Terry D., 'Humanitarian Intervention: Legality, Justice and Legitimacy', *The Global Community* 1 (2005) pp. 51-75.
Goodman, Ryan, 'Humanitarian Intervention and Pretext for War', 100 *American Journal of International Law* (2006) pp. 107-141.
Heine, Jorge, 'The Responsibility to protect: Humanitarian Intervention and the Principle of Non-intervention in the Americas', in Ramesh Thakur, Andrew F. Cooper, and John English, eds., *International Commissions and the Power of Ideas* (2005).
Henckaerts J.M., and L. Doswald-Beck, *Customary International Humanitarian Law*: Vol. I, *Rules* (2005).
Janzekovic, John, *The use of force in humanitarian intervention: morality and practicalities* (2006).
Johnstone, Ian, 'The Plea of "Necessity" in International Legal Discourse: Humanitarian Intervention and Counter-terrorism', 43 *Columbia Journal of Transnational Law* (2005) pp. 337-388.
Karoubi, Mohammad Taghi, 'Unilateral Use of Armed Force and the Challenge of Humanitarian Intervention in International Law', *Asian Yearbook of International Law*, Vol. 10 (2005) pp. 95-124.
Kartashkin, Vladimir A., 'Humanitarian Intervention in the Globalizing World', *Baltic Yearbook of International Law*, Vol. 5 (2005) pp. 27-40.
Krajewski, Markus, 'Special Theme: Humanitarian Intervention and other Use of Force?: Preventive Use of Force and Military Actions against Non-State Actors: revisiting the Right of Self-defence in Insecure Times', *Baltic Yearbook of International Law*, Vol. 5 (2005) pp. 1-26.
Last, David, 'Twisting Arms of Shaking Hands?: How to Put Peacekeepers Out of Business', in Natalie Mychajlyszyn and Timothy M. Shaw, eds., *Twisting Arms and Flexing Muscles: Humanitarian Intervention and Peacebuilding in Perspective* (2005).
Lee, Steven P, 'Human Rights and Humanitarian Intervention', in David A. Reidy and Mortimer N.S. Seller, eds., *Universal Human Rights: Moral Order in a Divided World* (2005).
Lepard, Brian D., 'Jurying Humanitarian Intervention and the Ethical Principle of Open-minded Consultation', in Terry Nardin and Melissa W. Williams, eds., *Humanitarian Intervention* (2006).
Lu, Catherine, 'Whose Principles? Whose Institutions?: Legitimacy Challenges for "Humanitarian Intervention"', in Terry Nardin and Melissa W. Williams, eds., *Humanitarian Intervention* (2006).
MacClelland, Justin, 'Seminar A: Humanitarian Intervention and Preemption', *International Peacekeeping*, Vol. 9 (2005) pp. 229-232.
MacFarlane, S. Neil, 'International Politics, Local Conflicts and Intervention', in Natalie Mychajlyszyn and Timothy M. Shaw, eds., *Twisting Arms and Flexing Muscles: Humanitarian Intervention and Peacebuilding in Perspective* (2005).
Machielse, A.J.M., *Noodweer in het strafrecht: een rechtsvergelijkende en dogmatische studie* (VU Amsterdam 1986). Thesis.
Mani, V.S., 'Humanitarian intervention today', 313 *Recueil des cours* (2005).
Manual of the Law of Armed Conflict, The (British Ministry of Defense 2004).
Martin, Rex, 'Walzer and Rawls on Just Wars and Humanitarian Interventions', in Steven P. Lee, ed., *Intervention, Terrorism, and Torture: Contemporary Challenges to Just War Theory* (2007).
Matlary, Janne Haaland, *Values and weapons: from humanitarian intervention to regime change?* (2006).
McQueen, Carol, *Humanitarian intervention and safety zones: Iraq, Bosnia and Rwanda* (2005).

Medinger, Jason Daniel, 'The Holy See, Historicity, and Humanitarian Intervention: Using Integrative Jurisprudence to inform Contemporary Practice', 41 *Texas International Law Journal* (2006) pp. 39-66.

Mehta, Pratap Bhanu, 'From State Sovereignty to Human Security (via Institutions?)', in Terry Nardin and Melissa W. Williams, eds., *Humanitarian Intervention* (2006).

Molier, Gelijn, 'Humanitarian Intervention and the Responsibility to Protect after 9/11', 53 *Netherlands International Law Review* (2006) pp. 37-62.

Mychajlyszyn, Natalie, *Twisting arms and flexing muscles: humanitarian intervention and peacebuilding in perspective* (2005).

Nardin, Terry, *Humanitarian intervention* (2006).

Nardin, Terry, 'The Moral Basis of Humanitarian Intervention', in Stephen Chan and Cerwyn Moore, eds., *Theories of International Relations,* Vol. 2 (2006).

Norman, Richard, 'War, Humanitarian Intervention and Human Rights', in Richard Sorabji and David Rodin, eds., *The Ethics of War: Shared Problems in Different Traditions* (2006).

Orwin, Clifford, 'Humanitarian Military Intervention: Wars for the End of History?', in Ellen Frankel Paul, Fred D. Miller, Jr., and Jeffrey Paul, eds., *Justice and Global Politics* (2006).

Pawlowska, Karina, 'Humanitarian Intervention: transforming the Discourse', *International Peacekeeping* 12 (2005) pp. 487-502.

Pogge, Thomas, 'Moralizing Humanitarian Intervention: why Jurying fails and how Law can work', in Terry Nardin and Melissa W. Williams, eds., *Humanitarian Intervention* (2006).

Pradel, Jean, *Droit Penal Comparé* (2002).

Roth, Kenneth, 'War in Iraq: not a Humanitarian Intervention', in Richard Ashby Wilson, ed., *Human Rights in the "War on Terror"* (2005).

Scruton, Roger, 'National Interest and International Law', in Thomas Cushman, ed., *A Matter of Principle: Humanitarian Arguments for War in Iraq* (2005).

Seybolt, Taylor B., 'Humanitarian Military Intervention and the Quest for Legitimacy', in Henriette Riegler, ed., *Nation Building between National Sovereignty and International Intervention* (2005).

Shaw, Timothy M., 'Dilemmas of Peacekeeping at the Start of the Twenty-First Century: Conclusion', in Natalie Mychajlyszyn and Timothy M. Shaw, eds., *Twisting Arms and Flexing Muscles: Humanitarian Intervention and Peacebuilding in Perspective* (2005).

Shinko, Rosemary E., 'Postmodernism: a Genealogy of Humanitarian Intervention', in Jennifer Sterling-Folker, ed., *Making Sense of International Relations Theory* (2006).

Stacy, Helen, 'Humanitarian Intervention and Relational Sovereignty', in Steven P. Lee, ed., *Intervention, Terrorism, and Torture: Contemporary Challenges to Just War Theory* (2007).

Sulyok, Gábor, 'The Legality of Humanitarian Intervention under Traditional International Law', 46 *Acta Juridica Hungarica* (2005) pp. 221-248.

Sunga, Lyal S., 'The Role of Humanitarian Intervention in International Peace and Security: Guarantee or Threat?', in Hans Köchler, ed., *The Use of Force in International Relations: Challenges to Collective Security* (2006).

Tan, Kok-Chor, 'The Duty to protect', in Terry Nardin and Melissa W. Williams, eds., *Humanitarian Intervention* (2006).

Tan, Kok-Chor, 'The Unavoidability of Morality: a Commentary on Mehta', in Terry Nardin and Melissa W. Williams, eds., *Humanitarian Intervention* (2006).

Teson, Fernando, 'The Liberal Case for Humanitarian Intervention: (2003)', in Larry May, Eric Rovie, and Steve Viner, eds., *The Morality of War: Classical and Contemporary Readings* (2006).

Tesón, Fernando R., *Humanitarian intervention: an inquiry into law and morality*, 3rd edn. (2005).

Valek, Petr, 'Is Unilateral Humanitarian Intervention Compatible with the U.N. Charter?', 26 *Michigan Journal of International Law*, 2005, pp. 1223-1255.
Vukas, Budislav, 'Humanitarian Intervention and International Responsibility', in Maurizio Ragazzi, ed., *International Responsibility today: Essays in Memory of Oscar Schachter* (2005).
Whitman, Jim, 'Humanitarian Intervention in an Era of Pre-emptive Self-defence', 36 *Security Dialogue* (2005) pp. 259-274.
Wilkins, Burleigh, 'Humanitarian Intervention: Some Doubts: (2003)', in Larry May, Eric Rovie, and Steve Viner, eds., *The Morality of War: Classical and Contemporary Readings* (2006).
Williams, Melissa S., 'The Jury, the Law and the Primacy of Politics', in Terry Nardin and Melissa W. Williams, eds., *Humanitarian Intervention* (2006).
Wilson, Richard, *Human rights in the 'War on Terror'* (2005).
Winslow, Donna, 'Strange Bedfellows in Humanitarian Crises: NGOs and the Military', in Natalie Mychajlyszyn and Timothy M. Shaw, eds., *Twisting Arms and Flexing Muscles: Humanitarian Intervention and Peacebuilding in Perspective* (2005).
Wood, Michael C., 'Towards New Circumstances in which the Use of Force may be authorized?: the Cases of Humanitarian Intervention, Counter-Terrorism, and Weapons of Mass Destruction', in Niels Blokker & Nico Schrijver, eds., *The Security Council and the Use of Force: Theory and Reality: a Need for Change?* (2005).
Zacklin, Ralph, 'Beyond Kosovo: the United Nations and Humanitarian Intervention', 41 *Vanderbilt Journal of International Law* (2001) pp. 923-940.
Zajadlo, Jerzy, 'Humanitarian Intervention: Threat to International Order, Moral Imperative, or Customary Norm "in statu nascendi"?', *Polish Yearbook of International Law*, Vol. 27 (2006) pp. 33-48.

10. Fundamentalism and Clash of Cultures

Ali, Tariq, *The Clash of Fundamentalisms. Crusades, Jihads and Modernity* (2002).
Bassan, Tibi, *Im Schatten Allahs. Der Islam und die Menschenrechte* (2003).
Blankenhorn, David, et al., eds., *The Islam/West Debate: Documents from a Global Debate on Terrorism, U. S. Policy, and the Middle East* (2005).
Cook, David, 'The implications of "Martyrdom Operations" for Contemporary Islam', 32 *Journal of Religious Ethics* (2004) pp. 129-151.
Cook, David, *Understanding Jihad* (2005).
Darlympkc, Theodore, 'When Islam Breaks Down', in Theodore Darlymple, ed., *Our Culture, What's left of it* (2004).
Dershowitz, Alan, *Shouting Fire. Civil Liberties in a Turbulent Age* (2002).
Donnelly, Jack, 'Cultural Relativism and Universal Human Rights', 6 *Human Rights Quarterly* (1984) pp. 400-419.
Esposito, John L., *Unholy War. Terror in the Name of Islam* (2002).
Fareed, Zakaria, 'The Islamic Exception', in Fareed Zakaria, ed., *The Future of Freedom. Illiberal Democracy at Home and Abroad* (2003).
Fourest, Caroline and Venner, Fiametta, *Trois Croises. La Laicité à l'epreuve des Intégrismes Juif Chétien et Musulman* (2003).
Fukuyama, Francis, 'Nation Building 101', 293(1) *The Atlantic Monthly* (2004) pp. 159-162.
Fukuyama, Francis, 'The End of History?', in Paul Schumaker, Dwight C. Kiel and Thomas W. Heilke, eds., *Ideological Voices – an Anthology in Modern Political Ideas* (1997) pp. 409-417.

Fukuyama, Francis, 'The End of History?', 16 *The National Interest* (1989) pp. 3-18.
Fukuyama, Francis, 'The Neoconservative Moment', *The National Interest* (July 1, 2004).
Fukuyama, Francis, *State Building-Governance and World Order in the Twenty First Century* (2004).
Gardner, Martin, 'Beyond Cultural Relativism', in *The Night is Large. Collected Essays 1938-1995* (1996).
Gelner, Ernst, *Conditions of Liberty – Civil Society and Its Rivals* (1994).
Gelner, Ernst, 'Islam and Marxism: Some Comparisons', 67 *International Affairs* (1991) pp. 1-6.
Gelner, Ernst, *Postmodernism, Reason, and Religion* (1992).
Gensler, Harry, 'Cultural Relativism' in *Ethics* (1998).
Gerson, Mark, 'Security and Freedom: Making the World Safe with Ronald Reagen' in *The Essential Neoconservative Reader* (1996) pp. 161-207.
Gow, James, *Defending the West* (2005).
Hafez, Kai, *Islam and the West: The clash of Politicised Perceptions* (2000).
Haught, James, *Holy Hatred. Religious Conflicts of the 90's* (1995).
Howland, Courtney, *Religious Fundamentalism and the Human Rights of Women* (2001).
Howse, Brannon, *One Nation under Man? The Worldview War between Christians and the Secular Left* (2005).
Huntington, Samuel, 'The Clash of Civilizations?', *Foreign Affairs* (Summer 1993) pp. 20-49.
'Iran, too, wants to soothe the cartoons affair', *NRC Handelsblad* (21.1.2006).
'Islamic Court in India issues Death Sentence to Cartoonists', *Agence France Press* (20.2.2006).
Jacoby, Susan, *Freethinkers – A History of American Secularism* (2004).
Jansen, Johannes, *The Dual Nature of Islamic Fundamentalism* (1997).
Kepel, Gilles, *Fitna: Guerre au Coeur de l'islam* (2004).
Kepel, Gilles, *Jyhad. Expansion et Déclin de l'islamisme* (2000).
Kirsch, Jonathan, *God Against the Gods. The History of the War between Monotheism and Polytheism* (2004).
Krauthammer, Charles, *Democratic Realism: An American Foreign Policy for a Unipolar World*, The Irving Kristol Lecture (American Enterprise Institute, Washington DC 2004).
Krauthammer, Charles, 'Violence and Islam', *The Washington Post* (6.12.2002).
Laqueur, Walter, *Krieg dem Westen. Terrorismus im 21. Jahrhundert* (2003).
Lewis, Bernard, *The Crisis of Islam. Holy War and Unholy Terror* (2003).
Marshall, Paul, ed., *Radical Islam's Rules. The Worldwide Spread of Extreme Shari'a Law* (2005).
Nelson-Pallmeyer, Jack, *Is Religion killing Us? Violence in the Bible and the Quran* (2003).
Ostien, Philip, Jamila M. Nasir, and Kogelmann, Franz, eds., *The West and the Rest: Reflections on the Intercultural Dialogue about Shari'ah* (2005).
Pipes, Daniel, *The Rushdie Affair. The Novel, the Ayatollah and the West* (2003).
Rachels, James, *The Challenge of Cultural Relativism. The Elements of Moral Philosophy* (2003).
Raddatz, Hans-Peter, *Alllahs Frauen. Djihad zwischen Scharia und Demokratie* (2005).
Rohrlich, Wilfried, *Die Macht der Religionen, Glaubenskonflikte in der Weltpolitik* (2004).
Ruthven, Malise, *Fundamentalism. The Search for Meaning* (2004).
Sam Harris, *The end of Faith, Religion, Terror and the Future of Reason* (2005).
Samuel Huntington, *The Clash of Civilizations and the Remaking of World Order* (1996).
Selengut, Charles, *Sacred Fury. Understanding Religious Violence* (2003).
Sim, Stuart, *Fundamentalist World. The New Dark Age of Dogma* (2004).
Sorman, Guy, *Les Enfants de Rifaa, Musulmans et Modernes* (2003).

Spencer, Robert, *Islam Unveiled. Disturbing Questions about the World's Fastest-Growing Faith* (2002).
Spencer, Robert, *Onward Muslim Soldiers. How Jihad still Threatens America and the West* (2003).
Stelzer, Irwin, *Neoconservatism* (2005).
Thomas, Dominique, *Le Londonistan. Le djihad au Coeur de l'Europe* (2005).
Todorov, Tzvetan, *Le Nouveau Désordre Mondial d'un Européen* (2003).
Tibi, Bassam, *Der Neue Totalitarismus. Heiliger Krieg und Westliche Sicherheit* (2004).
Warraw, Ibn, *Leaving Islam Apostates Speak Out* (2003).

Part III

DOCUMENTS AND REFERENCES

A. Excerpts from International Conventions, Agreements, and Laws

1. The Briand Kellog Pact of 1928

BY THE PRESIDENT OF THE UNITED STATES OF AMERICA.
A PROCLAMATION.

WHEREAS a Treaty between the President of the United States of America, the President of the German Reich, His Majesty the King of the Belgians, the President of the French Republic, His Majesty the King of Great Britain, Ireland and the British Dominions beyond the Seas, Emperor of India, His Majesty the King of Italy, His Majesty the Emperor of Japan, the President of the Republic of Poland, and the President of the Czechoslovak Republic, providing for the renunciation of war as an instrument of national policy, was concluded and signed by their respective Plenipotontiaries at Paris on the twenty-seventh day of August, one thousand nine hundred and twenty-eight, the original of which Treaty, being in the English and the French languages, is word for word as follows:

THE PRESIDENT OF THE GERMAN REICH, THE PRESIDENT OF THE UNITED STATES OF AMERICA, HIS MAJESTY THE KING OF THE BELGIANS, THE PRESIDENT OF THE FRENCH REPUBLIC, HIS MAJESTY THE KING OF GREAT BRITAIN IRELAND AND THE BRITISH DOMINIONS BEYOND THE SEAS, EMPEROR OF INDIA, HIS MAJESTY THE KING OF ITALY, HIS MAJESTY THE EMPEROR OF JAPAN, THE PRESIDENT OF THE REPUBLIC OF POLAND THE PRESIDENT OF THE CZECHOSLOVAK REPUBLIC,

Deeply sensible of their solemn duty to promote the welfare of mankind;

Persuaded that the time has, come when a frank renunciation of war as an instrument of national policy should be made to the end that the peaceful and friendly relations now existing between their peoples may be perpetuated;

Convinced that all changes in their relations with one another should be sought only by pacific means and be the result of a peaceful and orderly process, and that any signatory Power which shall hereafter seek to promote its national interests by resort to war a should be denied the benefits furnished by this Treaty;

Hopeful that, encouraged by their example, all the other nations of the world will join in this humane endeavor and by adhering to the present Treaty as soon as it comes into force bring their peoples within the scope of its beneficent provisions, thus uniting the civilized nations of the world in a common renunciation of war as an instrument of their national policy;

Have decided to conclude a Treaty and for that purpose have appointed as their respective Plenipotentiaries:

THE PRESIDENT OF THE GERMAN REICH:
Dr Gustav STRESEMANN, Minister of Foreign Affairs;

THE PRESIDENT OF THE UNITED STATES OF AMERICA:
The Honorable Frank B. KELLOGG, Secretary of State;

HIS MAJESTY THE KING OF THE BELGIANS:
Mr Paul HYMANS, Minister for Foreign Affairs, Minister of State;

THE PRESIDENT OF THE FRENCH REPUBLIC:
Mr. Aristide BRIAND Minister for Foreign Affairs;

HIS MAJESTY THE KING OF GREAT BRITAIN, IRELAND AND THE BRITISH DOMINIONS BEYOND THE SEAS, EMPEROR OF INDIA:
For GREAT BRITAIN and NORTHERN IBELAND and all parts of the British Empire which are not separate Members of the League of Nations:
The Right Honourable Lord CUSHENDUN, Chancellor of the Duchy of Lancaster, Acting-Secretary of State for Foreign Affairs;

For the DOMINION OF CANADA:
The Right Honourable William Lyon MACKENZIE KING, Prime Minister and Minister for External Affairs;

For the COMMONWEALTH of AUSTRLIA:
The Honourable Alexander John McLACHLAN, Member of the Executive Federal Council;

For the DOMINION OF NEW ZEALAND:
The Honourable Sir Christopher James PARR High Commissioner for New Zealand in Great Britain;

For the UNION OF SOUTH AFRICA:
The Honourable Jacobus Stephanus SMIT, High Commissioner for the Union of South Africa in Great Britain;

For the IRISH FREE STATE:
Mr. William Thomas COSGRAVE, President of the Executive Council;

For INDIA:
The Right Honourable Lord CUSHENDUN, Chancellor of the Duchy of Lancaster, Acting Secretary of State for Foreign Affairs;

HIS MAJESTY THE KING OF ITALY:
Count Gaetano MANZONI, his Ambassador Extraordinary and Plenipotentiary at Paris.

HIS MAJESTY THE EMPEROR OF JAPAN:
Count UCHIDA, Privy Councillor;

THE PRESIDENT OF THE REPUBLIC OF POLAND:
Mr. A. ZALESKI, Minister for Foreign Affairs;

THE PRESIDENT OF THE CZECHOSLOVAK REPUBLIC:
Dr Eduard BENES, Minister for Foreign Affairs;

who, having communicated to one another their full powers found in good and due form have agreed upon the following articles:

ARTICLE I

The High Contracting Parties solemly declare in the names of their respective peoples that they condemn recourse to war for the solution of international controversies, and renounce it, as an instrument of national policy in their relations with one another.

ARTICLE II

The High Contracting Parties agree that the settlement or solution of all disputes or conflicts of whatever nature or of whatever origin they may be, which may arise among them, shall never be sought except by pacific means.

ARTICLE III

The present Treaty shall be ratified by the High Contracting Parties named in the Preamble in accordance with their respective constitutional requirements, and shall take effect as between them as soon as all their several instruments of ratification shall have been deposited at Washington.

This Treaty shall, when it has come into effect as prescribed in the preceding paragraph, remain open as long as may be necessary for adherence by all the other Powers of the world. Every instrument evidencing the adherence of a Power shall be deposited at Washington and the Treaty shall immediately upon such deposit become effective as; between the Power thus adhering and the other Powers parties hereto.

It shall be the duty of the Government of the United States to furnish each Government named in the Preamble and every Government subsequently adhering to this Treaty with a certified copy of the Treaty and of every instrument of ratification or adherence. It shall also be the duty of the Government of the United States telegraphically to notify such Governments immediately upon the deposit with it of each instrument of ratification or adherence.

IN FAITH WHEREOF the respective Plenipotentiaries have signed this Treaty in the French and English languages both texts having equal force, and hereunto affix their seals.

DONE at Paris, the twenty seventh day of August in the year one thousand nine hundred and twenty-eight.
[SEAL] GUSTAV STRESEMANN
[SEAL] FRANK B. KELLOGG
[SEAL] PAUL HYMANS

[SEAL] ARI BRIAND
[SEAL] CUSHENDUN
[SEAL] W. L. MACKENZIE KING
[SEAL] A. J. MCLACHLAN
[SEAL] C. J. PARR
[SEAL] J. S. SMIT
[SEAL] LIAM T.MACCOSGAIR
[SEAL] CUSHENDUN
[SEAL] G. MANZONI
[SEAL] UCHIDA
[SEAL] AUGUST ZALESKI
[SEAL] DR EDWARD BENES

Certified to be a true copy of the signed original deposited with the Government of the United States of America.

FRANK B. KELLOGG
Secretary of State of the United States of America

AND WHEREAS it is stipulated in the said Treaty that it shall take effect as between the High Contracting Parties as soon as all the several instruments of ratification shall have been deposited at Washington;

AND WHEREAS the said Treaty has been duly ratified on the parts of all the High Contracting Parties and their several instruments of ratification have been deposited with the Government of the United States of America, the last on July 24, 1929;

NOW THEREFORE, be it known that I, Herbert Hoover, President of the United States of America, have caused the said Treaty to be made public, to the end that the same and every article and clause thereof may be observed and fulfilled with good faith by the United States and the citizens thereof.

IN TESTIMONY WHEREOF, I have hereunto set my hand and caused the seal of the United States to be affixed.

DONE at the city of Washington this twenty-fourth day of July in the year of our Lord one thousand nine hundred and twenty-nine, and of the Independence of the United States of America the one hundred and fifty-fourth
HERBERT HOOVER
By the President:
HENRY L STIMSON
Secretary of State

2. UN Charter (signed on 26.6.1945)

Article 2
The Organization and its Members, in pursuit of the Purposes stated in Article 1, shall act in accordance with the following Principles.

1. The Organization is based on the principle of the sovereign equality of all its Members.
2. All Members, in order to ensure to all of them the rights and benefits resulting from membership, shall fulfill in good faith the obligations assumed by them in accordance with the present Charter.
3. All Members shall settle their international disputes by peaceful means in such a manner that international peace and security, and justice, are not endangered.
4. All Members shall refrain in their international relations from the threat or use of force against the territorial integrity or political independence of any state, or in any other manner inconsistent with the purposes of the United Nations.
5. All Members shall give the United Nations every assistance in any action it takes in accordance with the present Charter, and shall refrain from giving assistance to any state against which the United Nations is taking preventive or enforcement action.
6. The Organization shall ensure that states which are not Members of the United Nations act in accordance with these Principles so far as may be necessary for the maintenance of international peace and security.
7. Nothing contained in the present Charter shall authorize the United Nations to intervene in matters which are essentially within the domestic jurisdiction of any state or shall require the Members to submit such matters to settlement under the present Charter; but this principle shall not prejudice the application of enforcement measures under Chapter Vll.

Article 51
Nothing in the present Charter shall impair the inherent right of individual or collective self-defence if an armed attack occurs against a Member of the United Nations, until the Security Council has taken measures necessary to maintain international peace and security. Measures taken by Members in the exercise of this right of self-defence shall be immediately reported to the Security Council and shall not in any way affect the authority and responsibility of the Security Council under the present Charter to take at any time such action as it deems necessary in order to maintain or restore international peace and security.

3. Additional Protocol to the Geneva Conventions of 12 August 1949, and relating to the Protection of Victims of International Armed Conflicts (Protocol 1), adopted on 8.6.1977

Article 82

Legal advisers in armed forces
The High Contracting Parties at all times, and the Parties to the conflict in time of armed conflict, shall ensure that legal advisers are available, when necessary, to advise military commanders at the appropriate level on the application of the Conventions and this Protocol and on the appropriate instruction to be given to the armed forces on this subject.

For the full text see:
<http://www.unhchr.ch/html/menu3/b/93.htm>

4. Article 31 of the Rome Statute of the International Criminal Court

Article 31
Grounds for excluding criminal responsibility

1. In addition to other grounds for excluding criminal responsibility provided for in this Statute, a person shall not be criminally responsible if, at the time of that person's conduct:
   (a) The person suffers from a mental disease or defect that destroys that person's capacity to appreciate the unlawfulness or nature of his or her conduct, or capacity to control his or her conduct to conform to the requirements of law;
   (b) The person is in a state of intoxication that destroys that person's capacity to appreciate the unlawfulness or nature of his or her conduct, or capacity to control his or her conduct to conform to the requirements of law, unless the person has become voluntarily intoxicated under such circumstances that the person knew, or disregarded the risk, that, as a result of the intoxication, he or she was likely to engage in conduct constituting a crime within the jurisdiction of the Court;
   (c) The person acts reasonably to defend himself or herself or another person or, in the case of war crimes, property which is essential for the survival of the person or another person or property which is essential for accomplishing a military mission, against an imminent and unlawful use of force in a manner proportionate to the degree of danger to the person or the other person or property protected. The fact that the person was involved in a defensive operation conducted by forces shall not in itself constitute a ground for excluding criminal responsibility under this subparagraph;
   (d) The conduct which is alleged to constitute a crime within the jurisdiction of the Court has been caused by duress resulting from a threat of imminent death or of continuing or imminent serious bodily harm against that person or another person, and the person acts necessarily and reasonably to avoid this threat, provided that the person does not intend to cause a greater harm than the one sought to be avoided. Such a threat may either be:
   (i) Made by other persons; or
   (ii) Constituted by other circumstances beyond that person's control.

2. The Court shall determine the applicability of the grounds for excluding criminal responsibility provided for in this Statute to the case before it.

3. At trial, the Court may consider a ground for excluding criminal responsibility other than those referred to in paragraph 1 where such a ground is derived from applicable law as set forth in article 21. The procedures relating to the consideration of such a ground shall be provided for in the Rules of Procedure and Evidence.

5. Article 41 Dutch Criminal Code, Translation of Louise Rayar and Stafford Wadsworth, The American series of foreign codes, Colorado 1997

Article 41 of the **Criminal Code**:
"Appropriate force, when possible, preceded by a warning, should be applied only if the objective cannot be achieved by other means". Deadly force may only be used in situations involving a threat to the life or safety of the officer or the public."

6. European Convention for the Protection of Human Rights and Fundamental Freedoms as amended by Protocol No. 11 with Protocol Nos. 1, 4, 6, 7, 12 and 13

Article 2
Right to life

1. Everyone's right to life shall be protected by law. No one shall be deprived of his life intentionally save in the execution of a sentence of a court following his conviction of a crime for which this penalty is provided by law.

2. Deprivation of life shall not be regarded as inflicted in contravention of this article when it results from the use of force which is no more than absolutely necessary:
   (a) in defence of any person from unlawful violence;
   (b) in order to effect a lawful arrest or to prevent the escape of a person lawfully detained;
   (c) in action lawfully taken for the purpose of quelling a riot or insurrection.

Article 3
Prohibition of torture
No one shall be subjected to torture or to inhuman or degrading treatment or punishment.

Article 8
Right to respect for private and family life

1. Everyone has the right to respect for his private and family life, his home and his correspondence.

2. There shall be no interference by a public authority with the exercise of this right except such as is in accordance with the law and is necessary in a democratic society in the interests of national security, public safety or the economic well-being of the country, for the prevention of disorder or crime, for the protection of health or morals, or for the protection of the rights and freedoms of others.

B. ICJ Decisions

1. Case concerning Armed Activities on the Territory of the Congo (*Democratic Republic of the Congo* v. *Uganda*) 19.12.2005

SELF-DEFENCE IN THE LIGHT OF PROVEN FACTS

106. The Court has already said that, on the basis of the evidence before it, it has not been established to its satisfaction that Uganda participated in the attack on Kitona on 4 August 1998 (see paragraph 71 above). The Court has also indicated that with regard to the presence of Ugandan troops on Congolese territory near to the common border after the end of July 1998, President Kabila's statement on 28 July 1998 was ambiguous (see paragraph 51 above). The Court has further found that any earlier consent by the DRC to the presence of Ugandan troops on its territory had at the latest been withdrawn by 8 August 1998 (see paragraph

53 above). The Court now turns to examine whether Uganda's military activities starting from this date could be justified as actions in self-defence.

107. The DRC has contended that Uganda invaded on 2 August 1998, beginning with a major airborne operation at Kitona in the west of the DRC, then rapidly capturing or taking towns in the east, and then, continuing to the north-west of the country. According to the DRC, some of this military action was taken by the UPDF alone or was taken in conjunction with anti-government rebels and/or with Rwanda. It submits that Uganda was soon in occupation of a third of the DRC and that its forces only left in April 2003.

108. Uganda insists that 2 August 1998 marked the date only of the beginning of civil war in the DRC and that, although Rwanda had invited it to join in an effort to overthrow President Kabila, it had declined. Uganda contends that it did not act jointly with Rwanda in Kitona and that it had the consent of the DRC for its military operations in the east until the date of 11 September 1998. 11 September was the date of issue of the "Position of the High Command on the Presence of the UPDF in the DRC" (hereinafter "the Ugandan High command document") (see paragraph 109 below). Uganda now greatly increased the number of its troops from that date on. Uganda acknowledges that its military operations thereafter can only be justified by reference to an entitlement to act in self-defence.

109. The Court finds it useful at this point to reproduce in its entirety the Ugandan High Command document. This document has been relied on by both Parties in this case. The High Command document, although mentioning the date of 11 September 1998, in the Court's view, provides the basis for the operation known as operation "Safe Haven". The document reads as follows:
"WHEREAS for a long time the DRC has been used by the enemies of Uganda as a base and launching pad for attacks against Uganda;
AND WHEREAS the successive governments of the DRC have not been in effective control of all the territory of the Congo;
AND WHEREAS in May 1997, on the basis of a mutual understanding the Government of Uganda deployed UPDF to jointly operate with the Congolese Army against Uganda enemy forces in the DRC;
AND WHEREAS when an anti-Kabila rebellion erupted in the DRC the forces of the UPDF were still operating along side the Congolese Army in the DRC, against Uganda enemy forces who had fled back to the DRC;
NOW THEREFORE the High Command sitting in Kampala this 11th day of September, 1998, resolves to maintain forces of the UPDF in order to secure Uganda's legitimate security interests which are the following:
1. To deny the Sudan opportunity to use the territory of the DRC to destabilize Uganda.
2. To enable UPDF neutralize Uganda dissident groups which have been receiving assistance from the Government of the DRC and the Sudan.
3. To ensure that the political and administrative vacuum, and instability caused by the fighting between the rebels and the Congolese Army and its allies do not adversely affect the security of Uganda.
4. To prevent the genocidal elements, namely, the Interahamwe, and ex-FAR, which have been launching attacks on the people of Uganda from the DRC, from continuing to do so.

5. To be in position to safeguard the territory integrity of Uganda against irresponsible threats of invasion from certain forces."

110. In turning to its assessment of the legal character of Uganda's activities at Aru, Beni, Bunia and Watsa in August 1998, the Court begins by observing that, while it is true that those localities are all in close proximity to the border, "as per the consent that had been given previously by President Kabila", the nature of Ugandan action at these locations was of a different nature from previous operations along the common border. Uganda was not in August 1998 engaging in military operations against rebels who carried out cross-border raids. Rather, it was engaged in military assaults that resulted in the taking of the town of Beni and its airfield between 7 and 8 August, followed by the taking of the town of Bunia and its airport on 13 August, and the town of Watsa and its airport at a date between 24 and 29 August.

111. The Court finds these actions to be quite outside any mutual understanding between the Parties as to Uganda's presence on Congolese territory near to the border. The issue of when any consent may have terminated is irrelevant when the actions concerned are so clearly beyond co-operation "in order to ensure peace and security along the common border", as had been confirmed in the Protocol of 27 April 1998.

112. The Court observes that the Ugandan operations against these eastern border towns could therefore only be justified, if at all, as actions in self-defence. However, at no time has Uganda sought to justify them on this basis before the Court.

113. Operation "Safe Haven", by contrast, was firmly rooted in a claimed entitlement "to secure Uganda's legitimate security interests" rather than in any claim of consent on the part of the DRC. The Court notes, however, that those most intimately involved in its execution regarded the military actions throughout August 1998 as already part and parcel of operation "Safe Haven".

114. Thus Mr. Kavuma, the Minister of State for Defence, informed the Porter Commission that the UPDF troops first crossed the border at the beginning of August 1998, at the time of the rebellion against President Kabila, "when there was confusion inside the DRC" (Porter Commission document CW 01/02 23/07/01, p. 23). He confirmed that this "entry" was "to defend our security interests". The commander of the Ugandan forces in the DRC, General Kazini, who had immediate control in the field, informing Kampala and receiving thereafter any further orders, was asked "[w]hen was 'Operation Safe Haven'? When did it commence?" He replied "[i]t was in the month of August. That very month of August 1998. 'Safe Haven' started after the capture of Beni, that was on 7 August 1998." (CW/01/03 24/07/01, p. 774.) General Kazini emphasized that the Beni operation was the watershed: "So before that . . . 'Operation Safe Haven' had not started. It was the normal UPDF operations – counter-insurgency operations in the Rwenzoris before that date of 7 August, 1998." (CW/01/03 24/07/01, p. 129.) He spoke of "the earlier plan" being that both Governments, in the form of the UPDF and the FAC, would jointly deal with the rebels along the border. "But now this new phenomenon had developed: there was a mutiny, the

rebels were taking control of those areas. So we decided to launch an offensive together with the rebels, a special operation we code-named 'Safe Haven'." General Kazini was asked by Justice Porter what was the objective of this joint offensive with the rebels. General Kazini replied "[t]o crush the bandits together with their FAC allies" and confirmed that by "FAC" he meant the "Congolese Government Army" (CW/01/03 24/07/01, p. 129).

115. It is thus clear to the Court that Uganda itself actually regarded the military events of August 1998 as part and parcel of operation "Safe Haven", and not as falling within whatever "mutual understandings" there had previously been.

116. The Court has noted that within a very short space of time Ugandan forces had moved rapidly beyond these border towns. It is agreed by all that by 1 September 1998 the UPDF was at Kisangani, very far from the border. Furthermore, Lieutenant Colonel Magenyi informed the Porter Commission, under examination, that he had entered the DRC on 13 August and stayed there till mid-February 1999. He was based at Isiro, some 580 km from the border. His brigade had fought its way there: "we were fighting the ADFs who were supported by the FAC".

117. Accordingly, the Court will make no distinction between the events of August 1998 and those in the ensuing months.

118. Before this Court Uganda has qualified its action starting from mid-September 1998 as action in self-defence. The Court will thus examine whether, throughout the period when its forces were rapidly advancing across the DRC, Uganda was entitled to engage in military action in self-defence against the DRC. For these purposes, the Court will not examine whether each individual military action by the UPDF could have been characterized as action in self-defence, unless it can be shown, as a general proposition, that Uganda was entitled to act in self-defence in the DRC in the period from August 1998 till June 2003.

119. The Court first observes that the objectives of operation "Safe Haven", as stated in the Ugandan High Command document (see paragraph 109 above), were not consonant with the concept of self-defence as understood in international law.

120. Uganda in its response to the question put to it by Judge Kooijmans (see paragraph 22 above) confirms that the changed policies of President Kabila had meant that co-operation in controlling insurgency in the border areas had been replaced by "stepped-up cross-border attacks against Uganda by the ADF, which was being re-supplied and re-equipped by the Sudan and the DRC Government". The Court considers that, in order to ascertain whether Uganda was entitled to engage in military action on Congolese territory in self-defence, it is first necessary to examine the reliability of these claims. It will thus begin by an examination of the evidence concerning the role that the Sudan was playing in the DRC at the relevant time.

121. Uganda claimed that there was a tripartite conspiracy in 1998 between the DRC, the ADF and the Sudan; that the Sudan provided military assistance to the DRC's army and to anti-Ugandan rebel groups; that the Sudan used Congo airfields to

deliver materiel; that the Sudan airlifted rebels and its own army units around the country; that Sudanese aircraft bombed the UPDF positions at Bunia on 26 August 1998; that a Sudanese brigade of 2,500 troops was in Gbadolite and was preparing to engage the UPDF forces in eastern Congo; and that the DRC encouraged and facilitated stepped-up cross border attacks from May 1998 onwards.

122. The Court observes, more specifically, that in its Counter-Memorial Uganda claimed that from 1994 to 1997 anti-Ugandan insurgents "received direct support from the Government of Sudan" and that the latter trained and armed insurgent groups, in part to destabilize Uganda's status as a "good example" in Africa. For this, Uganda relied on a Human Rights Watch (hereinafter HRW) report. The Court notes that this report is on the subject of slavery in the Sudan and does not assist with the issue before the Court. It also relied on a Ugandan political report which simply claimed, without offering supporting evidence, that the Sudan was backing groups launching attacks from the DRC. It further relies on an HRW report of 2000 stating that the Sudan was providing military and logistical assistance to the LRA, in the north of Uganda, and to the SPLM/A (by which Uganda does not claim to have been attacked). The claims relating to the LRA, which are also contained in the Counter-Memorial of Uganda, have no relevance to the present case. No more relevant is the HRW report of 1998 criticizing the use of child soldiers in northern Uganda.

123. The Court has next examined the evidence advanced to support the assertion that the Sudan was supporting anti-Ugandan groups which were based in the DRC, namely FUNA, UNRF II and NALU. This consists of a Ugandan political report of 1998 which itself offers no evidence, and an address by President Museveni of 2000. These documents do not constitute probative evidence of the points claimed.

124. Uganda states that President Kabila entered into an alliance with the Sudan, "which he invited to occupy and utilise airfields in north-eastern Congo for two purposes: delivering arms and other supplies to the insurgents; and conducting aerial bombardment of Uganda towns and villages". Only President Museveni's address to Parliament is relied on. Certain assertions relating to the son of Idi Amin, and the role he was being given in the Congolese military, even were they true, prove nothing as regards the specific allegations concerning the Sudan.

125. Uganda has informed the Court that a visit was made by President Kabila in May 1998 to the Sudan, in order to put at the Sudan's disposal all the airfields in northern and eastern Congo, and to deliver arms and troops to anti-Ugandan insurgents along Uganda's border. Uganda offered as evidence President Museveni's address to Parliament, together with an undated, unsigned internal Ugandan military intelligence document. Claims as to what was agreed as a result of any such meeting that might have taken place remain unproven.

126 Uganda informed the Court that Uganda military intelligence reported that in August 1998 the Sudan airlifted insurgents from the WNBF and LRA to fight alongside Congolese forces against RPA and RCD rebels. The Court observes that, even were that proven (which in the Court's view is not the case), the DRC

was entitled so to have acted. This invitation could not of itself have entitled Uganda to use force in self-defence. The Court has not been able to verify from concordant evidence the claim that the Sudan transported an entire Chadian brigade to Gbadolite (whether to join in attacks on Uganda or otherwise).

127. The Court further observes that claims that the Sudan was training and transporting FAC troops, at the request of the Congolese Government, cannot entitle Uganda to use force in self-defence, even were the alleged facts proven. In the event, such proof is not provided by the unsigned Ugandan military intelligence document, nor by a political report that Uganda relies on.

128. Article 51 of the Charter refers to the right of "individual or collective" self-defence. The Court notes that a State may invite another State to assist it in using force in self-defence. On 2 August 1998 civil war had broken out in the DRC and General Kazini later testified to the Porter Commission that operation "Safe Haven" began on 7-8 August 1998. The Ugandan written pleadings state that on 14 August 1998 Brigadier Khalil of the Sudan delivered three planeloads of weapons to the FAC in Kinshasa, and that the Sudan stepped up its training of FAC troops and airlifted them to different locations in the DRC. Once again, the evidence offered to the Court as to the delivery of the weapons is the undated, unsigned, internal Ugandan military intelligence report. This was accompanied by a mere political assertion of Sudanese backing for troops launching attacks on Uganda from the DRC. The evidentiary situation is exactly the same as regards the alleged agreement by President Kabila with the Sudanese Vice-President for joint military measures against Uganda. The same intelligence report, defective as evidence that the Court can rely on, is the sole source for the claims regarding the Sudanese bombing with an Antonov aircraft of UPDF positions in Bunia on 26 August 1998; the arrival of the Sudanese brigade in Gbadolite shortly thereafter; the deployment of Sudanese troops, along with those of the DRC, on Uganda's border on 14 September; and the pledges made on 18 September for the deployment of more Sudanese troops.

129. It was said by Uganda that the DRC had effectively admitted the threat to Uganda's security posed by the Sudan, following the claimed series of meetings between President Kabila and Sudanese officials in May, August and September 1998. In support of these claims Uganda referred the Court to a 1999 ICG report, "How Kabila lost his way"; although not provided in the annexes, this report was in the public domain and the Court has ascertained its terms. Reliance is also placed on a political statement by the Ugandan High Command. The Court observes that this does not constitute reliable evidence and in any event it speaks only of the reason for the mid-September deployment of troops. The Court has also found that it cannot rely as persuasive evidence on a further series of documents said to support these various claims relating to the Sudan, all being internal political documents. The Court has examined the notarized affidavit of 2002 of the Ugandan Ambassador to the DRC, which refers to documents that allegedly were at the Ugandan Embassy in Kinshasa, showing that "the Sudanese government was supplying ADF rebels". While a notarized affidavit is entitled to a certain respect, the Court must observe that it is provided by a party in the case and provides at best indirect "information" that is unverified.

130. The Court observes that it has not been presented with evidence that can safely be relied on in a court of law to prove that there was an agreement between the DRC and the Sudan to participate in or support military action against Uganda; or that any action by the Sudan (of itself factually uncertain) was of such a character as to justify Uganda's claim that it was acting in self-defence.

131. The Court has also examined, in the context of ascertaining whether Uganda could have been said to have acted in self-defence, the evidence for Uganda's claims that from May 1998 onwards the frequency, intensity and destructiveness of cross-border attacks by the ADF "increased significantly", and that this was due to support from the DRC and from the Sudan.

132. The Court is convinced that the evidence does show a series of attacks occurring within the relevant time-frame, namely: an attack on Kichwamba Technical School of 8 June 1998, in which 33 students were killed and 106 abducted; an attack near Kichwamba, in which five were killed; an attack on Benyangule village on 26 June, in which 11 persons were killed or wounded; the abduction of 19 seminarians at Kiburara on 5 July; an attack on Kasese town on 1 August, in which three persons were killed. A sixth attack was claimed at the oral hearings to have occurred at Kijarumba, with 33 fatalities. The Court has not been able to ascertain the facts as to this latter incident.

133. The DRC does not deny that a number of attacks took place, but its position is that the ADF alone was responsible for them. The documents relied on by Uganda for its entitlement to use force in self-defence against the DRC include a report of the interrogation of a captured ADF rebel, who admits participating in the Kichwamba attack and refers to an "intention" to obtain logistical support and sanctuary from the Congolese Government; this report is not signed by the person making the statement, nor does it implicate the DRC. Uganda also relies on a document entitled "Chronological Illustration of Acts of Destabilisation by Sudan and Congo Based Dissidents", which is a Ugandan military document. Further, some articles in newspapers relied on by Uganda in fact blame only the ADF for the attacks. A very few do mention the Sudan. Only some internal documents, namely unsigned witness statements, make any reference to Congolese involvement in these acts.

134. The Court observes that this is also the case as regards the documents said to show that President Kabila provided covert support to the ADF. These may all be described as internal documents, often with no authenticating features, and containing unsigned, unauthenticated and sometimes illegible witness statements. These do not have the quality or character to satisfy the Court as to the matters claimed.

135. In oral pleadings Uganda again referred to these "stepped up attacks". Reference was made to an ICG report of August 1998, "North Kivu, into the Quagmire". Although not provided in the annexes, this report was in the public domain and the Court has ascertained its terms. It speaks of the ADF as being financed by Iran and the Sudan. It further states that the ADF is "[e]xploiting the incapacity of the Congolese Armed Forces" in controlling areas of North Kivu with neighbour Uganda. This independent report does seem to suggest some Sudanese support

for the ADF's activities. It also implies that this was not a matter of Congolese policy, but rather a reflection of its inability to control events along its border.

136. Uganda relies on certain documents annexed by the DRC to its Reply. However, the Court does not find this evidence weighty and convincing. It consists of a bundle of news reports of variable reliability, which go no further than to say that unconfirmed reports had been received that the Sudan was flying military supplies to Juba and Dungu. The Court has therefore not found probative such media reports as the IRIN update for 12 to 14 September 1998, stating that Hutu rebels were being trained in southern Sudan, and the IRIN update for 16 September 1998, stating that "rebels claim Sudan is supporting Kabila at Kindu". Neither has the Court relied on the (unreferenced and unsourced) claim that President Kabila made a secret visit to Khartoum on 25 August 1998 nor on the extract from Mr. Bemba's book *Le choix de la liberté* stating that. Sudanese soldiers were in the DRC, under the command of the Congolese army, to defend the area around Gbadolite.

137. Nor has the Court been able to satisfy itself as to certain internal military intelligence documents, belatedly offered, which lack explanations as to how the information was obtained (e.g. Revelations of Commander Junju Juma (former commanding officer in the ADF) of 17 May 2000, undated Revelations by Issa Twatera (former commanding officer in the ADF)).

138. A further "fact" relied on by Uganda in this case as entitling it to act in self-defence is that the DRC incorporated anti-Ugandan rebel groups and Interahamwe militia into the FAC. The Court will examine the evidence and apply the law to its findings.

139. In its Counter-Memorial, Uganda claimed that President Kabila had incorporated into his army thousands of ex-FAR and Interahamwe *génocidaires* in May 1998. A United States State Department statement in October 1998 condemned the DRC's recruitment and training of former perpetrators of the Rwandan genocide, thus giving some credence to the reports internal to Uganda that were put before the Court, even though these lacked signatures or particulars of sources relied on. But this claim, even if true, seems to have relevance for Rwanda rather than Uganda.

140. Uganda in its oral pleadings repeated the claims of incorporation of former Rwandan soldiers and Interahamwe into special units of the Congolese army. No sources were cited, nor was it explained to the Court how this might give rise to a right of self-defence on the part of Uganda.

141. In the light of this assessment of all the relevant evidence, the Court is now in a position to determine whether the use of force by Uganda within the territory of the DRC could be characterized as self-defence.

142. Article 51 of the United Nations Charter provides: "Nothing in the present Charter shall impair the inherent right of individual or collective self-defence if an armed attack occurs against a Member of the United Nations, until the Security Council has taken measures necessary to maintain international peace and

security. Measures taken by Members in the exercise of this right of self-defence shall be immediately reported to the Security Council and shall not in any way affect the authority and responsibility of the Security Council under the present Charter to take at any time such action as it deems necessary in order to maintain or restore international peace and security".

143. The Court recalls that Uganda has insisted in this case that operation "Safe Haven" was not a use of force against an anticipated attack. As was the case also in the *Military and Paramilitary Activities in and against Nicaragua (Nicaragua* v. *United States of America)* case, "reliance is placed by the Parties only on the right of self-defence in the case of an armed attack which has already occurred, and the issue of the lawfulness of a response to the imminent threat of armed attack has not been raised" (*I.C.J. Reports 1986*, p. 103, para. 194). The Court there found that "[a]ccordingly [it] expresses no view on that issue". So it is in the present case. The Court feels constrained, however, to observe that the wording of the Ugandan High Command document on the position regarding the presence of the UPDF in the DRC makes no reference whatever to armed attacks that have already occurred against Uganda at the hands of the DRC (or indeed by persons for whose action the DRC is claimed to be responsible). Rather, the position of the High Command is that it is necessary "to secure Uganda's legitimate security interests". The specified security needs are essentially preventative – to ensure that the political vacuum does not adversely affect Uganda, to prevent attacks from "genocidal elements", to be in a position to safeguard Uganda from irresponsible threats of invasion, to "deny the Sudan the opportunity to use the territory of the DRC to destabilize Uganda". Only one of the five listed objectives refers to a response to acts that had already taken place – the neutralization of "Uganda dissident groups which have been receiving assistance from the Government of the DRC and the Sudan".

144. While relying heavily on this document, Uganda nonetheless insisted to the Court that after 11 September 1998 the UPDF was acting in self-defence in response to attacks that had occurred. The Court has already found that the military operations of August in Beni, Bunia and Watsa, and of 1 September at Kisangani, cannot be classified as coming within the consent of the DRC, and their legality, too, must stand or fall by reference to self-defence as stated in Article 51 of the Charter.

145. The Court would first observe that in August and early September 1998 Uganda did not report to the Security Council events that it had regarded as requiring it to act in self-defence.

146. It is further to be noted that, while Uganda claimed to have acted in self-defence, it did not ever claim that it had been subjected to an armed attack by the armed forces of the DRC. The "armed attacks" to which reference was made came rather from the ADF. The Court has found above (paragraphs 131-135) that there is no satisfactory proof of the involvement in these attacks, direct or indirect, of the Government of the DRC. The attacks did not emanate from armed bands or irregulars sent by the DRC or on behalf of the DRC, within the sense of Article 3 *(g)* of General Assembly resolution 3314 (XXIX) on the definition of aggression, adopted on 14 December 1974. The Court is of the view that, on the evidence

before it, even if this series of deplorable attacks could be regarded as cumulative in character, they still remained non-attributable to the DRC.

147. For all these reasons, the Court finds that the legal and factual circumstances for the exercise of a right of self-defence by Uganda against the DRC were not present. Accordingly, the Court has no need to respond to the contentions of the Parties as to whether and under what conditions contemporary international law provides for a right of self-defence against large-scale attacks by irregular forces. Equally, since the preconditions for the exercise of self-defence do not exist in the circumstances of the present case, the Court has no need to enquire whether such an entitlement to self-defence was in fact exercised in circumstances of necessity and in a manner that was proportionate. The Court cannot fail to observe, however, that the taking of airports and towns many hundreds of kilometres from Uganda's border would not seem proportionate to the series of transborder attacks it claimed had given rise to the right of self-defence, nor to be necessary to that end.

FINDINGS OF LAW ON THE PROHIBITION AGAINST THE USE OF FORCE

148. The prohibition against the use of force is a cornerstone of the United Nations Charter. Article 2, paragraph 4, of the Charter requires that: "All Members shall refrain in their international relations from the threat or use of force against the territorial integrity or political independence of any state, or in any other manner inconsistent with the Purposes of the United Nations". Article 51 of the Charter may justify a use of force in self-defence only within the strict confines there laid down. It does not allow the use of force by a State to protect perceived security interests beyond these parameters. Other means are available to a concerned State, including, in particular, recourse to the Security Council.

Separate Opinion by Judge Parra-Aranguren:

21. Paragraph 130 of the Judgment states "that it has not been presented with evidence that can safely be relied on in a court of law to prove that there was an agreement between the DRC and the Sudan to participate in or support military action against Uganda; or that any action by the Sudan (of itself factually uncertain) was of such a character as to justify Uganda's claim that it was acting in self-defence".

22. In this respect I wish to make reference to the statement by the Chief Prosecutor on the Uganda arrest warrants, dated 14 October 2005, because it is in the public domain and the Court may ascertain its terms. The statement announces that the pre-trial Chamber II of the International Criminal Court has unsealed five warrants of arrest in the Uganda situation, because it considered there to be sufficient evidence that the concerned persons have committed crimes against humanity and war crimes; it is recalled therein that the Lord's Resistance Army (LRA) has killed, abducted, enslaved and raped the people of northern Uganda for 19 years, that more than 50 missions were made to Uganda, in small groups

of two or three, to investigate the situation, and that among other facts, it was established that Joseph Kony is the absolute leader of the LRA and that he directs all of the LRA operations from his bases in the Sudan.

Dissenting Opinion by Judge ad hoc Kateka:

29. As regards the LRA, I wish to underscore the inter-connectivity of the events in the Great Lakes region. The Sudan had been sponsoring the LRA that for nearly 20 years had caused massive and grave violations of human rights and international humanitarian law in northern Uganda. This has led the Prosecutor of the International Criminal Court to indict five leaders of the LRA for crimes against humanity. The Sudan was ferrying the LRA rebels to the DRC in order to create "another frontier" in its conflict with Uganda. It has also been said that Zaire's attempt to evict Congolese Tutsi triggered the Congo crisis. These examples show that the situation in the DRC has an internal, regional and international dimension. Another dimension of the inter-connectivity of events in the region is that the Hima people are to be found in the DRC, Rwanda, Burundi and Uganda. The various pogroms in Rwanda and Burundi led to massive inflows of refugees into Uganda and Tanzania in the 1960s. Hence instability in one country creates instability in another owing to the ethnic composition of the people. In this situation it is not easy to tell whether a person belongs to this or that ethnic group.

2. Case concerning Military and Paramilitary Activities in and against Nicaragua (*Nicaragua* v. *United States of America*) 27.6.1986 (Merits)

The judgment by the ICJ on the merits of this case is a classic on the issue of [collective] self-defence and deserves to be consulted in integro. The sheer length of the judgment precludes insertion in this volume. Therefore, reference is made here to the ICJ website.

<http://www.icj-cij.org/docket/index.php?p1=3&p2=3&k=66&case=70&code=nus &p3=90>

3. Oil Platforms (*Islamic Republic of Iran* v. *United States of America*) 16.11.2003 (Merits)

43. The Court will thus examine first the application of Article XX, paragraph 1 *(d)*, of the 1955 Treaty, which in the circumstances of this case, as explained above, involves the principle of the prohibition in international law of the use of force, and the qualification to it constituted by the right of self-defence. On the basis of that provision, a party to the Treaty may be justified in taking certain measures which it considers to be "necessary" for the protection of its essential security interests. As the Court emphasized, in relation to the comparable provision of the 1956 USA/Nicaragua Treaty in the case concerning *Military and Paramilitary Activities in and against Nicaragua,* "the measures taken must not merely be such as tend to protect the essential security interests of the party taking them, but must be 'necessary' for that purpose"; and whether a given measure is "necessary" is "not purely a question for the subjective judgment of the party" (*I.C.J. Reports 1986*, p. 141, para. 282), and may thus be assessed by the Court. In the present case, the question whether the measures taken were "necessary" overlaps with

the question of their validity as acts of self-defence. As the Court observed in its decision of 1986 the criteria of necessity and proportionality must be observed if a measure is to be qualified as self-defence (see *I.C.J. Reports 1986*, p. 103, para. 194, and paragraph 74 below).

44. In this connection, the Court notes that it is not disputed between the Parties that neutral shipping in the Persian Gulf was caused considerable inconvenience and loss, and grave damage, during the Iran-Iraq war. It notes also that this was to a great extent due to the presence of mines and minefields laid by both sides. The Court has no jurisdiction to enquire into the question of the extent to which Iran and Iraq complied with the international legal rules of maritime warfare. It can however take note of these circumstances, regarded by the United States as relevant to its decision to take action against Iran which it considered necessary to protect its essential security interests. Nevertheless, the legality of the action taken by the United States has to be judged by reference to Article XX, paragraph 1 *(d)*, of the 1955 Treaty, in the light of international law on the use of force in self-defence.

45 The United States has never denied that its actions against the Iranian platforms amounted to a use of armed force. Some of the details of the attacks, so far as established by the material before the Court, may be pertinent to any assessment of the lawfulness of those actions. As already indicated, there were attacks on two successive occasions, on 19 October 1987 and on 18 April 1988. The Court will examine whether each of these met the conditions of Article XX, paragraph 1 *(d)*, as interpreted by reference to the relevant rules of international law.

[....]

51. Despite having thus referred to attacks on vessels and aircraft of other nationalities, the United States has not claimed to have been exercising collective self-defence on behalf of the neutral States engaged in shipping in the Persian Gulf; this would have required the existence of a request made to the United States "by the State which regards itself as the victim of an armed attack" (*I.C.J. Reports 1986*, p. 105, para. 199). Therefore, in order to establish that it was legally justified in attacking the Iranian platforms in exercise of the right of individual self-defence, the United States has to show that attacks had been made upon it for which Iran was responsible; and that those attacks were of such a nature as to be qualified as "armed attacks" within the meaning of that expression in Article 51 of the United Nations Charter, and as understood in customary law on the use of force. As the Court observed in the case concerning *Military and Paramilitary Activities in and against Nicaragua*, it is necessary to distinguish "the most grave forms of the use of force (those constituting an armed attack) from other less grave forms" (*I.C.J. Reports 1986*, p. 101, para. 191), since "In the case of individual self-defence, the exercise of this right is subject to the State concerned having been the victim of an armed attack" (*ibid.*, p. 103, para. 195). The United States must also show that its actions were necessary and proportional to the armed attack made on it, and that the platforms were a legitimate military target open to attack in the exercise of self-defence.

[....]

57. For present purposes, the Court has simply to determine whether the United States has demonstrated that it was the victim of an "armed attack" by Iran such as to justify it using armed force in self-defence; and the burden of proof of the facts showing the existence of such an attack rests on the United States. The Court does not have to attribute responsibility for firing the missile that struck the *Sea Isle City*, on the basis of a balance of evidence, either to Iran or to Iraq; if at the end of the day the evidence available is insufficient to establish that the missile was fired by Iran, then the necessary burden of proof has not been discharged by the United States.

4. Legal Consequences of the Construction of a wall in the Occupied Palestinian Territory Advisory Opinion 9.7.2004

138. The Court has thus concluded that the construction of the wall constitutes action not in conformity with various international legal obligations incumbent upon Israel. However, Annex I to the report of the Secretary-General states that, according to Israel: "the construction of the Barrier is consistent with Article 51 of the Charter of the United Nations, its inherent right to self-defence and Security Council resolutions 1368 (2001) and 1373 (2001)". More specifically, Israel's Permanent Representative to the United Nations asserted in the General Assembly on 20 October 2003 that "the fence is a measure wholly consistent with the right of States to self-defence enshrined in Article 51 of the Charter"; the Security Council resolutions referred to, he continued, "have clearly recognized the right of States to use force in self-defence against terrorist attacks", and therefore surely recognize the right to use non-forcible measures to that end (A/ES-10/PV.21, p. 6).

139. Under the terms of Article 51 of the Charter of the United Nations:

"Nothing in the present Charter shall impair the inherent right of individual or collective self-defence if an armed attack occurs against a Member of the United Nations, until the Security Council has taken measures necessary to maintain international peace and security".

Article 51 of the Charter thus recognizes the existence of an inherent right of self-defence in the case of armed attack by one State against another State. However, Israel does not claim that the attacks against it are imputable to a foreign State. The Court also notes that Israel exercises control in the Occupied Palestinian Territory and that, as Israel itself states, the threat which it regards as justifying the construction of the wall originates within, and not outside, that territory. The situation is thus different from that contemplated by Security Council resolutions 1368 (2001) and 1373 (2001), and therefore Israel could not in any event invoke those resolutions in support of its claim to be exercising a right of self-defence. Consequently, the Court concludes that Article 51 of the Charter has no relevance in this case.

140. The Court has, however, considered whether Israel could rely on a state of necessity which would preclude the wrongfulness of the construction of the wall. In this regard the Court is bound to note that some of the conventions at

issue in the present instance include qualifying clauses of the rights guaranteed or provisions for derogation (see paragraphs 135 and 136 above). Since those treaties already address considerations of this kind within their own provisions, it might be asked whether a state of necessity as recognized in customary international law could be invoked with regard to those treaties as a ground for precluding the wrongfulness of the measures or decisions being challenged. However, the Court will not need to consider that question. As the Court observed in the case concerning the *Gabčíkovo-Nagymaros Project (Hungary/Slovakia)*, "the state of necessity is a ground recognized by customary international law" that "can only be accepted on an exceptional basis"; it "can only be invoked under certain strictly defined conditions which must be cumulatively satisfied; and the State concerned is not the sole judge of whether those conditions have been met" (*I.C.J. Reports 1997*, p. 40, para. 51). One of those conditions was stated by the Court in terms used by the International Law Commission, in a text which in its present form requires that the act being challenged be "the only way for the State to safeguard an essential interest against a grave and imminent peril" (Article 25 of the International Law Commission's Articles on Responsibility of States for Internationally Wrongful Acts; see also former Article 33 of the Draft Articles on the International Responsibility of States, with slightly different wording in the English text). In the light of the material before it, the Court is not convinced that the construction of the wall along the route chosen was the only means to safeguard the interests of Israel against the peril which it has invoked as justification for that construction.

141. The fact remains that Israel has to face numerous indiscriminate and deadly acts of violence against its civilian population. It has the right, and indeed the duty, to respond in order to protect the life of its citizens. The measures taken are bound nonetheless to remain in conformity with applicable international law.

142. In conclusion, the Court considers that Israel cannot rely on a right of self-defence or on a state of necessity in order to preclude the wrongfulness of the construction of the wall resulting from the considerations mentioned in paragraphs 122 and 137 above. The Court accordingly finds that the construction of the wall, and its associated régime, are contrary to international law.

Separate Opinions and Declarations

Judge Higgins (Separate Opinion):

33. I do not agree with all that the Court has to say on the question of the law of self-defence. In paragraph 139 the Court quotes Article 51 of the Charter and then continues "Article 51 of the Charter thus recognizes the existence of an inherent right of self-defence in the case of armed attack by one State against another State". There is, with respect, nothing in the text of Article 51 that *thus* stipulates that self-defence is available only when an armed attack is made by a State. *That* qualification is rather a result of the Court so determining in *Military and Paramilitary Activities in and against Nicaragua (Nicaragua* v. *United States of America)* (*Merits, Judgment, I.C.J. Reports 1986*, p. 14). It there held that military action by irregulars could constitute an armed attack if these were sent

by or on behalf of the State and if the activity "because of its scale and effects, would have been classified as an armed attack . . . had it been carried out by regular armed forces" (*ibid.*, p. 103, para. 195). While accepting, as I must, that this is to be regarded as a statement of the law as it now stands, I maintain all the reservations as to this proposition that I have expressed elsewhere (R. Higgins, *Problems and Process: International Law and How We Use It*, pp. 250-251).

Judge Kooijmans (Separate Opinion):

35. *Self-defence* – Israel based the construction of the wall on its inherent right of self-defence as contained in Article 51 of the Charter. In this respect it relied on Security Council resolutions 1368 (2001) and 1373 (2001), adopted after the terrorist attacks of 11 September 2001 against targets located in the United States.

The Court starts its response to this argument by stating that Article 51 recognizes the existence of an inherent right of self-defence in the case of an armed attack by one State against another State (para. 139). Although this statement is undoubtedly correct, as a reply to Israel's argument it is, with all due respect, beside the point. Resolutions 1368 and 1373 recognize the inherent right of individual or collective self-defence without making any reference to an armed attack by a State. The Security Council called acts of international terrorism, without any further qualification, a threat to international peace and security which authorizes it to act under Chapter VII of the Charter. And it actually did so in resolution 1373 without ascribing these acts of terrorism to a particular State. This is the completely new element in these resolutions. This new element is not excluded by the terms of Article 51 since this conditions the exercise of the inherent right of self-defence on a previous armed attack without saying that this armed attack must come from another State even if this has been the generally accepted interpretation for more than 50 years. The Court has regrettably by-passed this new element, the legal implications of which cannot as yet be assessed but which marks undeniably a new approach to the concept of self-defence.

Judge Buergenthal (Declaration):

5. Whether Israel's right of self-defence is in play in the instant case depends, in my opinion, on an examination of the nature and scope of the deadly terrorist attacks to which Israel proper is being subjected from across the Green Line and the extent to which the construction of the wall, in whole or in part, is a necessary and proportionate response to these attacks. As a matter of law, it is not inconceivable to me that some segments of the wall being constructed on Palestinian territory meet that test and that others do not. But to reach a conclusion either way, one has to examine the facts bearing on that issue with regard to the specific segments of the wall, their defensive needs and related topographical considerations.

Since these facts are not before the Court, it is compelled to adopt the to me legally dubious conclusion that the right of legitimate or inherent self-defence is not applicable in the present case. The Court puts the matter as follows:

"Article 51 of the Charter . . . recognizes the existence of an inherent right of self-defence in the case of armed attack by one State against another State. However, Israel does not claim that the attacks against it are imputable to a foreign State.

The Court also notes that Israel exercises control in the Occupied Palestinian Territory and that, as Israel itself states, the threat which it regards as justifying the construction of the wall originates within, and not outside, that territory. The situation is thus different from that contemplated by Security Council resolutions 1368 (2001) and 1373 (2001), and therefore Israel could not in any event invoke those resolutions in support of its claim to be exercising a right of self-defence.

Consequently, the Court concludes that Article 51 of the Charter has no relevance in this case". (Para. 139.)

6. There are two principal problems with this conclusion. The first is that the United Nations Charter, in affirming the inherent right of self-defence, does not make its exercise dependent upon an armed attack by another State, leaving aside for the moment the question whether Palestine, for purposes of this case, should not be and is not in fact being assimilated by the Court to a State. Article 51 of the Charter provides that "Nothing in the present Charter shall impair the inherent right of individual or collective self-defence if an armed attack occurs against a Member of the United Nations . . ." Moreover, in the resolutions cited by the Court, the Security Council has made clear that "international terrorism constitutes a threat to international peace and security" while "*reaffirming* the inherent right of individual or collective self-defence as recognized by the Charter of the United Nations as reiterated in resolution 1368 (2001)" (Security Council resolution 1373 (2001)). In its resolution 1368 (2001), adopted only one day after the September 11, 2001 attacks on the United States, the Security Council invokes the right of self-defence in calling on the international community to combat terrorism. In neither of these resolutions did the Security Council limit their application to terrorist attacks by State actors only, nor was an assumption to that effect implicit in these resolutions. In fact, the contrary appears to have been the case. (See Thomas Franck, "Terrorism and the Right of Self-Defense", *American Journal of International Law*, Vol. 95, 2001, pp. 839-840.)

Second, Israel claims that it has a right to defend itself against terrorist attacks to which it is subjected on its territory from across the Green Line and that in doing so it is exercising its inherent right of self-defence. In assessing the legitimacy of this claim, it is irrelevant that Israel is alleged to exercise control in the Occupied Palestinian Territory – whatever the concept of "control" means given the attacks Israel is subjected from that territory – or that the attacks do not originate from outside the territory. For to the extent that the Green Line is accepted by the Court as delimiting the dividing line between Israel and the Occupied Palestinian Territory, to that extent the territory from which the attacks originate is not part of Israel proper. Attacks on Israel coming from across that line must therefore permit Israel to exercise its right of self-defence against such attacks, provided the measures it takes are otherwise consistent with the legitimate exercise of that right. To make that judgment, that is, to determine whether or not the construction of the wall, in whole or in part, by Israel meets that test, all relevant facts bearing on issues of necessity and proportionality must be analysed. The Court's formalistic approach to the right of self-defence enables it to avoid addressing the very issues that are at the heart of this case.

5. Legality of the threat or Use of Nuclear Weapons (Advisory Opinion 8.7.1996)

96. Furthermore, the Court cannot lose sight of the fundamental right of every State to survival, and thus its right to resort to self-defence, in accordance with Article 51 of the Charter, when its survival is at stake.

Nor can it ignore the practice referred to as "policy of deterrence", to which an appreciable section of the international community adhered for many years. The Court also notes the reservations which certain nuclear-weapon States have appended to the undertakings they have given, notably under the Protocols to the Treaties of Tlatelolco and Rarotonga, and also under the declarations made by them in connection with the extension of the Treaty on the Non-Proliferation of Nuclear Weapons, not to resort to such weapons.

97. Accordingly, in view of the present state of international law viewed as a whole, as examined above by the Court, and of the elements of fact at its disposal, the Court is led to observe that it cannot reach a definitive conclusion as to the legality or illegality of the use of nuclear weapons by a State in an extreme circumstance of self-defence, in which its very survival would be at stake.

[....]

105. For these reasons,

THE COURT,

(1) By thirteen votes to one,

Decides to comply with the request for an advisory opinion;

IN FAVOUR: *President* Bedjaoui; *Vice-President* Schwebel; *Judges* Guillaume, Shahabuddeen, Weeramantry, Ranjeva, Herczegh, Shi, Fleischhauer, Koroma, Vereshchetin, Ferrari Bravo, Higgins;

AGAINST: *Judge* Oda.

(2) *Replies* in the following manner to the question put by the General Assembly:

A. Unanimously,

There is in neither customary nor conventional international law any specific authorization of the threat or use of nuclear weapons;

B. By eleven votes to three,

There is in neither customary nor conventional international law any comprehensive and universal prohibition of the threat or use of nuclear weapons as such;

IN FAVOUR: *President* Bedjaoui; *Vice-President* Schwebel; *Judges* Oda, Guillaume, Ranjeva, Herczegh, Shi, Fleischhauer, Vereshchetin, Ferrari Bravo, Higgins;

AGAINST: *Judges* Shahabuddeen, Weeramantry, Koroma.

C. Unanimously,

A threat or use of force by means of nuclear weapons that is contrary to Article 2, paragraph 4, of the United Nations Charter and that fails to meet all the requirements of Article 51, is unlawful;

D. Unanimously,

A threat or use of nuclear weapons should also be compatible with the requirements of the international law applicable in armed conflict, particularly those of the principles and rules of international humanitarian law, as well as with specific obligations under treaties and other undertakings which expressly deal with nuclear weapons;

E. By seven votes to seven, by the President's casting vote,

It follows from the above-mentioned requirements that the threat or use of nuclear weapons would generally be contrary to the rules of international law applicable in armed conflict, and in particular the principles and rules of humanitarian law; However, in view of the current state of international law, and of the elements of fact at its disposal, the Court cannot conclude definitively whether the threat or use of nuclear weapons would be lawful or unlawful in an extreme circumstance of self-defence, in which the very survival of a State would be at stake;

IN FAVOUR: *President* Bedjaoui; *Judges* Ranjeva, Herczegh, Shi, Fleischhauer, Vereschetin, Ferrari Bravo;

AGAINST: *Vice-President* Schwebel; *Judges* Oda, Guillaume, Shahabuddeen, Weeramantry, Koroma, Higgins.

F. Unanimously,

There exists an obligation to pursue in good faith and bring to a conclusion negotiations leading to nuclear disarmament in all its aspects under strict and effective international control.

Done in English and in French, the English text being authoritative, at the Peace Palace, The Hague, this eighth day of July, one thousand nine hundred and ninety-six, in two copies, one of which will be placed in the archives of the Court and the other transmitted to the Secretary-General of the United Nations.

6. Certain Expenses of the United Nations (Advisory Opinion 20.7.1962)

<http://www.icj-cij.org/icjwww/idecisions/isummaries/iceunsummary620720.htm>

The Court considers that the kind of action referred to in Article 11 paragraph 2, is coercive or enforcement action. This paragraph, which applies not merely to general questions relating to peace and security, but also to specific cases brought before the General Assembly by a State under Article 35, in its first sentence empowers the General Assembly, by means of recommendations to States or to the Security Council, or to both, to organize peace-keeping operations, at the request, or with the consent, of the States concerned. This power of the General Assembly is a special power which in no way derogates from its general powers under Article 10 or Article 14, except as limited by the last sentence of Article 11, paragraph 2. This last sentence says that when "action" is necessary the General Assembly shall refer the question to the Security Council. The word "action" must mean such action as is solely within the province of the Security Council. It cannot refer to recommendations which the Security Council might make, as for instance under Article 38, because the General Assembly under Article 11 has a comparable power. The "action" which is solely within the province of the Security Council is that which is indicated by the title of Chapter VI1 of the Charter, namely "Action with respect to threats to the peace, breaches of the peace, and acts of aggression". If the word "action" in Article 11, paragraph 2, were interpreted to mean that the General Assembly could make recommendations only of a general character affecting peace and security in the abstract, and not in relation to specific cases, the paragraph would not have provided that the General Assembly may make recommendations on questions brought before it by States or by the Security Council. Accordingly, the last sentence of Article 11, paragraph 2, has no application where the necessary action is not enforcement action.

[...]

It is not necessary for the Court to express an opinion as to which article or articles of the Charter were the basis for the resolutions of the Security Council, but it can be said that the operations of OWGC did not include a use of armed force against a State which the Security Council, under Article 39, determined to have committed an act of aggression or to have breached the peace. The armed forces which were utilized in the Congo were not authorized to take military action against any State. The operation did not involve "preventive or enforcement measures" against any State under Chapter VI1 and therefore did not constitute "action" as that term is used in Article 11.

C. OTHER COURT DECISIONS

1. Permanent Court of Arbitration
Ethiopia-Eritrea Claims Commission
Partial Award for claims 1-8 (jus ad bellum). 19.12.05

11. The Commission turns next to Eritrea's second line of argument. In general, recourse to the use of armed force by one State against another is unlawful unless it is used in self-defense or occurs with the sanction of the Security Council pursuant to Chapter VII of the UN Charter. As the text of Article 51 of the Charter makes clear, the predicate for a valid claim of self-defense under the Charter is that the party resorting to force has been subjected to an armed attack. Localized border encounters between small infantry units, even those involving the loss of life, do not constitute an armed attack for purposes of the Charter. In that connection, the Commission notes that Eritrea did not report its use of armed force against Ethiopia on May 12, 1998 to the Security Council as measures taken in self-defense, as it would be obligated to do by Article 51 of the Charter in case of self-defense against armed attack.

2. Naulilaa Incident Arbitration (*Portugal* v. *Germany*)
2 RIAA 1001 (1928)

2. La nécessité d'une *proportion* entre la représaille et l'offense, paraît être reconnue dans la réponse allemande. Même si l'on admettait que le droit des gens n'exige pas que la représaille se mesure approximativement à l'offense, on devrait certainement considérer, comme excessives et partant illicites, des représailles hors de toute proportion avec l'acte qui les a motivées. Or, en l'espèce, – même sans tirer argument du précédent de Maziua, à raison duquel une certaine modération s'imposait, – il y a eu disproportion évidente entre l'incident de Naulilaa et les 6 actes de représailles qui l'ont suivi. *Les arbitres arrivent donc à la conclusion* que les agressions allemandes d'octobre, novembre et décembre 1914, à la frontière de l'Angola, ne peuvent être considérées comme représailles licites de l'incident de Naulilaa ou d'actes postérieurs des autorités portugaises, ce faute de motif suffisant, de sommation préalable et d'une proportion admissible entre l'offense alléguée et les représailles exercées.
ad E. Responsabilité de principe du Gouvernement allemand à raison des agressions à la frontière de l'Angola.
Les faits invoqués ne sont contestés que sur des questions de détails. Ces questions pourront avoir leur importance, lorsqu'il s'agira de déterminer la quotité d'indemnités dues: leur solution ne peut influer sur le principe de la responsabilité. Il est, dès lors, superflu d'analyser ici les témoignages. Il suffit de constater que, du 31 octobre au 18 décembre 1914, les forces allemandes ont

assailli et détruit plusieurs forts ou postes-frontière portugais. A côté des dégâts matériels, de fortes pertes, en tués, blessés ou prisonniers, ont été infligées aux garnisons portugaises. Enfin, la retraite des garnisons a entraîné la destruction volontaire d'autres installations militaires et elle a été suivie d'une révolte des indigènes. Cette révolte a causé des dommages considérables dans la province d'Huila, et n'a pu être réprimée qu'à la suite d'une expédition meurtrière et coûteuse.

3 *Oneryildiz* v. *Turkey*
ECHR Decision of 30.11.04

Due to the length of the decision, see:

<http://cmiskp.echr.coe.int/tkp197/view.asp?item=1&portal=hbkm&action=html&highlight=%D6nery%u0131ld%u0131z%20%7C%20v.%20%7C%20Turkey&sessionid=19781010&skin=hudoc-en>

D. Reports of International Commissions

1. International Law Commission
Report for 2001, 56th Session
Official Records Supplementary 10 (A/56/10) Chapter V

See: <http://untreaty.un.org/ilc/reports/2001/2001report.htm>

Pages 366-371:

CHAPTER V

INTERNATIONAL LIABILITY FOR INJURIOUS CONSEQUENCES ARISING OUT OF ACTS NOT PROHIBITED BY INTERNATIONAL LAW (PREVENTION OF TRANSBOUNDARY HARM FROM HAZARDOUS ACTIVITIES)

A. Introduction

78. The Commission, at its thirtieth session (1978), included the topic "International liability for injurious consequences arising out of acts not prohibited by international law" in its programme of work and appointed Mr. Robert Q. Quentin-Baxter Special Rapporteur.

79. The Commission, from its thirty-second (1980) to its thirty-sixth sessions (1984), received and considered five reports from the Special Rapporteur.
The reports sought to develop a conceptual basis and schematic outline for the topic and contained proposals for five draft articles. The schematic outline was set out in the Special Rapporteur's third report to the thirty-fourth session of the Commission in 1982. The five draft articles were proposed in the Special Rapporteur's fifth report to the thirty-sixth session of the Commission in 1984. They were considered by the Commission, but no decision was taken to refer them to the Drafting Committee.

80. The Commission, at its thirty-sixth session (1984), also had before it the following materials: the replies to a questionnaire addressed in 1983 by the Legal Counsel of the United Nations to 16 selected international organizations to ascertain whether, amongst other matters, obligations which States owe to each other and discharge as members of international organizations may, to that extent, fulfil or replace some of the procedures referred to in the schematic outline and a study prepared by the secretariat entitled "Survey of State practice relevant to international liability for injurious consequences arising out of acts not prohibited by international law".

81. The Commission, at its thirty-seventh session (1985), appointed Mr. Julio Barboza, Special Rapporteur for the topic. The Commission received 12 reports from the Special Rapporteur from its thirty-seventh (1985) to its forty-eighth session (1996).

82. At its forty-fourth session (1992), the Commission established a Working Group to consider some of the general issues relating to the scope, the approach to be taken and the possible direction of the future work on the topic. On the basis of the recommendation of the Working Group, the Commission at its 2282nd meeting on 8 July 1992 decided to continue the work on this topic in stages. First to complete work on prevention of transboundary harm and to proceed with remedial measures. The Commission decided that, in view of the ambiguity in the title of the topic, to continue with the working hypothesis that the topic deal with "activities" and to defer any formal change of the title.

83. At its forty-eighth session (1996), the Commission re-established the Working Group in order to review the topic in all its aspects in the light of the reports of the Special Rapporteur and the discussions held, over the years, in the Commission and make recommendations to the Commission.

84. The Working Group submitted a report which provided a complete picture of the topic relating to the principle of prevention and that of liability for compensation or other relief, presenting articles and commentaries thereto.

85. At its forty-ninth session (1997), the Commission established again a Working Group to consider the question of how the Commission should proceed with its work on this topic. The Working Group reviewed the work of the Commission on the topic since 1978. It noted that the scope and the content of the topic remained unclear due to such factors as conceptual and theoretical difficulties, appropriateness of the title and the relation of the subject to "State responsibility". The Working Group further noted that the Commission had dealt with two issues under the topic: prevention and international liability. In the view of the Working Group, these two issues were distinct from one another, though related. The Working Group therefore agreed that henceforth the issues of prevention and of liability should be dealt with separately.

86. Accordingly the Commission decided to proceed with its work on the topic "International liability for injurious consequences arising out of acts not prohibited by international law", dealing first with the issue of prevention under the subtitle .Prevention of transboundary damage from hazardous activities. The

General Assembly took note of this decision in paragraph 7 of its resolution 52/156.

87. At the same session, the Commission appointed Mr. Pemmaraju Sreenivasa Rao Special Rapporteur for this part of the topic.

88. At its fiftieth session (1998), the Commission received and considered the first report of the Special Rapporteur, and adopted on first reading a set of 17 draft articles on prevention of transboundary damage from hazardous activities.

89. In accordance with articles 16 and 21 of its Statute, the Commission transmitted the draft articles, through the Secretary-General, to Governments for comments and observations, with the request that such comments and observations be submitted to the Secretary-General by 1 January 2000.

90. At its fifty-first (1999) and fifty-second (2000) sessions, the Commission received and considered the second and third reports of the Special Rapporteur. The Commission also had before it comments and observations received from Governments. At its 2643rd meeting, on 20 July 2000, the Commission referred the draft preamble and revised draft articles to the Drafting Committee.

B. Consideration of the topic at the present session

91. At the present session, the Drafting Committee considered the draft articles which the Commission had referred to it last year. The Chairman of the Drafting Committee presented his report (A/CN.4/L.601, Corrs.1 (English only) and 2) at the 2675th meeting of the Commission held on 11 May 2001). At the same meeting, the Commission considered the report of the Drafting Committee and adopted the final text of a draft preamble and a set of 19 draft articles on Prevention of Transboundary Harm from Hazardous Activities.

92. At its 2697th, 2698th, 2699th and 2700th meetings, from 27 July to 2 August 2001, the Commission adopted the commentaries to the aforementioned draft articles.

93. In accordance with its Statute, the Commission submits the draft preamble and the draft articles to the General Assembly, together with a recommendation set out below.

C. Recommendation of the Commission

94. At its 2701st meeting, on 3 August 2001, the Commission decided, in accordance with article 23 of its Statute, to recommend to the General Assembly the elaboration of a convention by the Assembly on the basis of the draft articles on prevention of transboundary harm from hazardous activities.

D. Tribute to the Special Rapporteur, Mr. Pemmaraju Sreenivasa Rao

95. At its 2701st meeting, on 3 August 2001, the Commission, after adopting the text of the draft preamble and draft articles on prevention of transboundary harm from

hazardous activities, adopted the following resolution by acclamation:
The International Law Commission,
Having adopted the draft preamble and draft articles on prevention of transboundary harm from hazardous activities,
Expresses to the Special Rapporteur, Mr. Pemmaraju Sreenivasa Rao, its deep appreciation and warm congratulations for the outstanding contribution he has made to the preparation of the draft preamble and draft articles through his tireless efforts and devoted work, and for the results achieved in the elaboration of the draft preamble and draft articles on prevention of transboundary harm from hazardous activities.

96. The Commission also expressed its deep appreciation to the previous Special Rapporteurs, Mr. Robert Q. Quentin-Baxter and Mr. Julio Barboza, for their outstanding contribution to the work on the topic.

E. Text of the draft articles on Prevention of Transboundary Harm from Hazardous Activities

1. Text of the draft articles

97. The text of the draft preamble and draft articles adopted by the Commission at its fifty-third session are reproduced below.

PREVENTION OF TRANSBOUNDARY HARM FROM HAZARDOUS ACTIVITIES

The States Parties,
Having in mind Article 13, paragraph 1 (a) of the Charter of the United Nations, which provides that the General Assembly shall initiate studies and make recommendations for the purpose of encouraging the progressive development of international law and its codification,
Bearing in mind the principle of permanent sovereignty of States over the natural resources within their territory or otherwise under their jurisdiction or control, *Bearing also in mind* that the freedom of States to carry on or permit activities in their territory or otherwise under their jurisdiction or control is not unlimited,
Recalling the Rio Declaration on Environment and Development of 13 June 1992,
Recognizing the importance of promoting international cooperation,
Have agreed as follows:

Pages 377-380:

2. Text of the draft articles with commentaries thereto

98. The text of the articles, adopted by the Commission at its fifty-third session, with commentaries thereto are reproduced below.

PREVENTION OF TRANSBOUNDARY HARM FROM HAZARDOUS ACTIVITIES
General Commentary

(1) The articles deal with the concept of prevention in the context of authorization and regulation of hazardous activities which pose a significant risk of transboundary harm. Prevention in this sense, as a procedure or as a duty, deals with the phase prior to the situation where significant harm or damage might actually occur, requiring States concerned to invoke remedial or compensatory measures, which often involve issues concerning liability.

(2) The concept of prevention has assumed great significance and topicality. The emphasis upon the duty to prevent as opposed to the obligation to repair, remedy or compensate has several important aspects. Prevention should be a preferred policy because compensation in case of harm often cannot restore the situation prevailing prior to the event or accident. Discharge of the duty of prevention or due diligence is all the more required as knowledge regarding the operation of hazardous activities, materials used and the process of managing them and the risks involved is steadily growing. From a legal point of view, the enhanced ability to trace the chain of causation, i.e. the physical link between the cause (activity) and the effect (harm), and even the several intermediate links in such a chain of causation, makes it also imperative for operators of hazardous activities to take all steps necessary to prevent harm. In any event, prevention as a policy is better than cure.

(3) Prevention of transboundary harm arising from hazardous activities is an objective well emphasized by principle 2 of the Rio Declaration and confirmed by the International Court of Justice in its advisory opinion of 8 July 1996 on the *Legality of the Use by a State of Nuclear Weapons in Armed Conflict* as now forming part of the corpus of international law.

(4) The issue of prevention, therefore, has rightly been stressed by the Experts Group on Environmental Law of the World Commission on Environment and Development. Article 10 recommended by the Group in respect of transboundary natural resources and environmental interferences thus reads: "States shall, without prejudice to the principles laid down in articles 11 and 12, prevent or abate any transboundary environmental interference or a significant risk thereof which causes substantial harm - i.e. harm which is not minor or insignificant". It must be further noted that the well-established principle of prevention was highlighted in the arbitral award in the *Trail Smelter* case and was reiterated not only in principle 21 of the Stockholm Declaration and principle 2 of the Rio Declaration but also in General Assembly resolution 2995 (XXVII) of 15 December 1972 on cooperation between States in the field of the environment. This principle is also reflected in principle 3 of the 1978 draft Principles of Conduct in the Field of the Environment for the Guidance of States in the Conservation and Harmonious Utilization of Natural Resources Shared by Two or More States, which provided that States must .avoid to the maximum extent possible and ... reduce to the minimum extent possible the adverse environmental effects beyond its jurisdiction of the utilization of a shared natural resource so as to protect the environment, in particular when such utilization might: (a) cause damage to the environment which could have repercussions on the utilization of the resource by another sharing State; (b) threaten the conservation of a shared renewable resource; (c) endanger the health of the population of another State.

(5) Prevention of transboundary harm to the environment, persons and property has been accepted as an important principle in many multilateral treaties concerning protection of the environment, nuclear accidents, space objects, international watercourses, management of hazardous wastes and prevention of marine pollution.

PREVENTION OF TRANSBOUNDARY HARM FROM HAZARDOUS ACTIVITIES

Preamble

The States Parties,
Having in mind Article 13, paragraph 1 (a) of the Charter of the United Nations, which provides that the General Assembly shall initiate studies and make recommendations for the purpose of encouraging the progressive development of international law and its codification, *Bearing in mind* the principle of permanent sovereignty of States over the natural resources within their territory or otherwise under their jurisdiction or control, Decision 6/14 of the Governing Council of the United Nations Environment Programme (UNEP) of 19 May 1978, *Official Records of the General Assembly, Thirty-Third Session, Supplement No. 25* (A/33/25), annex I, reprinted in ILM, vol. 17 (1978), p. 1098. For a mention of other sources where the principle of prevention is reflected, see *Environmental Protection and Sustainable Development - Legal Principles and Recommendations* (footnote 904 above),

Bearing also in mind that the freedom of States to carry on or permit activities in their territory or otherwise under their jurisdiction or control is not unlimited,
Recalling the Rio Declaration on Environment and Development of 13 June 1992,
Recognizing the importance of promoting international cooperation,
Have agreed as follows:

Commentary

(1) The preamble sets out the general context in which the topic of prevention is elaborated, keeping in view the mandate given to the Commission to codify and develop international law.
Activities covered under the present topic of prevention require States to engage in cooperation and accommodation in their mutual interest. States are free to formulate necessary policies to develop their natural resources and to carry out or authorize activities in response to the needs of their populations. In so doing, however, States have to ensure that such activities are carried out taking into account the interests of other States and therefore the freedom they have within their own jurisdiction is not unlimited.

(2) The prevention of transboundary harm from hazardous activities should also be seen in the context of the general principles incorporated in the Rio Declaration and other considerations that emphasize the close inter-relationship between issues of environment and development. A general reference in preambular paragraph 3 to the Rio Declaration indicates the importance of the interactive nature of all the principles contained therein. This is without prejudice to highlighting specific principles of the Rio Declaration, as appropriate, in the commentaries to follow on particular articles.

2. International Law Commission 53rd session, 2001 Draft Articles on Responsibility of States for Internationally Wrongful Acts with commentaries

Article 21 - Self-defence

The wrongfulness of an act of a State is precluded if the act constitutes a lawful measure of self-defence taken in conformity with the Charter of the United Nations.

Commentary

(1) The existence of a general principle admitting self-defence as an exception to the prohibition against the use of force in international relations is undisputed. Article 51 of the Charter of the United Nations preserves a State's "inherent right" of self-defence in the face of an armed attack and forms part of the definition of the obligation to refrain from the threat or use of force laid down in Article 2, paragraph (4). Thus a State exercising its inherent right of self-defence as referred to in Article 51 of the Charter is not, even potentially, in breach of Article 2, paragraph (4). Convention on the Settlement of Investment Disputes between States and Nationals of Other States, Washington, United Nations, *Treaty Series,* vol. 575, p. 159, art. 27 (1).
See, e.g., International Covenant on Civil and Political Rights, United Nations, *Treaty Series,* vol. 999, p. 171, arts. 7; 8 (3); 14 (1) (g); 23 (3).

Cf. *Legality of the Threat or Use of Nuclear Weapons, I.C.J. Reports 1996*, p. 226, at p. 244, para. 38; p. 263, para. 96, emphasizing the lawfulness of the use of force in self-defence.

(2) Self-defence may justify non-performance of certain obligations other than that under Article 2, paragraph (4), of the Charter, provided that such non-performance is related to the breach of that provision. Traditional international law dealt with these problems by instituting a separate legal regime of war, defining the scope of belligerent rights and suspending most treaties in force between the belligerents on the outbreak of war. In the Charter period, declarations of war are exceptional and military actions proclaimed as self-defence by one or both parties occur between States formally at "peace" with each other. The Vienna Convention on the Law of Treaties leaves such issues to one side by providing in article 73 that the Convention does not prejudice "any" question that may arise in regard to a treaty ... from the outbreak of hostilities between States.

(3) This is not to say that self-defence precludes the wrongfulness of conduct in all cases or with respect to all obligations. Examples relate to international humanitarian law and human rights obligations. The Geneva Conventions of 1949 and Protocol I of 1977 apply equally to all the parties in an international armed conflict, and the same is true of customary international humanitarian law. Human rights treaties contain derogation provisions for times of public emergency, including actions taken in self-defence. As to obligations under international humanitarian law and in relation to non-derogable human rights provisions, self-defence does not preclude the wrongfulness of conduct.

See further A. McNair & A. D. Watts, *Legal Effects of War* (4th edn.) (Cambridge, Cambridge University Press, 1966), p. 579:

In *Oil Platforms (Islamic Republic of Iran* v. *United States of America), Preliminary Objection, I.C.J. Reports 1996*, p. 803, it was not denied that the Treaty of Amity of 1955 remained in force, despite many actions by United States naval forces against Iran. In that case both parties agreed that to the extent that any such actions were justified by self-defence they would be lawful.

As the Court said of the rules of international humanitarian law in the advisory opinion on the *Legality of the Threat or Use of Nuclear Weapons, I.C.J. Reports 1996*, p. 226, at p. 257, para. 79, they constitute intransgressible principles of international customary law.

On the relationship between human rights and humanitarian law in time of armed conflict, see ibid., p. 240, para. 25.

(4) The International Court in its advisory opinion on the *Legality of the Threat or Use of Nuclear Weapon*s provided some guidance on this question. One issue before the Court was whether a use of nuclear weapons would necessarily be a breach of environmental obligations because of the massive and long-term damage such weapons can cause. The Court said:

[T]he issue is not whether the treaties relating to the protection of the environment are or are not applicable during an armed conflict, but rather whether the obligations stemming from these treaties were intended to be obligations of total restraint during military conflict. The Court does not consider that the treaties in question could have intended to deprive a State of the exercise of its right of self-defence under international law because of its obligations to protect the environment. Nonetheless, States must take environmental considerations into account when assessing what is necessary and proportionate in the pursuit of legitimate military objectives. Respect for the environment is one of the elements that go to assessing whether an action is in conformity with the principles of necessity and proportionality. A State acting in self-defence is "totally restrained" by an international obligation if that obligation is expressed or intended to apply as a definitive constraint even to States in armed conflict.

(5) The essential effect of article 21 is to preclude the wrongfulness of conduct of a State acting in self-defence vis-à-vis an attacking State. But there may be effects vis-à-vis third States in certain circumstances. In its advisory opinion on the *Legality of the Threat or Use of Nuclear Weapons*, the Court observed that:
[A]s in the case of the principles of humanitarian law applicable in armed conflict, international law leaves no doubt that the principle of neutrality, whatever its content, which is of a fundamental character similar to that of the humanitarian principles and rules, is applicable (subject to the relevant provisions of the United Nations Charter), to all international armed conflict, whatever type of weapons may be used. *I.C.J. Reports 1996*, p. 226, at p. 242, para. 30.

See e.g., Convention on the Prohibition of Military or any other Hostile Use of Environmental Modification Techniques, United Nations, *Treaty Series*, vol. 1108, p. 151. *I.C.J. Reports 1996*, p. 226, at p. 261, para. 89.

The law of neutrality distinguishes between conduct as against a belligerent and conduct as against a neutral. But neutral States are not unaffected by the existence of a state of war. Article 21 leaves open all issues of the effect of action in self-defence vis-à-vis third States.

(6) Thus article 21 reflects the generally accepted position that self-defence precludes the wrongfulness of the conduct taken within the limits laid down by international law. The reference is to action "taken in conformity with the Charter of the United Nations". In addition, the term "lawful" implies that the action taken respects those obligations of total restraint applicable in international armed conflict, as well as compliance with the requirements of proportionality and of necessity inherent in the notion of self-defence. Article 21 simply reflects the basic principle for the purposes of chapter V, leaving questions of the extent and application of self-defence to the applicable primary rules referred to in the Charter.

E. UN General Assembly Resolutions

1. Resolution 56/83 (28.1.2002)

Resolution adopted by the General Assembly
[*on the report of the Sixth Committee (A/56/589 and Corr.1)*]
56/83. Responsibility of States for internationally wrongful acts

The General Assembly,

Having considered chapter IV of the report of the International Law Commission on the work of its fifty-third session, which contains the draft articles on responsibility of States for internationally wrongful acts,

Noting that the International Law Commission decided to recommend to the General Assembly that it should take note of the draft articles on responsibility of States for internationally wrongful acts in a resolution and annex the draft articles to that resolution, and that it should consider at a later stage, in the light of the importance of the topic, the possibility of convening an international conference of plenipotentiaries to examine the draft articles with a view to concluding a convention on the topic,

Emphasizing the continuing importance of the codification and progressive development of international law, as referred to in Article 13, paragraph 1 (*a*), of the Charter of the United Nations,

Noting that the subject of responsibility of States for internationally wrongful acts is of major importance in the relations of States,

1. *Welcomes* the conclusion of the work of the International Law Commission on responsibility of States for internationally wrongful acts and its adoption of the draft articles and a detailed commentary on the subject;

2. *Expresses its appreciation* to the International Law Commission for its continuing contribution to the codification and progressive development of international law;

3. *Takes note* of the articles on responsibility of States for internationally wrongful acts, presented by the International Law Commission, the text of which is annexed to the present resolution, and commends them to the attention of Governments without prejudice to the question of their future adoption or other appropriate action;

4. *Decides* to include in the provisional agenda of its fifty-ninth session an item entitled "Responsibility of States for internationally wrongful acts".

85th plenary meeting
12 December 2001

Annex
Responsibility of States for internationally wrongful acts

PART ONE
THE INTERNATIONALLY WRONGFUL ACT OF A STATE

Chapter I
General principles

Article 1 - Responsibility of a State for its internationally wrongful acts
Every internationally wrongful act of a State entails the international responsibility of that State.

Article 2 - Elements of an internationally wrongful act of a State
There is an internationally wrongful act of a State when conduct consisting of an action or omission:
(*a*) Is attributable to the State under international law; and
(*b*) Constitutes a breach of an international obligation of the State.

Article 3 - Characterization of an act of a State as internationally wrongful
The characterization of an act of a State as internationally wrongful is governed by international law. Such characterization is not affected by the characterization of the same act as lawful by internal law.

Chapter II
Attribution of conduct to a State

Article 4 - Conduct of organs of a State
1. The conduct of any State organ shall be considered an act of that State under international law, whether the organ exercises legislative, executive, judicial or any other functions, whatever position it holds in the organization of the State, and whatever its character as an organ of the central government or of a territorial unit of the State.

2. An organ includes any person or entity which has that status in accordance with the internal law of the State.

Article 5 - Conduct of persons or entities exercising elements of governmental authority
The conduct of a person or entity which is not an organ of the State under article 4 but which is empowered by the law of that State to exercise elements of the governmental authority shall be considered an act of the State under international law, provided the person or entity is acting in that capacity in the particular instance.

Article 6 - Conduct of organs placed at the disposal of a State by another State
The conduct of an organ placed at the disposal of a State by another State shall be considered an act of the former State under international law if the organ is acting in the exercise of elements of the governmental authority of the State at whose disposal it is placed.

Article 7 - Excess of authority or contravention of instructions
The conduct of an organ of a State or of a person or entity empowered to exercise elements of the governmental authority shall be considered an act of the State under international law if the organ, person or entity acts in that capacity, even if it exceeds its authority or contravenes instructions.

Article 8 - Conduct directed or controlled by a State
The conduct of a person or group of persons shall be considered an act of a State under international law if the person or group of persons is in fact acting on the instructions of, or under the direction or control of, that State in carrying out the conduct.

Article 9 - Conduct carried out in the absence or default of the official authorities
The conduct of a person or group of persons shall be considered an act of a State under international law if the person or group of persons is in fact exercising elements of the governmental authority in the absence or default of the official authorities and in circumstances such as to call for the exercise of those elements of authority.

Article 10 - Conduct of an insurrectional or other movement
1. The conduct of an insurrectional movement which becomes the new government of a State shall be considered an act of that State under international law.

2. The conduct of a movement, insurrectional or other, which succeeds in establishing a new State in part of the territory of a pre-existing State or in a territory under its administration shall be considered an act of the new State under international law.

3. This article is without prejudice to the attribution to a State of any conduct, however related to that of the movement concerned, which is to be considered an act of that State by virtue of articles 4 to 9.

Article 11 - Conduct acknowledged and adopted by a State as its own
Conduct which is not attributable to a State under the preceding articles shall nevertheless be considered an act of that State under international law if and to the extent that the State acknowledges and adopts the conduct in question as its own.

Chapter III
Breach of an international obligation

Article 12 - Existence of a breach of an international obligation
There is a breach of an international obligation by a State when an act of that State is not in conformity with what is required of it by that obligation, regardless of its origin or character.

Article 13 - International obligation in force for a State
An act of a State does not constitute a breach of an international obligation unless the State is bound by the obligation in question at the time the act occurs.

Article 14 - Extension in time of the breach of an international obligation
1. The breach of an international obligation by an act of a State not having a continuing character occurs at the moment when the act is performed, even if its effects continue.

2. The breach of an international obligation by an act of a State having a continuing character extends over the entire period during which the act continues and remains not in conformity with the international obligation.

3. The breach of an international obligation requiring a State to prevent a given event occurs when the event occurs and extends over the entire period during which the event continues and remains not in conformity with that obligation.

Article 15 - Breach consisting of a composite act
1. The breach of an international obligation by a State through a series of actions or omissions defined in aggregate as wrongful occurs when the action or omission occurs which, taken with the other actions or omissions, is sufficient to constitute the wrongful act.

2. In such a case, the breach extends over the entire period starting with the first of the actions or omissions of the series and lasts for as long as these actions or omissions are repeated and remain not in conformity with the international obligation.

Chapter IV
Responsibility of a State in connection with the act of another State

Article 16 - Aid or assistance in the commission of an internationally wrongful act
A State which aids or assists another State in the commission of an internationally wrongful act by the latter is internationally responsible for doing so if:
(*a*) That State does so with knowledge of the circumstances of the internationally wrongful act; and
(*b*) The act would be internationally wrongful if committed by that State.

Article 17 - Direction and control exercised over the commission of an internationally wrongful act
A State which directs and controls another State in the commission of an internationally wrongful act by the latter is internationally responsible for that act if:
(*a*) That State does so with knowledge of the circumstances of the internationally wrongful act; and
(*b*) The act would be internationally wrongful if committed by that State.

Article 18 - Coercion of another State
A State which coerces another State to commit an act is internationally responsible for that act if:
(*a*) The act would, but for the coercion, be an internationally wrongful act of the coerced State; and
(*b*) The coercing State does so with knowledge of the circumstances of the act.

Article 19 - Effect of this chapter
This chapter is without prejudice to the international responsibility, under other provisions of these articles, of the State which commits the act in question, or of any other State.

Chapter V
Circumstances precluding wrongfulness

Article 20 - Consent
Valid consent by a State to the commission of a given act by another State precludes the wrongfulness of that act in relation to the former State to the extent that the act remains within the limits of that consent.

Article 21 - Self-defence
The wrongfulness of an act of a State is precluded if the act constitutes a lawful measure of self-defence taken in conformity with the Charter of the United Nations.

Article 22 - Countermeasures in respect of an internationally wrongful act
The wrongfulness of an act of a State not in conformity with an international obligation towards another State is precluded if and to the extent that the act constitutes a countermeasure taken against the latter State in accordance with chapter II of part three.

Article 23 - Force majeure
1. The wrongfulness of an act of a State not in conformity with an international obligation of that State is precluded if the act is due to force majeure, that is the occurrence of an irresistible force or of an unforeseen event, beyond the control of the State, making it materially impossible in the circumstances to perform the obligation.

2. Paragraph 1 does not apply if:
(*a*) The situation of force majeure is due, either alone or in combination with other factors, to the conduct of the State invoking it; or
(*b*) The State has assumed the risk of that situation occurring.

Article 24 - Distress
1. The wrongfulness of an act of a State not in conformity with an international obligation of that State is precluded if the author of the act in question has no other reasonable way, in a situation of distress, of saving the author's life or the lives of other persons entrusted to the author's care.

2. Paragraph 1 does not apply if:
(*a*) The situation of distress is due, either alone or in combination with other factors, to the conduct of the State invoking it; or
(*b*) The act in question is likely to create a comparable or greater peril.

Article 25 - Necessity
1. Necessity may not be invoked by a State as a ground for precluding the wrongfulness of an act not in conformity with an international obligation of that State unless the act:
(*a*) Is the only way for the State to safeguard an essential interest against a grave and imminent peril; and
(*b*) Does not seriously impair an essential interest of the State or States towards which the obligation exists, or of the international community as a whole.

2. In any case, necessity may not be invoked by a State as a ground for precluding wrongfulness if:
(*a*) The international obligation in question excludes the possibility of invoking necessity; or
(*b*) The State has contributed to the situation of necessity.

Article 26 - Compliance with peremptory norms
Nothing in this chapter precludes the wrongfulness of any act of a State which is not in conformity with an obligation arising under a peremptory norm of general international law.

Article 27 - Consequences of invoking a circumstance precluding wrongfulness
The invocation of a circumstance precluding wrongfulness in accordance with this chapter is without prejudice to:
(*a*) Compliance with the obligation in question, if and to the extent that the circumstance precluding wrongfulness no longer exists;
(*b*) The question of compensation for any material loss caused by the act in question.

PART TWO
CONTENT OF THE INTERNATIONAL RESPONSIBILITY OF A STATE

Chapter I
General principles

Article 28 - Legal consequences of an internationally wrongful act
The international responsibility of a State which is entailed by an internationally wrongful act in accordance with the provisions of part one involves legal consequences as set out in this part.

Article 29 - Continued duty of performance
The legal consequences of an internationally wrongful act under this part do not affect the continued duty of the responsible State to perform the obligation breached.

Article 30 - Cessation and non-repetition
The State responsible for the internationally wrongful act is under an obligation:
(*a*) To cease that act, if it is continuing;
(*b*) To offer appropriate assurances and guarantees of non-repetition, if circumstances so require.

Article 31 - Reparation
1. The responsible State is under an obligation to make full reparation for the injury caused by the internationally wrongful act.

2. Injury includes any damage, whether material or moral, caused by the internationally wrongful act of a State.

Article 32 - Irrelevance of internal law
The responsible State may not rely on the provisions of its internal law as justification for failure to comply with its obligations under this part.

Article 33 - Scope of international obligations set out in this part
1. The obligations of the responsible State set out in this part may be owed to another State, to several States, or to the international community as a whole, depending in particular on the character and content of the international obligation and on the circumstances of the breach.

2. This part is without prejudice to any right, arising from the international responsibility of a State, which may accrue directly to any person or entity other than a State.

Chapter II
Reparation for injury

Article 34 - Forms of reparation
Full reparation for the injury caused by the internationally wrongful act shall take the form of restitution, compensation and satisfaction, either singly or in combination, in accordance with the provisions of this chapter.

Article 35 - Restitution
A State responsible for an internationally wrongful act is under an obligation to make restitution, that is, to re-establish the situation which existed before the wrongful act was committed, provided and to the extent that restitution:
(*a*) Is not materially impossible;
(*b*) Does not involve a burden out of all proportion to the benefit deriving from restitution instead of compensation.

Article 36 - Compensation
1. The State responsible for an internationally wrongful act is under an obligation to compensate for the damage caused thereby, insofar as such damage is not made good by restitution.

2. The compensation shall cover any financially assessable damage including loss of profits insofar as it is established.

Article 37 - Satisfaction
1. The State responsible for an internationally wrongful act is under an obligation to give satisfaction for the injury caused by that act insofar as it cannot be made good by restitution or compensation.

2. Satisfaction may consist in an acknowledgement of the breach, an expression of regret, a formal apology or another appropriate modality.

3. Satisfaction shall not be out of proportion to the injury and may not take a form humiliating to the responsible State.

Article 38 - Interest
1. Interest on any principal sum due under this chapter shall be payable when necessary in order to ensure full reparation. The interest rate and mode of calculation shall be set so as to achieve that result.

2. Interest runs from the date when the principal sum should have been paid until the date the obligation to pay is fulfilled.

Article 39 - Contribution to the injury
In the determination of reparation, account shall be taken of the contribution to the injury by wilful or negligent action or omission of the injured State or any person or entity in relation to whom reparation is sought.

Chapter III
Serious breaches of obligations under peremptory norms of general international law

Article 40 - Application of this chapter
1. This chapter applies to the international responsibility which is entailed by a serious breach by a State of an obligation arising under a peremptory norm of general international law.

2. A breach of such an obligation is serious if it involves a gross or systematic failure by the responsible State to fulfil the obligation.

Article 41 - Particular consequences of a serious breach of an obligation under this chapter
1. States shall cooperate to bring to an end through lawful means any serious breach within the meaning of article 40.

2. No State shall recognize as lawful a situation created by a serious breach within the meaning of article 40, nor render aid or assistance in maintaining that situation.

3. This article is without prejudice to the other consequences referred to in this part and to such further consequences that a breach to which this chapter applies may entail under international law.

PART THREE
THE IMPLEMENTATION OF THE INTERNATIONAL RESPONSIBILITY OF A STATE

Chapter I
Invocation of the responsibility of a State

Article 42 - Invocation of responsibility by an injured State
A State is entitled as an injured State to invoke the responsibility of another State if the obligation breached is owed to:
(*a*) That State individually; or
(*b*) A group of States including that State, or the international community as a whole, and the breach of the obligation:
(i) Specifically affects that State; or
(ii) Is of such a character as radically to change the position of all the other States to which the obligation is owed with respect to the further performance of the obligation.

Article 43 - Notice of claim by an injured State
1. An injured State which invokes the responsibility of another State shall give notice of its claim to that State.

2. The injured State may specify in particular:
(*a*) The conduct that the responsible State should take in order to cease the wrongful act, if it is continuing;
(*b*) What form reparation should take in accordance with the provisions of part two.

Article 44 - Admissibility of claims
The responsibility of a State may not be invoked if:
(*a*) The claim is not brought in accordance with any applicable rule relating to the nationality of claims;
(*b*) The claim is one to which the rule of exhaustion of local remedies applies and any available and effective local remedy has not been exhausted.

Article 45 - Loss of the right to invoke responsibility
The responsibility of a State may not be invoked if:
(*a*) The injured State has validly waived the claim;
(*b*) The injured State is to be considered as having, by reason of its conduct, validly acquiesced in the lapse of the claim.

Article 46 - Plurality of injured States
Where several States are injured by the same internationally wrongful act, each injured State may separately invoke the responsibility of the State which has committed the internationally wrongful act.

Article 47 - Plurality of responsible States
1. Where several States are responsible for the same internationally wrongful act, the responsibility of each State may be invoked in relation to that act.

2. Paragraph 1:
(*a*) Does not permit any injured State to recover, by way of compensation, more than the damage it has suffered;
(*b*) Is without prejudice to any right of recourse against the other responsible States.

Article 48 - Invocation of responsibility by a State other than an injured State
1. Any State other than an injured State is entitled to invoke the responsibility of another State in accordance with paragraph 2 if:
(*a*) The obligation breached is owed to a group of States including that State, and is established for the protection of a collective interest of the group; or
(*b*) The obligation breached is owed to the international community as a whole.

2. Any State entitled to invoke responsibility under paragraph 1 may claim from the responsible State:
(*a*) Cessation of the internationally wrongful act, and assurances and guarantees of non-repetition in accordance with article 30; and
(*b*) Performance of the obligation of reparation in accordance with the preceding articles, in the interest of the injured State or of the beneficiaries of the obligation breached.

3. The requirements for the invocation of responsibility by an injured State under articles 43, 44 and 45 apply to an invocation of responsibility by a State entitled to do so under paragraph 1.

Chapter II
Countermeasures

Article 49 - Object and limits of countermeasures
1. An injured State may only take countermeasures against a State which is responsible for an internationally wrongful act in order to induce that State to comply with its obligations under part two.

2. Countermeasures are limited to the non-performance for the time being of international obligations of the State taking the measures towards the responsible State.

3. Countermeasures shall, as far as possible, be taken in such a way as to permit the resumption of performance of the obligations in question.

Article 50 - Obligations not affected by countermeasures
1. Countermeasures shall not affect:
(*a*) The obligation to refrain from the threat or use of force as embodied in the Charter of the United Nations;

(*b*) Obligations for the protection of fundamental human rights;
(*c*) Obligations of a humanitarian character prohibiting reprisals;
(*d*) Other obligations under peremptory norms of general international law.

2. A State taking countermeasures is not relieved from fulfilling its obligations:
(*a*) Under any dispute settlement procedure applicable between it and the responsible State;
(*b*) To respect the inviolability of diplomatic or consular agents, premises, archives and documents.

Article 51 - Proportionality
Countermeasures must be commensurate with the injury suffered, taking into account the gravity of the internationally wrongful act and the rights in question.

Article 52 - Conditions relating to resort to countermeasures
1. Before taking countermeasures, an injured State shall:
(*a*) Call upon the responsible State, in accordance with article 43, to fulfil its obligations under part two;
(*b*) Notify the responsible State of any decision to take countermeasures and offer to negotiate with that State.

2. Notwithstanding paragraph 1 (*b*), the injured State may take such urgent countermeasures as are necessary to preserve its rights.

3. Countermeasures may not be taken, and if already taken must be suspended without undue delay if:
(*a*) The internationally wrongful act has ceased; and
(*b*) The dispute is pending before a court or tribunal which has the authority to make decisions binding on the parties.

4. Paragraph 3 does not apply if the responsible State fails to implement the dispute settlement procedures in good faith.

Article 53 - Termination of countermeasures
Countermeasures shall be terminated as soon as the responsible State has complied with its obligations under part two in relation to the internationally wrongful act.

Article 54 - Measures taken by States other than an injured State
This chapter does not prejudice the right of any State, entitled under article 48, paragraph 1, to invoke the responsibility of another State, to take lawful measures against that State to ensure cessation of the breach and reparation in the interest of the injured State or of the beneficiaries of the obligation breached.

PART FOUR
GENERAL PROVISIONS

Article 55 - Lex specialis
These articles do not apply where and to the extent that the conditions for the existence of an internationally wrongful act or the content or implementation of the international responsibility of a State are governed by special rules of international law.

Article 56 - Questions of State responsibility not regulated by these articles
The applicable rules of international law continue to govern questions concerning the

responsibility of a State for an internationally wrongful act to the extent that they are not regulated by these articles.

Article 57 - Responsibility of an international organization
These articles are without prejudice to any question of the responsibility under international law of an international organization, or of any State for the conduct of an international organization.

Article 58 - Individual responsibility
These articles are without prejudice to any question of the individual responsibility under international law of any person acting on behalf of a State.

Article 59 - Charter of the United Nations
These articles are without prejudice to the Charter of the United Nations.

2. Resolution 59/35 (16.12.2004)

Resolution adopted by the General Assembly
[*on the report of the Sixth Committee (A/59/505)*]
59/35. Responsibility of States for internationally wrongful acts

The General Assembly,

Recalling its resolution 56/83 of 12 December 2001, the annex to which contains the text of the articles on responsibility of States for internationally wrongful acts,

Emphasizing the continuing importance of the codification and progressive development of international law, as referred to in Article 13, paragraph 1 (*a*), of the Charter of the United Nations,

Noting that the subject of responsibility of States for internationally wrongful acts is of major importance in relations between States,

1. *Commends once again* the articles on responsibility of States for internationally wrongful acts to the attention of Governments, without prejudice to the question of their future adoption or other appropriate action;

2. *Requests* the Secretary-General to invite Governments to submit their written comments on any future action regarding the articles;

3. *Also requests* the Secretary-General to prepare an initial compilation of decisions of international courts, tribunals and other bodies referring to the articles and to invite Governments to submit information on their practice in this regard, and further requests the Secretary-General to submit this material well in advance of its sixty-second session;

4. *Decides* to include in the provisional agenda of its sixty-second session the item entitled "Responsibility of States for internationally wrongful acts".

65th plenary meeting
2 December 2004

3. The Effect of Armed Conflict on Treaties: an Examination of Practice and Doctrine Memorandum by the Secretariat A/CN.4/550 + A/CN.4/550/Corr/1

For A/CN.4/550 (95 pages) see:
<http://documents-dds-ny.un.org/doc/UNDOC/GEN/N05/226/28/pdf/N0522628.pdf?OpenElement>

For A/CN.4/550/Corr.1 see:

International Law Commission
Fifty-seventh session
Geneva, 2 May-3 June and 4 July-5 August 2005
The effect of armed conflict on treaties: an examination of practice and doctrine
Memorandum by the Secretariat
Corrigendum
1. Paragraph 70, seventh and eighth lines
For the outbreak of hostilities *read* incidents of hostile acts
2. Paragraph 102, sixth line
For leading up to *read* prior to

4. Resolution 2625 (XXV); 24.10.1970 Declaration on Principles of International Law Concerning Friendly Relations and Cooperations amongst States in Accordance with the Charter of the United Nations

1970

The General Assembly,

Recalling its resolutions 1815 (XVII) of 18 December 1962, 1966 (XVIII) of 16 December 1963, 2103 (XX) of 20 December 1965, 2181 (XXI) of 12 December 1966, 2327 (XXII) of 18 December 1967, 2463 (XXIII) of 20 December 1968 and 2533 (XXIV) of 8 December 1969, in which it affirmed the importance of the progressive development and codification of the principles of international law concerning friendly relations and co-operation among States,

Having considered the report of the Special Committee on Principles of International Law concerning Friendly Relations and Co-operation among States, which met in Geneva from 31 March to 1 May 1970,

Emphasizing the paramount importance of the Charter of the United Nations for the maintenance of international peace and security and for the development of Friendly relations and Co-operation among States,

Deeply convinced that the adoption of the Declaration on Principles of International Law concerning Friendly Relations and Co-operation among States in accordance with the Charter of the United Nations on the occasion of the twenty-fifth anniversary of the United Nations would contribute to the strengthening of world peace and constitute a landmark in the development of international law and of relations among States, in promoting the rule of law among nations and particularly the universal application of the principles embodied in the Charter,

Considering the desirability of the wide dissemination of the text of the Declaration,

1. Approves the Declaration on Principles of International Law concerning Friendly Relations and Co-operation among States in accordance with the Charter of the United Nations, the text of which is annexed to the present resolution;

2. Expresses its appreciation to the Special Committee on Principles of International Law concerning Friendly Relations and Co-operation among States for its work resulting in the elaboration of the Declaration;

3. Recommends that all efforts be made so that the Declaration becomes generally known. 1883rd plenary meeting, 24 October 1970

ANNEX [25 UN GAOR, Supp. (No. 28), UN Dec. A/5217 (1970), at 121]

DECLARATION ON PRINCIPLES OF INTERNATIONAL LAW CONCERNING FRIENDLY RELATIONS AND CO-OPERATION AMONG STATES IN ACCORDANCE WITH THE CHARTER OF THE UNITED NATIONS

The General Assembly,

PREAMBLE

Reaffirming in the terms of the Charter of the United Nations that the maintenance of international peace and security and the development of friendly relations and co-operation between nations are among the fundamental purposes of the United Nations,

Recalling that the peoples of the United Nations are determined to practise tolerance and live together in peace with one another as good neighbours,

Bearing in mind the importance of maintaining and strengthening international peace founded upon freedom, equality, justice and respect for fundamental human rights and of developing friendly relations among nations irrespective of their political, economic and social systems or the levels of their development,

Bearing in mind also the paramount importance of the Charter of the United Nations in the promotion of the rule of law among nations,

Considering that the faithful observance of the principles of international law concerning friendly relations and co-operation among States and the fulfilment in good faith of the obligations assumed by States, in accordance with the Charter, is of the greatest importance for the maintenance of international peace and security and for the implementation of the other purposes of the United Nations,

Noting that the great political, economic and social changes and scientific progress which have taken place in the world since the adoption of the Charter give increased importance to these principles and to the need for their more effective application in the conduct of States wherever carried on,

Recalling the established principle that outer space, including the Moon and other celestial bodies, is not subject to national appropriation by claim of sovereignty, by means of use or occupation, or by any other means, and mindful of the fact that consideration is being given in the United Nations to the question of establishing other appropriate provisions similarly inspired,

Convinced that the strict observance by States of the obligation not to intervene in the affairs of any other State is an essential condition to ensure that nations live together in peace with one another, since the practice of any form of intervention not only violates the spirit and letter of the Charter, but also leads to the creation of situations which threaten international peace and security,

Recalling the duty of States to refrain in their international relations from military, political, economic or any other form of coercion aimed against the political independence or territorial integrity of any State,

Considering it essential that all States shall refrain in their international relations from the threat or use of force against the territorial integrity or political independence of any State, or in any other manner inconsistent with the purpose of the United Nations,

Considering it equally essential that all States shall settle their international disputes by peaceful means in accordance with the Charter,

Reaffirming, in accordance with the Charter, the basic importance of sovereign equality and stressing that the purposes of the United Nations can be implemented only if States enjoy sovereign equality and comply fully with the requirements of this principle in their international relations,

Convinced that the subjection of peoples to alien subjugation, domination and exploitation constitutes a major obstacle to the promotion of international peace and security,

Convinced that the principle of equal rights and self-determination of peoples constitutes a significant contribution to contemporary international law, and that its effective application is of paramount importance for the promotion of friendly relations among States, based on respect for the principle of sovereign equality,

Convinced in consequence that any attempt aimed at the partial or total disruption of the national unity and territorial integrity of a State or country or at its political independence is incompatible with the purposes and principles of the Charter,

Considering the provisions of the Charter as a whole and taking into account the role of relevant resolutions adopted by the competent organs of the United Nations relating to the content of the principles,

Considering that the progressive development and codification of the following principles:

(a) The principle that States shall refrain in their international relations from the threat or use of force against the territorial integrity or political independence of any State, or in any other manner inconsistent with the purpose of the United Nations,

(b) The principle that States shall settle their international disputes by peaceful means in such a manner that international peace and security and justice are not endangered,

(c) The duty not to intervene in matters within the domestic jurisdiction of any State, in accordance with the Charter,

(d) The duty of States to co-operate with one another in accordance with the Charter,

(e) The principle of equal rights and self-determination of peoples,

(f) The principle of sovereign equality of States,

(g) The principle that States shall fulfil in good faith the obligations assumed by them in accordance with the Charter,

so as to secure their more effective application within the international community, would promote the realization of the purposes of the United Nations,

Having considered the principles of international law relating to friendly relations and co-operation among States,

1. *Solemnly proclaims* the following principles:

The principle that States shall refrain in their international relations from the threat or use of force against the territorial integrity or political independence of any State, or in any other manner inconsistent with the purpose of the United Nations

Every State has the duty to refrain in its international relations from the threat or use of force against the territorial integrity or political independence of any State, or in any other manner inconsistent with the purposes of the United Nations. Such a threat or use of force constitutes a violation of international law and the Charter of the United Nations and shall never be employed as a means of settling international issues.

A war of aggression constitutes a crime against the peace, for which there is responsibility under international law.

In accordance with the purposes and principles of the United Nations, States have the duty to refrain from propaganda for wars of aggression.

Every State has the duty to refrain from the threat or use of force to violate the existing international boundaries of another State or as a means of solving international disputes, including territorial disputes and problems concerning frontiers of States.

Every State likewise has the duty to refrain from the threat or use of force to violate international lines of demarcation, such as armistice lines, established by or pursuant to an international agreement to which it is a party or which it is otherwise bound to respect. Nothing in the foregoing shall be construed as prejudicing the positions of the parties concerned with regard to the status and effects of such lines under their special regimes or as affecting their temporary character.

States have a duty to refrain from acts of reprisal involving the use of force.

Every State has the duty to refrain from any forcible action which deprives peoples referred to in the elaboration of the principle of equal rights and self-determination of their right to self-determination and freedom and independence.

Every State has the duty to refrain from organizing or encouraging the organization of irregular forces or armed bands, including mercenaries, for incursion into the territory of another State.

Every State has the duty to refrain from organizing, instigating, assisting or participating in acts of civil strife or terrorist acts in another State or acquiescing in organized activities within its territory directed towards the commission of such acts, when the acts referred to in the present paragraph involve a threat or use of force.

The territory of a State shall not be the object of military occupation resulting from the use of force in contravention of the provisions of the Charter. The territory of a State shall not be the object of acquisition by another State resulting from the threat or use of force. No territorial acquisition resulting from the threat or use of force shall be recognized as legal. Nothing in the foregoing shall be construed as affecting:

(a) Provisions of the Charter or any international agreement prior to the Charter regime and valid under international law; or

(b) The powers of the Security Council under the Charter.

All States shall pursue in good faith negotiations for the early conclusion of a universal treaty on general and complete disarmament under effective international control and strive to adopt appropriate measures to reduce international tensions and strengthen confidence among States.

All States shall comply in good faith with their obligations under the generally recognized principles and rules of international law with respect to the maintenance of international peace and security, and shall endeavour to make the United Nations security system based on the Charter more effective.

Nothing in the foregoing paragraphs shall be construed as enlarging or diminishing in any way the scope of the provisions of the Charter concerning cases in which the use of force is lawful.

The principle that States shall settle their international disputes by peaceful means in such a manner that international peace and security and justice are not endangered

Every State shall settle its international disputes with other States by peaceful means in such a manner that international peace and security and justice are not endangered.

States shall accordingly seek early and just settlement of their international disputes by negotiation, inquiry, mediation, conciliation, arbitration, judicial settlement, resort to regional agencies or arrangements or other peaceful means of their choice. In seeking such a settlement the parties shall agree upon such peaceful means as may be appropriate to the circumstances and nature of the dispute.

The parties to a dispute have the duty, in the event of failure to reach a solution by any one of the above peaceful means, to continue to seek a settlement of the dispute by other peaceful means agreed upon by them.

States parties to an international dispute, as well as other States, shall refrain from any action which may aggravate the situation so as to endanger the maintenance of international peace and security, and shall act in accordance with the purposes and principles of the United Nations.

International disputes shall be settled on the basis of the sovereign equality of States and in accordance with the principle of free choice of means. Recourse to, or acceptance of, a settlement procedure freely agreed to by States with regard to existing or future disputes to which they are parties shall not be regarded as incompatible with sovereign equality.

Nothing in the foregoing paragraphs prejudices or derogates from the applicable provisions of the Charter, in particular those relating to the pacific settlement of international disputes.

The principle concerning the duty not to intervene in matters within the domestic jurisdiction of any State, in accordance with the Charter

No State or group of States has the right to intervene, directly or indirectly, for any reason whatever, in the internal or external affairs of any other State. Consequently, armed intervention and all other forms of interference or attempted threats against the personality of the State or against its political, economic and cultural elements, are in violation of international law.

No State may use or encourage the use of economic, political or any other type of measures to coerce another State in order to obtain from it the subordination of the exercise of its sovereign rights and to secure from it advantages of any kind. Also, no State shall organize, assist, foment, finance, incite or tolerate subversive, terrorist or armed activities directed towards the violent overthrow of the regime of another State, or interfere in civil strife in another State.

The use of force to deprive peoples of their national identity constitutes a violation of their inalienable rights and of the principle of non-intervention.

Every State has an inalienable right to choose its political, economic, social and cultural systems, without interference in any form by another State.

Nothing in the foregoing paragraphs shall be construed as affecting the relevant provisions of the Charter relating to the maintenance of international peace and security.

The duty of States to co-operate with one another in accordance with the Charter

States have the duty to co-operate with one another, irrespective of the differences in their political, economic and social systems, in the various spheres of international relations, in order to maintain international peace and security and to promote international economic stability and progress, the general welfare of nations and international co-operation free from discrimination based on such differences.

To this end:

(a) States shall co-operate with other States in the maintenance of international peace and security;

(b) States shall co-operate in the promotion of universal respect for, and observance of, human rights and fundamental freedoms for all, and in the elimination of all forms of racial discrimination and all forms of religious intolerance;

(c) States shall conduct their international relations in the economic, social, cultural, technical and trade fields in accordance with the principles of sovereign equality and non-intervention;

(d) States Members of the United Nations have the duty to take joint and separate action in co-operation with the United Nations in accordance with the relevant provisions of the Charter.

States should co-operate in the economic, social and cultural fields as well as in the field of science and technology and for the promotion of international cultural and educational progress. States should co-operate in the promotion of economic growth throughout the world, especially that of the developing countries.

The principle of equal rights and self-determination of peoples

By virtue of the principle of equal rights and self-determination of peoples enshrined in the Charter of the United Nations, all peoples have the right freely to determine, without external interference, their political status and to pursue their economic, social and cultural development, and every State has the duty to respect this right in accordance with the provisions of the Charter.

Every State has the duty to promote, through joint and separate action, realization of the principle of equal rights and self-determination of peoples, in accordance with the provisions of the Charter, and to render assistance to the United Nations in carrying out the responsibilities entrusted to it by the Charter regarding the implementation of the principle, in order:

(a) To promote friendly relations and co-operation among States; and

(b) To bring a speedy end to colonialism, having due regard to the freely expressed will of the peoples concerned;

and bearing in mind that the subjection of peoples to alien subjugation, domination and exploitation constitutes a violation of the principle, as well as a denial of fundamental human rights, and is contrary to the Charter.

Every State has the duty to promote through joint and separate action universal respect for and observance of human rights and fundamental freedoms in accordance with the Charter.

The establishment of a sovereign and independent State, the free association or integration with an independent State or the emergence into any other political status freely determined by a people constitute modes of implementing the right of self-determination by that people.

Every State has the duty to refrain from any forcible action which deprives peoples referred to above in the elaboration of the present principle of their right to self-determination and freedom and independence. In their actions against, and resistance to, such forcible action in pursuit of the exercise of their right to self-determination, such peoples are entitled to seek and to receive support in accordance with the purposes and principles of the Charter.

The territory of a colony or other Non-Self-Governing Territory has, under the Charter, a status separate and distinct from the territory of the State administering it; and such separate and distinct status under the Charter shall exist until the people of the colony or Non-Self-Governing Territory have exercised their right of self-determination in accordance with the Charter, and particularly its purposes and principles.

Nothing in the foregoing paragraphs shall be construed as authorizing or encouraging any action which would dismember or impair, totally or in part, the territorial integrity or political unity of sovereign and independent States conducting themselves in compliance with the principle of equal rights and self-determination of peoples as described above and thus possessed of a government representing the whole people belonging to the territory without distinction as to race, creed, or colour.

Every State shall refrain from any action aimed at the partial or total disruption of the national unity and territorial integrity of any other State or country.

The principle of sovereign equality of States

All States enjoy sovereign equality. They have equal rights and duties and are equal members of the international community, notwithstanding differences of an economic, social, political or other nature.

In particular, sovereign equality includes the following elements:

(a) States are juridically equal;

(b) Each State enjoys the rights inherent in full sovereignty;

(c) Each State has the duty to respect the personality of other States;

(d) The territorial integrity and political independence of the State are inviolable;

(e) Each State has the right freely to choose and develop its political, social, economic and cultural systems;

(f) Each State has the duty to comply fully and in good faith with its international obligations and to live in peace with other States.

The principle that States shall fulfil in good faith the obligations assumed by them in accordance with the Charter

Every State has the duty to fulfil in good faith the obligations assumed by it in accordance with the Charter of the United Nations.

Every State has the duty to fulfil in good faith its obligations under the generally recognized principles and rules of international law.

Every State has the duty to fulfil in good faith its obligations under international agreements valid under the generally recognized principles and rules of international law.

Where obligations arising under international agreements are in conflict with the obligations of Members of the United Nations under the Charter of the United Nations, the obligations under the Charter shall prevail.

GENERAL PART

2. *Declares* that:

In their interpretation and application the above principles are interrelated and each principle should be construed in the context of the other principles.

Nothing in this Declaration shall be construed as prejudicing in any manner the provisions of the Charter or the rights and duties of Members States under the Charter or the rights of peoples under the Charter, taking into account the elaboration of these rights in this Declaration.

3. *Declares further* that:

The principles of the Charter which are embodied in this Declaration constitute basic principles of international law, and consequently appeals to all States to be guided by these principles in their international conduct and to develop their mutual relations on the basis of the strict observance of these principles.

5. Resolution 3314 (XXIX); 14.12.1974
Definition of Aggression

Committee: 6

Vote: Adopted without a vote

Ref: 3105(XXVIII), 2967(XXVII), 2781(XXVII), 2644(XXV), 2549(XXIV), 2420(XXIII), 2330(XXII), 1181(XII), 895(IX), 688(VII), 599(VI)

The General Assembly,

Having considered the report of the Special Committee on the Question of Defining Aggression, established pursuant to its resolution 2330(XXII) of 18 December 1967, covering the work of its seventh session held from 11 March to 12 April 1974, including the draft Definition of Aggression adopted by the Special Committee by consensus and recommended for adoption by the General Assembly,[FN1]

Deeply, convinced that the adoption of the Definition of Aggression would contribute to the strengthening of international peace and security,

1. Approves the Definition of Aggression, the text of which is annexed to the present resolution;

2. Expresses its appreciation to the Special Committee on the Question of Defining Aggression for its work which resulted in the elaboration of the Definition of Aggression;

3. Calls upon all States to refrain from all acts of aggression and other uses of force contrary to the Charter of the United Nations and the Declaration on Principles of International Law concerning Friendly Relations and Cooperation among States in accordance with the Charter of the United Nations;[FN2]

4. Calls the attention of the Security Council to the Definition of Aggression, as set out below, and recommends that it should, as appropriate, take account of that Definition as guidance in determination, in accordance with the Charter, the existence of an act of aggression.

2319th plenary meeting

14 December 1974

ANNEX

Definition of Aggression

The General Assembly,

Basing itself on the fact that one of the fundamental purposes of the United Nations is to maintain international peace and security and to take effective collective measures for the prevention and removal of threats to the peace, and for the suppression of acts of aggression or other breaches of the peace,

Recalling that the Security Council, in accordance with Article 39 of the Charter of the United Nations, shall determine the existence of any threat to the peace, breach of the peace or act of aggression and shall make recommendations, or decide what measures shall be taken in accordance with Articles 41 and 42, to maintain or restore international peace and security,

Recalling also the duty of States under the Charter to settle their international disputes by peaceful means in order not to endanger international peace, security and justice,

Bearing in mind that nothing in this Definition shall be interpreted as in any way affecting the scope of the provisions of the Charter with respect to the functions and powers of the organs of the United Nations,

Considering also that, since aggression is the most serious and dangerous form of the illegal use of force, being fraught, in the conditions created by the existence of all types of weapons of mass destruction, with the possible threat of a world conflict and all its catastrophic consequences, aggression should be defined at the present stage,

Reaffirming the duty of States not to use armed force to deprive peoples of their right to self-determination, freedom and independence, or to disrupt territorial integrity,

Reaffirming also that the territory of a State shall not be violated by being the object, even temporarily, of military occupation or of other measures of force taken by another State in contravention of the Charter, and that it shall not be the object of acquisition by another State resulting from such measures or the threat thereof,

Reaffirming also the provisions of the Declaration on Principles of International Law concerning Friendly Relations and Cooperation among States in accordance with the Charter of the United Nations,

Convinced that the adoption of a definition of aggression ought to have the effect of deterring a potential aggressor, would simplify the determination of acts of aggression and the implementation of measures to suppress them and would also facilitate the protection of the rights and lawful interests of, and the rendering of assistance to, the victim,

Believing that, although the question whether an act of aggression has been committed must be considered in the light of all the circumstances of each particular case, it is nevertheless desirable to formulate basic principles as guidance for such determination,

Adopts the following Definition of Agression:[FN3]

Article 1

Aggression is the use of armed force by a State against the sovereignty, territorial integrity or political independence of another State, or in any other manner inconsistent with the Charter of the United Nations, as set out in this Definition.

Explanatory note: In this Definition the term "State":

(a) Is used without prejudice to questions of recognition or to whether a State is a member of the United Nations;

(b) Includes the concept of a "group of States" where appropriate.

Article 2

The First use of armed force by a State in contravention of the Charter shall constitute prima facie evidence of an act of aggression although the Security Council may, in conformity with the Charter, conclude that a determination that an act of aggression has been committed would not be justified in the light of other relevant circumstances, including the fact that the acts concerned or their consequences are not of sufficient gravity.

Article 3

Any of the following acts, regardless of a declaration of war, shall, subject to and in accordance with the provisions of article 2, qualify as an act of aggression:

(a) The invasion or attack by the armed forces of a State of the territory of another State, or any military occupation, however temporary, resulting from such invasion or attack, or any annexation by the use of force of the territory of another State or part thereof,

(b) Bombardment by the armed forces of a State against the territory of another State or the use of any weapons by a State against the territory of another State;

(c) The blockade of the ports or coasts of a State by the armed forces of another State;

(d) An attack by the armed forces of a State on the land, sea or air forces, or marine and air fleets of another State;

(e) The use of armed forces of one State which are within the territory of another State with the agreement of the receiving State, in contravention of the conditions provided for in the agreement or any extension of their presence in such territory beyond the termination of the agreement;

(f) The action of a State in allowing its territory, which it has placed at the disposal of another State, to be used by that other State for perpetrating an act of aggression against a third State;

(g) The sending by or on behalf of a State of armed bands, groups, irregulars or mercenaries, which carry out acts of armed force against another State of such gravity as to amount to the acts listed above, or its substantial involvement therein.

Article 4

The acts enumerated above are not exhaustive and the Security Council may determine that other acts constitute aggression under the provisions of the Charter.

Article 5

1. No consideration of whatever nature, whether political, economic, military or otherwise, may serve as a justification for aggression.

2. A war of aggression is a crime against international peace. Aggression gives rise to international responsibility.

3. No territorial acquisition or special advantage resulting from aggression is or shall be recognized as lawful.

Article 6

Nothing in this Definition shall be construed as in any way enlarging or diminishing the scope of the Charter, including its provisions concerning cases in which the use of force is lawful.

Article 7

Nothing in this Definition, and in particular article 3, could in any way prejudice the right to self-determination, freedom and independence, as derived from the Charter, of peoples forcibly deprived of that right and referred to in the Declaration on Principles of International Law concerning Friendly Relations and Cooperation among States in accordance with the Charter of the United Nations, particularly peoples under colonial and racist regimes or other forms of alien domination: nor the right of these peoples to struggle to that end and to seek and receive support, in accordance with the principles of the Charter and in conformity with the above-mentioned Declaration.

Article 8

In their interpretation and application the above provisions are interrelated and each provision should be construed in the context of the other provisions.

FOOTNOTES

1. Official Records of the General Assembly, Twenty-ninth Session, Supplement No. 19 (A/9619 and Corr. 1).

2. Resolution 2625 (XXV), annex.

3. Explanatory notes on articles 3 and 5 are to be found in paragraph 20 of the Report of the Special Committee on the Question of Defining Aggression (Official Records of the General Assembly, Twenty-ninth Session, Supplement No. 19 (A/9619 and Corr. 1). Statements on the Definition are contained in paragraphs 9 and 10 of the report of the Sixth Committee (A/9890).

6. Resolution 27 A (III); 10.12.1948 Universal Declaration of Human Rights

Article 2.

Everyone is entitled to all the rights and freedoms set forth in this Declaration, without distinction of any kind, such as race, colour, sex, language, religion, political or other opinion, national or social origin, property, birth or other status. Furthermore, no distinction shall be made on the basis of the political, jurisdictional or international status of the country or territory to which a person belongs, whether it be independent, trust, non-self-governing or under any other limitation of sovereignty.

7. Resolution 39/11 (12.11.1984) Declaration on the Right of Peoples to Peace

The General Assembly,

Reaffirming that the principal aim of the United Nations is the maintenance of international peace and security,

Bearing in mind the fundamental principles of international law set forth in the Charter of the United Nations,

Expressing the will and the aspirations of all peoples to eradicate war from the life of mankind and, above all, to avert a world-wide nuclear catastrophe,

Convinced that life without war serves as the primary international prerequisite for the material well-being, development and progress of countries, and for the full implementation of the rights and fundamental human freedoms proclaimed by the United Nations,

Aware that in the nuclear age the establishment of a lasting peace on Earth represents the primary condition for the preservation of human civilization and the survival of mankind,

Recognizing that the maintenance of a peaceful life for peoples is the sacred duty of each State,

1. *Solemnly proclaims* that the peoples of our planet have a sacred right to peace;

2. *Solemnly declares* that the preservation of the right of peoples to peace and the promotion of its implementation constitute a fundamental obligation of each State;

3. *Emphasizes* that ensuring the exercise of the right of peoples to peace demands that the policies of States be directed towards the elimination of the threat of war, particularly

nuclear war, the renunciation of the use of force in international relations and the settlement of international disputes by peaceful means on the basis of the Charter of the United Nations;

4. *Appeals* to all States and international organizations to do their utmost to assist in implementing the right of peoples to peace through the adoption of appropriate measures at both the national and the international level.

F. UN SECURITY COUNCIL RESOLUTIONS

1. Resolution 1373 (2001); 28.9.2001

Resolution 1373 (2001)
Adopted by the Security Council at its 4385th meeting, on 28 September 2001

The Security Council,
Reaffirming its resolutions 1269 (1999) of 19 October 1999 and 1368 (2001) of 12 September 2001,

Reaffirming also its unequivocal condemnation of the terrorist attacks which took place in New York, Washington, D.C. and Pennsylvania on 11 September 2001, and expressing its determination to prevent all such acts,

Reaffirming further that such acts, like any act of international terrorism, constitute a threat to international peace and security,

Reaffirming the inherent right of individual or collective self-defence as recognized by the Charter of the United Nations as reiterated in resolution 1368 (2001),

Reaffirming the need to combat by all means, in accordance with the Charter of the United Nations, threats to international peace and security caused by terrorist acts,

Deeply concerned by the increase, in various regions of the world, of acts of terrorism motivated by intolerance or extremism,

Calling on States to work together urgently to prevent and suppress terrorist acts, including through increased cooperation and full implementation of the relevant international conventions relating to terrorism,

Recognizing the need for States to complement international cooperation by taking additional measures to prevent and suppress, in their territories through all lawful means, the financing and preparation of any acts of terrorism,

Reaffirming the principle established by the General Assembly in its declaration of October 1970 (resolution 2625 (XXV)) and reiterated by the Security Council in its resolution 1189 (1998) of 13 August 1998, namely that every State has the duty to refrain from organizing, instigating, assisting or participating in terrorist acts in another State or acquiescing in organized activities within its territory directed towards the commission of such acts,

Acting under Chapter VII of the Charter of the United Nations,

1. *Decides* that all States shall:
(a) Prevent and suppress the financing of terrorist acts;
(b) Criminalize the wilful provision or collection, by any means, directly or indirectly, of funds by their nationals or in their territories with the intention that the funds should be used, or in the knowledge that they are to be used, in order to carry out terrorist acts;
(c) Freeze without delay funds and other financial assets or economic resources of persons who commit, or attempt to commit, terrorist acts or participate in or facilitate the commission of terrorist acts; of entities owned or controlled directly or indirectly by such persons; and of persons and entities acting on behalf of, or at the direction of such persons and entities, including funds derived or generated from property owned or controlled directly or indirectly by such persons and associated persons and entities;
(d) Prohibit their nationals or any persons and entities within their territories from making any funds, financial assets or economic resources or financial or other related services available, directly or indirectly, for the benefit of persons who commit or attempt to commit or facilitate or participate in the commission of terrorist acts, of entities owned or controlled, directly or indirectly, by such persons and of persons and entities acting on behalf of or at the direction of such persons;

2. *Decides also* that all States shall:
(a) Refrain from providing any form of support, active or passive, to entities or persons involved in terrorist acts, including by suppressing recruitment of members of terrorist groups and eliminating the supply of weapons to terrorists;
(b) Take the necessary steps to prevent the commission of terrorist acts, including by provision of early warning to other States by exchange of information;
(c) Deny safe haven to those who finance, plan, support, or commit terrorist acts, or provide safe havens;
(d) Prevent those who finance, plan, facilitate or commit terrorist acts from using their respective territories for those purposes against other States or their citizens;
(e) Ensure that any person who participates in the financing, planning, preparation or perpetration of terrorist acts or in supporting terrorist acts is brought to justice and ensure that, in addition to any other measures against them, such terrorist acts are established as serious criminal offences in domestic laws and regulations and that the punishment duly reflects the seriousness of such terrorist acts;
(f) Afford one another the greatest measure of assistance in connection with criminal investigations or criminal proceedings relating to the financing or support of terrorist acts, including assistance in obtaining evidence in their possession necessary for the proceedings;
(g) Prevent the movement of terrorists or terrorist groups by effective border controls and controls on issuance of identity papers and travel documents, and through measures for preventing counterfeiting, forgery or fraudulent use of identity papers and travel documents;

3. *Calls* upon all States to:
(a) Find ways of intensifying and accelerating the exchange of operational information, especially regarding actions or movements of terrorist persons or networks; forged or falsified travel documents; traffic in arms, explosives or sensitive materials; use of communications technologies by terrorist groups; and the threat posed by the possession of weapons of mass destruction by terrorist groups;

(b) Exchange information in accordance with international and domestic law and cooperate on administrative and judicial matters to prevent the commission of terrorist acts;
(c) Cooperate, particularly through bilateral and multilateral arrangements and agreements, to prevent and suppress terrorist attacks and take action against perpetrators of such acts;
(d) Become parties as soon as possible to the relevant international conventions and protocols relating to terrorism, including the International Convention for the Suppression of the Financing of Terrorism of 9 December 1999;
(e) Increase cooperation and fully implement the relevant international conventions and protocols relating to terrorism and Security Council resolutions 1269 (1999) and 1368 (2001);
(f) Take appropriate measures in conformity with the relevant provisions of national and international law, including international standards of human rights, before granting refugee status, for the purpose of ensuring that the asylum-seeker has not planned, facilitated or participated in the commission of terrorist acts;
(g) Ensure, in conformity with international law, that refugee status is not abused by the perpetrators, organizers or facilitators of terrorist acts, and that claims of political motivation are not recognized as grounds for refusing requests for the extradition of alleged terrorists;

4. *Notes* with concern the close connection between international terrorism and transnational organized crime, illicit drugs, money-laundering, illegal armstrafficking, and illegal movement of nuclear, chemical, biological and other potentially deadly materials, and in this regard *emphasizes* the need to enhance coordination of efforts on national, subregional, regional and international levels in order to strengthen a global response to this serious challenge and threat to international security;

5. *Declares* that acts, methods, and practices of terrorism are contrary to the purposes and principles of the United Nations and that knowingly financing, planning and inciting terrorist acts are also contrary to the purposes and principles of the United Nations;

6. *Decides* to establish, in accordance with rule 28 of its provisional rules of procedure, a Committee of the Security Council, consisting of all the members of the Council, to monitor implementation of this resolution, with the assistance of appropriate expertise, and *calls upon* all States to report to the Committee, no later than 90 days from the date of adoption of this resolution and thereafter according to a timetable to be proposed by the Committee, on the steps they have taken to implement this resolution;

7. *Directs* the Committee to delineate its tasks, submit a work programme within 30 days of the adoption of this resolution, and to consider the support it requires, in consultation with the Secretary-General;

8. *Expresses* its determination to take all necessary steps in order to ensure the full implementation of this resolution, in accordance with its responsibilities under the Charter;

9. *Decides* to remain seized of this matter.

2. How the SC Dealt with the Entebbe Situation
<http://www.un.org/News/Press/docs/1998/19980424.SC6508.html>

G. Classical Sources

1. CICERO

On Behalf of Milo. Ed. Watts, Cambridge (Ms.) and London 1964.

4.9-11 (ed. Watts at pp. 15-19)
And if there is any occasion (and there are many such) when homicide is justifiable, it is surely not merely justifiable but even inevitable when the offer of violence is repelled by violence. [...] There does exist therefore, gentlemen, a law which is a law not of the statute-book, but of nature; a law which we possess not by instruction, tradition or reading, but which we have caught, imbibed, and sucked in at Nature's own breast; a law which comes to us not by education but by constitution, not by training but by intuition – the law, I mean, that, should our life have fallen into a snare, into the violence and the weapons of robbers or foes, every method of winning a way to safety would be morally justifiable. When arms speak, the laws are silent; that is the famous *inter enim arma silent leges* – they bid none to await their word, since he who chooses to await it must pay an undeserved penalty ere he can exact a deserved one.
And yet most wisely, and, in a way, tacitly, the law itself authorizes self-defence; it forbids not homicide, but the carrying of a weapon with a view to homicide, and consequently when the circumstances of the case and not the carrying of the weapon was being investigated, the man who had employed a weapon in self-defence was not held to have carried that weapon with a view to homicide. So let this consideration be held in view, gentlemen, throughout the case; for I have no doubt that I shall make good my case for the defence, if you will bear in mind (and it is a fact that you cannot forget) that the slaying of a conspirator may be a justifiable act.

For a different version, see:
<http://www.uah.edu/student_life/organizations/SAL/texts/latin/classical/cicero/promilone1e.html#cfour>

H. Hebrew Sources

1. Babylonian talmud
Sanhedrin 72A

Do not take life - which God has made sacred - except for just cause. And if anyone is slain wrongfully, we have given his heir authority to demand retribution; but let him not exceed bounds in the matter of taking life, for he is helped by the law.

2. Maimonides

Code, Book xiv, "the Book of Judges", Treaties Five, Kings and their Wars, Chapter 5 (translation by Abraham M. Hershman, Yale Judaica Series, Vol III, 1949)

Kings and Wars

Chapter V

1. The primary war which the king wages is a war for a religious cause. Which may be denominated a war for a religious cause? It includes the war against the seven nations,

that against Amalek, and the war to deliver Israel for the enemy attacking him. Thereafter he may engage in an optional war, that is, a war against neighboring nations to extend the borders of Israel and to enhance his greatness and prestige.
2. For a war waged for a religious cause, the king need not obtain the sanction of the court. He may at any time go forth of his own accord and compel the people to go with him. But in case of an optional war, he may not lead forth the people save by a decision of the court of seventy-one.
3. He may break through (private property) to make a road for himself, and none may protest against it. No limit can be prescribed for the king's road; he expropriates as much as is needed. He does not have to make detours because someone's vineyard or field (is in the way). He takes the straight route and attacks the enemy.
4. It is a positive command to destroy the seven nations, as it is said: *But thou shalt utterly destroy them* (Deut. 20:17). If one does not put to death any of them that falls into one's power, one transgresses a negative command, as it is said: *Thou shalt save alive nothing that breatheth* (Deut. 20:16). But their memory has long perished.
5. So troo, it si said a positive command to destroy the memory of Amalek, as it is aid: *Thou shalt blot out the remembrance of Amalek* (Deut. 25:19). It is a positive command always to bear in mind his evil deeds, the waylaying (he resorted to), so that we keep fresh the memory of the hatred manifested by him, as it is said: *Remember what Amalek did unto see* (Deut. 25:17). The traditional interpretation of this injunction is: *Remember,* by word of mouth; *do not forget,* out of mind.
6. All provinces conquered by the king at the decision of the court are deemed a national conquest and become in all respects an integral part of the Land of Israel by Joshua, provided that they are annexed after the whole of Palestine, the boundaries of which are specified in the Bible, has been reconquered.
7. It is permitted to settle everywhere except in Egypt from the Great Sea to the west thereof, an area of four hundred square Persian miles, opposite Ethiopia and the wilderness. In all this territory it is forbidden to settle.
Three times the Torah admonishes us not to return to Egypt, as it is said: *Ye shall henceforth return no more that way* (Deut. 17:16); *And thou shalt see it no more again* (Deut. 28:68); *Ye shall see them again no more forever* (Exod. 14:13). Alexandria is included in the forbidden area.
8. It is permitted to go to Egypt on business or for the purpose of conquering it. The interdiction applies only to settling there; but the infraction of the negative command does not subject (the offender) to the penalty of flogging, because he is permitted to enter the land and his decision to reside there permanently does not involve a tangible act.
It appears to me that were the king of Israel with the approval of the Supreme Court to conquer Egypt, it would be permitted to settle there. The prohibition is directed only at individuals or at those who would take up their abode there while it is in the hands of the heathens, because the practices of the Egyptians are more corrupt than those of the inhabitants of all other lands, as it is said: *After the doings of the land of Egypt...shall ye not do* (Lev. 18:3).
9. It is forbidden to emigrate form Palestine and go abroad unless one goes to study the Law, or to marry a wife, or to rescue property from heathens, and then returns to Palestine. So too, one may leave on business. But one is forbidden to make one's home abroad, unless there is a famine in Palestine so severe that a *denar's* worth of wheat is selling at two *denar*. This holds good only if money is available and food is high. But if food is cheap and money scarce and one is unable to earn it and has no savings, one may go to any place where one can make a living. But though one is permitted to emigrate, if one does, the act is not conformity with the law of saintliness. Remember Mahlon and Chilion! They were the two great men of their generation. They left Palestine at a time of great distress; nevertheless, they incurred thereby the penalty of extinction.

10. The greatest of our Sages used to kiss (the rocks) on the borders of Palestine. They used to kiss the stone of the land and roll themselves in its dust, as it is written: *For thy servants take pleasure in her stones, and love her dusts* (Ps. 102:15).
11. The Rabbis said that the sins of him who lives in Palestine are forgiven, as it is written: *And the inhabitants shall not say: "I am sick"; the people that dwell therein shall be forgiven their iniquity* (Isa. 33:24). Even if one walks four cubits in it, one is assured of life in the world to come. So too, one who is buried there will obtain atonement; it is as though the place (where one lies) were an altar which effects atonement, as it is said: *And the land doth make expiation for His people* (Deut. 32:43). In (forecasting) punishment, (the prophet) says: *And thou thyself shalt die in an unclean land* (Amos 7:17). There is no comparison between one whom Palestine receives while he is living and one whom it receives after his death; nevertheless the greatest among our wise men brought their dead there. Think of Jacob, our father, and of Joseph, the righteous!
12. At all times one should live in Palestine even in a place the majority of whose population is heathen, and not live outside Palestine even in a place the majority of whose population is Jewish; for he who leaves Palestine is as though he would serve idolatry, as it is written: *I should not cleave unto the inheritance of the Lord, saying: Go, serve other gods* (I Sam. 26:19). In (predicting) punishment, the prophet says: *Neither shall they enter into the land of Israel* (Ezek. 13:9).
Just as it is forbidden to emigrate from Palestine to other lands, so it is forbidden to emigrate from Babylon to other lands, as it is written: *They shall be carried to Babylon, and there shall they be* (Jer. 27:22).

Epistle Addressed By Rabbi Moses Maimonides To Rabbi Samuel Ibn Tibbon p. 377

Let me premise one canon. Whoever wishes to translate, and purposes to render each word literally, and at the same time to adhere slavishly to the order of the words and sentences in the original, will meet with much difficulty; his rendering will be faulty and untrustworthy. This is not the right method. The translator should first try to grasp the sense of the subject thoroughly, and then state the theme with perfect clearness in the other language. This, however, can not be done without changing the order of the words, putting many words for one word, or *vice versa*, and adding or taking away words, so that the subject be perfectly intelligible in the language into which he translates. This method was followed by Honein ben Is'hak with the works of Galen, and his son Is'hak with the works of Aristotle. It is for this reason that all their versions are so peculiarly lucid, and therefore we ought to study them to the exclusion of all others. Your distinguished college ought to adopt this rule in all the translations undertaken for those honored men, and the heads of the congregation. And may God grant that the spread of knowledge among other communities of Israel be prompted by such works.

See link: <http://www.sacred-texts.com/jud/mhl/mhl19.htm>

3. The Mishna (Ethics of the Fathers)

Rabbi Shimon ben (son of) Gamliel said: "On three things does the world endure: justice, truth and peace, as the verse states, 'Truth and [judgments of] peace judge in your gates'" (Zechariah 8:16).

I. Arabic Sources

1. Islamic Quran – Surat al-Shura (42), 39, 41

See: <http://www.sacred-texts.com/isl/pick/042.htm>

39 And those who, when great wrong is done to them, defend themselves,

41 And whoso defended himself after he hath suffered wrong - for such, there is no way (of blame) against them.

J. Early Modern Sources

1. Balthazar Ayala

Three Books on the Law of War and on the Duties Connected with War and on Military Discipline (1582); Ed. Bate, 2 vols., Washington, D.C. 1912.

I.2.1 (ed. Bate at II p. 7)
Cicero lays it down that in a well-ordered Sate the laws of war should be scrupulously observed. Alike in beginning a war and in carrying it on and in ending it, law has a most important position and so has good-faith.

I.2.3 (ed. Bate at II p. 8)
War, therefore, is justifiable when its object is to procure peaceful existence and freedom from outrage, and when begun in such a way as that peace may appear to be its sole object.

I.2.6 (ed. Bate at II p. 8)
Just wars are, indeed, enjoined by the Law of Nations (jus gentium), and are permitted both by the canon law and by the law of God, for God himself ordered the Jews to make war on the Amorites and other peoples.

I.2.10 (ed. Bate at II p. 10)
Beside this, war may not be made save for just and necessary cause and there should be an entire absence of the passion to do hurt and of revengeful savagery and of the lust of conquest. [...]

I.2.11 (ed. Bate at II pp. 10-11)
Now the principal just causes of war are: the defence of our own empire, of our persons, of our friends, of our allies, and of our property; for no other warrant than the law of nature is needed to justify even private persons in defending themselves. [...]

A war is based on a just cause, again, when it is waged in order to regain from the enemy something which he is forcibly and unjustly detaining, in the same way as the authors of a wrong or harm done with private and not public intent are handed over to punishment. [...]

Another just cause of war is to take vengeance for some wrong which has been unjustifiable inflicted.

I.2.12 (ed. Bate at II p. 11)
And then a prince has a most just cause of war when he is directing his arms against rebels and subjects who abjure his sovereignty; for it is a heinous offense, against both God and the prince, for subjects to resist his authority, all power being from God alone.

I.2.33 (ed. Bate at II p. 22)
From the foregoing it may be gathered that our remarks so far also out just causes of war deal rather with considerations of fairness and goodness and propriety, and not with the character of the legal result which is produced.

I.2.34 (ed. Bate at II p. 22)
A war may in one sense be styled just and yet not be waged for a just cause; for the word 'just' has varying meanings (as Budaeus has remarked) and does not always indicate justice and equity but sometimes signifies a certain legal completeness.

2. Alberico Gentili

De jure belli Libri Tres (1612); Ed. Rolfe, 2 vols., Oxford 1933.

I.5.45 (ed. Rolfe at II. pp. 28-29)
To Cicero, who maintains that war is opposed to some law of humanity, by which we were born for union and not for discord, we may reply that war is not contrary to all human law; for example, that which provides that those who revolt from society and do not keep men's laws should be punished and forced to conform to those laws, statutes, and costumes. This fact too has a bearing upon our investigation, that wars are just even though so many things which come from them are evil, because their final aim is good, after the rebels have been forced to submit to reason. And since its aim is good, war itself is also good and just. And because all things have their own bounds, etc., all of which is from Aristotle.

I.13.92-94 (ed. Rolfe at II. pp. 58-59)
Now although I maintain that no natural cause for was exists, there are reasons because of which we undertake wars under Nature's guidance. For example, for defence and when we make war because something is refused us which Nature herself has bestowed upon mankind; and therefore war is resorted to, because a law of Nature is violated. We call defence, now necessary, now expedient, now honourable; yet in every case we should regard it as necessary. He who defends himself is said to act through compulsion. So says Baldus, who refuses to distinguish whether one is defending oneself, one's possessions, or one's subjects; or whether what is defended is near or at a distance. Thus one who is attacked by an armed enemy makes necessary defence, and his action is that of necessary defence; and so what does one against whom an enemy has been making preparations. And that such a one ought to be helped by his allies is rightly maintained by the aforementioned Baldus, while others hold the same opinion. [...]

But these things have nothing to do with justice. For to kill in self-defence is just, even though the one who kills may flee without danger and so save himself; and regardless of the question whether the one who slays in self-defence is of such condition that it would be disgraceful for him to flee, or not disgraceful. These views have been admitted in the case of private individuals, and I consider them still more valid with regard to states. Even the brutes are given the right of defence by nature, and we are persuaded and convinced of this right not by argument, but by some innate power. And it is necessary right; for what can be done against violence, says Cicero, without resort to violence? This is the most generally accepted of all rights. All laws and all codes allow the repelling of force by force. There is one rule which endures for ever, to maintain one's safety by any and every means. Every method of securing safety is honourable. This has been taught to philosophers by reason, to barbarians by necessity, to the nations by customs, to wild animals by Nature herself. This law is not written, but inborn.

3. Hugo Grotius

A. *Commentary on the Law of Prize and Booty* (c.1604); Ed. Williams, 2 vols., Oxford 1950.

Ch. I (ed. Williams 1950 at p. 3)
Justice consists in taking a middle course. It is wrong to inflict injury, but it is also wrong to endure injury. The former is, of course, the graver misdeed, but the latter is also to be avoided. Owing, however, to the fact that we are more frequently impelled toward the first extreme, the precept of regard for others is usually held up to us with excessive zeal, the implication being that we are by nature sufficiently inclined to care for ourselves. Nevertheless, the wise man does not belittle himself, nor does he neglect to avail himself of his own advantages, since no other person will use them more properly. By the same token, he will repel every injury to himself in so far as law and justice permit him to do so. Thus the truly good man will be free from *meionexia*, that is to say, from the disposition to accord himself less than his due.
To be sure, such a disposition, as long as the loss resulting from it affects no one save the individual in error, customarily excites more ridicule than reproach and is called folly rather than injustice. But if at any time private loss brings common peril in its train, then indeed, we must combat it with all our force, lest the public welfare be harmfully affected by the mistaken convictions of individual citizens. Under this head should be placed the weakness of those persons who betrayed their own possessions to the enemy because some conscientious scruple prevented them from fighting. We know about the Jewish Sabbaths and the Greek Moons. If there be other men who have not borne sufficiently in mind the famous epic passage, let them remember that:

There is no act more noble than defence
Of one's own land upon the battlefield.
[Hom. *Il.* 12.243]

Ch. II (ed. Williams 1950 at p. 9)
Therefore, since God fashioned creation and willed its existence, every individual part thereof has received from Him certain natural properties whereby that existence may be preserved and each part may be guided for its own good, in conformity, one might say, with the fundamental law inherent in its origin. From this fact the old poets and philosophers have rightly deduced that love, whose primary force and action are directed to self-interest, is the first principle of the whole natural order. Consequently, Horace should not be censured for saying, in imitation of the Academics, that expediency might perhaps be called the mother of justice and equity. For all things in nature, as Cicero repeatedly insists, are tenderly regardful of self, and seek their own happiness and security.
This phenomenon can be observed not only in the human race, but among the beasts also and even in connexion with inanimate objects, being a manifestation of that true and divinely inspired self-love which is laudable in every phase of creation.

Ch. II (ed. Williams 1950 at p. 10)
Accordingly from this combination of concepts two precepts of the law of nature emerge: first, that *It shall be permissible to defend [one's own] life and to shun that which threatens to prove injurious*; secondly, that *It shall be permissible to acquire for oneself, and to retain, those things which are useful for life.*

Ch. II (ed. Williams 1950 at p. 11)
But God judged that there would be insufficient provision for the preservation of His works, if He commended to each individual's care only the safety of that particular individual, without also willing that one created being should have regard for the welfare of his fellow beings, in such a way that all might be linked in mutual harmony as if by an everlasting covenant. Seneca has said: "You must needs live for others, if you would live for yourself." Love, then, is twofold: love for oneself, and love for others. In the former aspect, it is known as 'desire'; in the latter, as 'friendliness'.

Ch. VI (ed. Williams 1950 at p. 60)
Thus Solon (so we are told) laid down the doctrine that the state wherein each individual regards injuries to others as injuries to himself, will be a happy state. [...] It behoves us to defend with all our might the victims of unjust oppression, and not to leave them neglected; for the former course is just and good, whereas the latter is unjust and wicked.

Ch. VI (ed. Williams 1950 at p. 61)
If injury has been inflicted upon any person, it is fitting that we should take up arms, whether in self-defence or for the sake of kindred or benefactors; or again, if our allies have been wronged, it is fitting that we go to their aid. For that matter, even if other bonds are lacking, the universal fellowship of mankind and the communion established by nature, will still cause us to be affected in our turn by ills inflicted upon others. For human beings should not hold themselves aloof from anything that is of human import. Indeed, this maxim holds good to such an extent that great nations, as well as theologians and jurists of no slight authority, in many cases regard as punishable the negligence of those who have allowed some person to be injured when they could have prevented such injury.

Ch. VII (ed. Williams 1950 at p. 67)
Therefore, every [just] war must have its origin in one of four causes. The first of these is self-defence, which is based upon the First Law. For, as Cicero observes, '...the act [of homicide] is not only just but even necessary, when it represents the repulsion of violence by means of violence'. Many statements to the same effect are to be found in the works of various authors.

A second cause is defence of one's property, based upon the Second Law, which makes it permissible not only to offer resistance but also to dispossess others. Moreover, the term 'property' is to be understood not exclusively in a material sense, but as referring to every right, including that right to a good name which is justly the possession of virtuous persons and of which they ought by no means to be deprived.

A third cause – one, that a great many authorities neglect to mention – turns upon debts arising from a contract or from some similar source. [...]

The fourth cause arises from wrongdoing, and from every injury – whether of word or deed – inflicted with unjust intent. Augustine wrote: 'Just wars, indeed, are wont to be defined as those which avenge injuries.

Ch. VII (ed. Williams 1950 at pp. 68-69)
Therefore, in both kinds of warfare, [public and private,] one must consider the causes involved. Of these there are four kinds, as we have pointed out: for the authorities who hold that there are three just causes of war (defence, recovery, and punishment, according to their classification), fail to mention the not uncommon cause that arises whenever obligations are not duly discharged. Indeed, in so far as we are concerned with subject-matter, which is the same in warfare and in judicial trials, we may say that there should be precisely as many kinds of execution as there are kinds of legal action.

Ch. VII (ed. Williams 1950 at p. 70)
Therefore, in so far as concerns the persons who wage war voluntarily, that war has a just cause, wherein the said persons defend their lives or their property, or seek to recover the latter, or attempt to exact either payment of that which is due or punishment for wrongdoing.

Ch. VII (ed. Williams 1950 at p. 73)
For, on the basis of the First Law, which charges me to have a care for myself even in preference to others, I have the right to ward off an act of that kind by any means whatsoever. As Seneca says, 'Necessity, the great defence of human weakness, breaks down every law'. Indeed, as we observed at the outset, necessity is the first law of nature.

Ch. VIII (ed. Williams 1950 at p. 87)
The defect is of brief duration whenever our rights have not yet been violated but the matter does not permit of the delay necessary for judicial procedure. In the first place, then, as Baldus has said, whatever is expedient for self-defence in such cases, is likewise permissible; for a crisis that threatens our lives permits of no delay. The jurists, indeed, approve of everything done to ward off danger, or through fear of death, or for the protection of our persons, or in order to repel violence, in so far as it is impossible for us to defend ourselves becomingly or effectively in any other way. This contention is equivalent to that rule of blameless self-defence which is so frequently reiterated. Similarly, it is permissible for us to defend or recover our own property, even with the assistance of groups of men assembled for that purpose, but only if such action is taken at once. For after an interval during which there has been time to appear before a judge, force should no longer be used.

Ch. VIII (ed. Williams 1950 at p. 88)
As regards continuous lack of means for judicial settlement, the authorities maintain that there two ways in which such a defect may occur: it may be either a defect in law or a defect in fact. It is a defect in law when in a given place there is no one possessing jurisdiction, a state of affairs, which may exist in desert lands, on islands, on the ocean or in any region where the people have no government. The defect is one of fact whenever the person to whom jurisdiction properly pertains, is disregarded by those subject to him, or when he is not at leisure to conduct a judicial inquiry. In such cases, as Castrensis' rightly observes, the situation becomes very much what it was before states and courts of justice were established.

Ch. VIII (ed. Williams 1950 at p. 93)
To take one example, certain laws grant the power of direct self-defence and vengeance to private individuals, precisely on the ground that it is not easy to resist soldiers and collectors of public revenue through the medium of the courts; and these particular precepts

accordingly represent what we retain of natural law – the vestiges of that law, so to speak – in regard to punishment.

Ch. XII (ed. Williams 1950 at p. 267)
The causes above set forth certainly constituted just grounds for undertaking a war. In addition, however, we have observed that not every right [justifying belligerent measures] exists prior to the outbreak of war. There is a form of right, which arises in the midst of armed conflict and in defence whereof warfare is properly continued.
Defence of one's own life is included under this head. For when we are defending or attempting to recover our property, or seeking to obtain that which is our right, while our adversary offers armed opposition to such attempts on our part, it is evident that we, though innocent, are thus brought into peril of our lives. This situation constitutes the oldest and most just of the causes of war.

Ch. XIII (ed. Williams 1950 at p. 314)
There are two kinds of injustice: the kind characteristic of persons who inflict injury; and the kind characteristic of those who fail to ward off injury, when they are able to do so, from the victims upon whom it is inflicted. For he who neither repels nor resists injury when such resistance lies within his power, is as gravely at fault as if he were forsaking his parents or friends or native land, since (according to the aforesaid philosophers) the contention that one must have regard for one's fellow citizens but not for foreigners, is assuredly equivalent to repudiation of the universal bond of human fellowship, a bond which one cannot repudiate without being adjudged impious toward God Himself, the Author thereof. Our jurists, too, are of the opinion that the person responsible for such an omission shares in the guilt attaching to the injurious act; and the Church Fathers hold that he who has failed to resist injury to his fellow man is no less culpable than the individual who inflicts that injury.

Ch. XV (ed. Williams 1950 at p. 355)
.... A soldier's strength is measured by his cause:
Unless that cause be just, his shame will strike
The weapons from the soldier's very hands.
[…] The Dutch sailor knows that he is fighting in defence of the law of nations while his foes are fighting against the fellowship of mankind.

B. *On the Law of War and Peace* (c.1646); Ed. Kessinger Publishing, Whitefish 2004.

2. 1.1 (ed. Kessinger 2004 at p. 49)
The causes of war by which are meant the justifiable causes, are now to be considered. For in some cases motives of interest operate distinctly from motives of justice. Polybius accurately distinguishes these motives from each other, and from the beginning of the war, or that which gave occasion to the first acts of hostility; as was he case when Ascanius wounded the stag, which gave rise to the war between Turnus and Aeneas. But though here is an actual distinction between the justifiable causes, the pretexts, and the beginning of war; yet the terms used to express them are often confounded. For what we call justifiable causes, Livy, in the speech which he as put into the mouth of the Rhodians, calls beginnings. The Rhodian deputies said, 'You Romans profess to believe that your wars are successful, because they are just: or do you boast so much of their victorious issue, as of the just principles, upon which you take them.'

2.1.2.1-2 (ed. Kessinger 2004 at p. 50)
The grounds of war are as numerous as those of judicial actions. For where the power of law ceases, there war begins. Now there are methods in law to prevent intended injuries, as well as actions for those actually committed. For CIVIL INJURIES various methods of redress, or prevention are appointed by the law; and by the same power securities are provided to prevent the commission of crimes and misdemeanors. In civil cases, the party aggrieved may recover damages for the injuries sustained; and in crimes, which are offences against the public, the aggressor must submit to actual punishment. Plato, in his ninth book on laws, very properly makes the same distinction, as Homer had done before him. Now reparation or indemnity relates to what either does or did belong to us; which gives rise to real and personal actions. These ascertain our right to the damages, which are our due, either from an agreement, or from an injury received. A right which is termed in law a right by contract, or injury. Crimes, which are offences against society, are prosecuted by indictment, that is by an accusation in the name of the sovereign.

2.1.2.3-5 (ed. Kessinger 2004 at p. 51)
The justifiable causes generally assigned for war are three, defence, indemnity, and punishment, all which are comprised in the declaration of Camillus against the Gauls, enumerating all things, which it is right to defend, to recover, and the encroachment on which it is right to punish. There is an omission in this enumeration, unless the word recover be taken in its most extensive sense. For recovering by war what we have lost, includes indemnity for the past, as well as the prosecution of our claim to a debt. Plato has not omitted to notice this distinction, for he has said, 'that wars are made to punish not only oppression or robbery, but also fraud and deception'. With whom Seneca agrees; for to command payment of what you owe, he calls, 'an equitable sentence, stamped with the authority of the law of nations'. Indeed the form which was prescribed for the Roman heralds to use in declarations of war, bears exactly the same import. For therein the aggressor is charged with having neither given, paid, nor done what was due. Sallust in one of his fragments, has made a Tribune, in his harangue to the people, say, 'As a final settlement of all discussion; I demand restitution according to the law of nations'.

St. Augustin, in defining those to be just wars, which are made to avenge injuries has taken the word avenge in a general sense of removing and preventing, as well as punishing aggressions. This appears to be his meaning from the following sentence of the passage, in which he does not enumerate the particular acts, which amount to injury, but adds, by way of illustration, that 'the state or nation, which has neglected to punish the aggressions of its own subjects, or to make reparation for the losses occasioned by those aggressions, is a proper object of hostility and attack.' Prompted by this natural knowledge of right and wrong, the Indian King, as we are informed by Diodorus, accused Semiramis of having commenced war against him without having received any injury, Thus the Romans expostulated with the Senones, that they ought not to attack a people who had given them no provocation. Aristotle in the second book and second chapter of his Analytics, says, war generally is made upon those who have first done an injury. Quintus Curtius describes the Abian Scythians, as the best acquainted with the principles of justice of any of the Barbarians. For they declined having recourse to arm; unless provoked by aggression. A just cause then of war is an injury, which though not actually committed, threatens our persons or property with danger.

2.1.3 (ed. Kessinger 2004 at p. 52)
It has already been proved that when our lives are threatened with immediate danger, it is lawful to kill the aggressor, if the danger cannot otherwise be avoided: an instance, as it has

been shewn, on which the justice of private war rests. We must observe that this kind of defence derives its origin from the principle of self. preservation, which nature has given to every living creature, and not from the injustice or misconduct of the aggressor. Wherefore though he may be clear of guilt, as for instance a soldier in actual service, mistaking my person for that of another, or a madman in his frenzy, or a man walking in his sleep, none of these cases deprive me of the right of self-defence against those per. sons. For I am not bound to submit to the danger or mischief intended, any more than to expose myself to the attacks of a wild beast.

2.1.4.1 (ed. Kessinger 2004 at p. 52

It admits of some doubt, whether those, who unintentionally obstruct our defence, or escape, which are necessary to our preservation, may be lawfully maimed or killed. There are some, even Theologians, who think they may. And, certainly if we look to the law of nature alone, according to its principles, our own preservation should have much more weight with us, than the welfare of society. But the law of charity, especially the evangelical law, which has put our neighbour upon a level with ourselves, does not permit it.

2.1.4.2 (ed. Kessinger 2004 at p. 52)

Thomas Aquinas, if taken in a right sense, has justly observed, that in actual self-defence no man can be said to be purposely killed. Indeed, it may some times happen that there is no other way for a person to save himself, than by designedly doing an act, by which the death of an aggressor must inevitably ensue. Yet here the death of any one was not the primary object intended, but employed as the only means of security, which the moment supplied. Still it is better for the party assaulted, if he can safely do it, to repel or disable the aggressor than to shed his blood.

2.1.5.1-3 (ed. Kessinger 2004 at p. 52-53)

The danger must be immediate, which is one necessary point. Though it must be confessed, that when an assailant seizes any weapon with an apparent intention to kill me I have a right to anticipate and prevent the danger. For in the moral as well as the natural system of things, there is no point without some breadth. But they are themselves much mistaken, and mislead others, who maintain that any degree of fear ought, to be a ground for killing another, to prevent his SUPPOSED intention. It is a very just observation made by Cicero in his first book of Offices, that many wrongs proceed from fear; as when the person, who intends to hurt another, apprehends some danger to himself unless he tool, that method. Clearchus, in Xenophon, says, I have known some men, who partly through misrepresentation, and partly through suspicion, dreading one another, in order to prevent the supposed intentions of their adversaries, have committed the most enormous cruelties against those who neither designed, nor wished them any harm. Cato in his speech for the Rhodians, says, 'Are we to prevent them by doing first, what we say they intended to do to us?' On this subject there is a remarkable passage in Aulus Gellius, 'When a Gladiator prepares to enter the lists for combat, such is his lot that he must either kill his adversary, or be killed himself. But the life of man is not circumscribed by the hard terms of such an over-ruling necessity, as to oblige him to do an injury to prevent him from receiving one.' Quintilian has quoted a passage from Cicero, wherein the orator asks, 'Whoever made such a decision, or to whom could such a point be yielded without the most imminent danger, that you have a right to kill the person, by whom you say, you fear that you shall afterwards be killed yourself?' To which this passage of Euripides, may be applied, 'If your husband, as you say, intended to have killed you, you ought to have waited, till he actually did make the attempt.' Conformably to which Thucydides, in the first book of his history, has expressed himself in the following terms, 'The issue of war is uncertain, nor ought we to be so far transported by our fears, as to engage in immediate and open hostilities.' The same writer too in his luminous description of the dangerous factions, that had arisen in the Grecian states, condemns the approbation bestowed on the person, that injured or destroyed another from whom he himself apprehended injury or destruction. Livy says, 'Men, to guard against their alarms, make themselves objects of terror; averting the danger from their own heads, by imposing upon others the necessity of either doing or suffering the evil which they them selves fear.' Vibius asked a person, that appeared armed in the forum, 'Who gave you permission to shew your fear in this manner?' A question not inapplicable to the present subject, and much commended by Quintilian. Livia also in Dion says, that great infamy redounds to those, who by anticipation perpetrate the criminal act, which they fear.

2.1.5.4 (ed. Kessinger 2004 at p. 54)
Now if any one intend no immediate violence, but is found to have formed a conspiracy to destroy me by assassination, or poison, or by false accusation, perjury, or suborned witnesses, I have no right to kill him. For my knowledge of the danger may prevent it. Or even if it were evident that I could not avoid the danger without killing him; this would not establish my right to do so. For there is every presumption that my knowing it will lead me to apply for the legal remedies of prevention.

2.1.6 (ed. Kessinger 2004 at p. 54)
The next thing to be considered is, what must be said upon the mutilation of a limb. Now, as the loss of a limb, especially that of a principal limb in the body, is a grievous detriment, and nearly equal to the loss of life, to which may be added the probability of death ensuing from such a calamity; the lawfulness of killing any one, who makes such an attempt, if the danger cannot otherwise be avoided, scarce admits of a doubt.

2.1.7 (ed. Kessinger 2004 at p. 54)
Neither is there any more difficulty in allowing the same right for the personal defence of chastity, the preservation of which, both in the common estimation of men, and by the divine law, is deemed of equal value with life itself. We have an example of this in Cicero, Quintilian, and Plutarch, in the person of one of Marius's tribunes, who was killed by a soldier. Among the actions of women, who have defended themselves. Heliodorus records that of Heraclea, which he calls a just defence of her injured honour.

2.1.8 (ed. Kessinger 2004 at p. 54)
Though some, as it has been already said, admit the lawfulness of killing the person, who attempts with open violence to destroy one's life, yet they deem it more commendable to spare the life of another, even at the hazard of one's own. Yet to persons, in whose preservation the public interest is involved, they will grant an exemption from this rule of forbearance. Indeed it seems unsafe to impose upon ANY, whose lives are of importance to others, a rule of forebearance so contrary to all the principles of all law. This exemption therefore must be allowed to all vested with any public office, which makes them responsible for the safety of others; as the generals who conduct armies, or the rulers of the state, and many others in similar situations; to whom may be applied the lines of Lucan – 'When the lives and safety of so many nations depend upon yours, and so great a portion of the world has chosen you for its head; it is cruelty to expose yourself willfully to death.'

2.1.9.1 (ed. Kessinger 2004 at p. 54)
On the other hand it may happen, that the aggressor may be one whose person is rendered sacred and inviolable by all divine, human, and natural laws; which is the case with

respect to the person of the Sovereign. For the law of nature regards not only the principles of STRICT JUSTICE, but comprises other virtues also, as temperance, fortitude, and discretion, making the observance of them in certain cases, binding as well as honourable. To observe these we are bound also by the law of charity.

2.1.9.2 (ed. Kessinger 2004 at p. 55)
Nor is the truth of this argument at all weakened by what Vasquez has advanced, who maintains that the Sovereign who attempts the life of an individual loses, in reality, the character of Sovereign: a doctrine fraught with equal absurdity and danger. For sovereignty cannot any more than property be forfeited by any particular act of delinquency; unless it has been previously and expressly so enacted by the fundamental laws of the state, For such a rule of forfeiture, which would be productive of universal anarchy and confusion, never has been, or ever will be established among any civilized people. For the maxim, "that all government is framed for the benefit of the subject and not of the Sovereign," which Vasquez and many other writers lay down as a fundamental law, though it may be generally true in theory, is by no means applicable to the question. For a thing loses not its existence, by losing some part of its utility, Nor is there sufficient consistency in his observation, that every individual desires the safety of the commonwealth on his own account, and therefore every one ought to prefer his own safety to that of the whole state. For we wish for the public welfare not on our own account alone, but also for the sake of others.

2.1.9.3 (ed. Kessinger 2004 at p. 55)
The opinion of those who think that friendship arises from necessity alone, is rejected, as false, by the more sound Philosophers; as we feel a spontaneous and natural inclination towards friendly intercourse. Charity indeed often persuades, and in some instances commands us to prefer the good of many to our own single advantage. To which the following passage from Seneca is very applicable. 'It is not surprising that princes, and kings, or whatever name the guardians of the public welfare may bear, should be loved with a veneration and affection, far beyond those of private friendship. For all men of sober judgment, and enlarged information deem the public interest of higher moment than their own. Their attachment therefore must be warmest to the person on whom the well being and prosperity of the state depends.' And to the same effect, St. Ambrose in his third book of Offices, says, 'every man feels a greater delight in averting public than private danger.' Seneca, the writer already quoted, produces two instances, the one of Callistratus at Athens, and the other of Rutilius at Rome, who refused to be restored from banishment thinking it better for two individuals to suffer hardship, than for the public to be plunged into calamities.

2.1.11 (ed. Kessinger 2004 at p. 56)
The next object to be considered, relates to injuries affecting our property. In strict justice, it cannot be denied that we have a right to kill a robber, if such a step is inevitably necessary to the preservation of our property. For the difference between the value of life and property is overbalanced by the horror which a robber excites, and by the favourable inclination felt by all men towards the injured and innocent. From whence it follows, that regarding that right alone, a robber may be wounded or killed in his flight with the property, if it cannot otherwise be recovered. Demosthenes in his speech against Aristocrates, exclaims, "By all that is 'sacred' is it not a dreadful and open violation of law, not only of written law, but of that law which is the unwritten rule of all men, to be debarred from the right of using force against the robber as well as against the 'enemy' who is plundering your property?" Nor is it forbidden by the precepts of charity, apart from all consideration of divine and human

law, unless where the property is of little value, and beneath notice; an exception, which some writers have very properly added.

2.1.12.1 (ed. Kessinger 2004 at p. 56)
The sense of the Jewish law on this point is now to be considered. The old law of Solon, to which Demosthenes, in his speech against Timocrates, appeals, agrees with it. From hence the substance of the TWELVE TABLES, and Plato's maxim in his ninth book of laws were taken. For they all agree in making a distinction between a thief who steals by day, and the robber, who commits the act by night; though they differ about the REASON of this distinction. Some think this distinction arises from the difficulty of discerning by night, whether an aggressor comes with an intent to murder or steal, and therefore he ought to be treated as an assassin. Others think the distinction is made, because as it is difficult to know the person of the thief, there is less probability of recovering the goods. In neither case do the framers of laws seem to have considered the question in its proper light. Their evident intention is to prohibit the killing of any one, merely on account of our property; which would happen, for instance, by killing a thief in his flight in order to recover the goods he had stolen. But if our own lives are endangered, then we are allowed to avert the danger, even at the hazard of another's life. Nor is our having run into the danger any objection; provided it was done to preserve or to recover our goods, or to take the thief. For no imputation of guilt can attach to us in any of these cases, while we are employed in doing a lawful act, nor can it be said that we are doing wrong to another by exercising our own right.

2.1.12.2 (ed. Kessinger 2004 at p. 57)
The difference therefore made between a thief in the night and a thief in the day, arises from the difficulty of procuring sufficient evidence of the fact. So that if a thief is found killed, the person who says, that he was found by him with a destructive weapon, and killed by him in his own defence, will easily gain belief. For the Jewish law supposes this, when it treats of a thief in the act of piercing, or, as some translate it, with a stabbing instrument. This interpretation accords with the law of the twelve tables, which forbids any one to kill a thief in the day time, except he defend himself with a weapon. The presumption therefore against a thief in the night is that he defended himself in such a manner. Now the term weapon comprehends not only an instrument of iron, but as Caius interprets it is law, a club, or a stone. Ulpian on the other hand, speaking of a thief taken in the night, says that the person who kills him will incur no guilt, provided that in saving his property he could not spare his life, without en. dangering his own. There is a presumption, as it has been already observed, in favour of the person who has killed a thief taken in the night. But if there be evidence to prove, that the life of the person who killed the thief was in no danger; then the presumption in his favour fails, and the act amounts to murder.

2.1.12.3 (ed. Kessinger 2004 at p. 57)
The law of the twelve tables indeed required, that the person who took a thief either in the day time, or in the night, should make a noise that, if possible, the magistrates or neighbours might assemble to assist him and give evidence. But as such a concourse could more easily be assembled in the day time than in the night, as Ulpian observes upon the passage before quoted from Demosthenes, the affirmation of a person declaring the danger he was in during the night is more readily believed. To which an additional observation may be made, that, even under equal circumstances, the danger which happens by night can be less examined, and ascertained, and therefore is the more terrible. The Jewish law therefore, no less than the Roman, acting upon the same principle of tenderness forbids us to kill any one, who has taken our goods, unless for the preservation of our own lives.

2.1.16 (ed. Kessinger 2004 at p. 57)
What has been already said of the right of defending our persons and property, though regarding chiefly private war, may nevertheless be applied to public hostilities, allowing for the difference of circumstances. For private war may be considered as an instantaneous exercise of natural right, which ceases the moment that legal redress can be obtained. Now as public war can never take place, but where judicial remedies cease to exist, it is often protracted, and the spirit of hostility inflamed by the continued accession of losses and injuries. Besides, private war extends only to self-defence, whereas sovereign powers have a right not only to avert, but to punish wrongs. From whence they are authorised to prevent a remote as well as an immediate aggression. Though the suspicion of hostile intentions, on the part of another power, may not justify the commencement of actual war, yet it calls for measures of armed prevention, and will authorise indirect hostility. Points, which will be discussed in another place.

2.1.17 (ed. Kessinger 2004 at p. 58)
Some writers have advanced a doctrine which can never be admitted, maintaining that the law of nations authorises one power to commence hostilities against another, whose increasing greatness awakens her alarms. As a matter of expediency such a measure may be adopted, but the principles of justice can never be advanced in its favour. The causes which entitle a war to the denomination of just are somewhat different from those of expediency alone. But to maintain that the bare probability of some remote, or future annoyance from a neighbouring state affords a just ground of hostile aggression, is a doctrine repugnant to every principle of equity. Such however is the condition of human life, that no full security can be enjoyed. The only protection against uncertain fears must be sought, not from violence, but from the divine providence, and defensive precaution.

2.1.18.1. (ed. Kessinger 2004 at p. 58)
There is another opinion, not more admissible maintaining that the hostile acts of an aggressor, may be considered in the light of defensive measures, because, say the advocates of this opinion, few people are content to proportion their revenge to the injuries they have received; bounds which in all probability the party aggrieved has exceeded, and therefore in return becomes himself the aggressor. Now the excess of retaliation cannot, any more than the fear of uncertain danger, give a colour of right to the first aggression, which may be illustrated by the case of a malefactor, who can have no right to wound or kill the officers of justice in their attempts to take him, urging as a plea that he feared the punishment would exceed the offense.

2.1.18.2 (ed. Kessinger 2004 at p. 58)
The first step, which an aggressor ought to take, should be an offer of indemnity to the injured party, by the arbitration of some independent and disinterested state. And if this mediation be rejected, then his war assumes the character of a just war. Thus Hezekiah when he had not stood to the engagements made by his ancestors, being threatened with an attack from the King of Assyria on that account, acknowledged his fault, and left it to the King to assign what penalty he should pay for the offence. After he had clone so, finding himself again attacked, relying on the justice of his cause, he opposed the enemy, and succeeded by the favour of God. Pontius the Samnite, after restoration of the prizes had been made to the Romans, and the promoter of the war delivered up into their hands, said, 'We have now averted the wrath of heaven, which our violation of treaties had provoked. But the supreme being who was pleased to reduce us to the necessity of restoration, was not equally pleased with the pride of the Romans, who rejected our offer. What farther satisfaction do we owe to the Romans, or to Heaven, the arbiter of treaties? We do not

shrink from submitting the measure of YOUR resentment, or of OUR punishment to the judgment of any people, or any individual.' In the same manner, when the Thebans had offered the most equitable terms to the Lacedaemonians, who still rose higher in their demands, Aristides say, that the justice of the cause changed sides and passed from the Lacedaemonians to the Thebans.

2.22.4 (ed. Kessinger 2004 at p. 210)
Others make use of pretexts, which though plausible at first sight, will not bear the examination and test of moral rectitude, and, when stripped of their disguise, such pretexts will be found fraught with injustice. In such hostilities, says Livy, it is not a trial of right, but some object of secret and unruly ambition, which acts as the chief spring. Most powers, it is said by Plutarch, employ the relative situations of peace and war, as a current specie, for the purchase of whatever they deem expedient.

By having before examined and established the principles of just and necessary war, we may form a better idea of what goes to constitute the injustice of the same. As the nature of things is best seen by contrast, and we judge of what is crooked by comparing it with what is straight. But for the sake of perspicuity, it will be necessary to treat upon the leading points.

It was shewn above that apprehensions from a neigh. bouring power are not a sufficient ground for war. For to authorize hostilities as a defensive measure, they must arise from the necessity, which just apprehensions create; apprehensions not only of the power, but of the intentions of a formidable state, and such apprehensions as amount to a moral certainty. For which reason the opinion of those is by no means to be approved of, who lay down as a just ground of war, the construction of fortifications in a neighbouring country, with whom there is no existing treaty to prohibit such constructions, or the securing of a strong hold, which may at some future period prove a means of annoyance. For as a guard or against such apprehensions, every power may construct, in its own territory, strong works, and other military securities of the same kind, without having recourse to actual war. One cannot but admire the character, which Tacitus has drawn of the Chauci, a noble and high-spirited people of Germany, 'who, *he says*, were desirous of maintaining their greatness by justice, rather than by acts of ungovernable rapacity and ambition – provoking no wars, invading no countries, spoiling no neighbours to aggrandize themselves, – yet, when necessity prompted, able to raise men with arms in their hands at a moment's warning – a great population with a numerous breed of horses to form a well mounted cavalry and, with all these advantages, upholding their reputation in the midst of peace.'

2.22.6 (ed. Kessinger 2004 at p. 210)
Nor can the advantage to be gained by a war be ever pleaded as a motive of equal weight and justice with necessity.

2.23.13 (ed. Kessinger 2004 at p. 218)
From what has been said it will not be difficult to settle a much agitated question, whether, with respect to those, who are the principal movers of a war, there can be justice on both sides. For there are distinctions proper to be made in the various acceptations of the word JUST.

A thing is said to be just, either as to its causes, or its effects. The causes too may be confined either to justice in a PARTICULAR acceptation, or they may be extended so as to include under that name every kind of rectitude. Again, a particular acceptation may be divided into two kinds, one relating to the ACTION, and the other to the agent. An agent may be said to act justly, when, in what he does, he commits no breach of STRICT LAW, though his conduct may not be conformable to equity.

In a PARTICULAR acceptation of the word justice, with regard to a matter in dispute, it cannot in war, any more than in legal proceedings, apply to both sides. For there can be no moral principle, commanding us, under the same circumstances, both to Do, and to ABSTAIN from a particular action. It may happen indeed that neither of two belligerent powers may act unjustly. For no one can be charged with acting unjustly unless he knows that he is doing so; but there are many, who are not aware of the nature, extent, and consequences of their measures. Thus in a law-suit, both parties may sincerely believe that they have justice on their side. For many things both in law and fact, which would establish a right, may escape the notice of men.

In a GENERAL acceptation, an action may be called just, where the agent is free from every kind of blame. Yet in many cases an agent may deviate from the strict rules of legal justice, and be liable to no blame, when that deviation is owing to unavoidable ignorance, there having been neither time nor opportunity sufficient for him to know the substance, or perhaps existence of the law. So it may happen in law-suits, that both parties are free not only from the imputation of injustice, but from all blame, especially where either of them is litigating a matter not on his own, but on another's account; as for instance where a guardian is acting for his ward, he would not be authorized in abandoning even a doubted right. Aristotle says that in matters of disputed right neither side can be charged with injustice; conformably to which opinion Quintilian, observes that an upright pleader may be engaged on either side of the question. Aristotle further observes that passing a just judgment is an ambiguous term, signifying that a judge determines either according to the strict letter of the law, or according to the dictates of his own conscience. And, in another place, he has said that giving a wrong judgment through ignorance is no act of injustice.

But in matters of war and peace, where such weighty and varied interests on all sides are concerned, it would be difficult to obtain a judgment purely impartial, and abstracted from all personal motives, unless there be the most clear and undeniable evidence on the points in question.

If we denominate a thing to be just, from its effect in conferring certain rights, in this sense it is plain that in war there may be justice on both sides. In the same manner, a sentence not strictly legal, or a possession not perfectly just may nevertheless confer certain rights.

2.2.6.1 (ed. Kessinger 2004 at p. 64)
The next thing to be considered is the right, which men have to the common use of things, already appropriated; terms, in which at the first sight there appears to be some inconsistency, as it appears that the establishment of property has absorbed every right that sprung from a state of things held in common. But this is by no means the case. For the intention of those, who first introduce private property, must be taken into the account. And it was but reasonable to suppose, that in making this introduction of property, they would depart As little as possible from the original principles of natural equity. For if written laws are to be construed in a sense, approaching as nearly as possible to the laws of nature, much more so are those customs which are not fettered with the literal restrictions of written maxims. From hence it follows that in cases of extreme necessity, the original right of using things, as if they had remained in common, must be revived; because in all human laws, and consequently in the laws relating to property, the case of extreme necessity seems to form an exception.

2.2.6.2 (ed. Kessinger 2004 at p. 65)
Upon this principle is built the maxim that if in a voyage provisions begin to fail, the stock of every individual ought to be produced for common consumption; for the same reason a

neighbouring house may be pulled down to stop the progress of a fire: or the cables or nets, in which a ship is entangled, may be cut, if it cannot otherwise be disengaged. Maxims, none of which were introduced by the civil law, but only explained by it according to the rules of natural equity.

2.2.6.3 (ed. Kessinger 2004 at p. 65)
Now among Theologians also it is a received opinion, that if in urgent distress, any one shall take from another what is absolutely necessary for the preservation of his own life, the act shall not be deemed a theft. A rule not founded, as some allege, solely upon the law of charity, which obliges every possessor to apply some part of his wealth to relieve the needy; but upon the original division of lands among private owners, which was made with a reservation in favour of the primitive rights of nature. For if those who at first made the division had been asked their opinion upon this point, they would have given the same reason that has just been advanced. Necessity, says Seneca, the great protectress of human infirmity breaks through all human laws, and all those made in the spirit of human regulations. Cicero in his eleventh Philippic, says, that Cassius went into Syria, which might be considered as another's province, if men adhered to written laws, but if these were abolished, it would be considered as his own by the law of nature. In the sixth book and fourth chapter of Quintus Curtius, we find an observation, that in a common calamity every man looks to himself.

4. Francisco Suárez

Selections From Three Works (1621); Ed. Williams, 2 vols., Oxford 1944.

***Selections 1621* On Charity 13.4.1 (ed. Williams 1944 at vol. II, pp. 815-16)**

WHAT IS JUST CAUSE OF WAR, ON THE BASIS OF NATURAL REASON?

There was an old error current among the Gentiles, who thought that the right of nations were based on military strength, and that it was permissible to make war solely to acquire prestige and wealth; a belief which, even from the standpoint of natural reason, is most absurd.
Therefore I hold, first: that there can be no just war without an underlying cause of a legitimate and necessary nature. The truth of this conclusion is indubitable and clearly evident. Now, that just and sufficient reason for war is the infliction of a grave injustice which cannot be avenged or repaired by any other way. [...]
The first reason in support of such a conclusion is the fact that war is permissible [only] that a state may guard itself from molestation; for in other respects, war is opposed to the welfare of the human race on account of the slaughter, material losses, and other misfortunes which it involves; and therefore, if the cause in question should cease to exist, the justice of war would also cease to exist.
Secondly, in the war, men are despoiled of their property, their liberty, and their lives; and to do such things without just cause is absolutely iniquitous, for if this were permissible, men could kill one another without cause.
Thirdly, the sort of war which we are chiefly discussing is aggressive war, and it is frequently waged against non-subjects. Consequently, it is necessary that the latter shall have committed some wrong on account of which they render themselves subjects. Otherwise, on what account could they be deserving of punishment or subject to an alien jurisdiction?

***Selections 1621* On Charity 13.4.2 (ed. Williams 1944 at vol. II, p. 816)**
But, in order that this matter may be explained more clearly, there are several points which should be noted. First, it is not every cause that is sufficient to justify war, but only those

causes which are serious and commensurate with the losses that the war would occasion.

Selections 1621 **On Charity 13.4.3 (ed. Williams 1944 at vol. II, p. 817)**
Secondly, it must be noted that there are various kinds of injuries which are causes of a just war. These may be grouped under three heads. One of the heads would be the seizure by a prince of another's property, and his refusal to restore it. Another head would be his denial, without reasonable cause, of the common rights of nations, such as the right of transit over highways, trading in common, &c. The third would be any grave injury to one's reputation and honour. It should be added that it is a sufficient cause for war if an injury of this kind be inflicted either upon a prince himself or upon his subjects; for the prince is guardian of his state and also of his subjects. Furthermore, the cause is sufficient if the wrong be inflicted upon any one who has placed himself under the protection of a prince, or even if it be inflicted upon allies or friends.

Selections 1621 **On Charity 13.4.4 (ed. Williams 1944 at vol. II, p. 817)**
Thirdly, we must note that, in regard to an injury inflicted, two arguments may be alleged, [to justify a declaration of war]. The first is [that such a declaration is justifiable], in order that reparation for the losses suffered should be made to the injured party.

Selections 1621 **On Charity 13.4.5 (ed. Williams 1944 at vol. II, p. 818)**
Secondly, then, I hold that a war may also be justified on the ground that he who has inflicted an injury should be justly punished, if he refuses to give just satisfaction for that injury, without resort to war. This conclusion is generally accepted.

Selections 1621 **On Laws and God the Lawgiver II.17.6 (ed. Williams 1944 at vol. II, p. 329)**
Nevertheless, even this last explanation does not dispose of the difficulty. For, in the first place, according to these statements [the right] to repel force with force would have to be constituted not under the ius gentium, but under the natural law, since that right is not laid down in the precepts of the former system. The consequent is proved by the fact that such an act is common to men and to brute animals, and spring from the general inclination towards self-preservation. For just as reproduction arises from the natural inclination to preserve the species, so self-defence is the result of the innate tendency to preserve one's own life and one's own being; and both inclinations are common to men and to other animals, so that the act in question is wrongly classified under those sanctioned by the ius gentium.

5. Franciscus De Victoria

De Indis et de Iure Belli Relectiones (1696). Ed. Nys/Bate,Washington D.C. 1917.

On the Law of War **429 (ed. Nys/Bate at II. pp. 170-71]**

Fourth proposition: There is a single and only just cause for commencing a war, namely, a wrong received. The proof of this rests in the evidence on the authority of St. Augustine (Liber 83 Quaestionum, "Those wars are described as just wars", etc., as above) and it is the conclusion arrived at by St. Thomas (Secunda Secundae, qu. 40, art. I) and the opinion of the doctors. Also, an offensive war is for the purpose of avenging a wrong and of taking measures against an enemy, as said above. But there can be no vengeance where there is no preceding fault and wrong. [...] Also, a prince has no greater authority over foreigners than over his own subjects. But he may not draw his sword against his own subjects, unless they have done some wrong. Therefore not against foreigners either.

MIX
Papier aus verantwortungsvollen Quellen
Paper from responsible sources
FSC® C105338

If you have any concerns about our products,
you can contact us on
ProductSafety@springernature.com

In case Publisher is established outside the EU,
the EU authorized representative is:
Springer Nature Customer Service Center GmbH
Europaplatz 3, 69115 Heidelberg, Germany

Printed by Libri Plureos GmbH
in Hamburg, Germany